A Place
for
Summer

Official 1950 SCORE BOOK 10¢

Detroit Tigers

Briggs Stadium

A Place
for
Summer

A Narrative History of
Tiger Stadium

Richard Bak

Wayne State University Press Detroit

Great Lakes Books

A complete listing of the books in this series can be found at the back of this volume.

PHILIP P. MASON, *Editor*
Department of History, Wayne State University

DR. CHARLES K. HYDE, *Associate Editor*
Department of History, Wayne State University

02 01 00 99 98   5 4 3 2 1

Library of Congress Cataloging-in-Publication Data

Bak, Richard, 1954-
    A place for summer : a narrative history of Tiger Stadium /
Richard Bak.
        p.   cm. — (Great lakes books)
    Includes bibliographical references (p.) and index.
    ISBN 0-8143-2512-2 (alk. paper)
    1. Tiger Stadium (Detroit, Mich.)—History. 2. Detroit Tigers
(Baseball team)—History. I. Title. II. Series
GV416.D488B35 1998
796.357'06'877434—dc21   98-2509

To the memory of
Nancy (Maliszewski) Jabour
1957–1997

Ty Cobb and friends inside the dugout at Bennett Park.

Contents

Preface:
One Hundred Years and Counting   9

1. The Old Ball Game:
   The Rise of Baseball in Detroit, 1857–1895   13

2. Down on the Corner:
   Bennett Park, 1896–1911   51

3. Frank's Place:
   Navin Field, 1912–1937   117

4. The Fan Who Owned a Ballpark:
   Briggs Stadium, 1938–1960   181

5. Goalposts in the Outfield:
   Football at Michigan and Trumbull   247

6. Modern Love:
   Tiger Stadium, 1961–1997   291

   Postscript:
   An Empty Feeling   397

   Appendix A:
   Standings and Attendance at
   Michigan and Trumbull   401

   Appendix B:
   Opening Day at Michigan and Trumbull   407

   Bibliography   455

   Index   463

   Photo credits   483

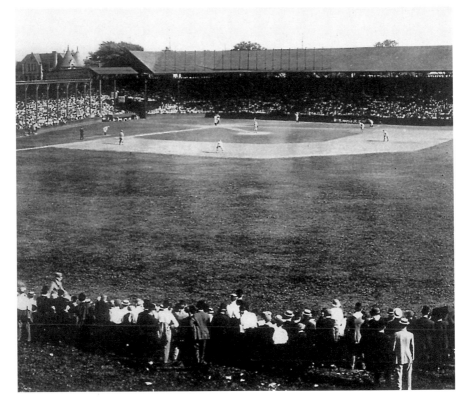

Michigan and Trumbull in the spring of 1911.

One Hundred Years and Counting

A NEW BASEBALL STADIUM will be built in downtown Detroit—that is a certainty; the only question involves its opening. The park is scheduled to be ready by the spring of 2000, which would deprive the Detroit Tigers of an unprecedented achievement. If the Tigers played at least one game at the corner of Michigan and Trumbull Avenues during the 2001 season, it would make the country's oldest sports address the site of big-league baseball for parts of three centuries. This would be a remarkable accomplishment, one unlikely to be replicated in our modern disposable age.

Not that the club itself is concerned with such arcanum. The institutional neglect of the old ballpark's unique history comes as no surprise to anyone who followed the drawn-out, bitter debate over a new stadium. What was to be gained by manufacturing nostalgia for a facility the team couldn't wait to flee? This attitude was apparent on April 28, 1996, when the Tigers played the Oakland Athletics on a cold, bright Sunday afternoon at Tiger Stadium. Although the team thoughtfully conveyed birthday greetings to several loyal fans via the scoreboard, it totally neglected what should have been the object of a major birthday blowout: the playing site itself. For the ground on which the teams were playing was the same that Detroit and Columbus players crossed exactly one hundred years earlier—April 28, 1896—when the Tigers played their first of an eventual seventy-eight-hundred-plus games at the corner of Michigan and Trumbull. It was called Bennett Park then, there were trees growing in the outfield, and fans arrived in buggies instead of automobiles. But all in all, if a six-year-old boy who had attended the first game down on the corner had returned as a 106-year-old man in 1996, he would have had little trouble recognizing the surroundings.

Researching and writing this book was hard work, but it proved a captivating voyage through the city's and the game's intertwined pasts. As a history buff and a long-time sports fan whose memories of Tiger Stadium stretch back thirty-five years, I found it fascinating to contemplate the central role the stadium at the corner of Michigan and Trumbull Avenues has played in the lives of millions of Detroiters. The original wooden facility, Bennett Park, was torn down over the winter of 1911–12 and the Tigers' home reincarnated as the concrete-and-steel Navin Field. Various stages of expansion and modernization followed, accompanied by two more name changes: Briggs Stadium in 1938 and then Tiger Stadium in 1961. Over the past century more than 105 million customers have passed through the turnstiles to watch the Tigers play. If the admissions to all of the other sporting, social, and civic events staged there over the years—high school, collegiate, and professional football games; prep and Negro-league baseball contests; political rallies; concerts; and boxing and soccer matches—were added to that number, the figure would probably exceed 135 million.

This narrative delivers a bit more than the title suggests. It takes the reader from baseball's beginnings in Detroit in the 1850s to the Tigers' 1997 season at Michigan and Trumbull. It covers a span of some 140 years and contains information about the nineteenth-century playing grounds that preceded Bennett Park, including the Woodward Avenue cricket grounds, the original Detroit Athletic Club, and Recreation and Boulevard parks, as well as an accurate sorting out of the many locations where the Tigers played bootleg games on Sundays at the turn of the century. Readers are also introduced to several relatively unknown figures from Detroit's baseball past, most notably George Vanderbeck, the controversial Californian responsible for establishing the Detroit franchise in 1894 and for moving the team to its present location two years later. Attendance records stretching back to the Tigers' Western League days were painstakingly added up and are presented here for the first time, as is a complete accounting of every opening day played since 1896. A separate chapter is dedicated to the story of the other cats who prowled the corner for so long, the football Panthers of the 1920s and the Lions, their more successful successor. Scores of vintage photographs, many rarely seen before, have been selected to illustrate the text. The result, I hope, is not only a lively history of Tiger Stadium, but also a well-rounded account of the relationship between the community, its teams, and the various fields, parks, and stadiums that served as common ground for generations of Detroiters.

Detroit's first enclosed ballyard, Recreation Park, in 1887.

CHAPTER ONE

The Old Ball Game

The Rise of Baseball in Detroit, 1857–1895

NYONE ATTEMPTING to trace the history of baseball in Detroit is obliged to lead off with a caveat. From this distance, no one can say with absolute certainty when the first game was played in the city—or anywhere else, for that matter. The popular fiction for years was that Abner Doubleday invented the game as a young man in upstate New York in 1839, after which the game quickly spread across the rest of the country. The latter is true enough; by 1861 baseball tournaments were held from New York to California and Detroiters were playfully experimenting with the game on skates at downtown ice rinks.

The former, however, is preposterous. Although Doubleday, who eventually gained a measure of fame as a Civil War general, tended to embroider his military exploits, even he would have arched an eyebrow at his designation as the paterfamilias of baseball, a posthumous honor assigned him in 1907 by a blue-ribbon committee investigating the game's origins. Certainly there is no concrete evidence that Doubleday ever held a baseball in his hand, or that the old soldier could even have distinguished one from a cannon ball.

The truth of the matter is that America's national pastime is a derivative of the English schoolyard game of "rounders," which by the early nineteenth century was being played in one form or another with great enthusiasm on both sides of the Atlantic. Participants freely experimented with the rules of play. Soon several variations of what came to be called "town ball" or "base ball" (later shortened to one word) had developed in the East.

The first printed references to baseball in Detroit date to the 1850s. However, since the town's merchant class was dominated by transplanted New Englanders, it is reasonable to assume that some citizens were aware of a form of ball called the "Massachusetts game" well before then. This version featured a square field with each side of the square sixty feet long and anchored by a base. The pitcher delivered the ball from the center of the square to the batter, who was positioned inside a four–foot square between first and fourth bases. Each side fielded between ten and twenty players and was allowed only one out, which occurred if the batter flied out, had his batted ball fielded on the first bounce, or was hit (soaked) by a fielder's throw while running the bases. One variation of the game required the winning side to score one hundred runs.

In the 1840s a New York City bank teller named Alexander Cartwright performed a major overhaul of the game. In 1845 he organized the Knickerbocker Baseball Club, complete with its own rule book. The "New York game" featured many of the elements of modern baseball. Nine players on each side played on a diamond with ninety–foot baselines, three bases, and a striker's point (home base). The pitcher was positioned forty–five feet away and tossed the ball underhand to the "striker" (batter) as gently and accurately as possible.* A player was out if he swung at and missed three pitches, had a fair ball caught on the fly, or had a foul ball fielded on the fly or on the first bounce. One significant change was the elimination of soaking; fielders now threw to the base ahead of the runner or tagged him with the ball. Then, as now, players batted in regular rotation, and three "hands lost" (outs) constituted one inning. The first side to score twenty–one runs won. The trendsetting Knickerbockers—who in 1849 also became the first team to wear uniforms—quickly developed the standard for other clubs around the country, including those in Detroit.

The first *recorded* baseball game in Detroit was played on the afternoon of August 15, 1857 at the corner of Adams Avenue and

---

* The object in the game's early years was to simply put the ball in play. Pitchers tossed the ball with no wrist snap, in a fashion similar to today's slow–pitch softball. However, it wasn't long before pitchers developed a variety of "unsportsmanlike" deliveries that baffled batters and horrified purists.

Richard Fyfe (left) and John S. Newberry were the opposing captains when the
Early Risers and Detroits played their historic match on the grounds of the Cass
farm in 1859. At the time, Newberry was a thirty–something gentleman on his
way to increasing his fortune in the railroad business. Like many of his
well–heeled contemporaries, he was just as interested in the game's social cachet
as in its recreational value. Fyfe, on the other hand, was a lowly shoe clerk and
"too busy working to devote much time to social matters." America offered
democratic opportunities that were personified by its new national pastime.
Honest labor soon earned Fyfe a coveted spot on the Detroits' roster and by the
end of the century made him one of the city's richest, best–known citizens.

Beaubien Street (where the J. L. Hudson warehouse stands today) by
"admirers of the 'good old Yankee sport,'" reported the *Detroit Free
Press*. At this point the game was already known to more than a few
leisure–minded Detroiters. But the fact that one of the participants,
Henry Starkey, was editor of the newspaper may explain why this particular game was mentioned in print. While the results of the intramural affair are unknown, the organizational attempts of what
became the Franklin Baseball Club apparently were successful. One
week later, members chose sides and played a doubleheader, after
which the club, "in compliance with an invitation, partook of a generous repast at the residence of Mr. Theodore Robinson."

Reports of the club's activities, which appear largely gastronomi-
cal in nature, quickly faded. In October 1858 several members
regrouped as the Detroit Baseball Club and joined the National

Association of Baseball Players, a New York–based organization of Eastern and Midwestern clubs devoted to preserving the game's pedigree. The roster included some of the city's leading citizens.

John S. Newberry, a wealthy thirty–three–year–old widower on his way to increasing his fortune in the railroad business, was president, captain, and played "short field," a shallow outfield position that evolved into shortstop. The roster also included first baseman William Craig, a grain merchant and future city council president; catcher E. E. Dumon, a prominent dentist; and pitcher David Peirce, a "man of means" who resided on fashionable Miami Avenue. Riding the bench was Dexter Ferry, then a bookkeeper in Howe's book shop on Jefferson and Bates; within a few years his fledgling seed business would blossom into the country's largest. The sixty members practiced three afternoons a week at a field on Grand River, west of Elizabeth Street, on a stretch of the Lewis Cass farm rented to Harvey King for use as a riding park and fairgrounds.

The following July, a second baseball club was organized. Named the Early Risers, it was comprised of twenty–two "young men employed in stores and offices, whose occupations prevent their taking any recreation during the day." They met three mornings a week at 4:00 a.m. and practiced in front of the Russell House, the city's leading hotel, at Michigan and Woodward Avenues. According to president and catcher Richard Fyfe, a twenty–year–old New York native eking out a living as a dollar–a–day shoe clerk, the Early Risers broke so many windows the team was finally given a flat rate on replacement glass.

It is possible that the Early Risers were organized with the idea of becoming serious competition for the Detroits, who were hungry for something other than intramural competition. Frank Folsom, one of the Early Risers' directors, was an officer and right fielder for the Detroits. Folsom and his father were wool buyers with offices in the *Detroit Free Press* building downtown. It is probable that some of the Early Risers clerked for the Folsoms and other members of the Detroits.

Whatever the connection, at 2:30 p.m. on August 8, 1859, the Early Risers and the Detroits squared off at the Cass farm (in the vicinity of what is today Cass Park) in the first match between rival ball clubs in the city's history. No illustrations of that historic match exist, although it is easy to imagine the scene. Seats were provided for the ladies, who protected their faces from the midday sun with parasols held high by gentlemen escorts in swallowtail coats. Carriages were parked in the far reaches of the playing field, where the horses grazed peacefully on the outfield grass. The playing action closely resembled a game of slow–pitch softball, as the pitcher carefully delivered the homemade leather ball according to the batter's instructions. Fielding gloves and other equipment were unheard of, but the players' positions were basically as they are today. The umpire, Captain W. V. Jones, undoubtedly wore a silk top hat and dispensed fines for such infractions as swearing or spitting tobacco.

The overmatched clerks were drubbed, 59–21, although "they took it in good part, consoling themselves with the recollection that they had an even share of the sport, as well as the opportunity of practicing with superior players," reported the *Free Press*. The Early Risers improved to the point that they lost a rematch by only three runs. By the time a third game rolled around, at least one clerk had progressed socially as well as athletically: Richard Fyfe was invited to join the Detroits, a first blush of prestige for the budding entrepreneur who became famous for his fourteen–story "shoe skyscraper" overlooking Grand Circus Park.

During the 1850s baseball was a gentleman's game, played interchangeably with what was still the country's most popular field sport, cricket. Today, curious Detroiters may watch cricket matches held Sundays on Belle Isle, but that's about it. One hundred and fifty years ago, cricket matches in progress could easily be found throughout the city. The British import carried a certain social cachet. In Detroit there were two major cricket teams, the Detroits and the Peninsulars. Members of both clubs planted their wickets on groomed fields on upper Woodward Avenue, a few blocks north of Grand Circus Park, on what was then the city's outer fringe.

Cricket resembles baseball. In fact, a good share of baseball's lingo and rules are derived from its cousin. In cricket, two teams consisting of eleven players each play two innings. The action centers around the pitch—the rectangular playing surface in the middle of the field—where a pair of batsmen defend their wickets from being knocked over by the opposing bowlers. When that happens, the batsman is declared out. (He can also fly out.) More likely, however, the batsman smokes the ball somewhere. When one batsman gets a hit, both batsmen race back and forth to each other's wickets until the ball is retrieved. A run is scored every time the two batsmen pass. Additional runs are awarded for grounding a ball out of the field or driving it past the flags that border the circular grounds. Since the team on the field must retire all eleven batsmen before batting themselves, hundreds of runs can be scored in a single inning.

Despite its popularity, cricket was doomed by its slow pace, interminable length and the rising tide of anti–British feeling that swept America during this period. One match often took two or more days to complete, an investment of time that neither the players nor the spectators were willing to make. While cricket remained a popular sport through the end of the century—in 1879 the world's best cricketers, the All–England Eleven, played a historic match against a squad of Detroit cricketers—it fell into disfavor in a young, virile nation desperately searching for a game that it could call its own.

A country of common men found it in baseball. The game's basic elements of throwing, hitting, and running appealed to something primeval in everyone. Hand someone a ball and his first impulse is to throw it. Give him a stick and he'll immediately want to swing it. Add to this the lung–searing joy of running with abandon after a fly ball or simply dashing from base to base, and it's clear why the game quickly passed from the manicured hands of a privileged few into the sweaty embrace of the masses.

Baseball took off like a spooked horse. Soon after the Detroits' match with the Early Risers, Michigan Central Railroad clerks and local printers formed clubs, followed by "a host of less pretentious organizations . . . under the particular patronage of the younger portions of a community." Left in the dust was cricket. Americans in their quest for a truly native identity were anxious to disavow most British influences in their culture. Detroit's Brother Jonathan Wicket Club reflected this mood of intense nationalism when in 1859 it voted to disband and reorganize as the Brother Jonathan Baseball Club. By then baseball was already widely hailed as "the game for young America."

The Civil War loomed. Rather than dampen enthusiasm for the game, however, four years of war (1861–1865) helped spread its popularity. Forty thousand Union soldiers watched a ball game on Christmas Day 1862; earlier that year, Abraham Lincoln took time off from his presidential duties to attend a game in Washington. Northern prisoners often challenged their Confederate guards to matches. Sergeant Lucius Shattuck of Plymouth, Michigan, who died on the first day of the Battle of Gettysburg, wrote to his sister earlier that members of the Twenty–fourth Michigan Infantry Regiment, most of whom hailed from the Detroit area, often whiled away their days in camp in Virginia playing ball. The large crowds that watched these camp games demonstrated baseball's great commercial potential. With urban populations willing to pay for entertainment, and facing little competition, baseball quickly developed into the first great American spectator sport in the years following the Civil War.

In August 1867 two dozen teams, including some from Canada and one from Allegheny, Pennsylvania, participated in a week–long baseball tournament at the cricket grounds on Woodward Avenue. Crowds of up to five thousand people attended the three–games–a–day affair. Promoters charged twenty–five cents for admission, and tacked on an extra fifty cents if a gentleman and his lady arrived in a buggy. Prizes were awarded for the longest throw and other competitions. To add to the festivities, the popular Detroit Light Guard band "discoursed sweet strains, both before the game and between each inning."

"A week of fine sport seems to have infused a mania for baseball into an otherwise staid and sober community," observed the *Free Press,* which typically devoted six of its eight front–page columns to each day's proceedings. "One hears little else on the street than discussions on the merits or demerits of clubs, umpires, etc." In 1869 more than one thousand teams operated nationwide; approximately one third belonged to the National Association.

The Detroit Baseball Club, which had either disbanded or suspended operations during the Civil War, was replaced by another group of local citizens who unimaginatively called themselves the Detroits. In December 1865 representatives from the Detroits and fifteen other clubs from eight states organized the Northwestern Association of Baseball Players in Chicago. The new organization adopted the constitution and amateur standards of the National Association.

In June 1866 the Detroits traveled to Rockford, Illinois, to participate in the Northwestern Baseball Tournament. The highly skilled nine crushed Pecatonica, 49–1, en route to the title match with the Excelsiors of Chicago. At stake were a solid gold baseball, municipal pride (confident Detroiters back home had raised two thousand dollars for the expected victory celebration) and the "national championship," championships during the amateur era being nearly as plentiful as today's softball trophies.

Reviewing accounts of the title match is rewarding, as it provides an early example of a team's home–field advantage, as well as a glimpse of the win–at–all–costs skulduggery already creeping into the game. The clubs were tied going into the eighth inning, when the Detroits pushed across a run to take a 10–9 lead. The Chicago club scored seven runs in the bottom of the final inning to win, 16–10. "During the playing of these innings the most intense excitement prevailed among the spectators," reported a Chicago daily. The play was rough and spirited. A batted ball dislocated Detroit first baseman Clark's finger and he was replaced. Although Clark's digit quickly healed, one teammate remained out of joint deep into old age. "The umpire beat us," claimed left fielder Dave Barry nearly forty years later. "He was . . . a member of the Chicago club. He allowed the pitcher to 'bowl'—that is, the pitcher would use a slight overhand motion in delivering the ball. Of course, everyone knows we had to deliver the ball underhand in those times, and the advantage that their pitcher had over us was enough to win the game." Added Barry: "That old grudge rankles deeply in our hearts yet."

As that early game illustrates, baseball had become a victim of its own popularity. As more Americans played and watched baseball, fans shouted for more games, better players, and winning teams. Promoters arranged tournaments where Association teams shared in gifts and gate receipts. The public clamor drove the true amateur to the sidelines. Those not completely disgusted with the game's crass commercialism were overwhelmed by the investment of time it suddenly required. It was one thing for a gentleman to take time off from his obligations to practice twice a week and play an occasional match; it was quite another to devote most of his waking hours to practice, travel, and competition.

Hypocrisy was an inevitable consequence of the drive for victory and profit. In 1860 the Brooklyn Excelsiors became the first club to make *sub rosa* payments to a player, setting in motion a practice that accelerated through the decade. Highly skilled players became baseball mercenaries, called "revolvers," who went from team to team, depending on which had the better offer. Businessmen, aware even then of the public relations value of backing a successful team, often replaced local talent with superior out–of–town players added to the company payroll as "clerk" or "warehouseman." Their real job, of course, was to play ball. In addition, "hippodroming," the throwing of games, gained widespread publicity and helped ruin public confidence in the game. The National Association banned such practices, but it was slow to identify and punish offenders.

The Detroits appeared to have resisted these temptations. Representing their fair city was regarded a rite of passage for young men like Ford Hinchman, Dexter Ferry, and James and Benjamin Vernor. In 1868 the team traveled by train or boat to Cincinnati, Cleveland, and Pittsburgh, and hosted such well–known teams as the Brooklyn Atlantics and the Unions of Morrisiana, New York. Covered seats accommodating two thousand people were erected on the Woodward Avenue grounds. Admission was twenty–five cents, and the Detroits customarily split the gate receipts with the visiting clubs.

Baseball in the late 1860s was decidedly more languid than it would later become. Teams typically took several days to travel to another city for a match. A certain protocol was followed, and the game merely served as the centerpiece of a foreign adventure that included hearty meals, touring the city in buggies, and various other planned events.

The dark–coated gentleman is the manager and the one holding the ball is the pitcher. Unfortunately, no other identification accompanies this photograph of an early Detroit baseball team. Various clues, however, suggest that these young men probably are members of the Aetna or Cass club of the early 1870s. Whatever the affiliation, it's interesting to note the absence of fielding gloves. Introduced in 1875, they didn't receive general acceptance until a decade later.

On one such trip in September 1867, the Detroits journeyed by steamship to Cleveland to play the Forest Citys. "You are now surprised at where I am & where I am going," Dexter Ferry wrote to his fiancee. "The facts are these. . . ."

I have felt so miserable for the past few days that I have not been fit for business & as Our Base Ball Club were going to Cleveland to play a match with a club of said city I thought it might benefit [my] health to cross the Lake & have a change of scene . . . here I am, in the cabin of the aforementioned Steamer writing a loving missive surrounded by a gay rolicking & as happy a company of young men as need be. The majority of them are unexceptionable, with one or two clowns & one or two Black Sheep which seems to be unavoidable as they are good Ball Players.

The following afternoon, after a fine dinner at the Kennard House and a carriage ride through the streets of Cleveland, the two sides squared off. Wrote Ferry: "There was thousands present to witness the game & Your Dexter was also chosen unanimously by both contesting clubs as Umpire of the day. This office he filled to their satisfaction, as at the close of the game both clubs gave him three hearty cheers, which was satisfying indeed as it was a trying position to do justice to both clubs while my sympathies of course was with the Detroit boys, which beat by a score of 37 to 25."

That evening, on their return trip across Lake Erie, the Detroits gathered inside the cabin "to draft a series of resolutions tendering the thanks of the Club & friends to the Captain, Clerk, & Steward of the boat for their courtesy, kindness, etc., etc. These resolutions were copied by the Chair (as the secretary's finger was sore from playing ball) & presented to the Captain & then our meeting adjourned."

Detroit fielded several other notable amateur nines, including the Cass, Aetna, and Excelsior teams. The Cass Baseball Club, which was formed in 1871, was perhaps the most talented, and won the informal state championship several times before it dissolved in 1889. In the absence of a professional team in Detroit, these clubs attracted quite a following, especially when they played amateur nines from sister cities like Jackson or hosted out–of–state professional clubs such as the Brooklyn Excelsiors and the Chicago White Stockings.

The Cass Club's 1878 season is typical of the era's amateur teams. In a fourteen–game schedule that ran from May 9 to September 29, the team racked up a 12–2 record playing local pickup teams, a professional club in Chicago, and amateur nines in Flint, Kalamazoo, and Owosso.

By the late 1870s most amateur clubs were semiprofessional in nature. The courtliness Dexter Ferry had savored just a few years earlier gave way to hot–blooded competition. Arguments on the field and fisticuffs in the stands were regular occurrences at the matches. A pair of games played by the Aetnas during the Centennial summer of 1876 are revealing. On June 22, the Aetnas visited London, Ontario, for a match with the Tecumsehs.

"To begin with," reported the *Free Press*, "there was a dispute over the sum of money to be paid the London club. It was settled in some way and the game began at half–past three o'clock. At the end of the second innings a change was made in umpires, and until the seventh innings the game was played in bad shape, so far as talk and ill behavior were concerned.

"At the end of the last half of the seventh innings the Londoners refused to go on with the game, as they wished to reach the evening train for Jackson. The umpire called the game and the crowd left in disgust. Where the responsibility of the lamentable fizzle rests is known only to the managers of both clubs, who tell such directly opposite stories of the disputes that it is impossible to decide. One thing is certain, and that is that Wood, of the Aetnas, and Latham, of the Tecumsehs, talked altogether too much and too loudly."

On July 26 the Aetnas hosted the Mutuals of Jackson. "The excitement was intense, and never before had there been on the Detroit base ball grounds so excited and indigent a crowd as these demanding the umpire's removal," observed the *Free Press*. "Storm after storm of hisses and groans were showered upon him, and finding that his manner of umpiring would be no longer tolerated by the spectators he very wisely withdrew, but not until he had grossly insulted the President of the Aetna Club . . . and had threatened to inflict personal injury to several of the members of the Detroit nine."

To cap an imperfect summer, several professionals were stranded in Detroit after promoters failed to pay their wages when their seasons ended in mid–November. A benefit banquet raised the funds to send them home.

Rowdyism and the encroachment of professionalism left a bad taste in the mouths of many. One Detroit paper recorded its disgust in an 1878 editorial: "Three years ago this city had the base ball mania, and the result was that the importation of paid professionals spoiled all interest in the game. Since that time there have been very few games and little interest shown." That year the Excelsiors disbanded and the Aetnas reorganized as a semipro team. Some of the disaffected young men helped form the Detroit Athletic Club (DAC) that December. The DAC's aim was to offer such "legitimate manly athletic sports" as fencing, boxing, tumbling, and rowing, while avoiding "those evils of a vain ambition to professionalism." The Cass Club applauded the new organization's noble mission and immediately challenged the DAC to a Christmas morning football game.

Despite the protestations of editorial writers and amateur sportsmen, professionalism was close to establishing a foothold in Detroit by late 1878. The country's first openly professional league, the National Association of Professional Baseball Players, organized in 1871. This loose confederation of Eastern and Midwestern teams lasted until 1875. A year after it folded, the National League began to operate clubs in some of the biggest cities in the country, including Cincinnati, Chicago, St. Louis, New York, and Philadelphia. The first enclosed ballpark, Brooklyn's Union Grounds, opened in 1862 and created a successful model for other cities. Union Grounds demonstrated the many benefits of enclosing a field and charging admission. Chief among them was a steady revenue stream for owners, who could then afford to regularly pay top players, and a higher quality audience, since the more raffish elements of society were unable or unwilling to pay for a ticket.

Attendance figures at National League contests impressed the local organizers of Recreation Park, a large multipurpose recreation center planned for the near east side. They reasoned that if Detroiters were disillusioned by the hypocrisy of paid amateurs, perhaps they would support an avowedly professional team. Horse racing was the only competition baseball faced as a spectator sport.

Accordingly, the Recreation Park Company hired W. M. Hollinger to organize a squad of professionals to serve as a paid attraction at the facility. Recreation Park opened May 10, 1879. Two days later, when Hollinger's Nine played against a team from Troy, New York, in front of a large crowd of paying customers, the transition was complete. Just twenty years after merchants and clerks had closed their businesses early for their historic match on the grounds of the Cass farm, the ideal of gentleman amateurs dabbling in baseball for recreation had been permanently shoved aside by the reality of imported professionals who played games for a living.

When Detroit's first professional baseball players took the field on May 12, 1879, dressed in cream–and–chocolate–colored caps and uniforms with red belts and stockings, they were probably unaware of the history they were making. So, for that matter, were the fifteen hundred Detroiters who had traveled by horseback, carriage, or on foot to Recreation Park that Monday afternoon. For many, the ball game was little more than a novelty, the visiting Troy Haymakers brought in (at a cost of $102.50, plus $25 for a brass band) to promote the real attraction—a facility touted as one of the best in the country.

Located on a section of the old Elijah Brush farm, one of the original eighteenth–century French land grants, Recreation Park was the first ambitious sports enterprise in a city whose name would one day become synonymous with professional sports of all types.

The general amusement park, located in the heart of today's Medical Center, extended along Brush Street from Brady Street to Willis Avenue, with the entrance and reception building two blocks east of Woodward on Brady. The baseball diamond was located at the south end of the field, while the north end contained a large cricket field. A three–quarter–mile trotting track encircled the grounds, which hosted lacrosse and croquet matches whenever baseball and cricket games were not being played. Additionally, the park featured a gymnasium, bowling alleys, tennis courts, an archery range, and a skating and curling rink. The entire eighteen–acre site was enclosed by a nine–foot fence, parts of which were later painted with colorful advertisements for such proprietors as clothier J. L. Hudson and the Garland Stove Company.

The facility's bathtub shape produced some peculiar dimensions. The outfield fence, which divided the cricket grounds from the ball field and essentially cut the park in half, stood more than 400 feet from the plate. But it was only about 230 feet from the plate to the dirt trotting track. The track itself was about 50 feet wide, meaning a 280–foot drive down the right–field foul line would clear the fence while a similarly placed hit to left would wind up in the grove of trees that separated the west end of the ball field from adjacent Harper Hospital.

Although the park was not built exclusively for baseball, it was widely regarded as one of the finest ball playing venues around. The turf was "smooth as a table," and the outfield was level with the infield—a rarity in those days. The covered wooden grandstand behind home plate held about a thousand people.

The directors and investors of the Recreation Park Company saw the multi–use facility as a fair risk. City dwellers, faced with the phenomenon of increased leisure time, were more concerned than ever with the consumptive urban lifestyle they led. Directors reasoned that Detroiters, if not moved to actively participate in the park's many attractions, might be enticed into watching others participate—in return for a little spare change, of course. After all, the average laborer now made slightly more than a dollar a day; skilled tradesmen, such as bricklayers, machinists, and carpenters, made twice that amount.

The president of the Recreation Park Company was James McMillan, an immigrant whose life story embodied the possibilities of nineteenth–century America. Born in Scotland in 1838 and raised in Hamilton, Ontario, McMillan came to Detroit in 1858 as the purchasing agent for the Detroit and Milwaukee Railroad. He became fast friends with John S. Newberry, who somehow found time among his many social and business activities to captain the Detroit Baseball Club that defeated the Early Risers in 1859.

While McMillan's prowess as a ballplayer is unknown, he displayed considerable business acumen. The railroad boom of the 1860s made him and Newberry rich men and primary sources of capital in a growing city. They invested in a series of business ventures that, among other things, obtained the city's telephone franchise in 1877 and, four years later, created the Edison Electric Light Company. Their many philanthropic activities included Grace Hospital, founded in memory of McMillan's oldest daughter Grace, who had died at a young age. As the leader of the state's Republican party, McMillan managed Newberry's successful campaign for Congress and later enjoyed a distinguished career himself as a U.S. senator.

Other Recreation Park Company directors included Treasurer George Hendrie, the owner of a trucking firm for whom McMillan had secured the lucrative franchise for the horse–driven Detroit City Railway; Secretary A. C. Bowman; and Vice President Alfred E. Brush, whose family owned the property on which most of the park rested. During the spring of 1879 the board wielded enough clout to convince the trustees of the adjoining property to surrender a hundred feet of wooded land to complete the ballfield. The entire grounds were donated by an obscure citizen named Walter Harper in 1859 to house a military hospital. After they received a formal request from the park directors on April 1, hospital trustees waited until May 6 to officially give their permission. Sixty workmen quickly moved in and leveled the trees, plowed the ground, and installed sod, drain tile, and water pipes. Within a week everything was ready for Detroit's first professional opening day.

The Hollinger Nine roster on May 12, 1879 included the following men. Their monthly salaries are in parentheses.

C	Emil Gross	($125)
P	Harry Salisbury	($125)
1B	Steve Libby	($100)
2B	Sam Barkley	($50)
3B	J. B. McSorley	($70)
SS	Tom Shaughnessy	($50)
LF	C. H. Morton	($55)
CF	P. N. Van Burkalow	($70)
RF	E. Swartwood	($55)

The Troy team scored two runs in the first inning and captured a 7–1 victory, spoiling the Hollinger Nine's debut. One observer saw reason for hope, however: "The fact that no runs were made by the

Two Detroit Wolverines of the 1880s. Like most nineteenth–century pitchers, George "Stump" Weidman (left) generally finished what he started, completing all but 12 of his 190 starts during his six seasons at Recreation Park. Second baseman Hardy Richardson (right) compiled a .330 average over three seasons with Detroit, second only to Dan Brouthers' .338 career mark as a Wolverine. In 1886 he hit 11 roundtrippers to tie Brouthers for the National League home–run title.

Troy club during their last five innings shows that the Detroits know how to play, and after practice together, good work may be looked for from them."

The Recreation Park team won the majority of its games in convincing fashion, hosting most games but sometimes traveling as far as Iowa and Illinois for contests. On one occasion they paid a well–regarded Kalamazoo club $111 (plus $6 for the umpire) to play

Detroit was still a community of pedestrians and horse–drawn buggies in the 1880s, as this shot of the intersection of Woodward and Michigan Avenues—about a ten–minute walk from Recreation Park—illustrates. Baseball fans in those days bought studio cards of their favorite players at the Eagle Art Gallery, or discussed the afternoon's game over an ice cream soda at Sanders (conspicuous by its striped awnings). Most players lived in downtown hotels. Because the players were more accessible, it was possible to get your picture taken with them, as illustrated by the top photograph. Notable are Wolverines Charles Getzien, Larry Twitchell (numbers 2 and 3 in the photo), Sam Thompson (number 10), and Frederick A. Cooke (number 6), the fan whose Cass Avenue drugstore is the setting for this photograph. Not everyone was enthralled with professional ballplayers, however. "Were it not for baseball the majority of these whiners and complainers would not be able to make a living," judged the *National Police Gazette* in 1886, "as they are too infernally lazy to make a success."

a three–game set at Recreation Park. The Hollinger Nine shut them out twice. Soon afterwards, the park team suddenly disbanded. Exactly why isn't clear, although crowds as low as two hundred people and a hefty monthly payroll of $700 probably convinced the park's owners that a ball club lacking a league affiliation would never be a profitable operation. The star battery of Salisbury and Gross immediately found employment in the National League.

Management worked hard to make the facility profitable. For example, a Professor Rulison launched his hot–air balloon from the baseball diamond, performing tricks on a trapeze bar as it rose into the sky. Professional women baseball teams were brought in, though customers—between yells of "Stretch her, Pinky, for all you're worth!" and "Sail in, old gal!"—pronounced the "bloomer girls" the "worst baseballists on record."

An interesting attraction was the electric promenade concert, where music lovers paid twenty–five cents to listen to a band on grounds lit by giant lamps and reflectors erected on the grandstand. The lighting equipment was the work of local tinkerer Charles Van Depoele. The band sat in the center of the diamond, where "the light illuminated the books of the musicians with a brilliancy equal to sunlight." Despite Van Depoele's lights and the park's penchant for novelty attractions, apparently no one thought of trying to play a baseball game underneath them. While the city was just starting to illuminate its streets with garishly painted hundred–foot–high electric towers, nighttime baseball would not arrive until the middle of the next century.

In 1881 recently elected Mayor William G. Thompson lit up the skies with the announcement that he had secured a franchise in the National League, which sought a western city to replace the ousted Cincinnati club. The mayor was ecstatic, convinced that Detroit's first major–league baseball team would be an unmatchable engineer of municipal pride and a winning business proposition, to boot. Thompson and his backers paid twenty thousand dollars for the franchise and arranged for the games to be played at Recreation Park.

Anticipating large crowds, officials expanded the grandstand to include a rooftop press box and seats for an additional five thousand people. Overflow crowds would be accommodated in time–honored fashion by placing them in the outfield and along both base lines. On these occasions, a semicircle of carriages and fans formed the perimeter of the outfield and special ground rules were put into effect. An outfielder would signal whenever a fair ball landed in the overflow; the batter was then awarded a two– or three–base hit, depending on what the opposing managers and umpire agreed to prior to the start of the game.

Mayor Thompson, an attorney and a meticulously barbered dandy who kept his "chew" in a silver tobacco box, dearly loved his growing horse–and–buggy town, whose 120,000 citizens in 1881 still lived within a three–mile radius of the original riverfront settlement. "When I ascended to the roof of the City Hall on a June or August day," he once rhapsodized, "it seemed to me as if Detroit was a city situated in the midst of a green forest. The trees that line every street and avenue made a most agreeable impression, not only upon strangers but upon Detroiters themselves." As the team's majority owner and president, Thompson kept the mayor's office as the franchise's official address. Hizzoner proudly labeled his club the Detroits, although newspapers were wont to call them the Wolverines.

During their first few seasons townspeople merely called the team bad. At 4 o'clock on the afternoon of May 2, 1881, the mayor's pride and joy took the field dressed in red–trimmed, light–gray uniforms with cardinal red belts and stockings. A crowd of 1,265 Detroiters paid between fifteen and sixty–five cents each to watch the first major–league game ever played in the city. The opposing team from Buffalo won, 6–4—a harbinger of troubles to come. The team led the pack until July, when it suddenly collapsed. Detroit ultimately finished fourth, but still posted a $12,440 profit on gross revenues of $35,000.

Although success was fleeting, the affection was genuine. Thus we read of one contest during that inaugural season: "During the game yesterday the home nine were presented with a basket of flowers each. A special floral ball was given to [Charlie] Bennett, and the genial Umpire Dick Higham was not forgotten."

There were other roses among the stinkweed. George "Stump" Weidman led the league with a 1.80 earned–run average in 1881, while George Derby split ninety–two decisions in two seasons before his arm gave out. Outfielder George Wood won the 1882 home run championship with seven round–trippers. But fellows like shortstop Sadie Houck and outfielder Mike Dorgan proved an embarrassment. Both were suspended for the entire 1882 season for "dissipation," the fashionable euphemism for excessive drinking and whoring. Adding to the foul odor was umpire Dick Higham, who proved to be a bit too genial. Mayor Thompson ordered him thrown out of the league after an investigation revealed the arbiter was in cahoots with a group of Detroit gamblers.

During their first five seasons the Wolverines consistently lost more games than they won, and never finished any higher than fourth. For a time they not only played like clowns, they dressed like them. In 1882 National League president William Hulbert pressured owners to outfit their players in white pants, belts, and ties, with the color of their caps and shirts determined by position. The second baseman wore orange and black, the pitcher baby blue, the catcher scarlet, and so on. The gaudily striped jerseys were made of heavy silk, which players complained were too uncomfortable—and ugly—to wear outdoors. Following this dizzying riot of colors had fans at Recreation Park feeling as if they were on hallucinogenics by the end of a game. The experiment was discontinued because of its expense to owners, but not before the color scheme produced a tidy profit for Hulbert's partner, sporting goods magnate Al Spalding, who had manufactured the detested "clown" shirts. All this grief proved too much for Mayor Thompson, who after two years of ownership sold the club to businessman Joseph H. Marsh.

The Wolverines fared no better under Marsh's ownership. In 1884 the team sank to an all–time low—they won only 28 times in 112 outings and finished dead last, 56 games behind pennant–winning Providence. That summer overhanded pitching was legalized, resulting in a slew of no–hitters, including the only ones ever pitched at Recreation Park. On August 4, Buffalo's great Jim "Pud" Galvin faced twenty-eight Detroit batters in an 18–0 trouncing; only an error prevented a perfect game. And on October 1, Detroit's Charles "Pretzels" Getzien hurled a six–inning, 1–0 no–no against Philadelphia.*

After several years of lackluster play and unimaginative ownership the Detroit franchise was in real danger of dissolving. To the forefront stepped Frederick K. Stearns, a former collegiate player and heir to his father's pharmaceutical business. Stearns, born in Buffalo in 1854, was a year old when his family came to Detroit. In 1871 Stearns helped organize the Aetna baseball club, an amateur nine from which he later resigned when it turned semipro. He attended the University of Michigan, where he played second base and captained the varsity squad in 1877. While he labored to learn the family business, he still found time to indulge his two other major passions: music (he played several instruments and founded U–M's Musical Sodality) and baseball. In 1885 he decided to invest in the Wolverines, becoming its majority shareholder and serving as president.

---

* During this period the rules governing the delicate balance between pitcher and batter continued to evolve through trial and error. The wrist snap was legalized in 1872, and opened the door for the development of the curve ball. Hitters regained the edge in 1881 when the distance between home plate and the pitcher's box was increased from forty-five to fifty feet. The 1884 rule change that allowed overhanded deliveries gave hurlers a big advantage, though batters continued to request a high or low pitch as late as 1886.

While the three–strike rule remained constant since 1879 (except for a short–lived experiment in 1887 when it took four strikes to fan a batter), it was a while before the game finally settled on its current formula of four balls for a walk. In 1879 nine balls constituted a base on balls. That number dropped over the next decade, from eight (1880) to seven (1881), six (1884), five (1886), and finally four (1889).

Recreation Park in 1886. Management charged fifty cents for general admission and seventy-five cents for reserved seats. The prices were doubled for the following year's postseason championship series with St. Louis.

At the end of the 1885 season Stearns purchased Buffalo's "Big Four" infield of first baseman Dan Brouthers, second baseman Hardy Richardson, shortstop Jack Rowe, and third baseman Jim "Deacon" White for the princely sum of eight thousand dollars. Added to a lineup that already featured catcher Charlie Bennett, outfielders Sam Thompson and Ned Hanlon, and pitchers Charles "Lady" Baldwin and Pretzels Getzien, the Wolverines just missed winning the pennant in 1886 by two–and–a–half games to Cap Anson's Chicago White Stockings.

As countless club owners have learned, nothing improves a sagging gate like a winning team. To take advantage of increased fan interest, Stearns expanded Recreation Park's seating capacity by installing bleachers that ran all the way from left field to the grandstand. A short, white picket fence separated the fans from the playing field. Additional bleachers were built halfway up the first–base line. Watching the Wolverines proved therapeutic for the park's neighbors as well. In 1884 Harper Hospital's original wooden structures were replaced by a modern facility, its main building constructed just beyond the park's left–field fence. It was the perfect spot for patients and hospital employees to watch the league's best offense unload on opposing pitchers.

With fans cheering from the bleachers, from wildcat stands erected outside the park, and from the roof and windows of Harper Hospital, the Wolverines led the league from start to finish in 1887, the first major–league club ever to do so. An unbeaten, preseason barnstorming tour and a torrid regular–season start produced forty–nine wins in the Wolverines' first fifty–one games, creating tremendous public interest. Stearns used his team's success to build a new reserved grandstand for the ladies. He also opened a box office inside a Woodward Avenue sporting–goods store and offered season tickets at twenty–five dollars for sixty–three home dates. (General admission tickets regularly cost fifty cents; reserved seats were seventy–five cents.) Detroiters could buy lithographs of their heroes at several downtown locations.

The Wolverines scored a league record 969 runs in 1887, an average of 8 runs per game. Much of the offense centered around future Hall of Famers Dan Brouthers and Sam Thompson. The twenty–nine–year–old Brouthers (pronounced "Broo–thers") was the top slugger of the nineteenth century. He batted .343 during his nineteen–year career (ninth–best of all–time) and won five batting titles for Buffalo, Boston, and Brooklyn. A big man, the six–foot, two–inch, 220–pound player had a keen eye (he's credited with coining the phrase, "Keep your eye on the ball") and a powerful swing. He once knocked a fan out of a tower with a home run blast. Brouthers, who topped the National League in two–base hits in all three seasons he played at Recreation Park, led the circuit with 153 runs scored and finished third in batting with a .338 mark.

Sam Thompson, a bear of a man who once split his pants legging out a double because Detroit couldn't find a uniform big enough to fit him, led the league with a .372 mark. The twenty–seven–year–old right fielder also knocked in a staggering 166 runs, 62 more than the runner–up. The good–natured Thompson proved as durable as he was popular. In 1906, when he was forty–six years old, Thompson played eight games alongside Ty Cobb and Sam Crawford in the Detroit Tigers' injury–depleted outfield.

During the regular season and the ensuing "world's series" with the St. Louis Browns of the American Association, crowds of up to nine thousand people swelled Recreation Park. It was a common sight to see the outfield ringed with carriages, horses, and knots of spectators. An outfielder chasing a ball into that overflow risked crushing a straw boater or sliding on a horse apple. But that was the charm of nineteenth–century baseball. It was fiercely competitive, yet was still wonderfully quaint.

A case in point was the public adoration of Charlie Bennett, one of only two Wolverines (field captain and center fielder Ned Hanlon was the other) to play for Detroit during its entire eight–year stay in the National League. Bennett, who hailed from New Castle, Pennsylvania, first sampled the city as a twenty–one–year–old member of the Aetnas in 1875 before breaking into the professional ranks with Worcester in 1878. He liked the people he met in Detroit, so much that when the city was awarded a major league franchise, he turned down an offer of more money from the Boston Beaneaters to become the first player to sign with the Wolverines.

An outstanding defensive catcher and a solid offensive threat (he hit better than .300 his first three seasons with Detroit) Bennett's health and batting statistics both declined sharply because of injuries. In 1886 he became the first backstop to wear a chest protector (concealing it under his uniform), but that did nothing for his hands. In those days mangled mitts were an occupational hazard for backstops, who caught barehanded or wore thin leather gloves. By the end of a game, the catcher's hands were covered with cuts and deep bruises, the ball was blood–stained and the catcher could barely feed himself at dinner. In 1886 and 1887 Bennett missed more than half of each campaign because of broken fingers. Bad luck followed him into the postseason, when he split a digit on a foul ball. "It did not seem anything unusual to Bennett or to his fingers," reported the *New York Times*.

> When he held up that battered right hand, with its fingers swollen and spread like a boxing glove, with rags tied around three of them, and a general appearance of having been run over by a freight–car about the entire hand, it did not seem as though there was room to split it in any new place. He went right on with his play . . . though the blood was reddening his hand and could be seen now and then to drip from his fingers. Bennett wears a look of patient suffering on his bronzed features. His hands have suffered so much that they have probably become case–hardened and ceased to feel. . . .

The *Times*'s reference to Bennett's being run over by a train later proved tragically prophetic. But with Dan Brouthers sidelined by an injured ankle, the battered catcher stoically remained in the lineup as Detroit took eleven of the fifteen postseason contests with St. Louis.

The 1887 world champs. Outer circle, clockwise from upper left: pitcher Charlie "Pretzels" Getzien, left fielder Hardy Richardson, first baseman Dan Brouthers, pitcher Charles "Lady" Baldwin, catcher Charlie Bennett, shortstop Jack Rowe, catcher Charlie Ganzel, pitcher Pete Conway, third baseman Jim "Deacon" White, second baseman Fred Dunlap. Inner circle: manager Bill Watkins, right fielder Sam Thompson, center fielder Ned Hanlon, and pitcher Larry Twitchell.

In 1888 the Recreation Park owners proudly hoisted the world- and
league-championship pennants captured by Detroit the previous season. By the end of the summer, however, the team had disbanded and
the players sold piecemeal.

The unprecedented championship tournament, correctly characterized as "the series that went on forever," lasted from October 10 through October 26 and dragged through eleven different parks in ten big–league cities. Only two games were played in Detroit.

Game three was held October 12. Nine thousand people watched in brisk weather as the home team pulled out a heart–pounding 2–1 victory in thirteen innings. Pretzels Getzien, who led the league in winning percentage with a 29–13 record, went the distance for Detroit. The German–born curveballer also stroked two hits and scored the winning run on the Browns' seventh error of the game.

By the time the Wolverines returned to Recreation Park two weeks later for the meaningless thirteenth game, the title had already been decided, so the four thousand fans in attendance were in a festive mood. In the fourth inning, Detroit was at bat. Suddenly, the action was halted as some sort of commotion behind the grandstand drew attention away from the game.

Fans were always interrupting games for presentations, but this one was special. For weeks supporters had circulated throughout the community, collecting money for a gift to honor faithful Charlie Bennett's meritorious service. Two puffing politicians pushed a wheelbarrow loaded with 520 silver dollars and topped by a floral horseshoe to the home plate. The crowd roared for Bennett to leave the bench. "Come out here, Charlie!" they yelled. "Come out here!"

Charlie obliged. Four thousand Detroiters roared even louder as their star catcher wheeled his treasure around the bases, followed by several smiling cops and a fife–and–drum corps playing "Yankee Doodle." Sheer bedlam reigned, reported the next day's paper, as "everybody got up and shouted themselves into hysterics."

This golden moment literally served as the Wolverines' last hurrah. Stearns, taking over the family business after his father's retirement, resigned as president of the club. The following season Detroit became the first club to issue rain checks. Maybe it should have been umbrellas. Bad luck rained down on the team, with injuries, dissension, and that old standby, dissipation, creating a fifth–place finish. After the season, club directors announced they were folding the franchise. They claimed they had lost $58,000, although skeptics believed the figure was the result of creative bookkeeping and not fan apathy. Business leaders talked of trying to save the team. "But they are too late," said the *Free Press*. "The men who have their money risked on the venture have come to the conclusion that Detroit as a baseball town is in that condition of reposeful indifference characteristic of a dead game cock, and they have determined to get out as nearly whole as possible." Over the winter the players were sold piecemeal, giving

investors a $135 return on their original $50 shares. Detroit was left
without major league ball for the next several years.

Bob Leadley, a Brooklyn native who had settled in Detroit in
1875, served as the Wolverines' secretary and treasurer from 1884 to
1888. After the team dissolved he convinced Merrill B. Mills, a
prominent figure in local stove and tobacco enterprises, to organize a
franchise in the new International Association. This minor league
originally consisted of three Canadian clubs—Hamilton, London and
Toronto—and five American clubs in Buffalo, Detroit, Rochester,
Syracuse and Toledo. In 1890 Grand Rapids and Montreal replaced
Buffalo and Hamilton; the franchise shifts were an indication of the
league's shaky status.

Leadley was manager and secretary of the Detroit nine, which
played two seasons at Recreation Park. Behind captain George
"Orator" Shaffer, an aging outfielder who had broken in with the
National League in 1877, Lev Shreve, a lanky young pitcher from
Kentucky, and shortstop Bobby Wheelock, Detroit won a champi-
onship in 1889. The team also featured some veterans of the National
League Detroits, including catcher Jake Wells and outfielder Charles
"Count" Campau, a descendant of one of the French families that
founded the city. However, attendance was poor throughout the cir-
cuit, and the following July the league collapsed.

At the same time that Detroit's International League representative was vainly trying to make it through the 1891 season, a local
entry popped up in the short–lived Northwestern League. An attraction was William "Rasty" Wright, an oversized twenty–eight–year outfielder born in nearby Birmingham. Wright, a murderous
minor–league hitter, served as manager. After opening the schedule
at Recreation Park, the club switched its home field to Riverside Park.
Little is known of the facility, which was built outside city limits, in
Hamtramck Township, with the intention of playing Sunday ball.
Riverside Park was located across from Belle Isle, between Jefferson
Avenue and the Detroit River, on land that today is Owens Park. To
the club's dismay, township authorities frustrated all attempts to play
on the Sabbath. Abysmal attendance caused the team to fold in early
June after playing only twenty–eight games.

Apart from demonstrating Detroiters' indifference over inferior
ball, these failures reflected the great instability and continuing
uncertainty of the professional game. Leadley, who managed
Cleveland to a second–place finish in 1892, was so unimpressed with
the National League's future he quit the club and found a job with
the Internal Revenue Service in Detroit. When he returned to baseball, it was as manager of the Detroit Athletic Club, one of the
strongest amateur clubs in the country.

The 1880s and 1890s were the heyday of athletic clubs in the U.S. Following the lead of the New York Athletic Club, organized in 1868, these represented the last gasp of amateurism in a country where sports were fast becoming professional. The Detroit Athletic Club, after operating out of the Y.M.C.A. for several years, leased land on the west side of Woodward between Canfield and Forest, site of countless amateur matches over the years. Members built a brick clubhouse there in 1888. Behind the clubhouse (where "good, moral influences abound within its walls"), a cinder track, ballfield, cricket grounds, and a covered grandstand took up most of the property from Woodward to Cass.

"Not only did the club on Woodward Avenue have the best club-house and field," remembered sportswriter Eddie Batchelor, "but it also achieved a social rating that helped to bring in the gifted performers on diamond, track, and gridiron." At various times the DAC Deltas included such budding civic and business leaders as outfielders John C. Lodge and Harry Jewett, shortstop William S. Crowley, third baseman John Kelsey, pitcher George Codd, and Frederick Stearns, who served as president from 1890 to 1894.

In 1889 the team won the city championship; the following year it grabbed the Amateur Athletic Union's national title, defeating the New Jersey Athletic Club in five games at the Polo Grounds in New York. George "Geep" Codd, a University of Michigan student and a future Detroit mayor and judge, pitched every game, winning the finale, 3–2. Codd pitched the Deltas into the finals again in 1891, but a dreadful mix–up in dates forced the Detroiters to forfeit the championship. The slightly built righthander led the DAC into the AAU finals for the third straight season in 1892. His catcher was Frank Bowerman, who went on to play for Detroit's Western League team in 1894 before enjoying a long career with the New York Giants. The Deltas traveled to Washington, D.C., and behind Codd and Bowerman, swept the eastern representatives for the national championship.

More titles might have followed, but the AAU decided to drop its sponsorship of baseball. Regardless, the DAC nine remained one of the best around for another couple decades. The 1909 lineup included future major leaguers Bill Lerchen, Nemo Seibold, Fred Blanding, and Chick Lathers. Even Ty Cobb took a turn, playing several games in 1906 as he worked himself back into shape after a lengthy illness.

The enthusiasm surrounding the DAC prompted some citizens to ask why a professional team wasn't representing the city. With the Washington club reportedly on the verge of folding, some campaigned for the National League to replace it with another franchise in Detroit.

"Detroit has not the remotest chance of getting back into the big leagues," one member of the National League's membership committee told the *Sporting News* in the fall of 1893. "It was no stayer when it was a member of the league and sold out at a considerable profit. Buffalo would be a good city if Washington decides to quit, but I would see no sense in leaving Washington merely to go to Detroit."

As it turned out, Washington remained in the National League, squelching any talk of a major league franchise in Detroit. That winter an energetic thirty–year–old Cincinnati sportswriter, Ban Johnson, visited the city to investigate the possibility of including Detroit in his reorganized Western League in 1894. Johnson envisioned his minor league ultimately becoming a major circuit similar to the all–powerful National League. Talks proved satisfactory, and soon afterwards Detroit became the most populous member of a Midwestern association that also included Grand Rapids, Indianapolis, Kansas City, Milwaukee, Minneapolis, Sioux City, and Toledo.

George Arthur Vanderbeck was the owner and president of the new team, which he optimistically announced would become "the cream of the league." That prompted some to call the team the Creams, though it wouldn't be long before they were known as the Detroit Tigers. The beefy, mustachioed, middle–aged Vanderbeck, previously involved with professional baseball in faraway Los Angeles, "understands the feelings of Detroit and the demands for good ball," reported one daily. "This he proposes to give us, if not with his present players, then with others."

Vanderbeck is an important but forgotten figure in the history of the Detroit Tigers. Not only did he bring professional baseball back to the city to stay, serving as the Tigers's owner for their first six seasons, he was responsible for moving the club to its present location at Michigan and Trumbull Avenues. Despite his historical significance, he remains a mystery. Biographical details are sketchy, although there appears to have been something about him that made a man want to count his fingers after a handshake.

Vanderbeck created some waves as head of the Los Angeles franchise in the California League, feuding with other league owners and arranging a postseason playoff without their permission. In December 1892 the magnates revoked Vanderbeck's license and dropped his franchise from the league. Nonetheless, with a seven–thousand–dollar surplus, the maverick owner was the only

Throughout the nineteenth century many Detroiters played cricket interchange-ably with baseball. This squad of cricketeers is perched on the steps of the Detroit Athletic Club's new clubhouse in 1889. The fellow wearing a derby and standing in the doorway is John C. Lodge, who also played outfield for the DAC's baseball team, played ball with several amateur teams, including the Cass Club, before beginning his political career in 1897. The longtime city council member obviously learned a little about pinch–hitting, as he twice filled in for resigning mayors in the 1920s before serving a full term himself. Like many others who came of age during the era of amateur competition, Lodge had little regard for the professional athletes of the twentieth century. In his old age he professed that he never "had the chance" to watch Charlie Gehringer play during his two decades with the Tigers, a startling but revealing admission for someone who lived and worked his entire life within walking distance of Michigan and Trumbull. Lodge finally retired from the city council in 1948 at age eighty–five and died two years later. The John C. Lodge Freeway was named for him, though Lodge, true to his horse–and–buggy roots, never learned how to drive a car.

one in the circuit to post a profit. The money presumably made it easier for him to poke around the country for a new beginning. After making some noise in the press about fielding a team in Toledo, Vanderbeck settled on Detroit. His base of operations was an office in the Hammond Building downtown. In time a white flag with a blue circle was raised from the roof whenever a home game was scheduled.

Newspapers referred to Vanderbeck's "California contingent," which moved seemingly en masse to Detroit. Nearly every man on the 1894 roster had played at one time or another on the West Coast, including first baseman Howard Earl, third baseman Bill Everett, pitchers George Harper and Lou Balsz, and outfielders James Burns and Joe McGucken. Some, such as second baseman Bob Glenalvin, right fielder Cliff Carroll, catcher Billy Kreig, and pitcher George Cobb, also were National League veterans or National League rejects, depending upon one's point of view. Cobb, a twenty–six–year–old righthander from San Francisco, lost a league–high thirty–seven games for Baltimore in 1892, an experience which undoubtedly influenced his decision to retire and go into business for himself on the coast. But Vanderbeck, by all accounts an energetic and persuasive man, convinced Cobb to leave California for Detroit. Reported the *News–Tribune*: "The fever is still with [Cobb] and as he expresses himself, 'In '94 I am with the champion Detroits.'"

Vanderbeck scheduled games at League Park (also known as Boulevard Park), a wobbly wooden structure at Helen and Champlain (later Lafayette), just outside of what was then the city's eastern limits. The neighborhood, located near the Belle Isle bridge, was served by three trolley lines and was only a ten–minute walk from City Hall.

Vanderbeck refurbished the park, which had a covered grandstand and open bleacher sections running along both foul lines. Seating capacity was about thirty–five hundred. According to one newspaper account, "the ground is well graded and the infield has a clay surface rolled very smoothly so that balls will land accurately." There was a dressing room for players who, once on the field, baked in the midday sun on uncovered benches. Thirsty players used a communal tin cup to quench themselves from a wooden water barrel.

Thousands of curious Detroiters positioned themselves in and around League Park for the Creams' home opener against Toledo on May 2. "In each of the little cottages on Helen Avenue a dozen frantic women bumped their heads against the window casings," observed a *News–Tribune* writer. "One fond mother held a wee baby seated on the second story window sill, and the little rascal . . . was

John Kelsey pitched and played third base for the DAC's national champions in 1892. In 1920 the millionaire industrialist bought a quarter-share of the Tigers for $250,000, an investment he held until his death seven years later.

nearly launched into kingdom come when Balsz made a home run hit over the fence." The Creams disappointed the estimated four thousand paying customers, as well as hundreds of others perched in trees and on rooftops, by losing 4–3. The novelty of watching a new team quickly wore off. The next day gaping holes appeared in the grandstand as attendance quickly leveled off to several hundred a game.

Detroit was occasionally criticized for not pulling its own weight attendance–wise, but in truth the Gay Nineties was a terrible time to launch a business of any kind. During the decade an estimated 40 percent of all organized baseball leagues failed to finish their first year. In 1892 hard economic times forced the American Association and National League to end their feuding and merge into one twelve–team circuit, the country's sole surviving major league. The following year a financial panic set off a nationwide depression that took several years to run its course.

Bob Glenalvin, an Indianapolis native who made his mark playing professionally in Chicago and Los Angeles, served as the second baseman and field captain of Detroit's first Western League team in 1894. After the club sustained a three-week losing streak early in the season, one local paper remarked: "The man has had so few occasions to smile."

By the time Vanderbeck's team debuted in the spring of 1894, most of Detroit's heavy industries had shut down or drastically cut back hours. In a city that now numbered some two hundred thousand people, more than twenty–five thousand workingmen— one–third of the labor force—were idle. The day before the Creams' opener at League Park, Thomas J. Navin, an attorney for the Michigan Liquor Dealers Protective Association (and the older brother of future club owner Frank Navin), estimated that the depression closed three hundred saloons and six houses of ill repute in the city. "The old–time rounders are beginning to wonder if they will recognize the town in the morning," remarked the *News–Tribune*. These were the days before government and industry provided safety nets for the unemployed, so private charities were overwhelmed by the poor and hungry. Conditions were so bad that Mayor Hazen S. Pingree sponsored vegetable gardens to provide food and jobs for the needy, an innovative if widely ridiculed public works program that thrust him into the national spotlight.

Despite the addition of outfielders Sam Dungan and Bob Campau, former National Leaguers who hit .447 and .370 respectively, Detroit finished a poor seventh in its first Western League sea-

Los Angeles business-
man George Arthur
Vanderbeck owned the
Detroit Tigers their first
six seasons, from 1894
through 1899.

son. The depression and bad baseball kept crowds small. All told,
about sixty thousand people made their way into League Park during
1894, an average of less than one thousand a game. The final gate was
boosted by a season–ending exhibition with the soon–to–be–famous
Baltimore Orioles, managed by Ned Hanlon and starring the likes of
Hughie Jennings, John McGraw, and Wee Willie Keeler. The visitors
demanded a guaranty that made Vanderbeck "curl up and shriek," but
a crowd of thirty– five hundred made it a profitable afternoon. As
expected, Baltimore won, 4–1. The big moment was when a bouquet
was brought out to Orioles first baseman Dan Brouthers. Like
Hanlon, Brouthers was a fondly remembered member of the city's
1887 championship team.

Several weeks later, Detroiters were stunned when they heard of
a tragic accident involving another old National League favorite,
Charlie Bennett. The former Wolverine catcher, who had helped lead
the Boston Beaneaters to three pennants after leaving Detroit, had
taken an off–season hunting trip to Kansas. At the Wellsville station
Bennett tried to board a moving train. He slipped and fell under the

wheels. His left foot was severed immediately and his badly mangled right leg was later amputated at the knee. Bennett's misfortune inspired widespread public sympathy. In a letter to *Sporting Life*, the recuperating Bennett thanked his fans and said that he was looking "forward to the time when I can stumble around with artificial limbs." When Detroit opened its 1895 campaign on May 1 against Toledo, the gritty ex–catcher was there to catch the ceremonial first pitch from Mayor Pingree.

By now the Detroit Creams were being referred to in some circles as the "Tigers." There has always been considerable speculation about how the team acquired a nickname that is nearly as old as the franchise itself. The first written mention of the name appeared in the April 16, 1895 edition of the *Detroit Free Press*, where editor Philip Reid wrote the headline, "Strouthers' Tigers Showed Up Very Nicely." On the same page a column of statistics was labeled, "Notes of the Detroit Tigers of 1895." Soon *Sporting Life* began using the name. By the following season, the team's first at Michigan and Trumbull, the hometown nine were frequently referred to in the local and national press as the Detroit Tigers. Thus they have been known ever since.

Why the Tigers? George Stallings, captain and field manager of the 1896 club, maintained years later that it was because he had dressed his troops in black–and–brown striped stockings that resembled tiger paws. But the *Free Press* headline proves the name arrived a full year before Stallings.

In sharp contrast to today's professional teams, which pay marketing wizards large sums to carefully and scientifically select a nickname, logo, and uniform colors with an eye to merchandising sales, nineteenth–century teams were under no such pressure. Many never had a nickname. Those that did typically acquired theirs informally, the result of an editor casting about for a way to save space or to create variety on the sporting page. Often a team was known by several sobriquets, a city's competing newspapers each endorsing its personal favorite. They were used interchangeably until one or the other finally caught the public's fancy and stuck.

The Tigers appellation enjoyed wide circulation in Detroit long before the Western League arrived. This was due to the Detroit Light Guard, an elite group that was the city's foremost military and social organization from the time it was formed in 1855 through the early part of the twentieth century. Comprised of many of Detroit's leading citizens, it honorably served the country during times of war and was a source of great community pride. The Guards earned their nickname during the Civil War, when they distinguished themselves at such battles as Bull Run, Antietam, Chancellorsville, and Gettysburg.

Boulevard Park, also known as League Park, was the Tigers' home their first two summers. The cramped eastside park was located at Helen and Lafayette near the Belle Isle bridge. As this picture demonstrates, not all of Boulevard Park's patrons were paying customers. By the end of the 1895 season, Tigers owner George Vanderbeck, fed up with freeloaders sneaking a peek at his players, sought a new playing site. He finally settled for property at the corner of Michigan and Trumbull Avenues.

In 1880 the Light Guard's gala birthday parade inspired the *Free Press* to headline its coverage, "THE TIGERS!" Two years later the militia formally adopted a tiger's head as its crest, which appeared on everything from flags to stationary. When the Light Guard Armory was built at the corner of Larned and Brush in 1897, a tiger's head was prominently carved on one of its exterior stone walls. Through the years several of the Guards, such as David R. Peirce, were involved with local baseball clubs, either as players or as directors.

Additionally, the renowned Light Guard band frequently performed at ball games, parades, and other community gatherings. The militia's high profile and status helped keep the name Tigers constantly in the public eye. In the nineteenth century, when matters of copyright were dealt with loosely, if at all, it is not surprising that the city's sole professional sports team would take on a nickname bearing a positive association with a proud community resource such as the Detroit Light Guard.*

Nearly sixty–three hundred fans attended the Tigers' 1895 opener, but as the season progressed Vanderbeck expressed dissatisfaction with League Park. Grass now covered what had been an all–clay field. But the park lacked drain tile, which meant that even a moderate rainfall flooded the diamond with ankle–deep water. Since "Vanderbeck has no duck boats for his players to move over the field," noted one sportswriter, this resulted in costly rainouts. Another irritation was the abundance of freeloaders. Unwilling or unable to pay a quarter for general admission, Detroiters hung like fruit from neighborhood trees, rooftops, and second–story windows. Rows of children pressed their eyes to cracks in the fences or took turns standing on each other's shoulders. If it was an interesting game, the neighborhood cop often claimed a knothole for himself. Enterprising teamsters pulled their wagons alongside the outfield fences and "filled them up with impecuniarious spectators who preferred stretching their necks three inches to paying the price of admission."

Like all Western League parks, Detroit's was narrow and cramped. While the exact dimensions are unknown, the fences in the deepest parts of right and left field were probably less than three hundred feet from the plate. The occasional overflow crowd shrunk those distances, turning routine fly balls into ground–rule doubles. The short distances down the foul lines caused Vanderbeck to erect a pair of white poles along the right and left field fences. Any ball hit over the fence through the two poles was declared a double, not a home run. Prior to the 1895 opener, Vanderbeck ordered the left–field fence moved back eighteen feet to the Helen Avenue gutter line, but the ball continued to bang around League Park like a marble in a shoebox. Scores of 17–9 and 12–8 were common. Twice that summer the Tigers scored fourteen or more runs during a single inning; on anoth-

---

* According to longtime Light Guard member John S. Bersey, the Detroit ball club eventually approached the militia for official permission to borrow its nickname and tiger's head logo. Exactly when this occurred isn't clear, but it was probably about 1900, not long after the Guard's triumphant return from the Spanish–American War. At the same time Ban Johnson was repositioning the Western League as a major league, which made the use of distinguishing nicknames necessary, since several cities contained both American League and National League teams. The Detroit Light Guard said yes to the Detroit team's pro forma request.

er occasion they scored twenty–four runs in a game. By the time the guns of summer stopped booming, Van Derbeck's legions had racked up nine hundred runs in 125 games, an average of more than seven runs per outing. Sam Dungan alone cracked out 228 hits en route to the batting title, while Bob Campau hit a solid .360. Despite that offense, the team finished fifth with a 59–66 record.

Because of a strictly enforced salary cap (no player was paid more than two hundred dollars a month) and a sinking fund that helped prop up poorer teams, the Western League was quickly recognized as a successful, stable enterprise. Of its eight charter members in 1894, all but two franchises fulfilled their original five–year commitments.

After realizing a profit during his first two seasons in Detroit, Vanderbeck sought larger accommodations. None were available. Aging Recreation Park finally shut its doors in 1894, and its valuable land was subdivided and sold. Other properties considered were either too expensive, too small, or too far off the beaten track to build on.

Vanderbeck then learned that a prime section of the old Woodbridge farm at the juncture of Michigan and Trumbull Avenues was available for lease. Known for years as Woodbridge Grove, it had been donated by William Woodbridge to the city for use as a public picnic grounds in the 1850s. In 1875 Woodbridge's son Dudley signed a twenty–year lease at five hundred dollars per year with the city, which needed a haymarket to service its western district. Many of the century–old trees were cut down, the ground leveled and paved with cobblestones, and farmers began bringing wagon loads of hay and lumber to Western Market to be weighed and sold under munic-ipal supervision.

In 1895 the city decided not to renew its lease on the property, and moved its operations to the recently opened Eastern Market on Gratiot Avenue. Vanderbeck capitalized on this bit of good fortune, and negotiated terms with Dudley Woodbridge to bring the Western League to Western Market. Papers were signed and hands were shook. Then, with the cool winds of the off–season whistling through Mayor Pingree's potato patches, the new tenant set about building a bigger and better place for summer at the northwest corner of Michigan and Trumbull Avenues.

April 28, 1896: A newspaper sketch artist recorded the Tigers' first league game at Michigan and Trumbull Avenues.

CHAPTER TWO

Down on the Corner

Bennett Park, 1896–1911

HUNDREDS OF YEARS AGO, the land that today surrounds Tiger Stadium was part of a vast primeval forest of ash, birch, hickory, maple, oak, cedar, and pine. Inside these shaggy woods Native American families hunted elk, turkey, moose, bear, and deer; picked strawberries, cranberries, and raspberries; and spread their blankets inside bark-covered huts. The future, in the form of Antoine de la Mothe Cadillac and one hundred soldiers and traders, arrived one July day in 1701. Beaching their canoes along the edge of the river, the French explorer and his men built a stockade, Fort Pontchartrain, in the vicinity of what today is Hart Plaza. Over time the centuries-old trees were toppled, fences were thrown across ancient trails, and the wheels of Western civilization began to slowly, inexorably grind away at millenniums of bow and arrow life.

Robert Navarre, a well-educated Frenchman, arrived in Detroit in 1734. Displaying a "pleasing personality and extraordinary ability," he handled the tiny fort's civic affairs for many years, serving as a royal notary and occasionally as a judge. In 1747 Navarre was awarded one of the narrow ribbon farms that fronted on the Detroit River and extended several miles inland. Although the British took control of the fort in 1760, Navarre was too valuable as an Indian expert and linguist to displace. When he died in 1791, his widow divided the property between their two oldest sons. One of them, Francis, was given a 103-acre section that included the future site of Tiger Stadium. In 1797 Francis Navarre sold the land to his cousin, Joseph Beaubien, a farmer and militiaman who in turn sold it to a large-souled Englishman named James May in 1810.

May played a variety of minor roles in early Detroit. He delivered the first U.S. troops to the fort aboard his schooner in 1796 and, seven years later, became the first licensed ferry operator on the Detroit River. After a fire destroyed all of Detroit in June 1805, May rounded up thousands of scorched chimney stones and built a large residence near the river. As Detroit rose from the ashes in the early nineteenth century, May's Mansion House served as jail, courthouse, and political gathering spot.

William Woodbridge, an Ohio native and a close friend of territorial governor Lewis Cass, stayed at the Mansion House upon his arrival in 1815. After renting the farm for a spell, Woodbridge bought the property in 1819, the same year he was elected the Michigan Territory's first congressional representative. After Michigan became a state in 1837, Woodbridge served first as a state senator, then as governor, and finally as a U. S. senator.

Woodbridge, the son of an American Revolutionary soldier, was a major figure during these formative years. Successively flying the flags of three nations—France, Great Britain, and the United States—Detroit remained little more than a trading post until the Erie Canal, completed in 1825, provided an unbroken water link between the overcrowded east and the rich, vacant lands of the West. Detroit quickly developed into a teeming port. Fifteen thousand people poured through "the gateway to the west" in 1830 alone. By 1837, an average of three steamships were arriving daily, with as many as 2,400 passengers disembarking on a single day. While many purchased wagons and immediately joined the throngs heading west, enough decided to forsake the frontier to raise Detroit's population from a mere 2,222 in 1830 to more than 21,000 by 1850.

Most of the early arrivals came from New York and New England. Collectively, they were known as "Bostonians," since many

The northwest corner of Michigan and Trumbull before baseball. A municipal market and a planing mill were the site's first tenants.

were middle-class merchants from Massachusetts. "It is probable, in proportion to its population, Detroit . . . has a larger percentage of New York and New England people than any other western city," Silas Farmer wrote in his history of early Detroit. "At one time it seemed as though all New England was coming."

Waves of German and Irish immigrants followed in the 1840s and 1850s. Woodbridge, Cass, and other landowners made a financial killing selling or leasing lots to families fleeing Ireland's potato famine. During this period many Irish settled in an area west of town dubbed Cork Town after County Cork in Ireland. This neighborhood of modest wood cottages produced generations of notable Detroiters, including the Bradys, whose front door opened on what is today third base at Tiger Stadium. James J. Brady would later recall his own experiences growing up poor in Corktown as part of his inspiration for starting the now-famous Goodfellows Fund for indigent children.

Two roads destined to become forever linked in local lore traversed the Woodbridge property. In 1836 the rough dirt road that marked the farm's eastern boundary became the western city limits of Detroit. In 1858 the north-south artery was named Trumbull Avenue after Woodbridge's father-in-law, John Trumbull, the author of *M'Fingal*, the most famous poem of the American Revolution.

Trumbull Avenue intersected with an old Indian footpath, the Sauk Trail, whose expansion Woodbridge supervised in the 1820s. The log-and-packed-dirt road eventually stretched through the wilderness all the way to Fort Dearborn (subsequently Chicago), almost three hundred miles to the west. It became a major route for merchants, farmers, trappers, and other travelers. Originally called Michigan Grand Avenue in 1807, and known outside of Detroit as the Chicago Road, its name was officially changed to Michigan Avenue in 1837.

Amusements in early Detroit were primitive by today's standards. Silas Farmer writes of merchants bowling cannon balls down Jefferson Avenue in the 1830s for fun, while an 1835 advertisement announced that "Two bears and one wild goose will be set up to be shot at, or chased by dogs" at Major David McKinstry's popular Michigan Garden. "Safe and pleasant seats will be in readiness for ladies and gentlemen," it added. The bears got on the scoreboard when one of them reportedly ate a Hamtramck boy outside his home in 1857, but outraged citizens recognized the attack for what it was: a final, random act of frontier mayhem in what was now an unmistakably urban community.

Detroit on the eve of the Civil War was an economically progressive city with a bustling waterfront, a thriving commercial district centered on Woodward Avenue, and a growing reputation for the manufacturing of stoves, cigars, paints, varnishes, pharmaceuticals, and railroad equipment. Plumes of smoke writhed from the chimneys of its many small factories and foundries, drawing scores of newcomers who daily disembarked steamships or tramped the plank roads leading into town. When William Woodbridge died in 1860, Detroit's population was approaching 50,000 people—an impressive figure at a time when three out of four Americans still lived in rural areas.

A few years before his death, Woodbridge gave his consent to have a wooded section of his property—the northwest corner of Michigan and Trumbull avenues—used as a public picnic grounds. Although at the time it stood on the western outskirts of town, citizens thought its shade trees and berries worth the long commute. Pretty soon Woodbridge had to hire a fellow named Captain Quigley to maintain the site, which Detroiters came to call Woodbridge Grove. In 1855 Woodbridge deeded the property to his nine-year-old granddaughter, Juliana Philinda Abbott. But after she was committed to an asylum in 1862, Woodbridge's son, Dudley, took over the property. As Detroit continued to grow in size, Dudley capitalized on the popularity of the site, leasing most of the grove to the city in 1875 for use as a haymarket and a dog pound. Twenty years later, as Western Market was abandoned in favor of Eastern Market, George Vanderbeck succeeded the city as the site's primary tenant.

George Vanderbeck was aware of the site's history as he arranged for his new ballpark to be built in the fall of 1895. He learned that the land he was leasing was covered with twenty-eight giant elm and oak trees, several of which dated back to well before the American Revolution. Some measured more than eight feet in circumference. According to legend, Ottawa chief Pontiac had held councils of war under their branches during the bloody uprising of 1763. Despite the trees' historical significance, most were toppled. The DeMan Brothers, who operated the planing mill adjacent to the new park's site, were hired to cut the trees into lumber. Vanderbeck spared eight of the forest giants. Three were located between the left-field foul line and the Michigan Avenue fence in an area set aside for carriages. The other five were left standing in the deep part of left-center field. The last of the trees remained through 1900, their gently swaying heads lending a tranquil and dignified air to the often calamitous proceedings.

As remarkable as the presence of trees on the playing field may seem today, one hundred years ago it was common enough to warrant barely a mention. With a clubhouse sitting square in center field, a scoreboard operator clambering up and down a ladder posting hand-painted numbers, and carriages, horses, and a standing-

Before construction on Bennett Park could begin in early 1896, workers first had to clear the site of several large trees. When the field was laid out, the cobblestones visible in the foreground were covered with a thin layer of loam.

room-only crowd frequently damming up behind them, outfielders in particular were used to dealing with obstacles. The challenge wasn't any easier for infielders and catchers, who contended with benches and equipment scattered along both foul lines, and the large broom (used to sweep off home plate) casually tossed to the side of the plate. There also was chance that the grounds keeper forgot his rake or a shovel in the grass, which could be big trouble for someone peeling after a ball and not remembering his surroundings. In this environment a few trees didn't make much difference, particularly in the dead ball era when long drives to the fences were uncommon.

Players soon discovered another hazard, unique to Western League parks. The haymarket site had been paved with cobblestones, which Vanderbeck decided to leave. He had several inches of loam—a mixture of clay, silt, and sand—spread over the stones. Its porous nature not only kept the outfield marshy days after a rainfall, it also allowed cobblestones to regularly work themselves up to the playing surface. The resultant bad hops and crazy bounces produced the familiar expression, "It hit another cobble," and split fingers, bruised shins, and anguished cries. Although the occasional cobblestone ceased to be a problem when the entire field was resurfaced in 1903, the overall cow-pasture look continued for many more years.

Vanderbeck's new park occupied about half of the area of today's Tiger Stadium. The planing mill stood on the other side of the right-field fence; the left-field fence ran parallel to National Avenue. Home plate was located near what is now Tiger Stadium's right-field corner, forcing batters to face the late afternoon sun melting into the rooftops along National Avenue. An L-shaped wooden grandstand was erected behind home plate and the third-base line. Bleachers were built along the first-base line, creating a total seating capacity of approximately five thousand. Fans bought tickets and entered the park at the main gate at Michigan and Trumbull.

Player accommodations, if not exactly luxurious, were considered more than adequate for the era. A clubhouse was built in the deepest part of center field, about 490 feet from the plate. Inside the Tigers dressed for games and, after the game ended, stood in line to use the single shower. Because of the cost involved, the all-wool uniforms were rarely laundered. Instead, blouses and knickers were rolled up and stored inside metal canisters until they were removed—damp, dirty and foul-smelling—for the next day's game. The clubhouse was off-limits to the visiting team, who dressed and showered in their hotel rooms. In a pinch the adjacent caretaker's shed served as a house of safety for the occasional umpire or player anxious to flee the crowd's wrath.

The twelve-foot-high wooden fence surrounding the park was built by Walker & Co., which was granted the exclusive right to sell advertising on the outside of the fencing. In time the bill posters competed with garishly painted ads for beer, cigars, clothing, and potions on the inside of the outfield fences, where they were visible to a captive audience for the entire nine innings.

As work on the park continued into the spring of 1896, some pondered the matter of what to call it. Suggestions addressed to

Vanderbeck came in the mail. Some of the names included American Beauty, Arena, Au Fait, Creighton, Diamond, Elk, Fairview, Knickerbocker, Michigan, Oakdale, Occidental, Olympia, and Vanderbeck. As with the team's nickname, popular usage informally decided the issue. Charlie Bennett, just a year after his accident, had returned for good to Detroit and was a familiar, extremely well-liked figure around town. Soon many people, including his friends in the press, dubbed the new grounds "Bennett's park." The name stuck.

Spring training was still a novelty, so Vanderbeck's players maneuvered around puddles and sawhorses throughout April as bad weather and construction delays threatened the scheduled 1896 home opener with Columbus. A scrimmage with the University of Michigan squad was arranged for Saturday, April 11, but a heavy rain the night before washed it out. Unfortunately for the collegians, Vanderbeck hadn't wired ahead, so the Wolverines disembarked from their train to discover a sea of mud awaiting them at the park. The U-M nine left grumbling, but the carpenters remained, raising the grandstand roof in time for the park-in-progress to host its inaugural game, an exhibition match between the Tigers and the Athletics, a local semiprofessional team.

At 3:35 p.m. on Monday, April 13, Umpire Popsay shouted "Play ball!" and the Athletics' star southpaw, Tony Ferry, threw the first pitch in competition at Michigan and Trumbull. The Tigers scored six runs in the top of the first and went on to rout the sandlotters, 30–3. The *Tribune* pronounced Bennett Park "vastly superior" to League Park. "Yesterday's game demonstrated that the old baseball grounds, when compared to Bennett park, are not in it. The spectacle of seeing easy hit fly balls sailing over the side fences is a thing of the past. It will be a long fair hit that will go over any fence on the new grounds."

Vanderbeck was so excited over the Tigers' marvelous spring record (only two losses and a tie in fifteen outings) that he announced come the regular season, his players would enter the field at a dead run from the center-field clubhouse and that a gong would sound the number of runs scored each inning.

Two weeks later, on the morning of Tuesday, April 28, 1896, players from the Detroit and visiting Columbus teams boarded festively decorated trolley cars and spent the next few hours touring downtown streets, acknowledging the citizenry's cheers and best wishes, before finally reaching Bennett Park. At 3:15 p.m., the Tigers' new manager and left fielder, George Stallings, led his team out onto the field, which was drying out slowly from the previous day's downpour. The sun shone and the fans beamed. At 3:30 Wayne County treasurer Alex McLeod strode out to the mound, where umpire Charlie Snyder tossed him a ball. To the joy of the six thousand people packed in the grandstand and bleachers, assembled in the outfield, and perched atop telegraph poles and trees, the ball hit the public servant in his stomach. McLeod picked the ball up and then lobbed the ceremonial first pitch to Charlie Bennett, who was supported by his old National League friend Snyder, at home plate.* The crowd roared and cannons boomed as the first century of baseball at Michigan and Trumbull officially began.

The Tigers, as was their habit for their stint in the Western League, batted first. At the time, the home team had the option of starting the game at bat or in the field. It wouldn't be until the middle of the next century that the custom of the visiting team batting first actually became a rule.

Fan involvement was evident from the start. Digging in against Bumpus Jones, Stallings lifted a fly ball toward the Columbus center fielder, a chap dubbed "Gold Brick" Butler, who—Pow!—barreled into a late-arriving fan just as he was about to make the catch. Both were knocked cold. Meanwhile, Stallings circled the bases for the first of an eventual ten thousand or so home runs hit down at the corner.

The Tigers, following their captain's lead, were off and running. They pounded Columbus, 17–2, and the largest opening-day crowd in the Western League went home happy.

The new surroundings evidently had a therapeutic effect. The Tigers won their first eight games at home and raced to a 14–2 start before they tumbled out of the clouds and settled into third place with an 80–59 record. Vanderbeck considered the season a success.

---

* Charlie Bennett remained a popular figure in Detroit for more than thirty years. The crippled former catcher caught the ceremonial first pitch at every home opener from 1895 to 1926, hobbling out to home plate on two artificial legs. Sam Thompson, who died in 1922, usually assisted his ex-teammate by holding his cane. In his final years Bennett painted china dishes, first as a hobby, and then as a way of making ends meet, despite his twisted, arthritic fingers, the product of years of barehanded receiving. "Many league catchers were known to wince in the closing innings of a hard fought game under the stings of a ball taken off the bat, but not Bennett," an admirer eulogized upon Bennett's death just a few weeks before the 1927 opener. "If he felt the punishment he took it as stoically as an Indian warrior."

Tigers captain George Stallings hit the first home run at
Michigan and Trumbull.

The team's first doubleheader at the corner—an Independence Day
sweep of Grand Rapids—drew a capacity crowd of 5,000. Total
attendance for the season was 122,148, meaning the park was about
one-third filled for every home date. The Tigers responded with
fifty-one wins and only twenty losses, a .718 home winning percentage that has been exceeded only once in the club's hundred-
year history.

  The following season the Tigers fell to fifth and attendance
dropped correspondingly to 101,500. On Decoration Day (today's
Memorial Day), they played their first morning/afternoon doubleheader, drawing 1,600 rooters for a morning game against
Minneapolis and another 5,000 for the second contest. In time the

idea grew to include the Fourth of July and Labor Day, and a holiday tradition was established that continued for many years. The club typically started the first game at 11 a.m., emptied the park after the final out, and then sold tickets to the afternoon affair, which usually began at 4:00 p.m. The whole day was wrapped in red-white-and-blue bunting, including lots of marching, flag waving, speechifying, and firecracker tossing.

In baseball histories of Detroit the Tigers' pioneering days in the Western League are given short shrift—if they are mentioned at all. This is because the six years of Ban Johnson's Western League (1894–99), as well as the inaugural season of his restructured American League (1900), were never recognized by latter-day records committees as major-league seasons. As far as the history books are concerned, the Tigers magically came into existence in 1901, the year the American League officially started play as a big-league cir-

Wayward George "Rube" Waddell wasn't in Detroit long, splitting eight decisions in 1898 before moving on. But the peripatetic fastball pitcher remained long enough to set a new Western League record with eleven strikeouts during one afternoon at Bennett Park.

cuit. Whether history remembers them as minor or major leaguers, those weren't ghosts hitting and catching the ball during those first five summers at Michigan and Trumbull.

Take, for example, Pat McCauley. His name doesn't strike a chord with even the most knowledgeable Tiger fans. But on August

6, 1897, the twenty-seven-year-old journeyman catcher from Massachusetts became the first player to hit for the cycle at Michigan and Trumbull, collecting a single, double, triple, and home run during a 17–5 rout of Kansas City. In the one hundred years since, only six other Tigers (and another six opposing players) achieved this rare feat.*

The most accomplished Tiger of the Western League years was right fielder Sam Dungan, a bald-headed Californian who spent three seasons in the National League before coming to Detroit. A paper hanger in Chicago in the off-season, he was more adept at wallpapering Bennett Park with base hits. For six seasons he was either at or near the top of the annual batting lists, including a couple of .400-plus seasons and a batting championship in 1899, when he hit .347.

The team's top moundsman during this period was Tommy Thomas, a six-foot, four-inch native of Shawnee, Ohio. Thomas led the staff with a 26–14 record in 1897 and a 20–19 mark in 1898 before moving on to St. Louis in the National League. Also on the roster were Harry Steinfeldt, destined to be the third baseman on the famous Chicago Cubs infield of Tinker, Evers, and Chance; pitcher Aloysius "Wish" Egan, who became the Tigers' longtime chief scout; Frank "Noodles" Hahn, later a consistent twenty-game winner with the Cincinnati Reds; and shortstop Norman "Kid" Elberfeld and outfielder Jimmy Barrett, both of whom continued to star with Detroit through its early American League days.

Another notable Tiger of the 1890s was George "Rube" Waddell, a wayward southpaw who pitched Detroit's home opener in 1898. On May 17, 1898, he set a single-game Western League strikeout record when he whiffed eleven Minneapolis batters at Bennett Park. He split eight decisions before jumping to a league in Canada. The following year he was back in the Western League, this time pitching Columbus past his former teammates on opening day at the corner. The irrepressible Waddell later carved out a Hall-of-Fame career with the Philadelphia Athletics. When he wasn't out

---

* The others: Bobby Veach (September 20, 1920 vs. Boston); George Sisler of St. Louis (August 13, 1921); Ray Schalk of Chicago (June 27, 1922); Bob Fothergill (September 26, 1926 vs. Boston); Bob Meusel of New York (July 26, 1928); Gee Walker (April 20, 1937 vs. Cleveland); Charlie Gehringer (May 27, 1939 vs. St. Louis); Joe Cronin of Boston (August 2, 1940); Hoot Evers (September 7, 1950 vs. Cleveland); Mike Hegan of Milwaukee (September 3, 1976); Frank White of Kansas City (August 3, 1982); and Travis Fryman (July 28, 1993 vs. New York).

The two biggest stars during the Tigers' Western League years were pitcher Tommy Thomas (top row, second from right) and outfielder Sam Dungan (middle row, extreme right), shown here in an 1899 team photo.

drinking beer or chasing fire engines, he was the best pitcher in the game—perhaps the best there ever was. Few remember that he once wore the Tigers' Olde English D on his uniform blouse.

Because of the Tigers' longevity at Michigan and Trumbull, it's easy to look back today and assume that professional baseball was somehow predestined to succeed in Detroit. Not so. One ongoing concern was rowdyism in and around the ball yard. Two incidents at Bennett Park offer a flavor of the times.

In an 1896 game against Grand Rapids, a fellow named Smink, the Grand Rapids catcher, innocently tried to replace the ball in play with one near the Tigers' bench. "He did not go far," observed a reporter, "for in a second Capt. Stallings had him by the throat and was choking him."

The players interfered and Stallings let go. Smink was not satisfied, for he followed Stallings into the [batter's] box, tripped him and threw him against a rake, the teeth of which ran into Stallings' cheek.

Stallings went for him, they clinched and then the members of the Detroit team ran to help their captain. Someone kicked Smink, another hit him on the head with a bat, and when he was dragged away by some of the cooler members of the team, he was willing to quit.

When the fight was over, Stallings was bleeding from a gash in the cheek and Smink was similarly decorated. Policemen crowded upon the ground, but too late to stop the fracas.

The following year, a decision against the Tigers' Burnett caused fans to riot on opening day at Bennett Park. The unfortunate umpire, a fellow named Ebright, barely escaped with his life. "Then there was a scene," reported the *Evening News*.

In less than a minute the umpire was surrounded by 18 or more wildly excited players. They brandished their fists under his nose, called him every name not in the dictionary, and made his life a burden. Ebright stalked around like a man in a dream. He did not know what to do or how to do it. Allen, Steinfeldt, Burnett and Trost led the Detroit kickers. The riot lasted for several minutes before Ebright mustered up courage enough to soak Burnett and Trost with fines of $25 apiece and put them out of the game.

The Indianapolis players had returned to their places on the field. Burnett, furiously angry, would not take his place on the bench.

"I'll punch your head after the game," he kept repeating to the umpire, using vile epithets, and shaking his fist under that individual's proboscis.

Detroit lost, and while Ebright was changing his coat near the Indianapolis players' bench Burnett walked over and without warning commenced to rain blows upon Ebright's head and shoulders. He hit him three or four times before the players interfered and dragged the furious Detroiter away.

The crowd became wildly excited. There were cries of "Slug him," "Kill the umpire," "Put a rope around his neck," etc. One lonely guardian of the peace came running across the field, watched Burnett walk away, and then grabbed Ebright by the arm and started to yank him off the field.

By this time the bleachers had begun to scale the fence on the grounds. Cushions aimed at the umpire were flying through the air. The policeman and his charge were surrounded by an angry mob. One enthusiastic fan managed to swat the umpire a heavy blow in the back of the neck. A second policeman grabbed him. The crowd surrounded the copper and made things so lively that he let his man go.

The Indianapolis players surrounded the policeman and the umpire, and by a lively swinging of their bats kept the crowd at bay until Ebright was hustled into the bus. Ebright, afraid of more missiles, crouched in the bottom. The Indianapolis players piled in, the driver whipped up his horses, and the bus tore down the street.

The mob did not discover where Ebright was hidden for a moment. Then they gave chase. It would have fared worse with Ebright had they caught him.

Such riotous episodes played into the hands of the small but vocal minority opposing Sunday ball, which was forbidden in Detroit and remained illegal in other parts of the country well into the twentieth century. Vanderbeck and subsequent Detroit owners, understanding that solvency depended in part upon arranging as many of the financially attractive Sunday dates as possible, fought a long battle with local authorities and ministers over the so-called "blue laws." *Why shouldn't workers and their families enjoy an afternoon at the ball park on their only day of rest?* they argued until they were, well, blue in the face.

Today it is difficult to imagine a summer Sunday without baseball, but in the nineteenth century a silent Sabbath was the norm in most communities. Ministers expected their congregants and their families to spend Sunday in peaceful, spiritual reflection instead of

partaking in such raucous amusements as baseball games or vaudeville houses. One man of the cloth spoke for all bluebloods when he
preached: "Aye, pound on the pearly gates with your baseball bat.
But if there is a shadow of a Sunday game on it, down to the eter-
nal roast you go!"

In Detroit, as elsewhere, ballplayers and patrons risked being
hauled off to jail if authorities decided to follow the letter of the
blue laws, state or local ordinances that in most cases were originally enacted to curb intemperance. Enforcement varied according
to custom. In some areas antiquated statutes remained on the
books well into the twentieth century. In Philadelphia,
Sabbatarians were able to keep Sunday ball out of their city until
the 1930s—an inconvenience, to say the least, for Philadelphia's
two major league teams.

Ironically, the formation of Detroit's first big-league team was a
direct result of the controversy surrounding Sunday ball. During the
fall of 1880 the Cincinnati team was thrown out of the National
League when it refused to stop scheduling Sunday dates and selling
liquor at its games. To fill the void, Detroit was awarded a franchise.
Throughout the 1880s the Wolverines played weekday and Saturday
afternoons at Recreation Park, but were always careful to observe the
state's blue laws which, thanks to local ministers and temperance leaders, were rigorously enforced. The National League lifted its ban in
1892 and allowed franchises to schedule Sunday dates as they saw fit.
But by this time Detroit had been out of the league for four years.

When the Tigers started Western League play in 1894, local
opposition to Sunday games was headed by William C. Maybury, an
attorney and a member of a prominent Detroit family. Maybury,
soon to be elected mayor (he would serve from 1897 to 1904), also
was the senior warden of St. Peter's Episcopal Church, whose nine-
ty-foot steeple rose dauntingly across the street from Bennett Park.
Vanderbeck desperately desired the lucrative Sunday games for his
ball club, but the formidable opposition of influential citizens like
Maybury convinced him to look well beyond city limits for a place
to stage them.

Vanderbeck first tested the waters on May 31, 1896, when he
arranged a match between his first-place Tigers and second-place
St. Paul at Athletic Park in Mount Clemens. Athletic Park was a spa-

cious, well-groomed facility that sat approximately two thousand people. Although located about twenty miles north of downtown Detroit—a considerable haul during those pre-automobile days—fans were well served by the Grand Trunk Railroad and Rapid Railway lines, each of which scheduled several runs out to the park.

The official attendance that afternoon was 3,483, the Tigers' largest crowd since the home opener. To ward off those who might interrupt the proceedings, Vanderbeck ostentatiously donated a sack containing three hundred dollars to an organization set up to aid the victims of a recent cyclone. Wisely, he waited until the ninth inning to do so, gambling that local authorities would not be insensitive enough to cancel the game prior to his act of charity. He was right. St. Paul won, 6–2, but Vanderbeck undoubtedly wore a smile when counting the gate receipts.

The following Sunday's game against Milwaukee was rained out, after which a circuit court order was issued forbidding the park owner and Vanderbeck from scheduling any more Sunday contests. Vanderbeck craftily circumvented the injunction by selling the club for a day. Since the new owner was not specifically named in the injunction, he was free to negotiate a lease for the July 26 game against Minneapolis.

"The sale is a genuine one," explained Vanderbeck, "and I have the money in the bank and the papers in my strong box. The team comes back into my possession Monday. I am not at liberty to give the name of the one-day purchase, as he has requested me not to mention it, but there is nothing of the fake about the deal. He takes it on speculation for what he can make out of it, and I shall not go near Mount Clemens.

"The game will count as a league game. At least I will not play it over. There is no reason why it should not count. It is just the same as if I sold the team to you or anyone else for the rest of the season, or for all time to come."

The game was a farce. Afraid of being raided, the umpire and most of Mount Clemens avoided the park. The players, nervously looking over their shoulders for policemen, didn't want to take the field. They finally agreed to an exhibition umpired by Detroit pitcher Jack Fifield and a Minneapolis player named Anderson. Fifteen hundred paying fans fumed as pitchers on both sides merely lobbed the ball up to the plate. "There will be a nice row raised about this," warned one irritated patron, "and if they ever catch Vanderbeck in this county on a week day they will make it hot for him."

Such extralegal threats, coupled with injunctions, forestalled future forays to Mount Clemens. By the time Vanderbeck finally risked a return, on June 13, 1897, only one thousand people showed up at Athletic Park to watch Detroit battle Kansas City. The same two teams played there again on August 8 before a crowd half that size. The following summer the Tigers didn't play a single Sunday game and suffered a 23 percent drop in attendance. Frustrated by his experiences in Mount Clemens, Vanderbeck searched for new Sunday grounds.

In the spring of 1899 he announced that the team would play several Sunday games at a park in River Rouge. The slapdash facility stood about five miles southwest of Bennett Park. The sandy, uneven diamond resembled a bog and the weed-choked outfield was an embarrassment, even by nineteenth-century standards. Although the Sabbath laws were in effect, enforcement was thought to be more relaxed "down on the farm," which was well outside Detroit's city limits.

Detroit's inaugural at the River Rouge grounds took place April 30, 1899, the Tigers grabbing a 6–4 decision over Columbus. Three thousand paid to get in; hundreds more clambered up fences and trees to get a free look. In June Sheriff Duff Stewart and a posse of deputies interrupted a Detroit-Minneapolis contest in the seventh inning. He announced to the grandstand that he would leave it up to the fans whether to suspend the game now or at the end of play.

"It is not my intention to interfere with the sport," Stewart explained, "but we want to test the law and find out whether Sunday baseball is legal." The issue remained unresolved. An Ecorse promoter named W. W. Harris continued to book Sunday dates for the Tigers throughout the season with little interference. In all, the Tigers played nine times on the spongy River Rouge grounds in 1899, drawing an average of 2,267 paying customers.

That year George Stallings, who had left the Tigers three years earlier to manage Philadelphia's National League club, returned to the fold. He brought with him a quick-tempered pipsqueak named Norman "Kid" Elberfeld to play shortstop. For the next few seasons their hellzapoppin' on-field antics proved a continual irritant to Ban

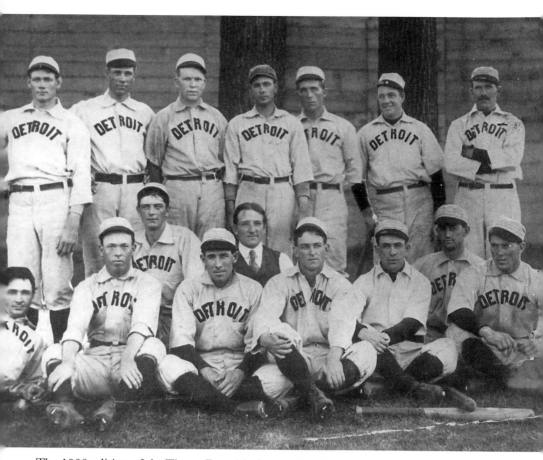

The 1900 edition of the Tigers, Detroit's first in Ban Johnson's new American League. Joe Yeager (seated, second from right) pitched and played the infield through 1903 without a glove, the last Tiger to play barehanded.

Johnson, who from day one strove to position his circuit as an order-ly alternative to the rowdy National League. In the meantime, Vanderbeck underwent a messy divorce from his wife, who hound-ed him for eighty-five hundred dollars in back alimony. Johnson saw the Detroit franchise as a mess. The players were undisciplined, the fans were unruly, ownership was distracted, and there were complaints about Bennett Park's lack of upkeep. Newspapers hinted at a pending change in management, but Vanderbeck squashed the rumors.

At the end of the 1899 season the National League dropped four of its twelve teams, a situation Johnson quickly capitalized on. On January 1, 1900, he met with Western League representatives in Chicago, where they formally renamed their eight-team circuit the American League. The name change in itself meant nothing, other than to suggest a broader scope of operations. But the subsequent announcement that Charles Comiskey's St. Paul franchise would relocate to Chicago (where the National League's Cubs played) and that the Grand Rapids club would move to Cleveland sounded an alarm to National League owners, who enjoyed a monopoly on the country's best players and most lucrative markets.

Johnson calmed their fears. He insisted his league would continue to obey the terms of the National Agreement, which among other things classified the American League as a minor league (thus making their players available to be drafted by major league clubs). Signatories to the National Agreement also were expected to respect the territorial rights of individual clubs and to honor the reserve clause that bound a player contractually to his team, essentially for as long as that team wished. In short the American League was still regarded as a minor circuit, albeit with a high-falutin' name, and they were expected to stay out of National League territory and not to raid any major-league rosters.

Vanderbeck did not attend the meeting. Nine weeks later, on March 6, 1900, the only owner the Tigers had ever known unloaded the club for twelve thousand dollars. Vanderbeck stayed in town another year or so, long enough to become involved with Thomas J. Navin and a few well-heeled backers in a serious effort to revive the old American Association and place a team in Detroit. When property owners around Bennett Park organized to thwart any potential land sales, Association supporters proposed to build a new park where the Detroit Athletic Club stood. Nothing came of any of it. It is unclear where George Arthur Vanderbeck went or what he did afterwards. His legacy is the ball team he brought to Detroit and the park he built for them to play in.

The Tigers' new owner was James D. Burns, a blustery, larger-than-life character who was bound to clash with Johnson. Quick to laugh and quicker to fight, the thirty-four-year-old Irish saloon keeper burnished his reputation during a run-in with Vanderbeck during the 1899 season. Burns had arranged to use Bennett Park for a social gathering of the Knights of Pythias when Vanderbeck, for one reason or another, changed his mind. Finding the entrance to the park locked, Burns grabbed an axe and, with several powerful swings, broke down the gate. The program continued as advertised.

"Everybody knows Jim," observed one newspaper when announcing the sale of the club. Burns, whose father had been a pioneer Detroit brick manufacturer responsible for many of the downtown buildings erected during the late nineteenth century, had once been the champion amateur boxer and wrestler of Michigan. In the 1890s he started in the liquor business, opening a saloon at 14 Michigan Avenue. It stood next to the Majestic Building on Woodward, the city's tallest building, and was a popular hangout for politicians, reporters, and assorted sporting types. He also ran the Cadillac Athletic Club, assisting two local boxers who later became world champions: middleweight Tommy Ryan and heavyweight Noah Brusso, who fought as Tommy Burns in tribute to his sponsor.

Burns, whose business interests during this period also included a brickyard on the family's fifty acres in Springwells Township, wound up owning the Tigers for only two years. In 1905 he became the first Democrat in fifty years to be elected Wayne County sheriff. After leaving office in 1908, he built the Burns Hotel at Cadillac Square and Bates Street. He sold it in 1917 and took over the popular Ste. Clair Hotel, which he operated until 1921. During this period he was a delegate to three Democratic national conventions. When he died in 1928, few would have argued against one newspaper's assessment that Jimmy Burns was "an all-around good fellow."

Burns retained Stallings, who had a share of the stock as manager, and arranged some minor improvements to the park. The ground around third base was unbearably rough, so the entire field was leveled. The bleachers down the first-base line were extended. Burns also moved Sunday games from River Rouge to a park hastily raised on his family's Springwell Township property, three miles west of Bennett Park. "Now the season can open with a clean slate," chirped one paper, "and everything ready to make the greatest of outdoor sports a big success in Detroit."

American League owners had hungrily snapped up scores of quality players thrown out of work when the National League trimmed four teams. Thus Detroit's 1900 lineup featured such new faces as third baseman Jim "Doc" Casey, outfielder Jim "Ducky" Holmes, pitcher John Cronin, and catcher Lew McAllister. All-purpose "Little Joe" Yeager was a crowd pleaser, pitching and playing a variety of infield positions through 1903 without a glove, the last Tiger to do so.

Unfortunately, this lineup did not prevent an embarrassing debut. On the afternoon of April 19, 1900, the Tigers donned their new black-trimmed white uni-

Before he was elected sheriff of Wayne County, Tigers owner Jim Burns often bent the law by holding Sunday games on his family's Springwells Township property.

forms, boarded a horse-drawn carriage, and rode triumphantly through downtown streets to Bennett Park. There they ushered in a new era of American League play with a basket of eggs, as Buffalo's Morris "Doc" Amole no-hit them, 8–0, in front of five thousand restless fans. The *Free Press* had the little dentists's dismal 4–10 lifetime record in mind when it moaned that it was "impossible to imagine anything more harrowing than the calamity that befell the Tigers."[*] Hobbled by injuries, Detroit still finished fourth and outdrew every team in the league except the pennant winner, Chicago.

---

[*] Since that afternoon eight other pitchers have twirled no-hitters on the Tigers' home turf: Frank Smith of Chicago (8–0 on September 6, 1905); George Mullin (7–0 vs. St. Louis on July 4, 1912); Earl Hamilton of St. Louis (5–1 on August 30, 1912); Hub Leonard of Boston (5–0 on June 3, 1918); Charlie Robertson of Chicago (2–0 on April 30, 1922); Bob Lemon of Cleveland (2–0 on June 30, 1948); Virgil Trucks (1–0 vs. Washington on May 15, 1952); and Nolan Ryan of California (6–0 on July 15, 1973). Robertson pitched a perfect game.

On October 14, 1900, shortly after the season ended, Ban Johnson and several select baseball men, including Charles Comiskey and Connie Mack, met in Chicago to organize a new American League that would jettison several weak sisters—Indianapolis, Kansas City, Buffalo, and Minneapolis—in favor of expanding into the east. The American League began play in 1901 with teams in four new cities: Boston, Philadelphia, Washington, and Baltimore. Johnson felt his organization was now strong enough to weather a confrontation with the established National League. He boldly withdrew from the National Agreement, unilaterally proclaimed the American League a major league, and announced player raids on the senior loop's rosters. A two-year brouhaha erupted, filled with threats, insults, recriminations, lawsuits, and court orders. Owners in both leagues tossed dollar bills around like confetti, inducing nearly two hundred players to jump teams, some more than once.

The off-field strife didn't deter Detroiters from turning out in a big way for the city's first major-league game since 1888. On opening day, April 25, 1901, the largest crowd yet to see a ballgame in Detroit overflowed the muddy field and pushed up against the backs of the fielders. Some scaled the fence and were chased in Keystone Kop fashion by bell-helmeted police. On this warm Thursday afternoon, 10,023 fans witnessed the greatest ninth-inning rally in the history of the major leagues.

Going into the bottom of the ninth, Milwaukee enjoyed a 13–4 lead, thanks in part to seven Detroit errors. Thousands left the park early in disgust; those that remained goaded the players and optimistically awaited a miracle finish.

They got it. Captain and third baseman Jim Casey (who like all off-season dentists was inevitably nicknamed "Doc") led off with a drive into the crowd that counted as a ground-rule double. Jimmy Barrett and Kid Gleason singled, and then Ducky Holmes, Pop Dillon, and Kid Elberfeld doubled in succession. The barrage accounted for five runs and sliced Milwaukee's advantage to 13–9.

With Elberfeld on second and no outs, Pete Husting came on in relief of starter Pete Dowling. Husting induced Bill Nance to ground out, but by now some of the fans who had left early had caught word of what was happening and were streaming back into

the park. The game was delayed several minutes while Detroit players tried to push back the throng pressing in on the backs of the
Milwaukee outfielders.

When play resumed, Husting walked catcher Fritz Buelow and
surrendered a single to pitcher Emil Frisk, which plated Elberfeld and
made the score 13–10. "At this stage of the game hats were being
thrown in the air, coats were flying and everyone was yelling themselves hoarse," reported the *Free Press*. "One man in the bleachers
threw up his coat and when it came down it was in two sections, but
he didn't care so long as Detroit was hitting the ball. . . ."

Doc Casey, up for the second time in the inning, beat out a bunt
to fill the bases, but then Husting struck out Barrett to put the
Brewers within one out of victory. They never got it. Gleason ripped
a sizzling grounder at third baseman Jimmy Burke, who fumbled it,
allowing Buelow to score. Burke's error on what should have been
the final out made the score 13–11. A few seconds later it was
13–12, as Holmes beat out another grounder to Burke as Frisk
scored. Up again stepped Dillon, who already had three doubles for
the afternoon. The Tigers' first baseman sent a Husting pitch
screaming over the left fielder's head and into the overflow. As
Dillon pulled into second with his record fourth double of the afternoon and the Brewers wailed about crowd interference, Casey and
Gleason raced home with the tying and winning runs for the Tigers'
amazing 14–13 victory.

"Dillon was the hero of the day," said the *Free Press*, "and pan-
demonium broke loose when he made his last hit. The crowd surged
out onto the field and everybody wanted to pat the hero on the
back. The big first baseman was almost torn to pieces by the fans,
and finally he was picked up and carried around on the shoulders of
some of the excited spectators." One hour later, jubilant fans still
milled around, unwilling to surrender the lingering euphoria over
the Tigers' incredible major-league debut.

Opening day was a tough act to follow, but the Tigers came
close. They won their next three games at Bennett Park in similar
last-licks style, renewing the town's appetite for big-league ball. The
Tigers finished third at 74–61 in their first major-league season.
George Stallings fielded a scrappy congregation—too scrappy, as far
as Ban Johnson was concerned. To make matters worse, Stallings
and Burns argued frequently. By the end of the season Johnson's

constant disciplining of Stallings turned into a three-sided battle when Burns charged Stallings with secretly plotting to deliver the franchise to the National League. This was impossible, since Johnson had taken the precaution of putting 51 percent of the club's stock in his name. Stallings countered with accusations that Burns had performed some creative bookkeeping with the gate receipts. (Actually, given that baseball was largely a cash business, it was hard to find an owner in Detroit or anywhere else who didn't fudge the numbers.)

Newspaperman Malcolm Bingay wrote in his memoirs that Stallings and Burns "had a simple system of bookkeeping. Whichever one got to the cash box first got the money. George used to say that Jimmy would toss all the money to the ceiling and that which stuck there was his partner's share. Jimmy insisted that George was lacking even in that element of sportsmanship. Salaries and taxes were considered useless annoyances."

Fed up with the bickering, Johnson forced Stallings and Burns out. On November 14, 1901, Burns sold the club to a syndicate headed by Samuel F. Angus, who made his money in the railroad and insurance businesses. Stallings sold his equity in the club for a big profit two days later.

Despite the welcome change in ownership, the Tigers' future remained doubtful. The 1900 census showed that, with almost 286,000 people, the city was the least populous in the league. Nearly that many had visited the park in 1901, a good showing that had netted a thirty-five-thousand-dollar profit for Burns. But in 1902 a seventh-place finish resulted in a 28 percent drop in attendance, and rowdyism continued to be a problem. During a weekend home series with Washington, for example, a different Tiger was ejected on Friday, Saturday, and Sunday. The last ejection resulted in a free-for-all at Burns Park, a Sunday venue that already earned an unsavory reputation because of its proximity to a saloon.

The Tigers might have continued to schedule Sunday games at River Rouge, but Burns understandably had a vested interest in moving the seventh-day site to his own property in Springwells Township. Burns Park was located on Dix, between Livernois and Waterman, about three miles from Bennett Park and just outside Detroit's western boundary. Today the site is a dreary looking industrial area, but its charm was no better a century ago. The park's

Garvey's Stockyard Hotel was adjacent to Burns Park at the corner of Waterman and Dix. The bar enjoyed land-rush business on game days, with drunken patrons contributing to the unsavory environment surrounding Sunday ball.

neighbor was a stockyard. A certain shift of the wind caused the nose of even the most indelicate spectator to crinkle.

The first game played there, an 11–5 loss to Indianapolis on May 6, 1900, offered a riotous beginning to the season. Grandstands had been erected for three thousand, but a nearly equal number of fans grew tired of waiting in the block-long line outside the park and clambered over the walls, ripped boards from the fences, or streaked past the harried gatekeepers. With no policemen on hand to control the mob, the field quickly took on back yard dimensions. The left and right fielders were completely surrounded by fans, while the catchers found themselves bumping up against a human backstop. After attempts to push the crowd back resulted in fistfights, both clubs finally agreed to ground rules that turned ordinary fly balls into a near-record total of three-base hits.

At game's end the rambunctious cranks celebrated by tossing hundreds of seat cushions back and forth between the grandstand and the field.

Over the next couple seasons, new bleachers and an enlarged grandstand removed the outfield, making ground rules unnecessary for most games at Burns Park. Despite consistently better-than-average gates, the Tigers abandoned their Sunday grounds after 1902. All told, they attracted 151,350 fans for thirty-four bootleg games at Burns Park (which also was known as West End Park). This was a handsome turnout of 4,451 per game. In explaining the club's decision to quit playing in Springwells, new owner Sam Angus stated that the rough field produced too many capricious bounces, making the game one of luck rather than skill.

The principle reason the Tigers left Burns Park after three summers, however, was its unsavory environment. Patrons tended to be coarser and more demonstrative than those at Bennett Park. Hardcore juveniles proved a nuisance, running off with balls and blatantly entering the grounds without paying. Walter O. Briggs, a budding industrialist destined to one day own the Tigers, was a regular patron of Burns Park. "Those were the days!" he reflected once in his old age. "That's when Jim Burns and George Stallings owned the club, and George was manager. Why, you used to see more fights there on a Sunday afternoon than you see now in the big leagues in five years. The players fought each other and the fans; the fans fought the gate tenders; and the tenders fought the ground keeper. The customers would come out all ginned up; fights started before a ball was pitched, lasted throughout the game, and continued long afterwards."

Briggs undoubtedly remembered the afternoon against Washington when a bad call against the home team caused angry fans to surround the umpire; Detroit players were forced to escort him from the park, knocking down three hoodlums in the process. The park had always attracted its fair share of gamblers, drunkards, and pickpockets, many of whom flocked to the bar inside the adjacent Garvey's Stockyard Hotel immediately after the game. The thought of thirsty players rubbing elbows with these disreputable characters gave Ban Johnson, who had never been enamored with how the Detroit franchise comported itself under

Vanderbeck's and Burns's ownership, one more reason to seriously consider shifting it east.*

It was no secret that Johnson wanted to install a team in Pittsburgh to compete with the National League Pirates, who had just won their second straight pennant. For a year rumors floated that the Tigers would be relocated, much as Johnson moved the Milwaukee franchise to St. Louis in 1902 to take on the crosstown Cardinals. Sam Angus, many claimed, was just a caretaker for the Tigers until a similar move to the Steel City could be worked out.

What finally saved the Tigers was the National League's suit for peace. In January 1903 the circuits agreed to end their costly war and sign a new National Agreement that recognized the American League as the country's second major league. That fall, the first modern "world's series" between the two leagues was held, the

---

* On April 14, 1903, Angus met with Johnson in Detroit and agreed to reschedule the Tigers' first Sunday game of the new season to a Friday. He also talked seriously of transferring other Sunday dates to grounds in Ohio. Meanwhile, some locals suggested that new trotting tracks being built at Clark Park and in Grosse Pointe might be ideal. The debate grew. Toledo "plays Sunday ball down town," argued the *Free Press:* "However, local custom, local feeling, governs this sort of thing, and it will be a very long time before it will be possible to play baseball anywhere near the center of Detroit. But the question of religious feeling cannot enter into the argument that if we are to have Sunday baseball at all, we should have it on a field that is more convenient that West End Park, with its long ride, its necessarily slow car service, and the temptation to the weaker one to tarry at the bar while waiting for the crowd to thin out, in preference to going directly home, as he would were the grounds somewhere within reason. Adding that "If we must go out of the city for our Sunday ball, West End Park is as good a place as any," the paper still concluded that "it would be the real thing to play in town."

The real thing was still several years off. Between 1903 and 1906 the Tigers played no Sunday games anywhere in the Detroit area. When either Chicago or St. Louis came to town for a weekend series, the home stand was interrupted for a quick overnight train trip to the visitors' park for a Sunday game, since baseball on the Sabbath was allowed in those cities. Otherwise the Tigers and their visitors rested on the seventh day, the players typically passing time in their rooms, hotel lobbies, or on Belle Isle until resuming play on Monday. During this period the Tigers experimented with Sunday dates in Grand Rapids, Toledo, and Columbus, Ohio—communities that maintained a more tolerant view of ballplayers laboring on the Sabbath. The Tigers were considered the home team in all of these neutral site games.

The first one, played May 24, 1903 in Grand Rapids, attracted 6,000 fans. The Tigers defeated Washington, 5–4. Later that season the Tigers twice traveled to Toledo, losing 7–3 to Philadelphia on June 28 before 4,500 and then beating New York, 12–8, on August 16. Toledo native George Mullin got the win as 3,506 looked on. Two years later, Detroit traveled to Columbus to play a two-game set with Boston. On Saturday, July 23, 1905, Cy Young pitched Boston past the Tigers, 6–1. The next day about 5,000 people packed Neil Park to watch Boston win again, this time by a 7–1 score. This marked the fiftieth and final occasion since 1896 that the Tigers played an official Sunday "home" game outside of Bennett Park, averaging just under 4,000 paid admissions per contest.

beginning of a grand tradition that was interrupted twice: in 1904, when the haughty New York Giants refused to meet the American League representative, and in 1994, when labor problems canceled America's oldest postseason tournament.

One of the accord's provisions was that the American League, in return for being allowed to abandon Baltimore in favor of New York, would not field a team in Pittsburgh. This completed the Western League's remarkable metamorphosis from a Midwestern minor league to a geographically diverse major league. It also signaled the start of a half-century of stability. Not until 1954, when the St. Louis Browns became the Baltimore Orioles, would the American League experience another franchise shift.

Detroit followers breathed a sigh of relief. The Tigers would remain at Michigan and Trumbull. The irony is that for all the uncertainty associated with the franchise since it first fielded a team in 1894, Detroit was the only city to survive the circuit's various permutations between 1899 and 1903:

1899	1900	1901	1903
Western League (minor league)	American League (minor league)	AmericanLeague (major league)	American League (major league)
Detroit	Detroit	Detroit	Detroit
Milwaukee	Milwaukee	Milwaukee	St. Louis
St. Paul	Chicago	Chicago	Chicago
Kansas City	Kansas City	Boston	Boston
Indianapolis	Indianapolis	Philadelphia	Philadelphia
Minneapolis	Minneapolis	Washington	Washington
Buffalo	Buffalo	Baltimore	New York
Grand Rapids	Cleveland	Cleveland	Cleveland

A benefit of the 1903 peace agreement was that Detroit was allowed to keep two players it had pirated from the National League: outfielder "Wahoo Sam" Crawford and pitcher Bill Donovan. Both quickly became Bennett Park favorites and were instrumental in making Detroit the first American League team to win three consecutive pennants.

Crawford, a former barbering student from Wahoo, Nebraska, was no stranger to Bennett Park fans, having first played there as a member of Grand Rapids' Western League team. Moving on to Cincinnati, the powerful, slope-shouldered slugger led the National

League with sixteen homers in 1901. He topped the American League in round-trippers six years later. More typically, his power during these dead ball years translated into three-base hits (312 of them, more than anyone in big-league history), inside-the-park home runs (a record fifty-one during his career), and tremendously long fly outs. "I have seen right fielders, playing against the fence, catch five fly balls off Crawford's bat in one game," recalled Harry Salsinger, longtime sports editor of the *Detroit News*, "five fly balls that would have cleared the fence any time after . . . the jackrabbit ball was introduced."

Wild Bill Donovan gained his sobriquet from his scatter-armed pitching and aggressive base running, not his lifestyle. The genial pitcher enjoyed the night life and good company and operated a popular billiards hall downtown during his playing days. Donovan topped the National League with twenty-five wins for Brooklyn in 1901, a feat he duplicated with Detroit in 1907. Years later, when Frank Navin owned the Tigers, he kept two photographs of his favorite ballplayer in his office. "Yes, there was a pitcher!" Navin would say admiringly. "What a heart!"

Navin, whose background will be fleshed out in the next chapter, entered the story about this time. In 1902 he was a thirty-one-year-old clerk in Sam Angus's office when the insurance agent bought the club and promoted him to bookkeeper. After two seasons, Angus's failing business interests forced him to shop around for a buyer. Chiefly through Navin's efforts, on January 22, 1904 Angus sold his interest in the team to William H. Yawkey, the twenty-eight-year-old heir to his recently deceased father's $10-million lumber fortune. In return for brokering the deal, Navin received five thousand dollars, or 10 percent of the fifty-thousand-dollar purchase price. (Another version insisted Navin won the money in an all-night poker game, a plausible scenario considering his love of gambling and skill with cards.)

Navin moved to the front office, which in those cozy days meant he served as secretary, treasurer, advertising manager, main ticket seller and whatever other title circumstances or his playboy boss chose to confer upon him. Yawkey regarded his ownership of the Tigers as a lark, occasionally treating his players to a drunken night on the town to break a slump, or slipping a hundred-dollar bill into a favorite's pocket to recognize a job well done. He left most of the

The earliest known action shot from Bennett Park. New York Highlanders third baseman Wid Conroy leapt to catch an errant throw during a 1903 game.

day-to-day details of the business to Navin. As the team prospered, Yawkey allowed him to buy up stock.

Navin survived an early power struggle with another up-and-coming baseball executive, Ed Barrow, who later became famous for managing the Boston Red Sox to a championship and then masterminding the New York Yankees' dynasty. The beetle-browed, two-fisted Barrow served as field manager and general manager of the Tigers for almost two years. Arguably the greatest judge of talent the game has ever known, Barrow left Detroit late in the 1904 season, but not before laying the groundwork for the 1907–08–09 pennant winners.

Navin "was a great baseball man," Barrow later reflected, "but as young men in Detroit we just couldn't see eye to eye. I eventual-

The Bennett Park entrance may be seen down the street from the Trumbull Avenue police station. Judging by the empty streets and bored youngsters, the Tigers were not at home this day.

ly resigned because of differences with Navin, but I think I left them the nucleus of their pennant-winning team." While Barrow sold his twenty-five-hundred dollars' worth of stock to Yawkey for a mere fourteen hundred dollars, "Navin held on to his and eventually became one of the wealthiest men in baseball."

Eighteen-year-old Ty Cobb (right) confers with Manager Bill Armour some time during his rookie season, 1905.

In 1905 two of the biggest crowd favorites ever to play at Bennett Park arrived: Herman "Germany" Schaefer and Tyrus Raymond Cobb. In terms of intelligence and personality, there could hardly have been two more dissimilar teammates. But each in his own wonderfully singular way regularly brought the crowd to its feet.

The twenty-eight-year-old Schaefer first stepped foot in Bennett Park while playing with Kansas City in the Western League. Cobb, ten years younger, was plucked off the Augusta, Georgia team in late August, just days after his mother accidentally shot to death his revered father. Many speculated since that the tragedy provided the psychological trip wire that transformed the "Georgia Peach" (a nickname coined by the *Free Press*'s Joe S. Jackson in 1906) into the emotionally troubled person he often appeared to be.

Bennett Park's clown prince, Herman "Germany" Schaefer.

While Cobb was educated and humorless, Schaefer was coarse and mirthful. The second baseman's shenanigans gave the impression that there was nothing but tumbleweed blowing between his ears. Cobb's mind was so focused it could practically bend spoons. Both men also were scrappy, creative, highly competitive, and fine base runners. Schaefer actually out stole Cobb during three of the five seasons they played together.

Fans enjoyed teasing Schaefer. "Back to Germany!" they yelled good-naturedly. Or, "You forgot all you ever knowed!"

"There is always something worth while when Schaefer is on the lot," observed Harry Salsinger. In the bandbox confines of Bennett Park, the pock-marked Chicagoan played to the crowd like a vaude-villian. His antics included tightrope-walking the baselines and car-rying an umbrella out to his position during a rainfall. Once, protesting an umpire's decision to continue a game when darkness enveloped Bennett Park, he trotted out to second base with a lit lantern in hand. On another occasion he forced a rule change when, standing on second, he decided to steal first base. It wasn't as goofball a move as it might appear; Schaefer was hoping to draw a throw, thus giving the runner on third a chance to score. It was the kind of scientific baseball Cobb loved—one reason, perhaps, that he counted Schaefer among his few friends on the team.

"As a drawing card Herman ranks second only to Cobb," said Salsinger. "He is the best comedian in baseball, past or present. Any stage piece without comedy cannot be a success. The

Hughie Jennings managed the Tigers from 1907 to 1920, the longest tenure of any Detroit manager until Sparky Anderson.

public wants comedy in its sports as well as the thrills. Schaefer gives the comedy, Cobb the thrills."

Cobb was considered the odd half of this baseball couple. He came to Detroit a high-strung teenager with a pronounced Southern accent. When he threatened to replace a favorite in the starting lineup, a small clique of veterans made life unbearable for him. He grew so alienated he took refuge in the caretaker's shed at Bennett Park before games; eventually he suffered a nervous breakdown and missed a month of his first full season while he recuperated at a Pontiac asylum. Manager Bill Armour had no clue as to how to handle one of the game's rising stars.

In 1907, however, a new manager, Hughie Jennings, arrived on

the scene. The red-haired, generously freckled Pennsylvanian started life as a ninety-cent-a-day coal miner, but eventually earned a law
degree at Cornell. A student of the old school of baseball, Jennings
mastered his craft playing shortstop for the famous Baltimore
Orioles teams in the late 1890s, which included John McGraw and
Willie ("Hit 'em where they ain't") Keeler. As the Tigers' manager,
the popular, ever-smiling Jennings earned a reputation for his
coaching-box antics. He pulled up handfuls of grass, clenched his
fists, and kicked a leg into the air, yelling all the while "Here we
are!" and "That's the boy!" Soon these shouts of encouragement
were shortened to "Ee-yah!" and "Attaboy!" He survived a near-
fatal beaning, a head-long plunge into an empty concrete pool, an
auto accident that killed two others, and a long battle with alco-
holism during his tough and colorful life. The "Ee-Yah Man" suc-
cumbed to tuberculosis in 1928, eight years after his final season
managing the Tigers. His fourteen seasons at the helm and 1,131
victories remained club records until Sparky Anderson came along
a couple of generations later.

Jennings recognized he had little to teach Cobb, so he simply
turned him loose on the diamond. The first of three straight pennants and eight consecutive batting titles followed.

Many myths about Cobb survive. The most pervasive is that he
sharpened his spikes. Cobb didn't deny the allegation (a 1908
invention of New York sportswriters) until after he retired; he
believed it gave him a psychological edge to have infielders and
catchers worry about possible disembowelment when they should
have concentrated on tagging him out. The story added to his
already heavily soiled reputation. An unrepentant bigot, he was
involved in a series of shameful racial episodes. He had a volcanic
temper, so that even the most innocuous slight could cause exple-
tives to flow like lava. His early experiences with big leaguers caused
him to be suspicious and a loner. He was cheap, jealous, and aloof.

Despite these very real faults, Cobb was not a bloody-fanged
ogre. Many knew him as a charitable, sentimental, and loyal friend.
He dispensed stock tips freely, pyramiding his own shrewd invest-
ments into a small fortune even as he played ball. He loved to
instruct others in the nuts and bolts of batting and base running. No
one who saw his scarred, bloody legs and hips, rubbed raw from
sliding on the cement-like infields, ever doubted his physical
courage.

"Wahoo Sam" Crawford inside his 1907 Cadillac.

Today Cobb's character flaws appear to all but obscure his genius as a player. He perfected a variety of slides, especially the fade away, a maneuver that was absolutely contrary to his cleats-in-the-midsection reputation. Instead of jamming his spikes straight into a base, the long-accepted method, he typically contorted his body away from an infielder's tag and at the last moment tucked a toe or hand into a distant corner of the base as he slid past.

On the base paths Cobb was "daring to the point of dementia," marveled one reporter. It was not unusual for Cobb to score from second base on a ground out, or to steal his way around the bases. (He once did it on three consecutive pitches against Philadelphia.) During his career he stole home an unbelievable fifty-four times (nearly twice as many as anyone else in major league history) and set an American League record with forty-seven inside-the-park home runs. His whole idea, he explained, was to upset and befuddle the opposition at every opportunity. His audacity was contagious, setting teammates and fans on fire. "Hold onto your pants!" Germany Schaefer would yell from the bench after Cobb had swiped another base. "Or he'll steal those too!" Even when Cobb was caught he served warning to jittery fielders: I'll be back. "His determination was fantastic," recalled Philadelphia catcher Rube Bressler. "I never saw anybody like him. It was *his* base. It was *his* game. Everything was his. The most feared man in the history of baseball."

Sam Crawford was never close to Cobb; in fact, the two rarely spoke to each other unless absolutely necessary. But even Wahoo Sam gave the devil his due. Ty was the master of the unexpected, he once related, and together he and Cobb gave Detroit fans something to talk about over that evening's meal.

"A lot of times Cobb would be on third base and I'd draw a base on balls," he said, "and as I started to go down to first I'd sort of half glance at Cobb, at third. He'd make a slight move that told me he wanted me to keep going—not to stop at first, but to keep on going to second. Well, I'd trot two-thirds of the way to first and then suddenly, without warning, I'd speed up and go across first as fast as I could and tear out for second. He's on third, see. They're watching him, and suddenly there I go, and they don't know what the devil to do.

"If they try to stop me, Cobb'll take off for home. Sometimes they'd catch him, and sometimes they'd catch me, and sometimes they wouldn't get either of us. But most of the time they were too paralyzed to do anything, and I'd wind up at second on a base on balls. Boy, did that ever create excitement. For the crowd, you know; the fans were always wondering what might happen next."

Cobb was always thinking. Players often commented on his nervous habit of kicking the base he was standing on. It was no superstition. He was pushing the bag another inch or two closer to his next stop. That inch just might serve as the telling difference between being called out and arriving safe.

Cobb grew livid whenever he was accused of being a dirty player. True, he bowled over infielders and catchers, gave the hip check to pitchers fielding bunts, and agitated on the base paths and at bat, looking to give himself—and his team—that one tiny advantage in the suffocating crucible of big-league competition. However, it is generally forgotten that in this age of Darwinian dead-ball baseball, when squeezing out a single run often was enough to win a game, so did most other players. But no one was as brilliant for as long as Cobb. In twenty-four seasons, all but the final two spent in Detroit, Cobb accumulated 4,191 base hits and 892 stolen bases, including 96 in one season (1915). All three of these major-league records were eventually broken, but significantly it took three separate men to do it. No one, however, will ever match his dozen batting titles, .367 lifetime batting average, or blowtorch intensity.

Cobb was only twenty years old when he propelled the Tigers to the 1907 pennant. He batted .350 to lead the league; behind him was Sam Crawford, who hit .323. A key addition was long-armed first baseman Claude Rossman, who was deadly effective on the hit-and-run play. The mound staff boasted three twenty-game winners—Bill Donovan (25–4), Ed Killian (25–13), and George Mullin (20–20)—and a near-miss in Ed Siever (19–10). This top-flight quartet accounted for all but one of the Tigers' ninety-two victories and put them in the World Series against the powerful Chicago Cubs of Tinker-to-Evers-to-Chance fame.

That summer, as Detroit took on the characteristics of a modern urban community, a combination of factors finally brought Sunday ball to the corner of Michigan and Trumbull. These included a more liberal view toward Sunday recreation and a red-hot team pursuing the city's first pennant in twenty years. The fact that new mayor George Codd and many of the city's aldermen, including James Vernor, John Lodge, and Charlie McCarthy, were great fans (Navin gave them all free season passes) also encouraged Navin to try to make Detroit the fourth major-league city after St. Louis, Chicago, and Cincinnati to regularly host Sunday games.

It also helped that Jim Burns had been elected sheriff of Wayne County. Complicating matters, however, was Navin's long-standing feud with Frank H. Croul, a successful businessman, inveterate gambler, and—to Navin's chagrin—the newly appointed police

A wide-angle view of the crowd that turned out to watch the fifth game of the 1907 World Series between the Tigers and Cubs. Chicago won, 2–0, to close out the series.

commissioner. Several years earlier, Navin made book at Alvord's gambling joint when Croul wagered five hundred dollars on a horse. Croul's horse came in at three-to-one, but when he tried to collect Navin returned the bet, explaining that it had been placed too late. Croul branded Navin a crook. Now Navin needed the cooperation of the local police department to ensure the success of Sunday baseball. He had to find a way to circumvent Croul's ire.

According to newspaperman Malcolm Bingay, Croul promised not to interfere if Navin agreed to settle the old gambling argument. "He's going to pay, and pay plenty, for what he did to me that night at Alvord's," Croul told Bingay. Detroit's top cop made Navin write a fifteen-hundred-dollar check to Croul's attorney, who equally divided the money among three charities: the Protestant Orphan Asylum, Salvation Army, and Little Sisters of the Poor.

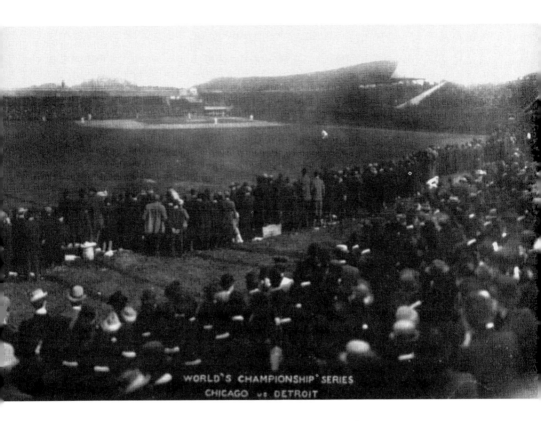

WORLD'S CHAMPIONSHIP SERIES
CHICAGO vs DETROIT

On August 18, 1907, the Tigers played their first Sunday game at Bennett Park, and beat the New York Highlanders, 13–6. The record crowd of 9,635 included the mayor, police chief, and county sheriff. Afterwards some aldermen suggested putting the question of Sunday ball on the ballot in September. "Many arguments are heard for and against Sunday baseball and the public will never be satisfied until the question is decided one way or another," said one. "If Sunday baseball is not consistent with the law it should be stopped by the police department, but if the law is not clear on the point I believe the matter should be submitted to the people."

Detroit played two more Sundays at Michigan and Trumbull in 1907 without incident. The issue didn't make it onto the ballot in September. Nonetheless Navin, gambling that pennant fever would drown out any protesting clergy and aldermen, scheduled eight Sunday dates in 1908. He was rewarded with crowds ranging from 7,900 to 12,500. Both Police Commissioner Croul and Sheriff Jim Burns maintained their indifference. Business owners vocalized their support, noting that Sunday games provided much-needed recreation for their workers. In 1909, as the Tigers clawed their way to an unprecedented third straight American League pennant and baseball fever reached an all-time high, ten Sunday games produced crowds between 8,600 and 18,478. Except for a few dwindling protests from the city's older citizens, these proceeded without incident. For all intents and purposes, the holy war over Sunday ball was over.*

The 1907 World Series, only the fourth played between the two rival leagues, opened in Chicago, where a passed ball by catcher Charlie "Germany" Schmidt allowed former Tiger Harry Steinfeldt to score the Cubs' tying run on what should have been the final out. The game, eventually called because of darkness, went into the books as a 3–3 tie, but it proved a disheartening loss to the Tigers. The Cubs won two games, 3–1 and 5–1, in as many days, before both teams boarded the train for Detroit.

The city's first postseason game since 1887 attracted 11,306 people to Bennett Park on a rainy Friday afternoon. Chicago breezed past the home nine, 6–1, scoring three runs in the seventh inning without once hitting the ball out of the muddy infield. The following day, October 12, only 7,370 turned out in the raw weather to watch the Cubs wrap up the championship behind Mordecai "Three Finger" Brown's seven-hit shutout, 2–0. The Cubs completely shut down the Tigers, limiting the majors' top offense to five runs and Cobb and Crawford to a combined .220 average. More

---

* An ugly brouhaha the following summer nearly killed Sunday ball. After George Moriarty was tagged out trying to steal home for the final out in a 3–2 loss to Boston, Red Sox catcher Bill Carrigan spit a mouthful of tobacco juice into Moriarty's face. Moriarty took a poke at Carrigan and suddenly the battle was on. Navin, who saw the worst fears of Sabbatarians realized, climbed atop the dugout and pleaded for calm as policemen, players, and hundreds of fans fought their way to the clubhouse door. For the next hour a mob milled outside, talking earnestly of sizing Carrigan's neck for a noose. Carrigan finally was spirited through the crowd disguised in the caretaker's overalls. Moriarty was slapped with a hundred-dollar fine by Ban Johnson, but the expected uproar from the "goo-goos"—Good Government Advocates—was little more than a squeak. Sunday ball, which had just been legalized in neighboring Ohio, had become too firmly entrenched at Michigan and Trumbull to be dislodged by a squirt of tobacco juice. By 1918 Michigan's blue laws were expunged from the books. The infidels in knickers and spikes had won, freeing future generations of Tiger stars to strut their stuff in front of the home folks seven days a week.

Cigar-chomping millionaire playboy Bill Yawkey sat back and let Frank Navin (right) run the club during the years of their partnership.

demoralizing than the outcome was the expected loser's share of the receipts. However, Bill Yawkey generously kicked $15,000 into the pot, giving each Tiger $1,946 for less than a week's work.

Some criticized the lack of support the Tigers received. As pennant fever gripped the city, more fans visited Bennett Park in 1907 than ever before. Nonetheless, the team still finished second from last in league attendance, barely out drawing last-place Washington. The sea of empty seats for the series was an embarrassment. For years, Detroit was widely thought of as a poor baseball town. Between 1902 and 1907, the team's attendance often plunged to 200,000 under the league average.

"The attendance at the two games in Detroit was a serious reflection on the patriotism of the citizens," observed *Chicago Tribune* writer Cy Sanborn. "There is only one conclusion to be drawn from Detroit's attitude toward its champions, and that is the well-known adage that a city of that size will not stand for a loser, and I look for the disappearance of Detroit from the major-league map within a few years. Even with President Yawkey's strong box and civic pride behind the club there, it will not satisfy the other seven clubs to carry along a city which will not make a losing club profitable nor a great success out of a winner."*

To Sanborn's chagrin, Yawkey betrayed some of the same indifference. On September 24, 1907, the press announced that Navin had acquired a half-interest in the team for twenty thousand dollars. Yawkey, who was moving to New York (where he would quadruple his fortune to $40 million), magnanimously lent Navin the money for the down payment and named him president. The young multimillionaire remained a silent partner until he died of a heart attack in the spring of 1919.

Navin, now fully in charge of the team's affairs, ignored comments about Detroit's fair-weather fans. Encouraged by the prospects for the city and his team, Navin unveiled a major expansion that doubled the park's capacity for 1908. After purchasing the planing mill property, he moved the right-field fence back to accommodate a two-thousand-seat bleacher section. The general admission seats sold for twenty-five cents. Reserved seating was increased

---

* Possibly adding to Sanborn's orneriness were the Bennett Park press facilities, which were primitive. Sportswriters climbed a ladder to the roof of the first-base pavilion and attempted to write while dodging raindrops, snowflakes, and dive-bombing pigeons. Fed up with the crass treatment received at Bennett and other big league parks, writers in town to cover the following year's World Series between the Tigers and Cubs organized. On October 14, 1908, they formed the Baseball Writers Association during a meeting at the Pontchartrain Hotel. One of the prime movers was Joe S. Jackson of the *Detroit Free Press,* a worldly, hard-drinking journalist who first dubbed Ty Cobb "the Georgia Peach" two years earlier. Jackson served a decade as president of the organization, which is still going strong.

from five thousand to eight thousand seats by connecting the main grandstand to the first-base pavilion and the quarter-stand behind third base. The main structure was extended several rows downward. One thousand of the seats sold at seventy-five cents, the balance at fifty cents. Because the addition encroached on the field, the diamond was moved about forty feet toward the outfield. The ground lost was more than compensated for by the space gained in right field, resulting in a larger overall playing surface.

At one point during this ambitious renovation Navin ran afoul of the American Federation of Labor (AFL), a union that was struggling to maintain its influence in a predominantly open-shop town. The AFL charged the Tigers' boss employed nonunion carpenters to shingle his grandstand roof. Both sides fired salvoes at each other. Navin pled ignorance, which seems dubious given his notoriously penurious ways, but eventually AFL leaders issued a statement that "they were satisfied that Mr. Navin is not antagonistic to union labor." The AFL canceled its threatened boycott of Bennett Park and work proceeded.

With increased seating capacity, a full slate of Sunday dates, and a red-hot pennant race, the Tigers attracted 436,199 customers in 1908, shattering the previous summer's attendance record. Only the New York and Philadelphia teams, playing in two of the country's most populous cities, drew more.

The large crowds that flocked to watch the Tigers contained a new classification of laborers: auto workers. It's an odd fact that baseball at Michigan and Trumbull and the automobile arrived within weeks and blocks of each other. For the next several years news of both were covered in the sporting pages of the local dailies, forging a symbiotic relationship between many Detroiters' two favorite pastimes: baseball and motoring.

Charles Brady King was the first to drive a horseless carriage in Detroit, maneuvering his "peanut roaster" along Jefferson Avenue on March 6, 1896, seven weeks before Bennett Park opened. King's nocturnal adventure earned but a single paragraph in the next day's *Free Press*, which observed that the "apparatus seemed to work all right, and went at the rate of five or six mile an hour at an even rate of speed." Then in the early morning hours of June 4, as a light rain threatened that day's game between Detroit and Kansas City, a thirty-year-old lighting engineer named Henry Ford drove his pony-

Bennett Park overflowed for an important series in 1908, a season that saw four teams battle down to the wire for the pennant.

sized quadri cycle through downtown's cobble-stoned streets. Three years later, Ransom Olds opened the city's first car factory on East Jefferson near the Belle Isle Bridge, a few hundred feet from League Park, the Tigers' original playing venue. Olds' handcrafted models cost $2,382 apiece, which was about double the salary of any Western League Tiger. But the automobile quickly graduated from an expensive novelty to an affordable necessity, so that even ballplayers could soon be seen "scorching" past Michigan and Trumbull in their Cadillacs, Owens, and Paige-Grahams, scaring horses and turning young women's heads. In the process of this unprecedented socioeconomic revolution the character of Detroit was irreversibly changed. The "Paris of the West," the leafy, conservative, tightly knit community whose mercantile and civic affairs had long been oiled by old Yankee money, was made over into the Motor City, a clanging, smoke-belching, concrete-ringed metropolis where the population doubled every ten years and work signs had to be posted in several languages.

"That the automobile industry has been one of the most potent factors in aiding Detroit's growth and prosperity is certain," observed the *Free Press* in September 1908, just as Henry Ford readied the launch of his revolutionary Model T. "Its beneficial influence has not ended here, however, for the product of its factories has made Detroit famous the world over as the home of the high grade motor car, and the place where not only is life worth living but that strives to make it worth while for others less fortunately situated geographically."

Although the newspaper didn't specifically identify them, among those "less fortunately situated geographically" at the time were American League fans in Chicago, Cleveland, and St. Louis, who watched in dismay as Detroit squeaked past for its second straight pennant. Once again Cobb (.324) and Crawford (.311) placed first and second on the league's batting list. And once again the Tigers were manhandled in five games by the Chicago Cubs in the World Series.

Bennett Park hosted the October 10 opener, a see-saw affair that exhausted the 10,812 fans on hand with the tension by game's end. Trailing 5–1 in the seventh, the Tigers rallied to take a 6–5 lead into the ninth. But rookie knuckle-baller Ed "Kickapoo" Summers, who led the staff with twenty-four victories during the season, inexplicably blew up in the final frame. He surrendered six straight hits as the Cubs scored five runs for a 10–6 victory.

The teams split the next two games in Chicago and then reassembled at Michigan and Trumbull on October 13. Three Finger Brown, who in twenty innings spanning two World Series did not allow a single Tiger to cross the plate, took a mere ninety-five minutes to toss a 3–0 shutout in front of 12,907 bored spectators. The following day, a chilly Wednesday, Orvie Overall required even less time—eighty-five minutes, the shortest series game on record—

Opposing managers Frank Chance and Hughie Jennings review the ground rules with umpires Tom Connolly (second from left) and Bill Klem prior to the start of the 1908 World Series' first game at Bennett Park. For the second October in a row, the Cubs made short work of the Tigers.

to dispose of the Tigers, 2–0. Adding insult to injury was the record low turnout of 6,210 people. To this day, no postseason game has ever drawn fewer people.

In 1909 The Tigers gained a third shot at a world's championship, winning a then-record ninety-eight games while outlasting Philadelphia. George Mullin won twenty-nine of them, the best in the majors. The entire infield was revamped: tiny Donie Bush played his first full season at shortstop, newcomer George Moriarty handled third base, and second baseman Jim Delahanty and first baseman Tom Jones came over in August trades that saw an old favorite, Germany Schaefer, leave town.

The notion of baseball as a metaphor for life received a boost early that season from William J. Cameron, whose famous editorial, "Don't Die on Third," was inspired by a game at Bennett Park. Cameron, who was born in Hamilton, Ontario in 1878, arrived in Detroit when he was nine. As a youth he listened for hours to the phonograph recordings of famous orators and was determined that he too would grow up to be a great speaker. By the early 1900s he was a familiar figure at dinners and Sunday services. His finely crafted passages eventually landed him a job as an editorial writer for the *Detroit News*. While serving in that capacity he attended a game between the Tigers and Cleveland Indians during the spring of 1909.

Perched on third base was George Moriarty, the Tigers' aggressive third baseman bought for five thousand dollars the previous winter from the New York Highlanders. Moriarty later enjoyed a long career as an American League umpire and managed the Tigers in 1927 and 1928. On this afternoon, however, the Detroit captain was more concerned about breaking a 2–2 deadlock. With two outs and a good-hitting pitcher, George Mullin, at bat, he broke for home, beating the catcher's tag by an eyelash and giving the Tigers a dramatic 3–2 victory.

On May 17, 1909, readers of the *Detroit News* discovered that Cameron had transformed Moriarty's daring dash into a moral lesson about the rewards of initiative:

> Moriarty was at third.
>
> Much as it meant to have advanced that far, nothing had been accomplished by it. Three-quarter runs are not marked up on the score boards. Third base runs never raised a pennant. Third base is not a destination, but the last little way station on the way home. It is better not to run at all than to run to third and "die." . . .
>
> It is 90 feet from third to home. Sometimes that 90 feet is a leaden mile, sometimes a mere patter of lightning-like steps. If it is a mile to you, you are a failure, and the great circle of specta-

A scorecard from the 1910 season at Bennett Park.

tors groans for your incompetency; if it is but a lightning streak, you are the great man of the baseball day. . . .

Now the Cleveland pitcher is "winding up" his arm—round and round it swings—he poises himself—there is yet a fraction of a second in which he can recall his intended throw—Moriarty is crouched like a tiger about to spring—Now! Now!

There is a white streak across the field!

A cloud of dust at the home plate!

The umpire stands with his hands extended, palms downward.

A bursting roar of acclaim echoes and re-echoes across the space of the park. Again and again it bursts forth in thrilling electric power. Thirty-six thousand eyes strain toward the man who is slapping at the dust from his white uniform.

MORIARTY IS HOME!

All the world's a baseball diamond. You are one of the players. Perhaps you have reached first by your own efforts. It may be that the sacrifices of your parents and friends have enabled you to reach second. Then on someone's "long fly" into the business world—a "fly" that was not "long" enough to prevent him going out—or someone's fluke on the rules of simple moral-

George Moriarty (left) and Germany Schaefer, 1909.

ity and square dealing, you have advanced to third. The opposition against you at third is stronger than at either first or second. At third you are to be reckoned with. Your opponents converge all their attention on you. Pitchers and catcher, coaches and opposing fans, are watching to tip off your plans and frustrate them. From third you become either a splendid success or dismal failure.

Don't die on third . . . .

Any fool could have led off spectacularly, but only a trained body and an alert mind could have stolen home right under the nose of the catcher whose hands were closing over the ball. Even a game means work. Work itself is a game and has its rules as its sudden openings. So, don't die on third. Bring to third every bit of your honest strength; study conditions; postpone thinking of your luck until you hear the umpire call "Safe."

Then you'll score all right.

Eventually Cameron's homilies caught auto tycoon Henry Ford's attention. In 1920 he became the editor of the *Dearborn Independent*, ghost-writing Ford's infamous anti-Semitic articles. Later he hosted the popular *Ford Sunday Evening Hour* radio program during the 1930s, delivering speeches on a variety of subjects. Cameron was an eloquent speaker and chronic drinker who often showed up for these live broadcasts under the influence. Amazingly, nary a burp or a slurred syllable passed his lips during eight years on the air. Ford was so moved by his interlocutor's words that he made sure they received wide circulation. A staggering 45 million booklets containing Cameron's best editorials and speeches eventually were published. As a result, "Don't Die on Third" ranks with Francis P. Church's classic "Yes, Virginia, There is a Santa" heart-tugger as one of the most frequently reprinted editorials of this century. Upon retirement, Cameron moved to Oakland, California, where he died at home in August of 1955. Following his own advice, the author of "Don't Die on Third" waited until the fourth of the month to pass away.

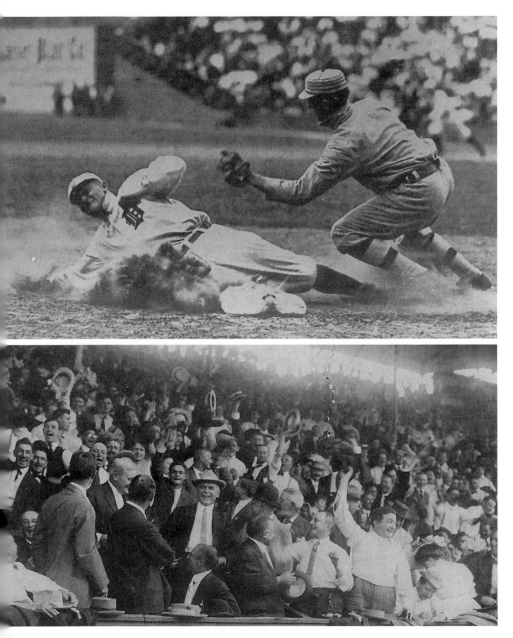

Cobb's hellzapoppin' style regularly brought Detroit fans to their feet. Here he slides in under the tag of Philadelphia's Jack Barry during a 1909 contest at Bennett Park.

The Tigers, as inspired by Moriarty's spirited play as Cameron was, were particularly effective at Michigan and Trumbull in 1909. They set still-standing club records for home victories (57) and winning percentage (.750). On a long home stand in August they won fifteen of sixteen contests. Cobb hit .604, averaged one stolen base per game, and accidentally spiked Philadelphia third baseman Frank Baker in an incident that through the years grew in infamy. Cobb, who was his usual brilliant, controversial self all season, seemed to save his best for the home crowd. Having hit only one home run at Bennett Park in his previous four seasons, he had six—all inside-the-park jobs—at Michigan and Trumbull in 1909. He added three more on the road to give him his only home-run crown and the third leg of baseball's mythical Triple Crown of batting. In addition to leading the league in batting (.377) and RBIs (107), he claimed another stolen base title with seventy-six steals.

The Tigers faced a new postseason opponent in the Pittsburgh Pirates, led by Honus Wagner. Thirteen years older than Cobb, the quiet, good-humored shortstop won the seventh of eight batting titles and led the National League in runs batted in. With his barrel chest, bowed legs, and thick dangling arms, Wagner was an odd-looking physical specimen, but despite his ungainly looks he also excelled in the field and on the base paths. Baseball fans in both cities eagerly awaited this confrontation between the game's two greatest stars.

The Pirates hosted the first two games in their spanking new Forbes Field. The cavernous stadium, built on a cow pasture, was representative of the new age of ballpark architecture. Made of concrete and steel, it was both fireproof and elegant. Elevators, telephones, grandstand lighting, upper-deck ramps, and ladies' restroom attendants were a few of the stadium's amenities. "For architectural beauty, imposing size, solid construction and public comfort and convenience," said the *Reach Baseball Guide*, "it has not its superior in the world."

After splitting the first two games, the teams moved to Bennett Park on October 11 for game three. The Pirates hammered out an 8–6 verdict on that frigid, windy Monday, scoring five runs in the opening frame before many in the record crowd of 18,277 had a chance to order their first box of Cracker Jack. However, the following day Mullin whitewashed Pittsburgh, 5–0, in front of 17,036 chilled fans. The victory—the Tigers' first at home in three World

Series—knotted the fall classic at two games apiece. After the teams returned to Forbes Field, the Pirates unknotted matters with an 8–4 win, and the action shifted to Bennett Park for the balance of the series.

Undoubtedly expecting the worst, many fans stayed home. Only 10,535 saw one of the most hotly contested series games ever. At one point George Moriarty walked over to a Pittsburgh runner standing on third base and, without provocation, pulled off his cap and slapped him over the head with it, after which the two players started kicking each other in the shins.

Pittsburgh exploded for a quick 3–0 lead at the top of the first off Mullin, but the Tigers refused to roll over. They tied the score in the fourth, and then added single runs in the fifth and sixth to take a 5–3 lead into the top of the ninth.

Mullin surrendered singles to the first two batters, bringing the go-ahead run to the plate in the person of Owen "Chief" Wilson. The Pirates' right fielder dropped a bunt in front of the plate, and then collided with Tom Jones as the first baseman reached for the throw from catcher Germany Schmidt. Jones was knocked cold, Wilson was safe at first, and as the ball trickled into right field one runner scored and the other pulled up at third.

Sam Crawford came in from center field to replace Jones, who after ten minutes of unconsciousness was finally hauled off the field on a stretcher. It was now a one-run affair. Mullin, pitching with runners on first and third and nobody out, induced the next batter to hit a grounder to Crawford. The runner on third, Bill Abstein, charged home. Crawford's throw arrived moments before Abstein's flashing spikes cut Germany Schmidt, who doggedly held on to make the tag for the first out.

Ed Abbaticchio came on to pinch hit. With two strikes and the crowd howling, Abbaticchio swung and missed Mullin's next offering as Wilson suddenly lit out for third. Schmidt fired to Moriarty in time to get Wilson, who flew in with spikes high. The double play ended the game and preserved a draining 5–4 victory, but the excitement continued, as Wilson and Moriarty angrily kicked at each other and players heatedly discussed each other's ancestry.

The bad feelings carried over into game seven, played two days later on October 16 in front of 17,562 Detroiters. The first batter up, Bobbie Byrne, was plunked by Bill Donovan's pitch. A couple of

Cobb presents a lonely figure in right field during the 1909 World Series against Pittsburgh. Daring Detroit fans are perched on rooftops and utility poles outside the park.

minutes later Byrne left the game with a sprained ankle after going hard into third base. Moriarty was also hurt on the play and left the game the next inning.

Meanwhile, Wild Bill couldn't find the plate, walking six batters and allowing two runs before Mullin pinch-hit for him in the third. The Tigers' workhorse, unable to find any zip in his tired right arm, gave up the final six runs in the Pirates' 8–0 romp. For the third year in a row, the Tigers closed out the World Series by getting shut out in front of the home folks. Doing the honors this time around was Charles "Babe" Adams, an unheralded twelve-game winner who picked up his third straight victory over Detroit. Cobb, outhit by Wagner .333 to .231, was so furious he kicked his bat halfway to the dugout.

Although undoubtedly aching inside, outwardly Frank Navin remained his usual undemonstrative self. Financially buoyed by three straight pennant-winning seasons, he paid off the balance of his debt to Bill Yawkey and sought to invest some of his profits into further expanding his ballpark. He added three thousand seats for 1910, increasing capacity to thirteen thousand. The main grandstand gained two small additions, one down each foul line. Always careful to pass the cost of capital improvements to the consumer, Navin increased the price of a reserved ticket to one dollar.

Navin also built a passageway beneath the grandstands leading from the dugout to the clubhouse. Previously, pitchers yanked from the game hustled past the crowd on what newspapers delicately called "the path of sighs." Disgraced pitchers often dodged verbal abuse and an occasional thrown bottle from ill-tempered fans. Navin's timing for this innovation was impeccable, as the Tigers collapsed that summer, missing a shot at a fourth pennant. Attendance dipped by nearly one hundred thousand, a consequence of the team's third-place finish.

After the 1910 season Navin once again looked for ways to add more seats. But plans to build a right-field grandstand were abandoned when property owners along Cherry Street demanded more money. Navin refused to meet their demands and opened the 1911 season with permanent bleacher sections in right and left fields.

Adding to Navin's frustration was his never-ending battle with the city's most notorious freeloaders, the wildcat fans.

Wildcat stands, the towering bleacher sections built outside a ballpark's fences, remained a feature of the city's baseball landscape for over thirty years. When Detroit fielded a National League team at Recreation Park in the 1880s, an enterprising citizen named John Deppert, Jr., built some bleachers atop his barn, which stood on the south side of Leland Street just outside the first-base line. Depending on the attractiveness of the opposition, between twenty-five and one hundred people gathered there each home date to watch the Detroit Wolverines. Deppert charged a bargain-basement admission fee, usually a dime, that undercut the Wolverines' ticket price of fifty cents. Deppert even sold lemonade, nuts, and apples to his guests from a concession stand.

The wildcat stands behind the left-field fence were a nuisance for most of the sixteen summers the Tigers played at Bennett Park.

The ball club tried a variety of strategies to foil Deppert, including raising additional boards and large cloth screens. Deppert simply built his bleachers higher as needed. Finally, the team sued, claiming it was being deprived of profits that were desperately needed to meet its monthly operating expenses of about three thousand dollars.

Judge J. Logan Chipman of the Superior Court of Detroit heard the case on September 19, 1885. Deppert's lawyer effectively turned the tables on the complainant during his response to the complaint. He told the court that the games were "a great nuisance, in that they collect and draw together the worst elements of society who congregate outside of the grounds, and tramp upon the adjacent property, and insult women and children." Moreover, "often the ball is knocked over the fence, and great injury is done to the adjoining premises in getting the ball back . . . by drawing together the crowds, who climb upon and attempt to look through the high fence, there have often occurred fights and brawls, and obscene and blasphemous language has been used to such an extent that the owners of adjacent premises have been compelled to call on the police, and arrests have been made."

On February 17, 1886, Judge Chipman ruled against the baseball club. The Wolverines appealed to the Michigan Supreme Court on April 13, 1886. Nine days later the court upheld the decision, noting that the ball club did not enjoy exclusive rights to conduct baseball games and that it couldn't tell its neighbors what they could or could not do with their property. One of the three justices dissented, calling Deppert's enterprise an "obnoxious nuisance" filled with "perverse ingenuity." But Deppert was free to operate his rooftop bleachers until the park finally closed in 1893.

Undoubtedly emboldened by Deppert's success, property owners around Bennett Park erected their own stands. A few popped up on Cherry Street, which ran behind the planing mill property in back of right field, and on Michigan Avenue, which ran parallel to the third-base line. But these were far from the action, affording only distant, partial views. For the diehard fan with only a nickel in his pocket, these cheap seats were his sole recourse. For a long time, the garret of a tumbledown building on Michigan Avenue was packed with as many as seventy-five patrons.

The choicest wildcat stands sprang up in the back yards on National Avenue, which ran behind the left-field fence. These offered a full view of the game. At any given time five or six of these stands operated a brisk business. Typically, a roof barn formed the foundation; the main part of the bleachers stood twenty feet above the barn and accommodated between fifty and sixty fans. A superstructure ten feet higher seated about thirty more. Another fifteen or so spectators perched on the barn roof itself. Each wildcat stand held a crowd of about one hundred people. Admission fees of a dime netted the operator up to ten dollars a game.

"The barns on which the stands are built are no longer barns, but more like primitive reception lobbies," a visitor once observed. "They have their door tenders to collect the numerous dimes, their floors and stairs are swept clean, and horses, hay, oats, etc., are absolutely unknown to them."

Who inhabited these primitive sky boxes? A reporter profiled these "oddest of the baseball cranks":

He differs radically from the bleacher rooter, although he is every whit as interested in the game. In fact, it would seem that he is more interested in baseball than the regular park patrons, because he will daily risk breaking his bones by climbing in the air among rafters to perch on a rickety platform 50 feet above terra firma.

The "wildcat fan" is a critical, discriminating individual, well versed in baseball lore and thoroughly posted on the fine points of the game. He has an eagle eye, being able to discern instantly the exact way in which the closest plays are effected. He differs from the bleacher and grandstand "fans" in that he is generally quiet and undemonstrative. It is seldom, indeed, that the spectators in the ball park hear a yell from the faraway wildcat stands. The distance from the diamond is probably the cause of the wildcat fan's quietness. Rooters yell during a game in order to encourage the players or "rattle" an opposing pitcher. They know that the players can hear what they say. In the wildcat stands it is different. It would have to be a tremendous yell that would carry to the diamond, and it requires an exceptional piece of fielding or batting to arouse that yell. . . .

One feature of these stands is the way every occupant keeps the score. Some of them keep the entire score, including runs, hits, errors, extra base hits, double plays, etc., and the next day compare scores with the newspapers in order to see if the sporting editors made any mistakes. A few of the "fans" had copies of the score card which is given away in front of the grounds, but most of them seemed to prefer pieces of cardboard, or the edge of a newspaper. Three or four had small sticks whittled even on one side and carefully marked with spaces for every inning.

Wildcatters, most of whom were young, lower-class males, were not noted for their perfect comportment. They whistled at women, insulted their boyfriends, and fought among themselves. In 1906 the *Detroit Journal* reported that Patrolman George Green complained to the chief of police "that the wildcat spectators have been making it a practice to expectorate tobacco on those who pass through the alley while taking a short cut to the grounds." As proof, Green produced his tobacco-stained uniform.

George Vanderbeck tried cutting off the wildcatters' view by hanging strips of canvas along the left-field fence. But "the owners of the stands promptly built higher, and it was a merry war for awhile," reported a daily. Vanderbeck's successor, rough-and-tumble Jim Burns, probably recognized a few familiar faces in the stands, so he did nothing but attempt to make operators pay an amusement license fee. The courts held that such a fee was illegal.

Subsequent owners continually took the operators to court, hoping to secure an injunction, but the Deppert case invariably was trotted out as precedent. The only victories came when the fire marshall closed a stand as a safety hazard. Once the operator brought his structure up to standard, he was free to re-open. Navin figured that the wildcat stands when full represented about four hundred lost admissions, and hung canvas during the Tigers' pennant-winning 1907–09 seasons. Angry wildcatters retaliated by hurling rotten vegetables and bottles to disrupt the games. Navin eased off, though photographs of the 1909 World Series clearly show canvas flapping in the faces of his freeloading adversaries. Their antics over the next couple of summers contributed to his growing desire to raze Bennett Park. To make room for the new ballpark, the block of houses on the east side of National would have to be purchased and demolished—and with them, the barns and towers would come tumbling down, too. The wrecking ball, not the courts, ended the in-your-face reign of the neighborhood's resourceful wildcat operators.

Sam Crawford digs in against New York's Ray Caldwell in the home half of the seventh on May 12, 1911. Moments earlier, Cobb had electrified fans by stealing home on Caldwell and catcher Ed Sweeney.

A somewhat livelier cork-centered ball was introduced in 1911, accounting in part for the Tigers' torrid start. Most fans loved the new sphere, which seemed to have doubled in cylinders. The ball bounced all over Bennett Park that summer. There even was a new target to aim for: the Bull Durham chewing tobacco sign in right-center field. A batter hitting the bull received fifty dollars from the company, about a week's salary for many big leaguers. "I hit my first home run off of George Mullin in 1911," recalled Ray Fisher, a decent-hitting pitcher for the New York Highlanders. "I socked that baby over the fence. But I was mad because I missed the sign. A foot lower and I would've had just a double, but I would've been fifty dollars richer."

That summer, for the fifth consecutive year, the Tigers led all American League teams in runs scored on their home turf. A bushel came on June 18, when a Bennett Park audience witnessed the biggest comeback in major-league history. Trailing 13–1 in the bottom of the sixth against the White Sox, the Tigers roared back to win, 16–15. The rally was part of a 31–9 spurt that inspired Detroiters to dream of another World Series appearance. However, Philadelphia came back strong in August and wound up handily winning its second straight pennant.

Applying salve to the disappointment were the performances of Cobb and Crawford, both of whom enjoyed their finest all-around season. Crawford whacked the ball at a .378 clip and knocked in 115 runs, second only to Cobb. Cobb, whose record forty-game hitting streak was finally snapped by Chicago's Ed Walsh in the morning game of a sweltering Fourth of July doubleheader at Bennett Park, won a fifth straight batting crown with a gaudy .420 average, his highest ever. He swiped eighty-three bases and had personal highs in hits (248), doubles (47), triples (24), runs (147), and RBI (144). For the second consecutive year Cobb was awarded a Chalmers automobile by local manufacturer Hugh Chalmers. In 1910 he had earned it by winning a close and controversial batting race with Cleveland's Nap Lajoie. This time he received a new model in recognition of being voted by sportswriters as the league's finest performer.

Frank Navin saw nearly 485,000 fans pass through the turnstiles in 1911, but now he dreamed of far greater numbers cheering lustily and comfortably in a modern showpiece. During the 1909 World Series Pittsburgh accommodated nearly thirty thousand per game in Forbes Field, roughly twice the number that had been squeezed into Bennett Park. Forbes Field was just one of several new stadiums replacing the old, dangerous, and cramped wooden facilities of the nineteenth century. Philadelphia's Shibe Park and St. Louis's Sportsman's Park had both opened the same year as Forbes, followed by Chicago's Comiskey Park in 1910. Boston's Fenway Park and Cincinnati's Crosley Field were scheduled to open in 1912. Down the road were Brooklyn's Ebbets Field (1913) and Chicago's Wrigley Field (1914).

Navin spoke wistfully of a new field beginning in 1908, but it wasn't until the summer of 1911 that he was able to buy out the last

Charlie Bennett, pictured here late in life, caught the ceremonial first pitch at every home opener from 1895 to 1926.

of the property owners on National and Cherry streets and finally act on his vision. A man who loved cards and horses, Navin didn't consider the considerable capital investment involved much of a gamble. Detroiters at one time had been ambivalent about their baseball team, but with a perennial contender and the game's top draw playing in their own back yard a dependable and sizable fan base was created. As "Dynamic Detroit" continued to grow exponentially in population and stature thanks to the auto industry, civic and business leaders increasingly talked of a ballpark worthy of Detroit's rank among America's great cities.

Over the winter of 1911–12, the fifteen-year-old wooden park was demolished and replaced with a modern concrete-and-steel structure. The Tigers' owner resisted naming the park after himself, but friends and Bill Yawkey finally prevailed. Navin Field opened for business in the spring of 1912, a new facility that was a tribute to progress and the community's growing love affair with its baseball team.

A fan's camera caught Ty Cobb at Navin Field in 1917.

CHAPTER THREE

Frank's Place

Navin Field, 1912–1937

A S ORIGINALLY PLANNED, April 18, 1912 was to have been a double-grand-slam day for Frank Navin. Not only was it his forty-first birthday, but his new ballpark was to be dedicated with considerable hoopla before a contest against the Cleveland Indians. Unfortunately, the weather did not cooperate. Heavy rains washed out the affair. Although the game could have been played the following day, a Friday, Navin canceled it. The official explanation was wet grounds. The truth was that the Tigers' boss, like most gamblers, was extremely superstitious. The man who always put his left shoe on first and avoided cross-eyed people at all costs simply refused to christen Navin Field on what he considered the bad-luck day of the week. The grand opening was rescheduled for Saturday, April 20, the same day Fenway Park would be unveiled in Boston.

Work crews raced to finish the job. Wooden Bennett Park had been easily demolished the previous October, shortly after the 1911 season ended. The Osborn Engineering Company, a Cleveland firm

Frank Navin.

that was the country's leading builder of ballparks, designed the new concrete-and-steel structure. Hunkin & Conkey, also of Cleveland, served as the general contractor. Major subcontractors included Detroit Architectural Iron Works and the John D. Templeton Company of Detroit, which installed the wiring and fixtures.

The park slowly took on a recognizable shape over the winter, as contractors battled time and the elements. March snows delayed the pouring of concrete in the giant horseshoe-shaped grandstand, which stretched about two hundred feet down each foul line. As opening day approached, two hundred men labored practically around the clock laying ten tons of concrete onto the giant frame-work. A covered pavilion connected each end of the grandstand to the outfield corners. When completed, the park seated twenty-three thousand people, nearly five times the capacity of Bennett Park when it was built fifteen years earlier. Navin Field cost co-owners Navin and Bill Yawkey three hundred thousand dollars. Today, an identical project would cost about $50 million.

Amidst the frenzy of last-minute preparations, Navin may have engaged in some private reflection. His reputation among ballplay-ers was that of a dispassionate nickel-nurser, but sentiment bubbled just below the surface of this stone-faced man. Those close to him described him as a warm, charitable person, someone with a whim-sical sense of humor who was loyal almost to a fault to family, friends, and favorite ballplayers. "I wish I could let my feelings out like some other men," he once confessed, "but I just can't."

Navin's older brother, Thomas, had passed away fifteen months before the celebration. The Navin brothers were born in Adrian, Michigan, into a large Irish family headed by a railroad worker and his wife. Tom, a former seminary student, was elected mayor of Adrian at the age of twenty-six. In 1885 family pride turned to pub-lic disgrace when he was sentenced to ten years for embezzling twenty-two thousand dollars. After serving nearly six years at Jackson Prison, he was pardoned in late 1890. He moved to Detroit and set up a law practice; eventually he headed the city's Republican machine.

Sometime in the early 1890s Frank followed Tom to Detroit, where he graduated from a business college and then earned a law degree from the Detroit College of Law. Frank put himself through night school by working as a clerk with the city and also as a croupi-er in local gambling houses. With his brother's help he ran for pub-lic office, but was quickly defeated in the election for justice of the peace. "We're still trying to find the fourteen men who voted for him," Tom joked.

At the turn of the century Frank found work in the office of Samuel Angus, selling insurance before his ability with numbers got him promoted to bookkeeper. At this time Tom became the first Navin family member to involve himself with professional baseball, spearheading the ill-fated attempt to resurrect the American

Association and place a team in Detroit. This was two years before Angus's purchase of the Tigers serendipitously started Frank on his career with club's front office. Frank kept his brother close by, retaining him as club counsel until Tom suddenly died of apoplexy just before Christmas in 1910.

While owning a pennant winner and building a modern ballpark guaranteed a certain amount of respectability and prestige among those willing to overlook the Navin family's foibles, some insisted that Frank Navin had missed his true calling. His teachers and classmates considered him "the best student ever to enter their institution," said newspaperman Malcolm Bingay. "What he might have made of himself as a barrister nobody knows because he turned all that magnificent power of absorption and concentration into the study of making money from the horses and professional poker."

Frank Navin loved and knew horses. He was a common sight around area racetracks, sometimes wagering several thousand dollars on a single race. He rode every day for exercise and owned several racehorses. He was much more cautious with his money when hammering out player contracts. During these sessions Navin's poker face served him well. He occasionally used questionable tactics to gain the upper hand. When Ty Cobb, his number-one gate attraction, was being wooed by the rival Federal League, Navin ordered Cobb's telegrams intercepted and sent to his home so he could keep abreast of negotiations.

Navin, a bald, corpulent, pasty-faced man who eschewed tobacco and alcohol but loved sweets, emerged as one of the most respected owners in baseball. He became a trusted confidant of Kenesaw Mountain Landis after the white-haired federal judge was named the game's first commissioner. Landis, brought on board in late 1920 to clean up the game after the Black Sox scandal, conveniently overlooked his friend's peccadillos.

Although Navin's early judgment of talent was sometimes weak—he rejected a rawboned fast ball pitcher named Walter Johnson, for example—his knowledge of the game expanded along with his waistline. "Navin was one of the few owners who knew the playing end of the game as well as he knew the business end," observed Harry Salsinger. "Few of his players ever matched him in his understanding of the technical aspects of the game. He made a study of baseball and knew more about pitching than anyone

Navin Field during the spring of 1912, shortly before its opening.

around. He never criticized his players, except if he felt they were lazy and weren't putting out their best effort. For this reason, they liked playing for him. None of them got rich but they always felt he was fair in dealing with them."

On the evening of April 19, 1912, the Detroit Board of Commerce hosted a banquet saluting Navin and Yawkey for their commitment to baseball and to the city. The banquet demonstrated how far the Detroit Baseball & Amusement Company (its official name) had come in just a few years. Once rumored to be moving to Pittsburgh, the franchise stabilized and prospered to such an extent that it was considered a community resource, its fortunes intertwined with the growing city it represented.

E. S. Barnard, vice president of the visiting Cleveland Indians, scoffed at past claims that Detroiters wouldn't support the home nine. "I always claimed that Detroit was not the poor ball town it has the reputation of being, but the reason attendance was not in proportion to the other cities in the league was because of the lack of accommodations at the small park."

Saturday arrived cool and hazy. Many of the dignitaries who attended the previous night's dinner rode out to the park in carriages, followed by members of both teams, a marching band, and a small army of fans. Officially, 24,382 men, women, and children poured into the park, but estimates of the afternoon's attendance reached 26,000. Most sat in the yellow-painted wooden slat seats; others stood in the roped-off outfield.

Navin Field was a sight to behold. It covered an area nearly twice the size of Bennett Park. With no circus bleachers or other obstacles to clutter the outfield, there was a symmetry to the field and more space to play. The new outfield dimensions were 365 feet down the right-field line, 400 feet to center, and 340 feet down the left-field line. A giant American flag flew from the 125-foot-high flagpole in center field. The flagpole still dominates Tiger Stadium's skyline and remains the tallest obstacle ever built in fair territory inside a major-league park.

Fans pointed to the giant scoreboard in left field, where out-of-town scores were easily read from any point inside the park. Players praised the large green panel in center field, an innovation that provided a wonderful backdrop for hitters. Batters also appreciated the reconfiguration of the diamond. At Bennett Park, home plate had been located at what was now the right field corner, so that by the end of the game the setting sun shone directly into the batter's eyes. Now the right fielder had to contend with the problem. Some fans joked about the long walk to get to one's seat; others reminisced about Bennett Park's chumminess. Overall Frank Navin's new ballpark was declared a smashing success. A *Detroit News* headline expressed the prevailing opinion: "Fan Verdict: SOME Park."

It also was some game. Cleveland's Shoeless Joe Jackson scored the first run at Navin Field in the opening frame, but in the bottom of the inning Cobb countered with his signature play, stealing home on Vean Gregg's high pitch to Del Gainor. Catcher Ted Easterly futilely tried to tag Cobb, who executed his famous fade-away slide. Cobb's steal of home was his first of eight that season, still the all-time record. Curiously, all occurred in Detroit, where fans had grown to anticipate such daredevil shenanigans.

Dependable old George Mullin netted his ninth start in the last ten openers and went all the way, pitching out of several jams as the Tigers rallied to tie the game at five runs apiece. In the bottom of the eleventh inning, with two runners on base, Mullin rapped a two-out single between the shortstop and third baseman and sent Detroiters home happy with a 6–5 victory.

Two months after Navin Field was christened, Detroit remained in a party mood. In June the Census Bureau announced that Michigan now officially led the country in auto production—reason enough, city fathers thought, to throw a party. And not just any party, but a summer event ballyhooed as the largest carnival ever attempted. Thus was born "Cadillaqua," a civic orgy designed to let everyone know that Detroit had finally arrived. For one week in July, the city tooted its own horn with an unending stream of fireworks, costume pageants, and other events, including a five-thousand-car parade down Woodward Avenue. Cadillaqua even had its own official song, "A Real, Live Regular Town", published by Jerome Remick & Co., the local version of Tin Pan Alley.

Come along, join the throng, get in line, Molly mine
We are going to old Detroit town
For it's a hummer in summer, a town that's a comer
And we'll be there Molly, Sweet Molly Brown
The train is waiting on the railroad track
Come let's honor Cadillac
Here we are in my car, right in town, Molly Brown
And tomorrow we'll see Ty Cobb at bat . . . .

For baseball fans, the summer proved to be more of a bummer than a hummer. The once-mighty Tigers fell to sixth place. Although Cobb won his sixth straight batting title, an incident involving his climbing into the stands at New York's Hilltop Park to assault a fan contributed to the dour season. The infamous episode resulted in the entire Tigers team striking to protest Cobb's suspension and forced Navin to hurriedly field a makeshift lineup of sandlotters in Philadelphia. It also forced owners to install ushers inside the ballparks to curb crowd unruliness.

Detroiters did not crowd the gates that first summer at Navin Field. Attendance fell by about 20 percent from the previous year, the last at Bennett Park. It dropped further in 1913 when the Tigers once again finished sixth. In addition, Navin contended with the possibility of an intracity rivalry siphoning off even more customers. In 1913 there was speculation that the Federal League, which began operating the following spring, would place a team in Detroit. The heavily bankrolled eight-team circuit, the only serious threat to the major leagues during this century, folded two years later, but not before building first-class parks in several cities, including Chicago's Wrigley Field. The recent opening of Navin Field prevented the construction of another new park in Detroit. Local backers also were discouraged by the refusal of John Roesink, a downtown clothier and major supporter of semipro baseball, to rent or sell his east-

Navin Field's grand opening on April 20, 1912. Some twenty-six thousand watched the exciting extra-inning victory, causing a reporter to observe that "only eight cities in the state have as many inhabitants as there were fans within the concrete walls of the Tigers' new home."

side Mack Park. For these and other reasons, the Federal League stayed out of Detroit.

The 1910s were lean years for the Tigers, at least on the field. Except for 1915, when they became the first second-place team to win one hundred games, and 1916, when they once again finished second to Boston, the Tigers were a middle-of-the-pack team. Shortstop Donie Bush, left fielder Bobby Veach, and hurlers George "Hooks" Dauss and Harry Coveleski were legitimate stars. The supporting cast was thin, though. The pressure to win eventually over-

George Mullin, who started nine home openers for the Tigers, was the logical choice to take the mound for the first game at Navin Field. In twelve seasons with Detroit the stout-hearted pitcher compiled 209 wins and frequently played the outfield or pinch-hit between starts. He also split six World Series decisions. His greatest single moment came on July 4, 1912, Mullin's thirty-second birthday, when he pitched a no-hitter against St. Louis. It was the first no-hitter ever pitched by a Tiger at the corner.

whelmed Hughie Jennings. The once-animated manager now often appeared listless and glassy-eyed in the coaching box, the result of trying to find solace in the bottle.

At the box office, though, the team usually drew well above the league average. Helping the gate were the European immigrants who continued to stream into the city to man the assembly lines. When the First World War shut off the spigot, industrial recruiters brought thousands of Southern blacks to Detroit. The Great Migration profoundly affected Detroit's racial composition. Between 1910 and 1920 the city's black population mushroomed from 6,000 to 41,000; the sevenfold increase was the largest in the nation. By the end of the 1920s the number of Detroit blacks tripled to 120,000.

In 1919 the Tigers led the league in attendance for the first time, drawing 643,805 fans and netting Navin a reported $110,000 profit while finishing fourth. That spring Navin became full owner of the club after Bill Yawkey died, but he soon brought on two more silent partners. In 1920 John Kelsey and Walter O. Briggs, baseball-loving industrialists who had some idle money lying around, bought quarter-shares of the club for $250,000 apiece. The extra cash would come in handy as Navin once again looked to expand his park.★

Throughout the summer of 1920 Navin Field fans hooted and called for a new manager. The Tigers lost ninety-three games; only the woeful Philadelphia Athletics kept the team out of the basement. To no one's surprise, after fourteen years as the Tigers' manager, Jennings was fired. Kelsey and Briggs undoubtedly had something to do with Jennings' dismissal, as well as with the hiring of his replacement, Ty Cobb.

Cobb initially rejected his old friends' overtures to manage the Tigers. After sixteen big-league seasons he was drained. He also was independently wealthy and considering retirement. He was reminded the one honor that had eluded him during his illustrious career was a World Series championship. Seeing his close friend Tris Speaker savoring another series win as player-manager of the

★ John Kelsey, third baseman and pitcher for the Detroit Athletic Club when it won a national championship in 1892, was a well-loved figure around town. He was a millionaire without airs, once caught washing his own socks in a hotel sink during a business trip to New York. He also was a hands-off shareholder. To fend off questions he carried around cards that read, "Ask Navin. He's the owner."

Bobby Veach (far right) is part of a pregame gathering of Boston and Detroit players watching Sam Crawford wing one from the first-base line at Navin Field. It was Veach's misfortune to play the outfield at the same time as Crawford, Cobb, and Harry Heilmann, three Hall of Famers who had nothing on the quiet Kentuckian. In three of his six seasons with Detroit Veach passed 100 RBI and led the circuit three times. In 1919 he batted .355 and led the loop in hits, doubles, and triples, although few people outside Detroit noticed his feats.

Cleveland Indians in 1920 may have finally persuaded Cobb to attempt the same with Detroit. Managing was a new challenge for Cobb, something all accomplished men craved as they grew older. And Cobb was offered a bundle: thirty-five thousand dollars, about seven times the average salary of a major-league player in those days. On December 18, 1920, his thirty-fourth birthday, Cobb finally accepted the offer.

Babe Ruth is pictured here in his first appearance in
Detroit, in 1915. Years before he became baseball's top
slugger, the Red Sox pitcher was recognized as the top
southpaw in the American League.

During the First World War, new recruits assembled at Navin Field before leaving for training camp.

Cobb managed the team with moderate success for six seasons, from 1921 through 1926. This was a period of radical change inside and outside the ball yard. Detroit was now the fourth-largest city in the country, with a population of over one million people. The physical problems associated with building and maintaining a modern industrial metropolis made the Roaring Twenties an especially reckless, rollicking decade in the Motor City.

Prohibition, the law of the land from 1918 to 1933, was particularly troublesome in Detroit. An estimated twenty-five thousand blind pigs, twenty times the number of legal establishments closed by Prohibition, slaked the thirst of the populace. This number did not include the untold thousands of citizens who brewed their own hooch in basements, attics, barns, and closets. "The town was completely wide open," recalled crime reporter Jack Carlisle. "Everybody was drinking themselves goofy."

Navin Field employees updated park patrons and visiting ballplayers about the availability of liquid refreshments or, in certain

Prior to the 1923 season, an upper deck was added to the grandstand that increased the ballpark's seating capacity to twenty-three thousand fans. Tons of sandbags were used to test the decking.

cases, provided the goods themselves. Bernard Joseph, who grew up on the east side near Harper and Gratiot, remembered that Prohibition "turned many ordinary citizens into lawbreakers," including his enterprising father, Walter. The Josephs operated a still in their basement, the parts bought from the neighborhood hardware store. "The front bedroom closet of our home contained boxes of small bottles and corks," said Joseph. "I spent hours playing with them and snacking on treats I found in one of the boxes. Although I have no personal memories of this, stories were told of my dad filling the bottom of the box with bottles of hootch, covering them with a layer of snack packages and then selling the stuff at Navin Field."

The city's premier bootleggers, the all-Jewish Purple Gang, were big sports fans. The young, nattily dressed thugs could be seen in choice seats at Navin Field, shouting encouragement to players, some of whom later bumped into them at favorite nightspots.

Fans line up to buy tickets for a home opener some time in the mid-1920s. In 1923 the club drew nine hundred thousand for the first time; the following season the Tigers became the second big-league team to reach the million mark in attendance.

Players like George Dauss and Harry Heilmann were well-known rounders. Heilmann secured his reputation by once driving his Austin roadster, a gift from fans on Harry Heilmann Day at Navin Field, down the stairs of a basement speakeasy and up to its bar, whereupon he ordered a drink.

The changes that baseball experienced were only slightly less tumultuous. After the First World War trick pitches were phased out, and umpires were authorized to use several fresh balls a game. Before this a dirty, lopsided ball—fouled with tobacco juice, wax, spit, and cuts from enterprising pitchers—was usually kept in play the entire game. The baseballs were made of more tightly wound yarn, which meant they traveled greater distances when struck. Also, the outfield fences of the new parks being built were not nearly as far back as in the old fields, resulting in more balls being whacked over or against the fences. The national pastime, long a game of pitching and defense, was turned on its head by the sudden emphasis on offense.

The chief benefactor was the New York Yankees' charismatic colossus, George Herman "Babe" Ruth. The bulb-nosed, spindly-legged outfielder, once a superb pitcher with the Red Sox, hit the ball far and often. In 1920, during his first season in Yankee pinstripes, Ruth bashed fifty-four home runs, and then followed that up with fifty-nine in 1921. His total for those two seasons was only five less than Cobb compiled during his entire twenty-four-year career. Fans flocked to Navin Field hoping to see Ruth crush the ball; Cobb, standing in center field and hearing the home crowd cheer his rival, burned a slow fuse. His jealousy was understandable. For years he had been the game's number-one creative genius, competitive spirit, and gate attraction, but now someone else was lighting up the corner of Michigan and Trumbull.

The Cobb-Ruth rivalry enlivened Navin Field during most of the 1920s. On one infamous Friday afternoon—June 13, 1924—the feud exploded into a full-scale riot at Michigan and Trumbull. It began when the Yankees' Bob Meusel was struck by a pitch, presumably on Cobb's orders. Both benches emptied, Cobb and Ruth crashing headlong into each other like a pair of runaway locomotives. Hundreds of Detroit fans joined in the melee, ripping seats loose from their concrete moorings and hurling them onto the field. The police joined in the half-hour battle, before the contest was forfeited to New York.

Despite the fracas, Ruth loved playing in Detroit. There was, of course, the proximity of good drink and willing women to recommend the Motor City, which rivaled Al Capone's Chicago as the most wide-open town in the country during the 1920s. There also was the park where, on June 8, 1926, Ruth hit the longest of his 714 career home runs—possibly the longest home run ever hit by any-

This page from a 1924 rotogravure section shows some of the principal characters in the superheated rivalry between the Tigers and Yankees. That summer the two teams engaged in a free-for-all at Navin Field, resulting in one of the few forfeits in big-league history.

one. Ruth unloaded in the fifth inning off Lil Stoner. The shot carried over the right-center-field fence, skimmed the tops of several parked cars on Cherry Street, and then rolled a few more blocks until a boy on a bicycle caught up with it. The official distance was tabulated at 626 feet, but at least one sportswriter estimated it had traveled between 800 and 850 feet before it finally stopped.

Ruth's wallops amazed even accomplished sluggers like Detroit's nineteenth-century star, Sam Thompson. One afternoon early in Ruth's career, Thompson was seated in John Kelsey's box at Navin Field when the Babe hit a monstrous shot.

"Sam, does that remind you of one of your long hits?" asked Kelsey.

"Huh," responded Big Sam. "The longest I ever hit, compared with this one, was a bunt."

Bunts were passé during the new age of offense that Ruth ushered in. Home runs were the name of the game—except at Navin Field. During Cobb's tenure as manager the visiting team out-homered the Tigers by a two-to-one margin in Detroit. Johnny Bassler was emblematic of the Tigers' offense during the 1920s, which was long on singles but short on homers. Between 1921 and 1927 the catcher hit a composite .308, but managed only one round-tripper in 2,240 at-bats.

Cobb, stubbornly clinging to the memory of hard-fought 3–2 games of yore where a squeeze play, hit-and-run, or steal of home typically decided the outcome, ordered his troops to play one base at a time, despite their obvious lack of interest or skill in doing so. Once, after the Tigers won a 16–15 slugfest over the White Sox at Navin Field, Harry Salsinger commented, "If the Tigers are going to insist on using the sacrifice bunt, something that none of the successful clubs do, then it would be an excellent idea to teach the players to bunt."

It wasn't entirely Cobb's fault. Players resisted his instruction, not so much because they disliked him (most did), but because they quickly caught on that adulation and fat contracts were not readily forthcoming to those who practiced the suddenly quaint art of scientific baseball. Upper-cutting, swing-from-the-heels sluggers—now, that was what kept the turnstiles humming.

Cobb tried to sabotage the visiting team's sluggers. "Ty was sly," said Neil Conway, the park's grounds keeper for thirty years. "When a slugging club would come to Detroit, Ty would have me install temporary bleachers in the outfield so that balls hit out there would be ground-rule doubles instead of homers. When the regulation stands were only half full Ty made the whole ground crew sit in the temporary seats so the umpires wouldn't have them removed."

Although the "Tygers" featured one of the majors' heaviest-hitting lineups, they were undermined by mediocre pitching. If Cobb couldn't teach pitching (and in Cobb's defense not many managers can), he could show someone how to properly apply ash to horsehide. "In all modesty," he once said, "I could teach hitting."

The 1921 edition of the Tigers hit a blistering .316, still the American League record. In four of Cobb's six years at the helm, the team hit .300 or better. Under his tutelage Detroit led the loop in batting in 1921 and 1924, in scoring in 1924 and 1925, and boasted the individual batting champion in 1921, 1923, 1925, and 1926. Cobb, who'd gathered his twelfth and final batting crown in 1919, didn't win any of them. Despite his advanced age and scarred, battered wheels, he was not a doddering old man. Weighed down by the pressures of running the team on the field, he still hit a collective .365 as player-manager and averaged eighty-eight RBI a season.

Cobb's prize pupil was Harry Heilmann, a six-foot, one-inch, two-hundred-pound product of San Francisco's sandlots who ran like a man trying to extract his feet from wet cement. A line-drive-hitting righthander, Heilmann heeded Cobb's advice to move his feet closer together and to hold the bat far down on the handle, the barrel resting against his shoulder. In 1921 Heilmann outhit the old master himself, .394 to .389, to win his first of four batting championships. He won additional crowns in 1923 (.403), 1925 (.393), and 1927 (.398), the year after Cobb left the team. Heilmann's lack of speed probably shaved a good ten points off his .342 career average and cost him three .400 seasons, but he impressed enough voters to be elected to the Hall of Fame a few months after his death from cancer in 1951.

Cobb, a big fan of scientific fads, fancied himself an amateur psychologist. Looking to light a fire under Bobby Veach, the easygoing Kentuckian who had been a fixture in Detroit's outfield since 1913, he instructed Heilmann to heckle Veach unmercifully from the on-deck circle whenever he was at the plate. Cobb assured Heilmann he would explain everything to Veach after the season ended. Heilmann did as he was told, and the feud resulted in Veach establishing personal highs in hits (207), home runs (16) and RBI (128) while batting .338. The trio of Veach, Heilmann, and Cobb hit a combined .374 and knocked in 368 runs in 1921. No American League outfield has ever driven in more runs in a season. But Cobb, in a hurry to return to Georgia, never got around to explaining the mission to Veach. When Heilmann tried to apologize, Veach warned his antagonist not to "come sucking around me with that phony line." The two remained on the outs until Veach left the club three years later.

Despite such mixed results, Cobb never tired of playing mind games. The following season, on April 30, 1922, he did his best to rattle the concentration of Charlie Robertson, a rookie righthander taking the hill for the Chicago White Sox. Robertson went on to an undistinguished major-league career (a 49–80 record and 4.44 ERA over eight seasons with three clubs) but on this afternoon at Navin Field the twenty-six-year-old Texan was perfect. He retired twenty-seven Tigers in a row, striking out six and allowing only six fly balls to the outfield. Herman Pillette was nearly as good for the home team, but he gave up a second-inning single to Earl Sheely that gave Robertson all the support he needed in a 2–0 victory.

Robertson hurled the modern era's third perfect game despite the jeers and taunts of twenty-five thousand fans and the disruptive tactics of Cobb and Heilmann, who stopped play to protest that the White Sox pitcher was doctoring the ball. Umpires found no fault with Robertson and, as the game wore on, neither did the fans. By the ninth inning Robertson's composure won the Navin Field crowd over. When he set down Danny Clark, Clyde Manion, and Johnny Bassler for the final outs of the game, fans stormed past the police and the roped-off outfield and carried the rookie off the field on their shoulders. Robertson's gem, just his second big-league win, remains the only perfect game ever pitched at the corner of Michigan and Trumbull.

The Tigers' batting carnival made them the biggest draw on the road after the Yankees and inspired a record number of people to enter Navin Field in 1922: 861,206. It was the first of three consecutive seasons when Detroit would attract more fans than any other league team except New York. Over the winter of 1922–23 Frank Navin had the grandstand double-decked, increasing seating capacity to 29,000. "Of course," sportswriter Fred Lieb reported, "Navin quietly raised the seat prices by two bits." He also built a rooftop press box, a luxury item then only to be found at magnificent Yankee Stadium, which opened in 1923. That season another new attendance mark was set at Michigan and Trumbull, as more than 911,000 passed through the turnstiles, including a record opening-day turnout of 36,000. Temporary bleachers were set up all around the outfield to accommodate the throng. "Detroit is simply baseball crazy," declared the *Sporting News*. The craziness grew to epic proportions in 1924, when Detroit joined the Yankees as the only teams ever to draw over one million customers. Twice that summer an estimated 40,000 people overflowed Navin Field to watch the home nine battle Babe Ruth and company.

Cobb gained personally, because his contract called for him to receive ten cents for every ticket sold over seven hundred thousand. But the Tigers' box office success had little effect on the team's on-field fortunes. Cobb went to his grave insisting that the Tigers' owner had deprived the team of a pennant or two by his refusal to purchase the key additions that might have pushed the Tigers past the hated Yankees, who won four pennants during Cobb's tenure as manager.

"Cobb wanted to buy Johnny Neun from the American Association to play first base," said pitcher Eddie Wells, remembering how regular Lu Blue's broken ankle probably cost Detroit the flag in 1924. "But old Frank Navin, I don't think he wanted to win a pennant. He'd have to pay us too much money. He wanted to stay in second, third place." Neun finally joined Detroit the next year, but by then the team was struggling to stay out of the second division.

By the middle of 1926, his sixth season at the helm, Cobb had surrendered center field to Heinie Manush (who edged Babe Ruth for the batting crown with a .378 mark) and spent his afternoons directing from the safety of the dugout, where the booing of restless fans was muffled by concrete. At the end of the year he announced his retirement as manager and player. Shortly thereafter, the allegations of a disgruntled former Tiger, Dutch Leonard, became public. Leonard's charges that Cobb and Speaker helped fix a game at Navin Field at the end of the 1919 season rocked the baseball world, but they were soon found groundless by Judge Landis. Hoping to restore his reputation, Ty signed with the Philadelphia Athletics, for whom he played the final two seasons of his career.

When Cobb next visited Detroit in 1927, this time wearing a uniform blouse with an elephant rather than an Olde English D on it, the Tigers had introduced radio broadcasts and a new manager to Navin Field. Ty Cobb Day brought out almost thirty thousand people to the corner. Cobb shook hands with George Moriarty, who gave up his umpiring job to succeed his former teammate as manager, graciously accepted a new car and floral horseshoe from admirers, and then held up the game as he signed autographs in the roped-off outfield. It was a civic love fest for the man who remains the centerpiece of baseball history at Michigan and Trumbull.

A few weeks later, the aging Georgia Peach chose his old stomping grounds for the site of a milestone hit. On July 19, he cracked a two-base hit off Sam Gibson. It was his four thousandth career base hit, a monumental figure that to this day only one other player— Pete Rose—reached.

While Cobb's historic hit attracted scant attention at the time (few newspapers in that less record-fixated age even mentioned it), Johnny Neun's feat of a few weeks earlier still had some fans buzzing. On May 31 the Tigers' first baseman had pulled off an unassisted triple play, which ranks with perfect games as one of the rarest sights on a baseball diamond. What made Neun's feat even more extraordinary was that it came a day after Pittsburgh's Johnny Cooney had turned the same trick against the Chicago Cubs. Neun, who enjoyed his one good season with Detroit that summer with a .324 average and five stolen bases in a game (still the team record), read of Cooney's feat before suiting up for the Tigers' home game with Cleveland. That afternoon, at the top of the ninth, with Cleveland runners on first and second and nobody out, Neun speared a line drive hit by Homer Summa. He quickly tagged Charlie Jamieson, who'd been caught off first, and then raced to touch second base, retiring Glenn Myatt. The triple play preserved a 1-0 victory and put Neun in the books. According to Eddie Wells, Neun ran off the field shouting "Triple play unassisted! Triple play unassisted!" One recollection featured Neun yelling "I'm running into the Hall of Fame!" Despite Neun's prediction, neither he nor the ball ever made it into the shrine at Cooperstown. But it was a nice try.

Michigan and Trumbull wasn't the only corner jumping with base-ball action during the 1920s. At Mack and Fairview Avenues on the city's east side, the Detroit Stars of the Negro National League per-formed their magic in front of crowds just as enthusiastic and knowledgeable as those found across town.

"We used to fill that Mack Park on Sundays," recalled Ted "Double Duty" Radcliffe, who played three seasons with the Stars. "They'd be lined up on the streets when we opened the gates. We could only get seven or eight thousand in the place, but there were some days that we'd outdraw the Tigers."

The Detroit Stars were bankrolled by Andrew "Rube" Foster, a former pitching phenomenon turned baseball promoter. In 1919, a year before he launched his eight-team circuit, he stocked the Stars with several players from his Chicago American Giants, arguably the greatest black team of all-time. Among those transferred were outfielder Pete Hill, pitcher Bill Gatewood, and catcher Bruce Petway. Petway, who succeeded Hill as player-manager in 1922, cemented his reputation as the game's first great black backstop when he threw out Ty Cobb attempting to steal in an exhibition game in Cuba in 1910.

Detroit's roster included many other star players. First baseman Edgar Wesley led the league in home runs three times and in batting with a .424 average in 1925. The battery of Andy "Lefty" Cooper and Leon "Pepper" Daniels stayed intact for almost a decade. The center field spot was ably filled by Norman "Turkey" Stearnes, a taciturn Nashville native who established nearly all of the team's records during his nine seasons. Stearnes, a legitimate Hall-of-Fame candidate, topped the Negro National League in homers six times in a Detroit uniform. After moving on to Chicago, he added a bat-ting championship and a seventh home run title in the 1930s. "If you didn't pitch it in the right place to him, he would just hit the ball out of that park just about every time he came up," the peri-patetic pitcher, Leroy "Satchell" Paige, said of Stearnes. "He was one of the greatest hitters we ever had. He was as good as Josh Gibson. He was as good as anybody ever played baseball."

Although franchises came and went, the Stars proved to be one of the Negro National League's most stable teams, existing thirteen consecutive seasons (1919–31) before finally collapsing during the Depression. They were supported by a black population that grew

The Detroit Stars inside Mack Park, 1921.

from 6,000 in 1910 to 120,000 twenty years later. Nearly all were squeezed into the sixty square blocks known as "Black Bottom" on the city's near east side.

The Stars' first president was John "Tenny" Blount, a local numbers racketeer who managed affairs for Foster. In 1925, shortly before Foster was institutionalized with severe mental problems (he died five years later), the team was sold to John Roesink, a well-known downtown clothier whose signs were familiar sights in and around Navin Field and Mack Park. Roesink, who helped introduce pro football to Detroit a few years earlier, was only the second white owner in Foster's otherwise all-black league.

The Stars played their first eleven seasons at Mack Park, which Roesink—a big sponsor of amateur and semipro athletics—opened in 1910. The wooden facility was a modest park typical of the era. A covered grandstand ran from first base to third base and seated about six thousand, not counting those daring souls who perched on the roof. Clubhouses were under the right-field stands. The outfield fences, painted with advertisements for Roesink's three stores, were inviting, especially to left-handed batters. It was only 325 feet down the right-field line, accounting for the Stars' dynamic duo of Wesley and Stearnes leading the loop in home runs six times between them during the 1920s.

White newspapers rarely reported on the games at Mack Park, although sportswriters often ventured down to see what all the excitement was about. In 1922 the *Free Press*'s Eddie Batchelor reported that the crowd was "by no means confined to the Afro-American" fan.

> White fans make up an appreciable proportion of attendance, some drawn by their interest in the game and some by their desire to hear the comedy that sparkles through the whole performance. Many Tiger fans transfer their allegiance to the Negro league when the Navin Field aggregation is out of town.
>
> It is a boisterous, merry, but thoroughly well-behaved crowd. Nobody seems to take the game so seriously as the average patron of the major league contests. The players to be sure fight tooth and nail, putting more bite into their efforts than many of the big leaguers do when there is nothing much at stake.

Just how good were Negro leaguers compared to their white counterparts? The results of many exhibition games between the two reveal that the black teams more than held their own. In October 1923 the St. Louis Browns ended the American League campaign in Detroit with a series against the Tigers. Before heading home, the Browns played the Stars in a three-game series at Mack Park. Performing in front of capacity crowds, the Stars rallied from five-run deficits to win the first two games before finally losing the last game. In 1930 the Stars reportedly approached Tiger owner Frank Navin about scheduling an exhibition series between the city's two professional teams. Navin, who had rented his park to black teams as early as 1916, refused. He believed he had nothing to gain and everything to lose in accepting such a challenge.

A disastrous fire broke out at Mack Park on July 7, 1929, prior to a big Sunday doubleheader with the Kansas City Monarchs. Workers were drying out the wet field with gasoline when the right-field stands suddenly exploded into flames. Thanks to the alert efforts of ballplayers, who freed the dam of terrified spectators by yanking down the protective chicken-wire screen enclosing the

Mack Park after its disastrous fire in 1929.

grandstand, nobody was killed. But 220 people were injured, dozens with broken bones and severe burns. While the exact cause of the blaze was never determined, Detroit's blacks blamed Roesink for carelessly storing gas cans under the grandstand. The fire caused twelve thousand dollars' worth of damage to the park and the Stars transferred their home games to Dequindre Park, a sandlot field at Dequindre and Modern.

The following summer Roesink moved the team into a football-style stadium he had built in Hamtramck, the predominantly Polish working-class community that rested entirely within Detroit's borders. The concrete structure, alternately called Hamtramck Stadium and Roesink Stadium, was erected on the site of a lumber yard in an area bounded by Gallagher, Roosevelt, Jacob, and Conant. It exuded little of the charm or intimacy of Mack Park. A ten-foot-high, corrugated-steel fence ringed the stadium. The oblong configuration produced a short left field (315 feet from home plate) but an almost unreachable right field (407 feet) and center field (515 feet).

The dimensions helped the pitching staff shave almost two full runs off its 1929 earned run average, but it also short-circuited the team's traditional left-handed power. Home runs dropped from 73 to 32, with Stearnes hitting but three round-trippers in 1930. Nonetheless, during their first year at Hamtramck Stadium the Stars enjoyed their best season ever. They just missed winning the Negro National League pennant, dropping the last two games of a seven-game playoff with the St. Louis Stars at home.

Hamtramck Stadium was built just blocks from Dodge Main, suggesting that Roesink hoped to attract both white fans and industrial teams from the area to his park. The Depression dampened Roesink's plans. Distracted by hard times and a long boycott by black fans still angry about the Mack Park fire, the haberdasher sold the club after the 1930 season to Everitt Watson, the city's foremost black racketeer.

Before that, however, Roesink made local baseball history. On June 28, 1930, the Kansas City Monarchs brought their portable lighting system to Hamtramck Stadium. That evening the Monarchs beat the Stars, 17–4, in the first night baseball game ever played in the Detroit area. Ten thousand people were on hand for the event. Six telescoping poles with floodlights towered fifty feet above the field. Other lights were placed on the roof. The 100-kilowatt generator was powered by a noisy, gas-guzzling 250-horsepower motor placed in center field. During the game players tip-toed around cables snaking through the grass. "It was very exciting," said Bobbie Robinson, who played third base for the Stars that night. "It was the first time I'd played under the lights. But it was kind of rough. The generators would go down and the lights would start to dim, and then they'd start back up and the lights would get bright again."

The lights went out for good midway through the following summer. The Negro National League, crippled by hard times and its founder's death, collapsed after a dozen seasons. Subsequent attempts to place a black big-league team in Detroit—the Wolves in 1932 and revived versions of the Stars in 1933 and 1937—all failed. Two rival circuits, the Negro National and Negro American leagues, managed to prosper until the majors' desegregation following the Second World War stripped the rosters of their best players.

Mack Park continued as the home of sandlot baseball and softball games until it was torn down in the 1960s. Today the Fairview Greens apartment complex occupies the site. Hamtramck Stadium still stands and is used primarily for high-school football games. While neither venue can boast the long tradition of Tiger Stadium, both showcased—if only for a short while—some of the finest baseball talent Detroiters have ever seen.

For all the criticism Ty Cobb received as manager, it's a fact that the Tigers went in the tank soon after he left. For six seasons beginning in 1928, Detroit finished in the second division. On September 25, 1928, in a contest with Boston, the soon-to-be-fired George Moriarty looked around Navin Field and commented on the smallest crowd ever to attend an American League game at Michigan and Trumbull: 404 people. For the year, attendance at the corner was off by nearly 300,000.

That winter, in an attempt to add a little spice to the game, National League president John Heydler proposed adding a tenth man to the lineup, a designated batter who would hit for the pitcher. Navin and other owners and writers across the American League guffawed at this demand for county fair baseball. "The only virtue in the Heydler plan is that it would permit some ballplayers who can hit, but who are in danger of getting killed when they take their positions in the field, a chance to earn a living," opined a Detroit writer. "There have been a lot of these birds in the game from time to time, but there is no particular reason why they should be encouraged. In response to the observation that even a poor fielder must live, we retaliate with the simple query, why?"

Ironically, the American League introduced the designated hitter to baseball in 1973. This was far too late for the Tiger who could have served as the prototype, a six-foot, three-inch, 215-pound hit-

Dale "Moose" Alexander set a club record with twenty-five home runs in 1929. One day at Navin Field he also set a standard for the longest single, lining a ball off the center-field flagpole so hard that it was returned to the infield before the heavy-legged first baseman could chug to second base.

ting machine named Dale "Moose" Alexander. Under new manager Bucky Harris, the big right-handed first baseman, born on a tobacco farm near Greenville, Tennessee, pounded pitchers for twenty-five home runs, 137 runs batted in, and a .343 average in 1929. His 215 hits tied teammate and fellow rookie Roy Johnson for the league high; his home run total set a club record. The Tigers finished sixth in Harris's initial season, but they were fun to watch, leading the loop in runs (926) and batting (.299).

Alexander followed up with another superb season in 1930 (.326, 20, 135). By then some circles compared the lumbering, close-mouthed farm boy to Babe Ruth. The difference was that Ruth knew his way around a glove. Alexander spoke hopefully of repairing his fractured footwork around the bag. "I know I look bad," said Moose, who led all first basemen in errors his first two seasons. "I had the bad habit of getting my legs crossed at first. That's a serious difficulty, but I've had some good coaching and I'm getting so that I can reach for a ball without falling down."

Somewhere along the line Alexander lost the ability to put the ball in the seats. After a .325 season in 1931, where he hit only three home runs (but forty-seven doubles), Alexander was sent to the Red Sox early in the 1932 campaign. He won the batting title that year, hitting .367 splitting time between Detroit and Boston. The following year he burned his leg while receiving heat therapy for a sprained knee, and then dropped down into the minors for the rest of his career. He stayed in baseball as a minor-league manager and scout, raising a family not far from the Appalachian farm he'd been born on. "I just didn't have the ability," he reflected a few years before he died in 1979. "I couldn't run or field." But goodness, some Navin Field old-timers will tell you, that boy sure could hit.

Moose Alexander's fall in fortune paralleled that of the city whose name was scripted across his uniform blouse. The Great Depression settled in Detroit in the fall of 1929 and took its time leaving. Initially, many thought the economic downturn was no worse than any of the others that periodically afflicted the one-industry town. In 1930 the sixth-place Tigers experienced a 220,000 drop in attendance, still better than the league average, but a portent of what pitcher Elon "Chief" Hogsett called "the dirty thirties." For every four cars built in 1929, the year Hogsett joined the club, only one rolled off the line in 1932 during the depth of the

Ty Tyson at the mike in 1927. That summer the Tigers began broadcasting home games over radio station WWJ.

Depression. That year the near-collapse of Detroit's banks forced the city to pay its employees with scrip. Unemployed workers were fired on and killed when they marched on the Ford Rouge plant. Throughout the city idled laborers and their families battled stomach cramps, spoke earnestly of social change, and joked about the luxury of having center-cut bologna for dinner.

"The depression affected our family just like everyone else," remembered Barney McCosky, whose family had moved from Coal Run, Pennsylvania, to Detroit in 1922, when he was four. The McCoskys grew up in the southwest part of the city, near Schaefer and Fort Street. Barney emulated the batting stance of his boyhood hero, second baseman Charlie Gehringer, while starring in prep baseball during the 1930s. He emerged at the end of the decade as the Tigers' center fielder.

"Nobody had any money," he continued. "We took mustard sandwiches and ketchup sandwiches to school. We made sandwiches out of bananas. When supper time came we always had soup. Whoever

An exterior view of Navin Field and the surrounding neighborhood in 1928.

worked—that was my brother Tony and my dad—got the meat off the soup bone. Five brothers and four sisters. But we survived."

So did baseball, although barely. A bad team coupled with a crumbling economy played havoc with Navin's finances. Attendance at Michigan and Trumbull during this same period plummeted from 11,290 to 4,115 a game. One year Navin borrowed from the bank to send his team to spring training. He banned radio broadcasts from his park on weekends and holidays, afraid that "giving the game away" over the air would cut into the gate.

As overall attendance dropped from a record 10.1 million in 1929 to just 6.3 million in 1933, clubs scrambled for ways to shave costs and put people in the seats. The average player's salary

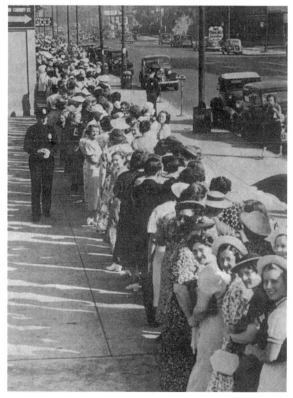

Female fans line up for a Ladies Day game in 1932. The Tigers pushed discounted seats especially hard during the thirties as an economic depression and a mediocre team caused attendance to plummet. Once inside the park, however, women were among the team's most boisterous and loyal supporters.

dropped 20 percent, to six thousand dollars. Playing managers became the rule, since it eliminated one spot on the roster. Doubleheaders, previously played primarily as a convenient way of making up rain outs, now became a regular feature of the schedule. Gimmicks such as footraces and milking contests were used to draw folks to the park. George Uhle, who pitched for Detroit between 1929 and 1933, recalled how Navin once staged a series of competitions the last home game of the season: "Fungo-hitting, circling the bases, fastest hundred-yard dash, four or five contests like that."

Bucky Harris came up to me and said, "Let's win at least one of these contests. Take a dozen balls home and bake them overnight. We'll win the fungo-hitting contest." Baking the baseballs made them lighter, so they'd go further when they were hit. As it turned out, that was the only contest we didn't win. No kidding. Joe Vosmik won it for Cleveland.

Anyway, the following year, the Missus was out at Navin Field with our daughter, who was about six or seven years old at the time. We were playing Boston. I went up to pinch-hit. I hit a line drive to right field, and at the last moment it curved away from the outfielder. It broke so fast, it went off his glove and they gave me a three-base hit.

My daughter turned to Helen and said, "Will they give Daddy a hit on that?"

"Sure," said Helen. "It was too hot to handle."

"Oh," said my daughter. "Did they bake that ball, too?"

There was a silver lining to the clouds that hung dark and low over the Motor City—the Depression was directly responsible for bringing Detroit its first pennant in a generation. Connie Mack, who owed $250,000 to Philadelphia banks, sold $275,000 worth of players to meet his obligations. One of them was Mickey Cochrane, who was sent to the Tigers on December 12, 1933 in exchange for $100,000 and a substitute catcher named Johnny Pasek. "Cochrane has been baseball poison for Detroit ever since he's been in the league," said Navin, pointing to the catcher's .500 batting average in eleven games at Navin Field in 1933. "I would rather have him with us than against us."

Walter Briggs, who often rewarded favorite players with a new suit of clothes, quietly provided Navin with the funds. "If

Cochrane's a success here," Briggs said, "he may be a bargain at that price."

The jug-eared, dark-faced catcher, nicknamed Black Mike as much for his fiery disposition as for his deeply tanned face, already had Hall-of-Fame credentials when he came to Detroit. He served as the inspirational leader of three straight pennant winners and two world championship teams in Philadelphia. He was the smartest signal-caller in the game, its best defensive catcher, and a consistent .300 hitter who frequently batted second or third in the lineup, an unheard-of spot for a catcher. And he brooked no nonsense, as Chief Hogsett once recalled.

"Ol' Mick never let you fall to sleep out there," said the mild-mannered, submarining southpaw, who had a few drops of Cherokee blood in his veins. "I remember sometimes I'd come into a game and feel like trying out a new pitch. Mickey would call for a fast ball and I'd cross him up. God! He'd come stormin' out halfway to the mound and fire that ball back to me.

"'Wake up, you big Indian son of a bitch!' he'd yell. I knew what he meant: Quit experimenting out there."

Two days after acquiring Cochrane, Navin traded John Stone to Washington for veteran Leon "Goose" Goslin, a temperamental outfielder who had back boned the only three pennants the Senators ever won. The future Hall of Famer already had one batting title and seven World Series home runs under his belt. His four full seasons in a Detroit uniform added to his reputation as one of the game's great clutch performers.

Cochrane and Goslin, two old pros who would not tolerate losing, turned the Tigers around. "They look like the old Tiger team as far as spirit goes," George Moriarty, who had returned to umpiring, said. "They've got the proper attitude. I believe that Detroit is finally getting what they wanted for many years—a fighting ball club."

It took awhile, though. "Cochrane was very discouraged and threatened to quit early," recalled Edgar Hayes of the *Detroit Times*. "He'd just never run into a team like this that was absolutely devoid of any winning tradition. They didn't know how to win. That was the big thing he had to do, to instill in them the confidence that you can win."

Win they did. Cochrane's troops baffled the experts, most of whom pegged the team as no better than fourth-place material. Under Cochrane's instruction the young pitching staff blossomed. Curveballer Tommy Bridges, who'd never won more than fourteen

The core of the team that delivered back-to-back pennants and a world's championship, arranged by their position in the batting order. From left are center fielder Jo-Jo White, catcher Mickey Cochrane, second baseman Charlie Gehringer, first baseman Hank Greenberg, left fielder Goose Goslin, shortstop Billy Rogell, right fielder Gee Walker, third baseman Marv Owen, and pitcher Schoolboy Rowe.

games, notched twenty-two—his first of three straight twenty-win seasons. Eldon Auker employed a wicked submarine-style delivery to compile a 15–7 record. The sensation of the staff—and the summer—was Lynwood "Schoolboy" Rowe, not long removed from the dusty diamonds of El Dorado, Arkansas. The towering righthander won twenty-four games, including sixteen in a row, tying a league record. When he wasn't taking his regular turn in the rotation and occasionally batting as high as seventh in the lineup (he hit .303), he was pitching relief or pinch-hitting.

"I eat a lot of vittles, climb that mound, wrap my fingers around the old baseball and say to it, 'Edna, honey, let's go,'" is how Rowe explained his success to a radio audience during his winning streak. In addition to invoking the name of his fiancee, Edna May Skinner,

Schoolie carried as many good luck charms on his person as his six-foot, four-inch frame could stand: a Canadian penny, a copper coin from the Netherlands, two Chinese trinkets, a rabbit's foot, a jade elephant figurine, and four feathers plucked from a three-legged rooster.

Then there were the G-Men: Goslin, Charlie Gehringer, and Hank Greenberg. All were huge crowd favorites. The schoolchildren yelled, "Yeah, Goose!" whenever Goslin—nicknamed for the size of his nose—trotted out to left field. As an old man talking into Larry Ritter's tape recorder, Goslin fondly recalled Detroit as the best baseball town he'd ever played in. "I loved it," he admitted. "We weren't allowed to throw balls into the stands, you know, but I'd always take four balls out with me, in my back pockets, when I went out for fielding practice. And just before I went back in, after I'd taken my throws, I'd sail them up to the kids."

Gehringer and Greenberg shared the right side of the infield. At thirty-one, Gehringer was an established star playing his twelfth big-league season. He was called "The Mechanical Man" for his seemingly effortless grace at second base. The gangly Greenberg, on the other hand, was eight years younger than his diamond mate and often appeared oafish handling plays at first base.

"In the field I could never figure out when to go for ground balls between first and second and when to leave them for Charlie," said Greenberg, who joined the Tigers in 1933. "I wanted to catch everything to prove to them I could do it, so I was going for balls I had no right to even try for. I remember I'd dive for one and it would bounce off my glove. Charlie would be standing there, right behind me, and he'd say, 'I could've gotten that one.' The man was amazing."

Both men were models of consistency at the plate. Gehringer, swinging from the left side, banged out line drives to all parts of the field and rarely whiffed. In 1934 Gehringer hit .356 (second only to Lou Gehrig) and led the American League in hits and runs. With his long, sweeping swing, the right-handed Greenberg broke existing club marks with twenty-six home runs and sixty-three doubles, tops in the majors. Combined, he and Gehringer drove in 266 runs, the best one-two RBI punch in baseball.

Detroiters, who had stayed away from the park for years, now packed Navin Field. Attendance tripled to more than 919,000, the

Auto pioneer Henry Ford and son Edsel meet the sparkplug of the Tigers' success, Mickey Cochrane, late in the 1934 season.

best in the majors, as the Tigers won 101 games, their most ever to that point. Writers recognized Cochrane's leadership and they voted him Most Valuable Player (MVP) despite Gehrig's Triple Crown year for the second-place Yankees.

Although the 1968 and 1984 teams were special in their own way, no Detroit team was as beloved by the city quite like the New Deal Tigers of the mid-1930s. Part of it had to with the long wait between

Mounted police were needed to control the overflow crowds that attended the hotly contested Tigers-Yankees games during the 1934 pennant race. In an action shot from an August contest at Navin Field, Lou Gehrig slides into third base in a cloud of dust while Marv Owen awaits the throw.

pennants; it had been twenty-five years since the 1909 squad had finished on top of the standings. The times, too, helped explain the idolatry. "Detroit is out of the depression," a prominent businessman proclaimed at a special banquet honoring Frank Navin. "Detroit is facing the future full of confidence. Detroit has forgotten such mundane things as banks, hard times, and unhappiness."

"That was one hell of a year," agreed Billy Rogell, as profane a sparkplug as Cochrane. "So much excitement. Goddamn, the World Series was over before I even realized I'd played in a World Series."

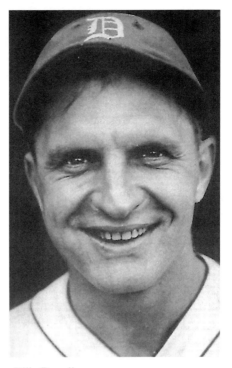

Billy Rogell.

The switch-hitting shortstop knocked in one hundred runs on just three home runs in 1934. Perhaps none was bigger than the one he drove in to win a classic midsummer showdown with the Yankees.

"This was late in July, and Navin Field was packed," he said. "They had the goddamn outfield roped off, mounted cops, everything. Lefty Gomez was pitching, and I think he'd only lost once or twice all season. At one point they were beating us 9–1 and we came back to win, 12–11. We scored four runs in the bottom of the ninth. Goslin doubled in a couple runs to tie it. I drove in the winning run. I hit a single between short and third, a line drive, and Goslin slid home safely.

"I only got to first base. I was jumping up and down, yelling 'Run, Goose! Run, Goose!' We beat 'em and that put us in first place. Jesus, after the game the fans stayed on the field and were yelling, cheering like you wouldn't believe."

After the game, however, Cochrane—ever the teacher—wanted to know why Rogell hadn't gone to second on the throw home.

There had only been one out and suppose Goslin had been nailed at the plate?

"I said, 'Excuse me,'" said Rogell. "He was right. That's where I should've been going on the throw home. But I was so excited, I was egging Goose on. I was saying, 'Put the wings on, boy, go like hell!'"

This kind of unbridled enthusiasm was infectious. Leading the cheers at Navin Field was a leather-lunged bug named Patsy O'Toole, dubbed "The Human Earache" for his unique ability to broadcast insults and rallying cries at a decibel level that made dogs howl three blocks from the park. Born Samuel Ozadowsky, O'Toole was a newsboy, prizefighter, whiskey salesman, and ticket seller before he joined Mayor Frank Murphy's inner circle as an errand boy. O'Toole typically clambered onto the roof of the Tigers' dugout to deliver his signature rallying cry: "Boy, oh boy, oh boy, oh boy! Keep cool wit' O'Toole!"

O'Toole declared all Tigers were "great guys" and their opponents were "bums." Once he went too far with Lefty Gomez. After the Tigers had knocked the nearly invincible Yankee pitcher out of that important game in July 1934, O'Toole's insults incited Gomez to make a beeline for him. It took several players to hold the angry man back.

A year earlier, O'Toole accompanied Frank Murphy to Washington, where they found themselves seated at a World Series game near President Franklin D. Roosevelt and Washington owner Clark Griffith. O'Toole's first blasts nearly blew FDR out of his seat. A Secret Service agent hurried to O'Toole's side. "I'm sure you'd like to do the President a favor," the agent said. "He'd like you to move to the other side of the field, and Mr. Griffith has already made the arrangements." Despite these periodic attempts to stifle him, O'Toole didn't stop until a throat operation, made necessary by twenty-five years of nonstop bellowing, permanently silenced one of the Tigers' most vocal fans.

O'Toole's annoying antics contributed to Detroit fans' unruly reputation. Seven years earlier, an out-of-town paper complained of Navin Field's company-picnic atmosphere: "Overflow crowds seem to be handled with less skill and foresight in Detroit than in any other big league center. Patrons strolled around and cops squatted contentedly on the grass." Harry Salsinger, the refined sports editor of the *Detroit News*, regularly criticized local fans for their lack of decorum.

This unsavory reputation was cemented during the 1934 World Series against St. Louis. The brash, free-spirited Gas House Gang Cardinals (who actually weren't called that until the following season) swaggered into town for the series opener. The Redbirds' roster was filled with stars: second baseman-manager Frankie Frisch, left fielder Joe "Ducky" Medwick, first baseman Ripper Collins, shortstop Leo Durocher, and third baseman Pepper Martin.

But the biggest star—and he was the first to admit it—was Jay Hanna "Dizzy" Dean, the swashbuckling, eccentric Arkansas farm boy who won thirty games with a fast ball as lively as his antics. Dean's younger brother, Paul, contributed nineteen wins, but he was happy to let Dizzy do the talking for the family. The afternoon before the opener, Dizzy paraded down Michigan Avenue from the Book-Cadillac Hotel to Navin Field, hundreds of fascinated fans in tow. Later he strolled unannounced into the Tigers' clubhouse, shook hands all around and introduced himself as "the Great Dean." He complimented the bemused Detroit stars, calling them such great hitters he doubted that he could strike out more than fifteen or twenty of them. He offered Greenberg the chance to feel the arm of "a real thirty-game winner" for free.

Detroit fans proved just as cocky. All around the town bartenders served special drinks. The Hanky Panky honored Greenberg with a blend of gin, vermouth, and orange flower; the Dizz Fizz featured two raw eggs in beer. At the Oriole Terrace, a singer crooned:

And so it's fall, come on play ball,
We'll beat those Deans,
Diz-zy and Paul,
We'll hit their pitches,
Those sons of bitches,
They're only farm boys.

Alvin "General" Crowder, a late-season pickup from Washington, got the call in the first game, played on October 3 before 42,505 late-arriving fans. The grizzled veteran's right arm was notable for the giant tattoo of a naked lady that stretched from his shoulder to his elbow, a souvenir of his Navy days during the First World War. Crowder pitched well enough to win, but on this afternoon Detroit's infield, which had set a still-standing big-league record by knocking in 462 runs between them, fell apart defensively, committing five errors in an 8-3 loss. Dizzy Dean scattered eight hits and struck out six. The all-purpose antagonist doubled in a run, scored two others, and along with his vocal teammates, kept up a constant barrage of irritating chatter.

The next afternoon the Cardinals' Bill Hallahan took a 2-1 lead into the bottom of the ninth, but a lead off single by Pete Fox sent the crowd of 43,451 to its feet. Schoolboy Rowe, who after a shaky start settled down to retire twenty-two batters in a row, bunted Fox to second. Gee Walker, pinch-hitting for Jo-Jo White, plated Fox for the tying run with a single to left. Three innings later, reliever Bill Walker walked Gehringer and Greenberg with one out. The remaining G-Man, Goose Goslin, slapped a single to right, scoring Gehringer for a heart-stopping 3-2 win.

The next three games were in St. Louis. Paul Dean turned back the Tigers, 4-1, in game three. But the Tigers rebounded to win games four and five by scores of 10-4 and 3-1, respectively. Having beaten Dizzy Dean in the pivotal fifth game, and returning to Detroit to close out the series, Detroit appeared to have a lock on its first world championship.

The 44,551 fans filing into Navin Field on October 8 to watch Rowe square off against Paul Dean in game six thought so. But a terrible call by American League umpire Brick Owens in the bottom of the sixth inning may have cost the Tigers the game and the series. Trailing 3-1 as they entered the frame, the Tigers rallied for a run and had Dean on the ropes. With runners on first and second and nobody out, Goslin attempted to sacrifice. Catcher Bill DeLancey threw the ball to third base hoping to get the lead runner. Cochrane easily beat the throw, as photographs later clearly showed, but Owens called him out. Detroit managed to tie the game, but St. Louis pushed across a run in the seventh to win, 4-3. Paul Dean, given fresh life, pitched out of deep jams in the eighth and ninth innings to record his second series triumph. Detroiters complained long and hard about the decision. "Cochrane's foot hit the bag and his knee was folded," maintained Tommy Bridges. "But Owens still called him out."

That evening ex-umpire Billy Evans sought to cheer up the Tigers' disconsolate owner. A seventh game, reminded Evans, meant at least an extra fifty thousand dollars in revenue.

Schoolboy Rowe shakes hands with Dizzy Dean as brother Paul "Daffy" Dean looks on before the start of the 1934 World Series at Navin Field.

"To hell with $50,000," snapped Navin. "I'd give the $50,000 and five times that much to have won today. I've been waiting thirty-five years to see Detroit win a world's championship, and here we have one within our grasp, and that umpire blows it for us."

Navin hid his petulance behind closed doors. The next day Detroit fans showed the world their ire. They watched uneasily as the showboating Cardinals, led by the irrepressible Dizzy Dean, rang up seven runs while batting around in the third inning off

Joe Medwick stands his ground as seventeen thousand disgruntled Detroit fans pelt him with fruit, vegetables, and other debris.

starter Eldon Auker. Dean, acting as if he was at a county fair instead of the seventh game of the World Series, contributed a double and a single in the inning, and then added a few handsprings and catcalls while on base. He mowed down the Tigers at bat, limiting them to six hits and no runs for the afternoon.

The crowd of 40,902, poised for a celebration, instead sulked. The mood grew uglier as the score climbed. In the sixth inning, Ducky Medwick bounced a ball off the right center-field bleachers, scoring Pepper Martin to make it 8–0. It was an easy triple, but third baseman Marv Owen, who had a reputation for juking runners, acted as if there would be a play. Medwick slid hard, and Owen stepped on his right foot.

"That's when he kicked me three times, called me a son of a bitch," Owen recalled years later. After Medwick got up and dusted himself off, he stuck his hand out. Owen, frustrated by the score, said, "Ah, bullshit with that." A few seconds later Medwick scored the Cardinals' ninth run on a single by Ripper Collins. When Medwick took his position in left field in the bottom of the sixth, the seventeen thousand displeased fans jammed into the temporary bleachers in left pelted him with fruit, vegetables, bottles, and anything else they could get their hands on. After a twenty-minute delay, Judge Landis ordered Medwick removed from the game to preserve the peace.

Paul Gallico, reporting for the *New York Daily News*, provided the best description of the uprising of October 9, 1934, one of the ugliest moments in the long history of baseball at the corner.

> I watched the crowd and Medwick and the pelting missiles through my field glasses, and it was a horrifying sight. Every face in the crowd, women and men, was distorted with rage. Mouths were torn wide, open eyes glistened and shone in the sun. All fists were clenched. Medwick stood grinning with his hands on his hips, just out of range of the bottles. A green apple rolled to his feet, and he fielded that, too. Umpires and attendants rushed out to left field and began picking up the mess. Medwick came back to the diamond. One cameraman ran out and leveled his box at the patch of inflamed and angry people all afire with mob hatred. In a moment cameramen were all over the field. Medwick and Pepper Martin began to play a little game of pop-ball between themselves, Martin making the ball bounce off his biceps into Medwick's hand and Medwick whipping it up behind his back to Martin. The crowd began to chant in a swelling, choleric chorus, "Take him out, take him out!"

For the second time Medwick started for his position, and the storm broke with renewed fury, with more bottles and less fruit. The outfield was covered with attendants with bags picking up the glassware as fast as it landed. One of them narrowly escaped being hit on the head. Someone in the dugout had sense enough to send out a sweater to Dizzy Dean, whose arm was getting cold.

Again Medwick returned to the diamond while the field was cleared, and then for the third time he tried to take his position. And he did a pretty brave thing. He trotted out and turned his back on the stands. Mobs are rank cowards, and the sight of courage inflames them beyond all reason. By far the most dangerous peal of rage broke from them this third time. Heavy milk bottles flew onto the field. The police stood quietly by against the fence along the bottom row and did nothing. "Take him out! Take him out!" The chant echoed and re-echoed like a football yell. Mickey Cochrane ran half way into left field, and with one gesture tried to pacify the mob. It had no more effect than throwing a pebble into the ocean. Cochrane returned to the diamond. The umpires walked around helplessly.

Judge Landis from his box beckoned to Medwick, Frisch, and Owen. They trotted into his box between home and first base. Umpire Klem joined them. There was a short discussion. Landis did the sane and reasonable thing. Flames were creeping near a powder mine. He extinguished that flame by asking Frisch to remove Medwick. Then only did this mad game continue.

During the next inning, Medwick, with a police escort, walked across the field and into the dugout. Once more the boos thundered. One more bottle was hurled at him, and then he vanished and the crowd was satisfied. Unheard-of in the annals of baseball, IT had worked its will, IT had taken an active and potentially terrible part in the game. When the thing was done, the poor Tigers had been soundly whipped by the humiliating score of 11 to 0.

Although the frustration of yet another postseason debacle wasn't apparent on his placid face, Frank Navin was beside himself. Four World Series, four losses, and each one of them had ended with his team getting blanked in its own park. "Are we destined never to win one of these things?" he lamented.

After three delays totaling about twenty minutes, commissioner Landis instructs St. Louis manager Frankie Frisch to yank Joe Medwick out of the game to restore order.

The Tigers proved they weren't a flash in the pan by winning a second straight pennant in 1935 with a 93–58 record, finishing three lengths ahead of the Yankees. Navin Field enjoyed another banner summer at the corner, with a record 1,034,929 people passing through the turnstiles.

That year Navin and local theater owner and producer J.J. Shubert veered from baseball to launch a summer-long operatic series, "Opera Under the Stars," at the ballpark. As they explained, the idea behind this civic project was to "provide the finest in musical entertainment at a price everyone can afford." This attempt to introduce culture to the masses came at a time when the venerable Detroit Opera House was two years away from being made over into a department store. The ambitious inaugural calendar included eleven operettas and musical comedies, beginning with *Rose Marie* on June 8. Week-long shows opened on Mondays with nightly performances, rain or shine, starting at 8:30 p.m. The stage and orchestra were situated on the infield and illuminated by portable lights. Ticket prices ranged from a quarter for a reserved seat in the back rows of the upper deck to $1.65 for lower-deck boxes. Despite the affordability, attendance figures proved discouraging. After Navin's death, "Opera Under the Stars" faded away.

Detroiters' true passion remained baseball. The heart and soul of the team continued to be snarling, cussing, black-faced Mickey Cochrane, who batted .319 in 1935, handled the pitching staff, and kept the rest of the team in line. "I'd watch him all game long," recalled Mary Bergen, whose family left their Saginaw farm to visit Navin Field once or twice each summer. "I couldn't keep my eyes off of him. He was just so dynamic."

The rest of the boys weren't too bad themselves. Bridges won twenty-one games while Rowe notched another nineteen victories and hit .312 for good measure. Once again the Tigers led the majors in runs (919) and batting (.290), paced by Greenberg, who topped the charts in home runs (36) and RBI (170) and was named Most Valuable Player. Gehringer pitched in with a .330 mark and 108 RBIs, just one less than Goslin.

Goslin, destined to be a World Series hero, inadvertently jolted the club out if its doldrums with his temper. With the team mired in sixth place in late May, he and Pete Fox got into an argument that cooled off into a silent, season-long duel. The quiet right fielder, rumored to be on the trading block at the time, took off on a thirty-four-game hitting tear that culminated in the best of his eight summers in Detroit. He hit .321, scored 116 runs, and stroked the ball at a .385 clip in the World Series against the Cubs.

Most of Detroit openly wished for a rematch with the Gas House Gang. But Chicago, led by twenty-game winners Bill Lee and Lon Warneke, second baseman Billy Herman, and first baseman Phil Cavaretta, overtook St. Louis down the stretch with a twenty-one-game winning streak.

The Cubs gave up home-field advantage to Detroit because they needed extra time to get Wrigley Field ready for the series. The change of venue didn't affect their play in the October 2 opener, when Warneke out pitched Rowe, 3–0, in front of a muted audience of 47,391. Detroiters' spirits were lifted the next day, however, when the Tigers scored four runs—two on a Greenberg home run—before the Cubs were able to retire a batter. Bridges went all the way in an 8–3 verdict before 46,742 fans.

The victory came with a price. In the seventh inning, Greenberg collided with catcher Gabby Hartnett in a play at the plate. X-rays revealed that the Tigers' bit gun had broken two bones; Greenberg was out for the rest of the series.

Navin ordered a move that was unpopular with his players. Marv Owen, a former minor-league first baseman, took over for Greenberg. Herman "Flea" Clifton, a good fielder but anemic hitter, was installed at third. Both had a terrible series at the plate, combining for one hit in thirty-six at-bats. But with Goslin moved up a notch in the order to Greenberg's customary cleanup spot, sandwiched between hot-hitting Charlie Gehringer and Pete Fox, the Tigers won two of three games at Wrigley Field to return home needing just one more victory to claim the title.

A noisy throng of 48,420 squeezed into Navin Field on October 7. Cochrane, Navin, and everyone else in Detroit had good cause to be wary that cool, sunny Monday. The team was in the same situation as the previous October, when the Cardinals bounced back to win games six and seven on the Tigers' turf. This time around, the Tigers broke the hex, setting off a citywide celebration that has had few equals.

The game was a heart-stopper. Detroit scratched out a run in the first off Larry French. Chicago tied the score in the third. Detroit regained the lead the following inning when Tommy Bridges' grounder scored Gee Walker, but then Bridges surrendered a two-run homer to Billy Herman in the fifth to make it 3–2, Chicago. The Tigers rallied in the bottom of the sixth. Billy Rogell doubled and rode home on Marv Owens' single, his only hit of the series, to knot the game at three apiece.

The game remained tied when Stan Hack opened the top of the ninth inning by tripling over Gee Walker's head in center. The crowd, sensing its dream was once again slipping away, suddenly

During the 1935 World Series between Detroit and Chicago, Navin Field's third deck accommodated hundreds of out-of-town sportswriters; photographers and newsreel cameramen were consigned to the roofs of the first- and third-base pavilions.

became so quiet that Cochrane's instructions to the infield were heard throughout the park. The Cubs stood on the top step of the dugout. All that was needed was the right kind of fly ball or grounder to bring Hack in.

Bridges bore down and snapped off a curve to strike out Billy Jurges for the first out. French, batting for himself, tapped the ball weakly back to the mound. Bridges checked the runner, and then tossed the ball to Owen at first base for the second out. The inning fizzled out completely when Augie Galan lifted an easy fly to Goslin. "When I think back to the 1935 World Series," Billy Herman recalled years later, "all I can see is Hack standing on third base, waiting for somebody to drive him in. Seems to me now he stood there for hours and hours."

In the bottom of the ninth Flea Clifton struck out, but then Cochrane singled off Herman's glove. Gehringer, up next, smoked a grounder at Cavaretta. The Cubs' first baseman knocked it down and retired Gehringer, as Cochrane took second on the play. This brought up Goslin, who predicted to the home-plate umpire, "If they pitch that ball over this plate, you can go take that monkey suit off."

Goslin slapped a French pitch toward right field. "It was one of those hits that begins dying the moment it leaves the bat," recalled Herman. "I ran out for it, Billy Jurges ran out for it, Frank Demaree came in from center for it, but nobody could quite catch up to it and it just dropped into the grass in center field, and Cochrane scored."

Cochrane jumped up and down on the plate several times, as if trying to keep a lid on the civic explosion that was about to occur. According to the *Reach Official American League Base Ball Guide*, within five minutes "everybody in Detroit knew that the Tigers had won and that Goose Goslin had batted in Mickey Cochrane with the winning run."

Then the inhabitants of this great city of more than a million began to boil. The street scenes that followed that night were never matched before in a World Series.

No city ever went as mad over baseball as Detroit. There was a rush to the central part of the city. Pedestrians blew tin horns and motorists honked those on the cars as they snailed through the downtown streets almost hopelessly clogged with the product that has earned Detroit worldwide fame.

The hotel where baseball headquarters had been established was a fair mark for the revelers. Police had to make lanes for arriving and departing guests. Facades of buildings were draped with ticker tape, the streets cushioned with confetti.

Departing guests never made their trains if they did not allow plenty of time, as taxis could make no headway in the milling streets thronged with merrymakers and autos. Traffic officers, helpless, gave up. They might as well have attempted to stop Pershing's armies in France.

Toward midnight the din increased instead of abating. The discharge of firecrackers and bombs, the staccato barks of back-firing cars and shrieks of sirens and blasts of horns kept on in continuous roar to early morning. Guests in downtown hotels could not sleep until three hours after midnight.

Even machine guns were rigged up in office windows to add to the noise. Natives of Detroit admitted that the noise and clamor were greater than on Armistice night.

When merrymakers through sheer exhaustion finally decided it was time for bed, the city looked as if a cyclone had hit it. All the next day, the whitewings were employed cleaning up the litter.

For the next several days Frank Navin could only smile and repeat over and over: "I've waited thirty years for this day."

Fueling the frenzy surrounding the New Deal Tigers was radio, with which owners like Navin maintained a love-hate relationship. During the years of the Depression and the Second World War, announcers Ty Tyson and Harry Heilmann enjoyed a popularity that in many cases exceeded that of the ballplayers whose heroics they described.

As the world inches closer to the day when baseball games will be staged inside a studio, not a stadium, it becomes increasingly more difficult to imagine a time when the instantaneous transmission of a sporting event was considered an absolute marvel, albeit a controversial one. Owners appreciated the revenue from selling rights to their games, of course. But there was always that gnawing fear that they were giving away a product fans traditionally paid money for. It wasn't until broadcast revenues slowly began to outstrip gate receipts in the 1960s that the last of these fears were put to rest.

In the 1890s, long before the advent of radio and television, telegraphy was the medium that transported fans outside the ballpark to that afternoon's game. Telegraph operators paid teams for

A hot dog vendor sells his wares to bleacherites during the 1935 World Series.

the right to transmit game reports to local pool rooms and saloons. As patrons quaffed beer, ate the free salted food, and invariably placed bets, employees charted the course of the game by reading the incoming ticker tape and recording the runners' movements around the bases on a chalkboard. It was crude and the atmosphere often was unsavory. However, in the case of important games thousands of citizens gathered in downtown streets to "watch" the action on large scoreboards, placed at an upper-story level so everyone could see.

"The newspaper scoreboards were the deluxe jobs," remembered newspaperman George Stark. "In addition to having a piece of chalk, the attendant was equipped with a megaphone. With the chalk he marked down the half-inning score, and through the megaphone he read off the detail of play, including runs, hits and errors, as carried over the Western Union lines." That was how many Detroiters "saw" the Tigers capture the 1908 pennant in Chicago on the last day of the season. Two years later, the Light Guard Armory advertised its coverage of "All Tiger Games Abroad," featuring "The New Realistic Paragon Automatic Scoreboard—The Only One in Detroit." This was "Enjoyed by either sex, old or young." By 1913, Western Union was paying the Tigers seventeen thousand dollars a season for the telegraphic rights to their games.

After the First World War a new phenomenon, radio, burst upon the scene. On August 5, 1921, Pittsburgh station KDKA broadcast the first baseball game, a contest between the Pirates and the Philadelphia Phillies. By the middle of the decade many major news and sporting events, including the World Series, were being aired live. Meanwhile, radio equipment sales boomed, jumping from $60 million in 1922 to nearly $1 billion seven years later. At the same time the country's first great national radio networks debuted: NBC in 1926, followed a year later by CBS.

The *Detroit News's* WWJ signed on as the country's first commercial radio station in 1920. The technology was now in place for the Tigers to begin broadcasts. But Frank Navin, who was spending heavily to expand Navin Field, figured they would cut into the turnstile counts—a view shared by many other owners. Starting in 1921, the Tigers set club attendance records four straight years, becoming only the second big-league team to draw one million paying customers in a single season. Navin finally was persuaded by the experience of University of Michigan football coach Fielding Yost, who in 1924 reluctantly allowed the Wolverines' games to be broadcast, and then watched in astonishment as attendance climbed.

WWJ began broadcasting Tiger games in 1927. Although the means to electronically transmit sound was now in place at Michigan and Trumbull, a public-address system was still a ways off. Line-up changes and other information of interest to those in attendance continued to be conveyed by an usher using a megaphone. Longtime Tigers follower Fred Smith remembered one game being interrupted that summer with the startling news that Charles Lindbergh had landed in Paris in *The Spirit of St. Louis*! Smith, then twelve years old, was unimpressed with history's first solo transatlantic flight. "I was annoyed that they disturbed the ball game even for a fraction of a minute with that announcement," he said.

Handling the play-by-play for that first broadcast was a droll, thirty-nine-year-old Pennsylvanian named Edwin "Ty" Tyson, who continued in that capacity through the 1942 season. Unlike many of his more loquacious colleagues, Tyson's descriptions of the games were spare. He often employed several seconds of dead air between pitches—a horror to broadcasters like Red Barber, who thought his "shortage of words at times bordered on being rude."

Tyson was extremely popular. When Judge Landis announced that Tyson would not be allowed to work the national broadcast of the 1934 World Series between Detroit and St. Louis (for which industrialist Henry Ford had paid a whopping one hundred thousand dollars to sponsor) because he was "too partial," the commissioner's office was deluged with six hundred thousand protest letters. The usually bull-headed Landis finally relented and allowed Tyson to do local coverage over WWJ. Tyson "didn't sound partial to me," said Barber. "He didn't use enough words between pitches and plays to give you an idea how he felt."

In 1934 Tyson acquired a rival in the booth. That year WXYZ president George W. Trendle, creator of such legendary Detroit-based programming as *The Lone Ranger* and *Call of the Yukon,* paid the Tigers twenty-five thousand dollars for the right to feed broadcasts via phone lines to five outstate stations collectively known as the Michigan Radio Network. Hired to announce the games for fifty dollars a week was former Tigers slugger Harry Heilmann, a familiar name to baseball fans and, unlike Tyson, a wonderful storyteller.

Heilmann originally lacked polish, but his folksy, laid-back style endeared him to listeners in Battle Creek and Saginaw. With cigarette in hand, he announced the action between anecdotes describing some incident that occurred in 1918 or 1925: "So here was Cobb on third and me standing there, wondering what that old bird was up to . . . A ball outside to Gehringer, Charlie almost went for it, two and one's the count . . . And ol' Ty finally called time and walked down to the batter's box to fill me in . . . There's ball three to Charlie, three and one . . . Well, I told Ty. . . ."

Like all broadcasters, Heilmann and Tyson used pet phrases. Tyson invariably described a high fly as being "hit up the smokestack." Heilmann, aware that one of his sponsors was an insect spray

Under the stewardship of Frank Navin and Walter Briggs, every ballpark employee was expected to be properly attired: the ground crew wore denim overalls and the cigarette girls were garbed in satin jackets and trousers.

called Bugaboo, described the same play: "There's a high fly ball to left. Goslin drifts under it and—Bugaboo!—another fly is dead!"

As late as 1951, all of the Tigers' away games aired on radio were reconstructed broadcasts. A Western Union operator in Chicago's Comiskey Park, for example, would tap out a skeletal description of the game in progress and transmit it to a studio in Detroit: "Greenberg up . . . S1C (*strike one called*) . . . B1W (*ball one wide*) . . . Out . . . High fly to deep left . . . York up . . . B1L (*ball one low*) . . . DP (*double play*) . . . Appling to Hayes to Bonura."

The operator in Detroit operator would translate the Morse code, type out the dispatches, and hand them to the play-by-play announcer, who then used every ounce of creativity he had to flesh out the dots and dashes: "Greenberg takes a look at Vern Kennedy's first pitch . . . It's a strike . . . Hank says something to Moriarty about that . . . Walker takes a short lead off of first . . . Here's Kennedy's next pitch . . . It's wide for a ball . . . One and one's the count on Hank . . . ."

With the sound of the telegraph key often clearly audible in the background, re-creations weren't meant to fool listeners. Many announcers used sound effects, but Tyson and Heilmann disdained such theatrics. Engineer Howard Stitzel, who entered the booth in 1948, remembers how a small crowd of fans often gathered in front of the TeleNews Theater on Woodward Avenue to watch him turn the dials for Heilmann as Ol' Slug dramatized the incoming ticker tape.

Although Frank Navin originally allowed most home games to be broadcast, the Depression and its effect on attendance caused him to reconsider his policy for several summers. He disallowed Sunday broadcasts from 1930 through 1932 and expanded the blackout to include all weekend games for the 1933 season. The sea of empty seats persuaded other owners to do likewise, which affected the number of away games that Detroit fans could listen to. Between 1932 and 1938 no re-creations of Tiger games in New York were broadcast, because the three big league team owners in that city banned all radio from their parks. It wasn't until after the Second World War that the Tigers finally began airing their complete schedule, though road games continued as re-creations. By 1955 all major league games, home and away, were broadcast live from the site and not from the studio.

After the 1935 World Series, newspapers reported that Navin had cleared $150,000 during the championship season, an amount he announced would be plowed back into expanding his ballpark. But on November 13, less than six weeks after realizing his life's ambition, the sixty-four-year-old owner suffered a heart attack while horseback riding at the Detroit Riding and Hunt Club on Belle Isle. He was rushed to Detroit Osteopathic Hospital in Highland Park, where he died shortly thereafter.

According to Briggs family lore, Navin's silent partner, upon hearing of the tragedy, immediately dispatched club secretary Harry Sisson to the hospital with a check equal to the book value of the club plus one hundred thousand dollars. "All my life I've wanted to own the Tigers," Walter Briggs explained. "If Navin isn't dead, they won't take the check." Asked later about this incident, Sisson wryly replied, "Maybe Mr. Briggs wanted to help them with the funeral expenses."

Mrs. Grace Navin accepted the one-million-dollar offer, but not on the spot. She buried her husband at Holy Sepulchre Cemetery, his burial vault guarded by two giant stone tigers.

Briggs continued the improvements to Navin Field over the winter of 1935–36. He once entertained the idea of planting ivy on the outfield walls, similar to Wrigley Field, but gave up on the idea after an outfielder lost a ball in the vines during the recently concluded World Series. Instead he instructed Osborn Engineering to design a double-decked grandstand extending down the first-base line into right field. The existing pavilion was demolished with no difficulty, but the proximity of Trumbull Avenue to the right-field fence was a cause for concern.

Osborn remedied the space problem by moving the right-field fence forty-two feet closer to the plate. However, the lower deck stands were still distressingly narrow. To compensate, Briggs ordered Osborn to widen the upper deck by ten feet in both directions. This accounted for the bulge in the park's outer wall along Trumbull and for the famous porch that hangs over right field. The addition increased seating capacity to thirty-six thousand. Not only was the distance down the right-field line pared to just 325 feet, a ball lifted high enough only had to travel 315 feet before plopping into the upper deck instead of the waiting outfielder's mitt—a cheap home run, complained generations of frustrated flyhawks, but a home run nonetheless.

Upon Cochrane's advice, who had assumed the additional responsibilities of general manager, Briggs shelled out seventy-five thousand dollars for Al Simmons, the former two-time batting champion and Cochrane's former teammate in Philadelphia. Simmons' batting magic had largely dissipated, but his ego and ill humor remained intact, and he was sent packing after one disappointing summer.

Nineteen thirty-six was a disappointing summer. The team ceremoniously raised its world championship banner one spring afternoon at Michigan and Trumbull, but it may just as well have been a flag of surrender. Greenberg re-injured his wrist in the twelfth game and missed the rest of the season, while Schoolboy Rowe battled arm problems and had to be satisfied with nineteen wins. General Crowder, beset by a stomach ailment, retired mid-season. The biggest loss was Cochrane. In June the high-strung catcher-manager-general manager, battling injuries, a crushing workload, dissension in the clubhouse, and the unreasonably high expectations of fans and management, suffered a nervous breakdown and was sent to a friend's western ranch for a long rest. Black Mike was replaced for several weeks by his coach, Del Baker. For the season the Tigers batted .300 as a team, averaged six runs a game, and finished a distant second to the Yankees.

Things grew worse in 1937. On June 25, Cochrane was struck in the temple by a Bump Hadley fast ball during a game at Yankee Stadium. The near-fatal beaning more than crushed the Tigers' pennant hopes, it ended Cochrane's playing career. Once again Del Baker stepped in while he recuperated. Although Cochrane returned to the bench, he was fidgety and foul-tempered. "He'd outguess himself," said Gehringer, who won the batting title (.371) and MVP award that year. "On the field he was able to make instantaneous decisions. Whether the beaning had any effect on it, I don't know."

Cochrane's injury gave Rudy York the opportunity he needed. The twenty-four-year-old utility player, the product of an impoverished childhood in Georgia, had bounced between third, first, and the outfield as the team tried to find a place for his lethal bat.

Charlie Gehringer digs in against Cleveland's Mel Harder in the 1937 opener as a battery of photographers kneels less than fifteen feet away. The upper deck in right field has been completed by now, but it won't be until after the season that the final phase of construction—the center field bleachers—will be started. The following April the expanded, double-decked ballpark will be renamed Briggs Stadium.

Writers described the hard-living, hard-faced York, who had some Cherokee blood, as "part Indian, part first baseman." Now he took over behind the plate, with startling results. In 104 games he hit thirty-five home runs and knocked in 103 teammates. He slammed eighteen home runs in August alone, setting a record for most round-trippers hit in a month.

In a year characterized by hundreds of sit-down strikes and bloody labor-management battles outside of the park (the infamous beating of Walter Reuther and fellow organizers at "the Battle of the Overpass" occurred the day after Cochrane's beaning), York and the rest of the Tigers faithfully reported to work every afternoon, providing sorely needed diversion. The team cranked out slightly more runs than it surrendered, its 935 runs and 150 round-trippers trailing only the mighty Yankees among all major-league teams. The team hit an aggregate .292, the best in baseball. On August 14, the Tigers pounded the St. Louis Browns for thirty-six runs during a doubleheader at Navin Field—the worst double drubbing in big-league history. Games like these reinforced the park's image as a batter-friendly environment. Due in part to the friendly right-field porch, that summer the home team and visitors combined for more runs (969, or nearly thirteen a game) and homers (149) than at any other ballpark. Four Tigers had two hundred hits—Greenberg, Gehringer, Pete Fox, and Gee Walker—and Greenberg knocked in 183 runs, missing Lou Gehrig's American League standard by one.

The result was a club-record gate of 1,072,276, the third time in four Depression summers that Navin Field had seated the most fans. The Tigers may have once again finished a poor second to the Yankees, and the local economy might still be more bust than boom, but under Frank Navin and Walter Briggs' stewardship Detroit had established itself as perhaps the best baseball town in America.

The American flag is run up the center-field flagpole at Briggs Stadium in front of a record opening-day crowd of 54,500 on April 22, 1938.

CHAPTER FOUR

The Fan Who Owned a Ballpark

Briggs Stadium, 1938–1960

L EGEND HAS IT that Walter O. Briggs' vow to one day own the Detroit Tigers came after he was frustrated in his attempts to buy tickets for the opening game of the 1907 World Series between Detroit and Chicago. He avidly supported the team all season, at one point being warned by umpire Tommy Connolly that he would be tossed out of Bennett Park if he didn't soften his objections to his decisions. When Briggs called on his regular-season supplier, downtown cigar-stand owner Mel "Straw Hat" Soper, for postseason tickets, he was told that there was nothing he could do. Every seat was taken.

Briggs sent Soper, straw hat in hand, to Frank Navin to personally plead his case. "And who in hell," asked the Tigers' boss, "is Walter Briggs?"

Navin found out after his tête-à-tête with the thirty-year-old industrialist. Briggs got his tickets. It also marked the first meeting between the two men who shaped the team's destiny for most of the first half of this century.

Walter O. Briggs made his millions building and painting car bodies for several major automakers. His fortune enabled him to buy a quarter-share of the Tigers in 1920 and 1927. Few knew he was Frank Navin's silent partner until he became sole owner after Navin died in 1935.

Navin liked what he saw. Briggs was the embodiment of the self-made man: rugged, occasionally profane, always supremely confident. Like Navin, Briggs' father had been a railroad employee, working as an engineer fifty years for the Michigan Central Railroad. Briggs began working in the car shops as a fifteen-year-old body trimmer. As a young man he joined a trim-and-paint shop owned by boyhood pal Barney Everitt. He moved from vice president to president. In 1909, two years after meeting the Tigers' owner, he became a boss himself, buying Everitt's firm and reorganizing it as the Briggs Manufacturing Company.

From a cramped two-story building on Clay Avenue the company rapidly grew into the country's largest independent manufacturer of car bodies. At its height sixteen plants, including nine in Detroit and one in England, employed forty thousand workers. Customers included such car makers as Ford, Packard, Hudson, Chalmers, and Chrysler. By 1920, when Briggs bought a quarter-share of the Tigers for $250,000, he was already a multimillionaire and an important man in Detroit. He was elected president of the

Detroit Athletic Club, the city's most exclusive men's club, in 1923, two years before Navin. At the time of his death he was a thirty-third-degree Mason and a Knight of Malta.

Briggs lived ostentatiously, keeping a forty-room house on fashionable Boston Boulevard and Walbri Hall, a 148-acre estate, in Bloomfield Hills. He also owned a palatial winter residence in Florida. As the Tigers' owner he always received a motorcycle escort to and from the park. On those afternoons when the lake breezes beckoned, Briggs listened to the game on the radio and occasionally phoned in suggestions from his yacht.

A handsome, energetic, positive man used to getting his way, Briggs was an enigma. He's been properly described as a philanthropist, sentimentalist, and an easy mark for children. One hundred thousand youths saw games for free at Briggs Stadium every summer. But to the blue-collar fathers of many of these kids, the Tigers' owner was more devil than benefactor. Briggs converted to Catholicism in 1937 at the age of sixty. Writers who openly reported about St. Hugo's, the church he built in Bloomfield Hills, also whispered of the apartment building constructed north of downtown, allegedly to house his mistresses. Briggs' reputation as an industrial employer was abysmal. He was the most despised labor boss in town. In the spring of 1927 a $2-million fire at his Harper Avenue plant killed at least twenty-one workers and horribly burned many more. It remains one of the deadliest and most controversial blazes in the city's history. Briggs was charged with ignoring unsafe working conditions by the labor press, which published a bitter poem, "Bodies by Briggs." The Mack Avenue plant, Briggs' largest, was already widely known as "the slaughterhouse." The industrialist's neglect was even more galling in the light of the $250,000 he paid that year to buy a quarter-share of the Tigers from John Kelsey's estate.

As economic conditions worsened in the 1930s, Briggs twice slashed wages at his Highland Park plant and resorted to paying workers only when the line was actually running—about two or three hours a day. In January 1933 nine thousand workers walked out and paralyzed Detroit's auto production. Briggs hired an army of strikebreakers and refused to meet with strike leaders. He eventually raised wages to twenty-five cents an hour, but by the time the ugly, violent affair was over half of the strikers had lost their jobs.

Briggs finally was forced to recognize the United Auto Workers in 1937. Thereafter, whenever a dispute arose between labor and management, the rank and file always picketed Briggs Stadium.

As the Tigers' boss, Briggs was impulsive and paternalistic. He overpaid his players, refused to trade his favorites, handed out overgenerous bonuses to unproven talent, and spent hundreds of thousands of dollars each year to pamper his park and its customers. He never strayed from his original statement that he was not in baseball to make money. His sole purpose, he insisted after taking over the club in 1936, was "to give Detroit the best team in the finest park in the country."

To that end he stationed attendants inside the immaculately clean restrooms, installed the majors' first underground sprinkler system, painted the seats and outside walls each year, and pioneered the use of nylon tarp to cover the field when raindrops started to fall. In rain delays Briggs was often spotted inside his private box next to the Tigers' dugout, timing the grounds keepers to see how fast they shielded his beloved playground.

Briggs, who had played sandlot ball when he was young, was no judge of talent. However, with his bankroll and super scout Wish Egan beating the bushes, he didn't have to be. Egan, who pitched for the Western League Tigers in the 1890s, was a familiar sight at Butzel Field, Northwestern Field, and scores of other diamonds then in heavy use throughout the city. Until his death in 1951, Egan was one of the game's great talent scouts, signing Barney McCosky, Walter "Hoot" Evers, Johnny Groth, Johnny Lipon, Art Houtteman, Billy Pierce, and Hal Newhouser off the sandlots.

Two decades before large bonuses became a common practice in the majors, Briggs ordered his general managers to throw huge wads of cash at prospects. In 1946 pitcher Lou Kretlow received thirty thousand dollars to sign with Detroit. Four years later, catcher Frank "Pig" House (so named for his fastidious dress and manicured nails) collected forty-five thousand dollars and two cars (at a time when most young Tigers couldn't afford one) for putting his name on the dotted line. Both were busts as pros. The original and most famous Briggs bonus baby was Dick Wakefield. In 1941 the University of Michigan standout was given a record fifty-two-thousand-dollar bonus and a new car in exchange for his signature. Wakefield, a .293 hitter during his seven seasons with Detroit, never lived up to expectations. But because he was a favorite of Briggs and his wife, he managed to stay with the club until 1949.

For all his demonstrated largesse and paternalism, Briggs was also mule-headed, meddlesome, impatient, and dictatorial in his dealings. He summarily rid the Tigers of two legends, Mickey Cochrane and Hank Greenberg, despite their contributions to the team, the city, and his own fortune. During the Second World War he refused twelve-game-winner Rufus Gentry's request for a one-thousand-dollar raise despite the manpower shortage. The promising pitcher, who like all major leaguers was bound to his team by the reserve clause in his contract, sat out the entire 1945 season and lost a year's salary and a substantial World Series check. He returned to pitch a total of ten innings during his last three years in Detroit.

"He could scare you," acknowledged Charlie Martin, who worked in the front office from 1923 to 1958 as the ticket manager and stadium manager. "You'd go into his office never knowing what to expect. He could really give it to you. But once you got inside of him, he wasn't too bad. He just demanded a lot from the people around him."

Briggs' blend of imperiousness and public spiritedness was much in evidence during 1938. After the 1937 season Briggs spent an estimated one million dollars to complete the expansion of his ballpark. After he ordered the third-base pavilion razed, a two-story grandstand that wrapped around the foul pole and continued into left field was built in its place, running parallel to Cherry Street (which had been closed by the city). There it met the double-decked bleachers in center. The additions increased seating capacity from 36,000 to 53,000 and made the field the first in baseball to be completely encircled by two decks. A new press box—the largest in the majors—hung below the grandstand roof and extended all the way from the overhang in right field to beyond third base.

A giant hand-operated scoreboard was installed above the upper-deck bleacher section; smaller electronic scoreboards were placed on the second-deck facing behind first and third bases. The bullpens were relocated beyond the fence in deep center field, which measured 440 feet from home plate. The other outfield dimensions were 340 feet to the left-field corner, 365 feet to left center, 370 feet to right center, and 325 feet down the right-field foul line.

Briggs removed his dead partner's name from the ballpark and renamed it after himself. Briggs Stadium officially opened to the public on April 22, 1938. Dedication day began with a reenactment of the 1901 opening day parade at Bennett Park, complete with buggies and horse-drawn hacks, and ended with the Tigers on the short end of a 4–3 score to Cleveland. In between was a bit of chaos among customers seeking a spot of sun on this nippy Friday.

"I'll never forget the day those stands opened," said Charlie Martin, who in 1923 had opened the team's first advance ticket office at LaFonde's Cigar Store on Griswold. "It was opening day and it was freezing. The people who bought tickets in the reserve sections around the infield saw the sun shining in these new stands and they went out there to sit.

"Now, the people in the street couldn't get into the bleachers and when Mr. Briggs saw this, he was really mad. He began screaming, 'Tear those new stands down—rip 'em down.' It took us a long while, but we finally got him quieted down."

Most in the record crowd of 54,500 pronounced the remodeled field an unqualified success. There was a certain harmony to the surroundings, from the lush blue-green grass to the freshly painted canoe-green wooden seats.

Unfortunately, disharmony characterized the first summer at Briggs' new sports palace. Mickey Cochrane's emotional and physical breakdowns ruined him in the eyes of many observers. Once a brilliant field leader, he had disintegrated into an indecisive bench manager, open to second-guessing from fans, reporters, players—and his owner. Briggs stood behind Cochrane when he traded the popular Gee Walker, but fans revolted, especially after the eight-player swap with the White Sox (which also included Marv Owen) failed to pay dividends. By the middle of the summer the club stood in fifth place and Briggs demanded answers.

On August 6, after the Tigers had suffered a second straight home loss to the Red Sox, Briggs called Cochrane to his office.

"Well, what is the alibi for today?" asked Briggs.

"To tell you the plain truth, Mr. Briggs, you haven't got the players to win," Cochrane replied.

"That's not what you said in the spring," Briggs shot back. "Maybe it isn't the players. Maybe you are the cause and it would help matters if you quit."

In just four and a half years in Detroit, Cochrane had become a part of the city's hagiography. He had delivered two pennants, two second-place finishes, and the Tigers' first world's championship. He'd received credit for practically singlehandedly lifting the city out of its funk during some of the worst days of the Depression. But now he was out, even as a large crowd of distraught Detroiters hurried to the airport to see him off.

Back at Michigan and Trumbull, Cochrane's old battery mate, Lefty Grove, joined the public outcry over the dismissal. "Mickey did more for baseball in four years here than Briggs can do in a lifetime," said the Red Sox pitcher. "Just look at the stadium—that's the stadium that Mickey Cochrane built."

The remainder of Cochrane's life was less than heroic. He drank and worked at a variety of bit roles in baseball, including that of a part-time scout. This most spirited of men lost his will to live after his only son was killed by a German artillery shell during the closing weeks of the Second World War. Black Mike was just fifty-nine when he died, bloated and broke, in 1962. "He never got over being let out as manager by Mr. Briggs," said Hank Greenberg. "Baseball is funny that way, especially for the great ones like Cochrane. He never got over the hurt. And this wasn't getting hit on the head by Bump Hadley. Mike's hurt was in the heart, not the head."

Greenberg regularly locked horns with Briggs, even after he had established himself as one of the game's greatest sluggers and a national hero to millions of American Jews. A warm, generous, and serious man affectionately dubbed "Hankus Pankus", he drew the admiration of many when he decided to sit out Yom Kippur during the heat of the 1934 pennant race. Eight days earlier, he had wrestled with the problem of whether to play on Rosh Hashana, the first day of the Jewish new year. A local rabbi consulted the Talmud, discovered that Jewish children had in ancient times played in the streets of Jerusalem, and gave Greenberg the green light to suit up. In typical dramatic style, he belted two solo home runs—the last in the bottom of the ninth—to beat the Red Sox, 2–1, at Navin Field. The *Free Press* ran a headline: "Leshono tovo tikosayva!" It was Yiddish for "Happy New Year!"

Nobody of any religion ever worked harder to make himself into a ballplayer than the towering, stoop-shouldered Greenberg. He was at the park hours before anybody else, paying local semipros out of

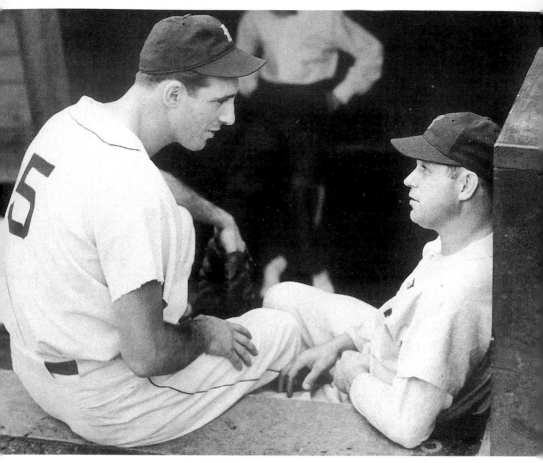

Hank Greenberg chats with Boston's Jimmie Foxx prior to a September 1938 game at Briggs Stadium. That summer Greenberg fell short of Babe Ruth's single-season home-run record by two, but still established a still-standing major-league record of thirty-nine four-baggers at home.

his pocket to pitch batting practice until his blistered hands could take no more. A small army of neighborhood kids fanned out in the seats and outfield, shagging balls in exchange for a quarter, a pass to that afternoon's game, or the chance to take a couple of swings themselves. He took countless throws and ground balls at first base, hoping to prove wrong one writer's contention that he "looked like an elephant trying to pick up marbles with his toes."

Greenberg's ethnicity and star status made him a special mark for bench jockeys and numb-skulled fans in every big-league city. But he played through the obscene taunts, an honest worker in a town that has always appreciated honest labor.

"You don't see players like him anymore," Bill O'Neill, who grew up near the park, reflected after Greenberg died of kidney cancer in 1986. "He was talented, but he was a great model for the kids, too. We used to see him walking up Michigan Avenue to games and he treated people like he was one of us. He was the first player ever to give a party for the ground crew. That's what kind of guy he was."

In 1938, as thousands of European Jews were herded into concentration camps and Father Charles Coughlin of Royal Oak broadcast anti-Semitic speeches during his radio show, the twenty-seven-year-old Greenberg captivated the country as he mounted an assault on Babe Ruth's single-season home run mark of sixty, set eleven years earlier. "The Detroit club never made any fuss about it," Greenberg recalled. "They didn't care about it even though I was getting good publicity for the club. I always felt that Walter Briggs . . . was almost pulling for me not to break Ruth's record, because it might mean $5,000 or $10,000 more in salary for me." Greenberg wound up with fifty-eight home runs, including thirty-nine at Briggs Stadium, still the most ever hit by a player in his home park. Sure enough, Briggs wanted his star slugger to play for the same salary the following season, explaining that he needed to paint the stadium. Greenberg held out for a five-thousand-dollar raise, and then hit thirty-three homers in 1939 as the club finished fifth under Del Baker. Although only one man in the majors hit more round-trippers, Briggs told new general manager Jack Zeller to trim ten thousand dollars off his contract offer to Greenberg.

That summer Detroit fans gave a warm send-off to one of baseball's most beloved figures. On May 2, 1939, the mighty Lou Gehrig, whose stalwart presence in the Yankees' lineup had convinced Greenberg to sign with Detroit instead of New York, played his final big-league game. Fred Rice, a young usher, was stationed right behind the Yankees' dugout.

"The Yanks were taking infield practice before the game, and Lou was at his usual first-base position," Rice remembered. "I watched intently as he took a ground ball, scooped it up and tossed it weakly to Bill Dickey, the Yankee catcher. Gehrig turned around,

Lou Gehrig rests on the dugout steps at Briggs Stadium on May 2, 1939, the afternoon his amazing playing streak came to an end.

walked off the field, and headed for the dugout. Our eyes met. I waved at him and said, 'Hi, Lou.' He smiled, waved back, and disappeared into the end of his career."

Too weak to play, Gehrig was not in that afternoon's starting lineup, and thus saw his remarkable playing streak of 2,130 consecutive games come to a halt. The fact was not missed by the midweek crowd of 11,739, which impulsively gave baseball's beloved Iron

Horse a two-minute standing ovation when he walked out to give the umpire the lineup card. "There was no shouting, just sustained applause," said Art Hill, a college student playing hooky from school that spring day. "But they were on their feet, which meant something in those days. A standing ovation was a ritual act, meant to honor a man's whole career, or some deed of superhuman courage or skill. It was important because it was unplanned; people knew when to do it—and when not to do it, which was most of the time."

Moments later, Gehrig was spotted crying on the bench. Unbeknownst to anyone, including Gehrig himself, he was wasting away from amyotrophic lateral sclerosis, a degenerative nerve disease that claimed his life two years later. "The saddest day of my young life was when that happened," said Rice. "It was the culmination of a sweet, memorable era."

During the Briggs era visitors to his ballpark were uniformly complimentary about the surroundings. "The outfield was just like a carpet," Roger "Doc" Cramer, a teammate of Cochrane's in Philadelphia, recalled. "You could dive for a ball out there and you'd scoot across that grass. You wouldn't stick in the ground. A lot of these ballparks, the ground gets a little wet and you wind up sticking your shoulder into it." That was how Cramer, who later played seven seasons in Detroit during the 1940s, once broke his collarbone diving into the unforgiving unforgiving outfield at Philadelphia's Shibe Park.

Hitters liked the solid-green outfield walls, which provided a dark, clutter-free background that allowed them to pick up the ball better. Ted Williams absolutely loved playing at Briggs Stadium. "I saw the ball better there," Boston's Hall-of-Fame left fielder explained. Of Williams' 521 career home runs, 55 were hit at Briggs Stadium, more than at any other enemy ballpark. That did not include one of his most famous, the dramatic ninth-inning blast that won the 1941 All-Star Game in Detroit.

"He could do whatever he wanted to do," recalled Barney McCosky, a fellow member of Williams' 1939 rookie class. "We used to talk about it on the bench: What would he hit if he played in Detroit, with that short right field? How many home runs would he hit? My God."

While no one will ever know the answer to that question, Williams provided a hint during his first game at Briggs Stadium. On May 4, 1939, the Boston Red Sox rookie awaited a 3–0 pitch from Roxie Lawson.

"You're not hitting, are you, Kid?" asked Rudy York, squatting behind the plate.

"I sure as hell am," responded Williams, who proceeded to blast the next pitch against the facing of the upper deck in right. York met him at the plate. "You weren't kidding, were you, Kid?" he said.

No, he wasn't. Later that afternoon, Williams teed off on Bob Harris and sent the ball arcing over the roof in right field, the first fair ball ever to make it completely out of Walter Briggs' new stadium. As Williams made his way around the bases, a disbelieving Billy Rogell asked, "What the hell you been eating?"* The unspoken but obvious answer: pitchers.

Claude Passeau was on the menu July 8, 1941, the date of the first All-Star Game in Detroit. The American League trailed the National League, 5–4, when Williams came to bat with runners on first and third and two out. With a count of two balls and one strike on him, and 54,674 people on the edge of their seats, Williams uncoiled on a belt-high fast ball and sent it screaming toward right field. Williams was afraid that he hadn't got enough wood on it. "But gee, it just kept going, up, up, way up into the right-field stands," he later remembered.

Well, it was the kind of thing a kid dreams about and imagines himself doing when he's playing those little playground games we used to play in San Diego. Halfway down to first, see-

---

* Through 1996, thirty balls have sailed completely out of the stadium since it was double-decked in 1938, all but three hit over the right-field grandstand. Williams' feat was duplicated by New York's Mickey Mantle (once each in 1956, 1958, and 1960); Norm Cash (once in 1961 and three times in 1962); Minnesota's Don Mincher (1964); Baltimore's Boog Powell (1969); Jim Northrup (1969); Jason Thompson (twice in 1977); Milwaukee's Cecil Cooper (1983); California's Reggie Jackson (1984); Ruppert Jones (1984); Lou Whitaker (1985); Kirk Gibson (1983, 1986, and 1994); Kansas City's George Brett (1988); Mickey Tettleton (twice in 1991); Chad Kreuter (1994); Melvin Nieves (1996); Toronto's Carlos Delgado (1996); and Tony Clark (1996). On August 3, 1962, Minnesota's Harmon Killebrew became the first player to hit a fair ball over the left-field grandstand, connecting off Jim Bunning. Frank Howard of Washington (1968) and Cecil Fielder (1990) were the only other batters to match Killebrew's feat.

ing that ball going out, I stopped running and started leaping and jumping and clapping my hands, and I was just so happy I laughed out loud. I've never been so happy, and I've never seen so many happy guys. They carried me off the field, [Joe] DiMaggio and Bob Feller, who had pitched early in the game and was already in street clothes, and Eddie Collins leaped out of the box seats and was there to greet me. I've got a picture of Del Baker, the Detroit manager, kissing me on the forehead. Somebody said, "Did you kiss the Kid?" and Del Baker said, "You damn right I did."

Sandwiched between Williams' 1939 and 1941 moonshots was the Tigers' equally improbable pennant-winning 1940 season. A club-record 1,112,693 fans poured through the turnstiles that summer to watch the Tigers unexpectedly edge Cleveland and the defending four-time world champion Yankees.

The Indians were managed by one-time Tiger Ossie Vitt, who proved no favorite with his troops. The players, chafing under Vitt's heavy hand, complained to management. This earned them the sobriquet "the Cleveland crybabies," in the press. During a crucial September series in Detroit, enterprising fans tied strings to baby bottles and dangled them from the upper deck over the Cleveland dugout.

At the same time some fans merrily rolled baby carriages across the top of the Cleveland dugout, Detroit batters received a huge assist from a spy in the outfield seats: Tommy Bridges, who a few days earlier had accidentally discovered that he could use his hunting rifle telescope to steal the signs from the catcher. After taking a couple of innings to master the code, Bridges retreated from the upper deck to the center field bullpen. There one Tiger picked up the signal, and then quickly passed the word to a teammate leaning against the fence. The batter, looking past the mound to center field, watched for a sign from the spotter's assistant. If it was a curve ball, he pulled his right hand down. If it was a fast ball, he kept it up.

"It was amazing how quickly you could pick it up," marveled Greenberg. "Of course, the batter was getting the signal as quickly as the pitcher was." Strangely enough, some players like Charlie Gehringer didn't want to know what was coming. But others,

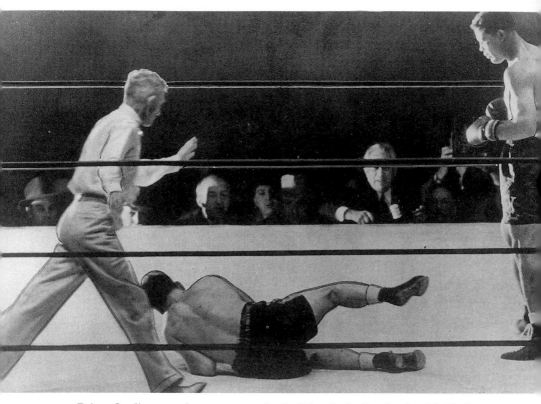

Briggs Stadium was home to several prizefights, including Joe Louis' title bout with Bob Pastor on the night of September 20, 1939. Detroit's famous Brown Bomber knocked out Pastor during the eleventh round in front of a damp crowd of thirty-three thousand fans.

including Greenberg, Rudy York, and Pinky Higgins, had a field day batting down the stretch.

The Tigers clinched the flag in Cleveland and finished the year at 90–64. Greenberg was the big gun in Detroit's major-league-leading offense (.286, 888 runs). Before the season he had leveraged a ten-thousand-dollar raise from General Manager Jack Zeller by agreeing to move from first base to left field. The move, designed to create a spot in the lineup for Rudy York, paid off. Greenberg hit .340 and topped the loop with 41 home runs, 50 doubles, and 150 RBI. He won his second MVP award, and became the first player to win it at different positions.

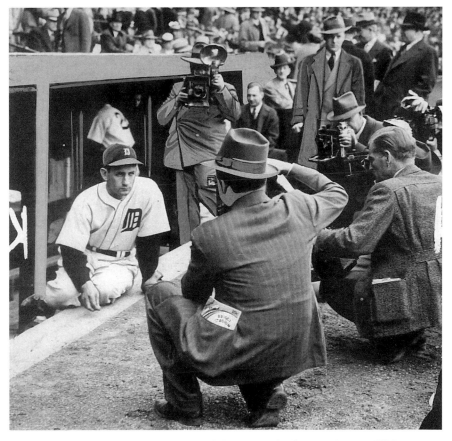

Charlie Gehringer, always a favorite of the press, the fans, and owner Walter Briggs, received the star treatment on his thirty-seventh birthday, celebrated one May Sunday in 1940. As part of the festivities ushers brought out a giant birthday cake.

York proved a capable replacement at first base, though it was worth the price of admission to watch him try to corral a pop-up. Batting in the fifth spot behind Greenberg, he hit .316 with 33 homers and 134 runs batted in. At thirty-seven, Gehringer still had enough pop left in his Louisville Slugger to hit .313. Double-play partner Dick Bartell, a veteran National Leaguer who replaced Billy Rogell after ten years as Detroit's short-fused shortstop, compensated for a weak bat with a flypaper glove. Barney McCosky hit .340 with a league-high 200 hits and 19 triples.

Bobo Newsom.

The ace of the staff was Norman Louis "Bobo" Newsom, a veteran of five teams in nine big-league campaigns when the Tigers traded for him in a ten-player swap with the Browns near the end of the 1939 season.

Gehringer called the gruff, bearlike righthander with the rubber arm and beet-red face "the biggest character on the Tigers." Cleveland pitcher and Hall of Famer Bob Feller agreed. "Newsom had this thing about not pitching if there was a scrap of paper on the mound. He'd stop the game and pick up any little piece of paper he saw, or have the ground crew come out on a windy day and pick up the loose hot dog wrappers."

Hoping to get Bobo off his game, Feller and teammate Ken Keltner stopped at a party store prior to a game at Briggs Stadium and bought a bag of confetti. At the end of every inning, Keltner

Detroit players, umpires, and Cincinnati's third-base coach watch a weakly hit grounder finally roll foul during the third game of the 1940 World Series, played in Detroit.

trotted from third base to the visitors' dugout, furtively sprinkling a couple of handfuls of confetti on the mound. "It looked like a blizzard out there," said Feller. "Newsom blew his stack immediately, stormed around the mound and refused to pitch. It took fifteen minutes for the ground crew to clean up the mound to Bobo's specifications."

After the fifth game of the 1940 World Series ends, part of the crowd of 54,093 cross the field and head for the exit. "In those days they didn't have a phalanx of guards keeping you from going on the field," recalled longtime fan Don Shapiro. "When the last out was made, everybody jumped over the box seats and walked across the field. You'd practice sliding into second base. Can you imagine that happening today? You put a foot on the field, you're thrown in the pokey."

When Newsom wasn't worrying about paper on the pitcher's mound, he kept the clubhouse alive with his perfect impersonation of the popular Amos 'n Andy radio show or drove teammates like Schoolboy Rowe nuts by nailing his shoes down to his locker and other pranks. "Good pitcher, though," Gehringer added. "He probably was on more ball clubs than anybody that ever pitched, but he certainly had a great arm and a great heart for the game. Pretty good beer drinker, but other than that, he really put it all out."

Newsom finished 1940 with a 21–5 record despite missing three weeks with a broken thumb. A couple of reclamation projects also came through. Rowe returned from the minors to post a 16–3 record, while Al Benton, moved from spot starter to strictly relief, saved seventeen games, tops in the circuit.

The Cincinnati Reds provided the opposition in the World Series. The team was forced to use forty-year-old coach Jimmie Wilson behind the plate after an injury relegated regular catcher Ernie Lombardi to spot duty. Newsom made short work of the Reds during the first game, played October 2 at Crosley Field. The Tigers won, 7–2, but jubilation turned to sorrow when Newsom's father, who had watched from the stands, died of a heart attack the following morning. That afternoon, while the Reds squared matters with a 5–3 victory, the Tigers' ace arranged for his father's funeral.

The middle three games moved to Briggs Stadium. On October 4, 52,877 Detroiters watched Tommy Bridges claim a 7–4 victory over Jim Turner. The big blows were two-run homers by York and Higgins. The next afternoon Paul Derringer, a twenty-game winner who had been routed in the opener, bounced back with a route-going five-hitter in a 5–2 Cincinnati win before 54,093.

The national spotlight fell on Bobo Newsom, who took the mound on October 6 with the series tied two games apiece. The press tried not to be melodramatic about Newsom, the man who had just returned from burying his father. Now, with tears in his eyes, he sought to give his team the edge in front of the greatest baseball crowd ever assembled in Detroit up to that point: 55,189 people. Pumped up by the emotion of the moment and by the volume of encouragement in Briggs Stadium, the grim-faced Newsom did as he promised. He "won one for Dad," spinning a magnificent three-hitter. His teammates, meanwhile, jumped on four Cincinnati pitchers for thirteen hits, including a home run by Greenberg, in an 8–0 thrashing.

The two teams traveled by train to Crosley Field to wrap up the series. The Tigers needed one more win. They never got it. Bucky Walters, a converted third baseman who had led the senior loop with twenty-two victories, threw a 4–0 shutout to even the series. Bobo Newsom, his right arm still weary after one day's rest, lost the

Ted Williams celebrates his famous home run in the 1941 All-Star Game in the Briggs Stadium clubhouse with New York Yankee Joe DiMaggio. "It was a wonderful, wonderful day for me," said Williams, who regarded Briggs Stadium as his favorite park to hit in.

closer, 2–1, to Derringer. The only consolation for the Tigers came when the series' receipts were counted up and divided. Although Crosley Field was one of the smallest venues in baseball, the three fifty-thousand-plus gates in Detroit—the first postseason crowds of that size anywhere outside of Yankee Stadium—helped produce a record pot. It was the culmination of a bittersweet year for Briggs, who had recently been stricken with polio. The disease paralyzed his legs and confined him to a wheelchair for the last twelve years of his life.

The following season the defending American League champs didn't even win half their games, and finished a distant fourth with a 75–79 record. Attendance fell by nearly a half-million. With the United States at the brink of war, a military draft took young men from all professions, including baseball. Hank Greenberg, much to the shock of the sporting public, entered the army in early May to begin six months of duty. He was the first major leaguer of any consequence to be drafted.

Without Greenberg, the Tigers' attack lost much of its power in 1941. Newsom slumped to a 12–20 record, prompting Briggs to tender him a contract for $12,500, a huge cut in pay from his previous salary of $34,000. Newsom sat out the spring of 1942 rather than sign, and soon the journeyman pitcher was once again on his way, this time sold to Washington.

When the 1942 season opened, the country had been at war for several months, the result of Japan's surprise attack on Pearl Harbor. Greenberg, released two days before the attack, immediately re-enlisted; four prime seasons passed before he returned to the game. Like most inductees and enlistees, Greenberg insisted that playing the national pastime took a back seat to serving his country.

The call to arms affected all teams. By 1945 about 5,400 of 5,800 major and minor league ballplayers served in the military. In addition to Greenberg, McCosky, and Wakefield, the Tigers lost catcher Birdie Tebbetts, outfielder Pat Mullin, shortstop Johnny Lipon, and pitchers Al Benton, Fred Hutchinson, and Virgil Trucks.

"Goddamn, we were lucky to get nine men to put on the field some times," said Doc Cramer, who took over center field in 1942. "We had guys on the field, to tell you the truth, I couldn't tell you who they were right now." Cramer remembered a draftee named Joe Orrell who one day took his physical examination before the game started. Everyone in the clubhouse figured the big pitcher was a goner. Not so. Orrell, classified 4-F, returned to Briggs Stadium halfway through the game.

"Joe, what happened?" someone asked.

"Oh," Orrell answered, "short war."

A view of Michigan and Trumbull in 1943. Note the streetcars, which would continue to transport fans to the park for another decade.

Beyond losing their best players to Uncle Sam, the Tigers made other sacrifices for the war effort, offering twenty-five cents in war stamps for every foul ball returned from the stands and raising almost seventy thousand dollars for war-related charities through exhibition games. To accommodate defense workers, the Tigers' owner (whose factories were retooled to produce tanks and aircraft parts) toyed with 5:00 and 6:00 p.m. starts, but the twilight affairs played havoc with everybody's eyes—players, fans, and especially umpires—and were poorly attended.

During this period the club experimented with Negro league contests. Negro league promoters typically put up a minimum one-thousand-dollar guarantee against 25 percent of the gate receipts when they rented major league parks. The ticket prices were the same as those charged to watch the big leaguers play, so the exhibitions generally were profitable for all involved. This was especially true in the Arsenal of Democracy, as national magazines had come to call Detroit. Defense work jobs swelled the city's black population from 150,000 to 300,000 during the decade, creating another baseball-starved community for the Tigers to tap into.*

---

* One of the most loyal of Detroit's black fans was Joe Louis, who grew up in Black Bottom, living and dying with the fortunes of the Tigers. He was a regular ballpark patron during the 1930s, even after he became the heavyweight champion of the world and a national hero from his knockouts of Primo Carnera and Max Schmeling. Briggs Stadium hosted several prizefights, including Louis's title bout with Bob Pastor on the evening of September 20, 1939. The Brown Bomber knocked out Pastor in the eleventh round in front of a damp crowd of thirty-three thousand. Walter Briggs eventually banned prizefights at the stadium because the crowds were too hard on his beloved grass.

On August 3, 1941, Briggs Stadium hosted a Sunday double-header between the Homestead Grays and Baltimore Elite Giants. Harry Salsinger, who considered the Negro leaguers' abilities on par with their white counterparts, also commented favorably on the behavior of the 27,949 fans in attendance. "It was, in fact, the best behaved crowd that has watched a doubleheader here all season. For once Briggs Stadium housed customers who refrained from littering the fringe of the outfield with waste paper." Six weeks later, 34,784 watched the legendary Satchel Paige strut his stuff for the equally famous Kansas City Monarchs.

Other black teams rented the stadium, including such well known nines as the New York Cubans and Chicago American Giants. Despite the profits to be made and the orderliness of the crowd, the sight of tens of thousands of blacks sitting in his beloved stadium must have been more discomfiting to Briggs than he origi-nally supposed. He had guards posted around the concession stands.

Briggs' prejudices were exacerbated by the terrible race riot that tore apart downtown Detroit. It began on the muggy Sunday night of June 20, 1943, not long after the Tigers had concluded a double-header with St. Louis at the corner. A series of minor altercations between several white sailors and black youths on the Belle Isle bridge fueled rumors that a white woman had been raped. The story that spread through the black entertainment district of Paradise Valley was that a black woman and her baby had been thrown over the side of the bridge. By the following morning businesses were torched, cars overturned, and unwary members of both races bru-tally attacked, some fatally.

Ballplayers were ordered to stay inside their apartments or hotel rooms, but some ventured outside. Doc Cramer strayed from his room at the Leland Hotel and watched in fascination as a policeman drilled a sniper "right between the eyes." Five thousand troops moved into Detroit and restored order, but not before 34 people—including 25 blacks—were killed and another 675 people injured. Property damage was assessed at $2 million.

Meanwhile, the Cleveland Indians arrived in town to begin a series. Monday had been a scheduled off day. Travel restrictions pre-vented Briggs from relocating the games, so he canceled Tuesday's game and rescheduled a makeup doubleheader on Wednesday, June 23. By that time the last of the rioting had been quelled. Briggs used

The 1943 race riot, which resulted in thirty-four deaths and $2 million in property damage, forced the Tigers to postpone an afternoon game with Cleveland. When the teams resumed play with a makeup doubleheader on Wednesday, June 23, hundreds of soldiers were posted in and around the stadium, including this contingent in the bleachers. It was the first time federal troops were used to guard a major-league game.

his influence to station three hundred armed soldiers throughout the stadium, the first and only time federal troops have been called on to serve in that capacity.

Under new manager Steve O'Neill the Tigers finished fifth in 1943 for the third straight year. In 1944 they lost twelve of their first thirteen games at home before finally coming alive. Paul "Dizzy" Trout, an intense righthander who led the circuit with twenty wins in 1943, was dazzling in 1944 with a 27–14 record. The bespectacled fast-baller, whose trademark was the red handkerchief jammed into his back pocket, led all hurlers in ERA (2.12), innings (352), complete games (33), and shutouts (7).

Even more sensational was equally intense lefthander Hal Newhouser. The plan had been for the talented Detroit native, who cracked the majors as an eighteen-year-old high school senior in 1939, to take his oath of service on the Briggs Stadium mound, but a heart murmur kept him out of combat boots. Instead his 29 victories and 187 strikeouts led the majors and earned him the MVP award. His 2.22 ERA, 312 innings, 25 complete games, and 6 shutouts were second only to Trout. Left fielder Dick Wakefield, who the year before batted .316 and topped the loop in doubles and hits, enjoyed the best, albeit abbreviated season of his career, batting .355 after receiving a ninety-day furlough from the navy.

The pennant race wound down to the final weekend. Detroit led St. Louis by a game. The Browns had to finish the season with a four-game set against the tough Yankees, but the Tigers were closing at home against last-place Washington. It appeared Detroit had a lock on the flag. However, the Tigers split a Friday doubleheader with the Senators while the Browns swept two from New York. Detroit and St. Louis were dead even. Both teams won on Saturday, as Newhouser notched his twenty-ninth victory. This meant the results of the final Sunday of the season, October 1, would determine whether there would be a special one-game playoff in Detroit the following afternoon or an outright champion crowned.

The odds favored the Tigers. But Emil "Dutch" Leonard, upset by a pregame telephone call from a drunk prankster who offered $1,500 if the Washington pitcher eased up against the home team, did just the opposite. The Tigers had beaten Leonard seven straight times entering the contest, but on this afternoon he was virtually untouchable. He tossed a four-hit, 4–1 gem in front of 45,565 restless fans. Trucks, who lost Friday's game, once again got stuck with the loss. Afterwards the Tigers huddled around a clubhouse radio and listened to the Browns beat the Yankees for the fourth time in three days. The Browns won the only pennant in their history by a single game. "That was a crusher, a real crusher," said second baseman Eddie Mayo, who Detroit had acquired on waivers from the Athletics. "Spoiled the whole winter for me."

Hank Greenberg and manager Steve O'Neill greet several soldiers in the stands. During the war years military personnel were given free passes to see their favorite players perform.

During the war, Walter Briggs urged fans to buy defense bonds with pennants and signs.

The war in Europe ended just a couple of weeks after the Tigers' 1945 home opener. Although the Pacific war continued until early September, hundreds of thousands of discharged GIs returned to the states. Thirty-four-year-old Hank Greenberg, after a four-year absence, returned to the Tiger lineup on July 1, 1945. The Tigers were playing a doubleheader against Philadelphia that afternoon and the Briggs Stadium crowd, the largest of the season, "was cheering like mad," recalled Greenberg, who resumed his old position in left field.

"After four years in the service, the greeting was nice," said Greenberg, "but it didn't matter all that much to me. I was just glad to be back alive. I just went out there to do my job." In the eighth inning of the first game, Hammerin' Hank cracked a home run, much to the delight of the partisan crowd. "Boy, it felt good to hit that one," he admitted to Bob Murphy of the *Detroit Times.*

Murphy wrote: "Hank confessed soon after joining the Tigers while serving his country here and in faraway places on the globe that he had many times lain awake at night and dreamed that someday he would return to Briggs Stadium . . . that someday he would park one in the left field seats and make that majestic trot round the bases. . . . "

In three months Greenberg hit thirteen homers and batted in sixty runs. He hit .311, the league's highest, but fell short of qualifying for the batting championship. Nonetheless, he helped Detroit's "nine old men" wheeze to the pennant by one game over the resurgent Senators. Their .575 winning percentage was the worst of any pennant winner yet, but no one in Detroit complained. The clincher came on the road, as Greenberg hit a ninth-inning grand slam during the first game of a season-ending doubleheader against St. Louis at muddy, rain-swept Sportsman's Park. Newhouser, who led the league in victories (25), innings (313), ERA (1.81), complete games (29), strikeouts (212), and shutouts (8), became the first (and so far, only) pitcher to be named Most Valuable Player two straight seasons. (The *Sporting News* opted for Eddie Mayo, who batted .285 and led all second basemen in fielding.)

The commissioner's office announced that, because of travel restrictions, the first three World Series games would be held in Detroit and the rest in Chicago. This put an unusual amount of pressure on the Tigers to win at least two of the games played on

The original plan was for Hall of Famer Hal Newhouser to take his oath of service on the mound at Briggs Stadium, but a heart murmur kept the Tigers' pitcher home for the duration. Newhouser, the only native Detroiter to go into the Hall of Fame as a Tiger, worked at a defense plant at night and carried the club on his strong left arm during the day. Here he stands by helplessly as Chicago Cub Don Johnson scores the first run of the 1945 World Series, the result of a passed ball.

their home turf. Their first game was abysmal—they were hammered 9–0 on October 3 in front of 54,637 frozen fans. Hank Borowy, who divided his twenty-one wins during the season almost evenly between the Yankees and the Cubs, demonstrated why Chicago had dealt for him, scattering six harmless singles. In contrast, Newhouser didn't make it out of the third inning, surrendering eight hits and seven earned runs.

The next day Cubs ace Hank Wyse, who had won twenty-two games, faced off against Virgil Trucks, who had received his discharge from the navy a week earlier, before 53,636 paying customers. It was a much warmer afternoon, but it still took time for the Tigers' muscle to get limber. With Chicago ahead 1–0 in the fifth, Doc Cramer lined a two-out single over third base, scoring shortstop James "Skeeter" Webb. Greenberg then crushed a three-run homer into the left-field seats to complete the scoring in the Tigers' 4–1 triumph.

Game three was a washout, as a record turnout of 55,500 dodged pregame raindrops and then sat through another lifeless performance by the home team. Claude Passeau threw the first one-hitter in series competition since 1906, and the Cubs won, 3–0. Only York's two-out single in the second and Bob Swift's lead-off walk in the sixth marred Passeau's near-perfect outing.

The Tigers' prospects did not look good. They were down, two games to one, and had to play the balance of the series in Chicago. Worse yet, they had been shut out twice and scored in just one of twenty-six innings played at Briggs Stadium. How would they fare on unfriendly soil?

The answer came within forty-eight hours. Detroit banged out 4–1 and 8–4 victories at Wrigley Field to seize a 3–2 series edge. With their fur against the wall, the Cubs won the exciting sixth game in twelve innings, 8–7, to set up the seventh-game showdown. Facing tired Hank Borowy, the Tigers exploded for five first-inning runs and claimed their second world's championship, 9–3, behind Newhouser's second series win.

Despite one wag's prediction that the competition was so poor neither team could win, Walter Briggs saw his Tigers emerge victorious in the last game of the last wartime season.

"Neither team missed a mistake that could possibly be made," summarized Malcolm Bingay's alter ego, Iffy the Dopester, in the

Free Press. "The only reason they didn't throw to more wrong bases was that there was only three to throw at. Pop flies went for two baggers, and Texas leaguers turned into triples. But our brave Tigers outsmarted them pesky Cubs. We let 'em play dumber baseball than we did. It was one of them kind of series where I never could tell whether it was great pitching or just bad hitting. They couldn't hit, they couldn't bunt, they couldn't field, they couldn't throw, or they couldn't run bases, on either side, according to Hoyle, but it was the most thrilling series I ever did watch. Mebbe Walter Briggs is right after all. The worse the game, the better it looks—or something like that. All I can say is that the lads fought every minute of play. They gave everything they had and for that reason nobody should shoot the piano player."

Although the celebrating wasn't as intense as that of V-J Day a few weeks earlier, it was vigorous enough. Tens of thousands of people waited at Michigan Central Station to greet the hometown team when the Tigers stepped off the train that night. "People were packed solid all the way from the station to the Book-Cadillac Hotel downtown," said Newhouser. "It was just a joy to walk off that train. I was also a little scared. They were grabbing at you, trying to congratulate us—I was afraid they were going to collapse on us. It was a great reception—something I'll never forget."

The championship came just in time for Briggs, who in his old age added arthritis and a hip injury to his list of ailments. He disregarded his doctor's orders and attended the team's victory banquet, despite being restricted to a wheelchair. He remained feisty and more determined than ever to continue the club's winning ways and to showcase what many called the most beautiful ballpark in America.

As an issue of *Detroit Tiger Tales,* the club's postwar newsletter, explained to fans: "No person in the stadium rejoices more over victory, or is sadder in defeat than the sole owner of the Tigers. The policy prevailing at Briggs Stadium, which is to give patrons the finest and cleanest play field in America, the best ball club that a most generous outlay of cash can provide and entertainment devoid of ballyhoo, has won the respect of visiting newspapermen and baseball officials, from all sections of the country. It is a policy inaugurated by Walter O. Briggs when he acquired the Detroit Baseball Club and which he has insisted on being followed since that time."

Barney McCosky (left) and George Kell at Briggs Stadium on May 24, 1946, shortly after the two had been traded for each other. "When I walked into the Detroit clubhouse I felt for the first time that I was playing for a big-league team," said Kell, who had been in the fourth season of toiling for the woeful Philadelphia Athletics. The marvelous defensive third baseman became a perennial All-Star during his seven seasons with Detroit, winning a batting title in 1949 and hitting .325 overall as a Tiger.

This was more than puffery. In many observers' eyes the Tigers were one of the most valuable franchises in baseball. While Briggs had enough money to treat the Tigers as a hobby, he had enough business savvy to make them profitable as well. During Briggs' first twenty-five years of involvement with the club (1920 through 1945) the Tigers posted profits of one hundred thousand dollars or more in all but eight seasons. Only the Yankees had done better. Twice during this period the Tigers exceeded five hundred thousand dollars, an achievement that only the Chicago Cubs matched. Over the next six seasons, Briggs' last as owner, the club maintained its high level of profitability, and cleared an average of nearly a quarter-million dollars annually. During this period ticket sales continued to account for between 75 and 80 percent of the team's revenues. Although Briggs first allowed television cameras into his park in 1947, the days of owners making tens of millions of dollars through the sale of broadcast rights was still a generation away.

Locally the Tigers were viewed as one of the community's greatest resources, an unmatchable engine of civic pride. After the World Series' win over the Cubs the *Detroit News* described "a strange, almost mystical connection between Detroit's fortunes in the world of sport and the state of the local mind and morale." That year the club had led the league in attendance for the sixth time in the last twelve seasons, drawing 1,280,341 fans and just missing the Yankees' 1920 major-league mark by 9,081 customers.

In the five seasons following their wartime championship—a period of unprecedented attendance gains throughout baseball—the Tigers averaged 1.6 million customers a summer, the best among all American League clubs. "It was a very special time in Detroit," explained Hoot Evers, a taciturn Missourian who roamed the outfield at Briggs Stadium for parts of nine seasons. "The war was over and everyone was getting back on their feet and they were getting into recreation. There was kind of a general craziness about baseball in the city."

Thanks to the sale of standing-room-only tickets, the crowds that flocked to Michigan and Trumbull were some of the largest on record. On four occasions in 1946 the team drew crowds of more than 56,000, including a record 57,235 on August 18 to watch a twin bill against the St. Louis Browns. Newhouser silenced those who criticized him as a wartime pitcher by winning twenty-six games against returning big leaguers in 1946, the third straight year he topped the majors in victories. His 1.94 ERA also was the best in the game. That summer Greenberg led the loop with 44 homers and 127 RBIs, and then was unceremoniously sold to Pittsburgh by the mercurial Briggs for reasons that were never fully explained. "I couldn't believe it," said Greenberg years later. "Detroit was my team. I identified 100 percent with the Tigers." Greenberg, soured by Briggs' treatment of him, enjoyed a measure of revenge. The Pirates made him the game's first one-hundred-thousand-dollar player. In 1947 attendance jumped by three hundred thousand in Pittsburgh and dropped by the same number at Michigan and Trumbull.

Despite the fan revolt over the loss of one of the city's most popular players, that year a new mark was set when 58,369 people piled into the park on Sunday, July 20 to watch the Tigers whip the Yankees twice. The Tigers prevailed in the opener, 4–1, and then took the second game, 12–11, in eleven innings. There were so many fans the club finally put some behind ropes in the outfield, a sight that hadn't been seen since the days of Navin Field. Others crowded into the wings of the third-story press box. It remains the largest crowd ever to watch a baseball game at Michigan and Trumbull.*

The Yankees always were a great draw in Detroit. Players admitted to being pumped up by the huge crowds squeezed into the dark green stands. One game stands out in the memories of every player and fan who was at Briggs Stadium on June 23, 1950. That warm summer evening, in a showdown for first place, the Tigers beat New York, 10–9, on Hoot Evers' dramatic inside-the-park home run in the bottom of the ninth inning.

* Of the Tigers' twenty largest home crowds in history, all but one occurred between 1940 and 1950. Was fan interest really that much greater in 1946–48, when the team averaged less than 1.6 million each season but still drew ten of its top dozen single-date crowds, than in the 1980s, when Tiger mania was at its crest and two-million gates became the norm? No, but changes in the team's seating policy, a series of park renovations, and the physical ramifications of postwar prosperity account for the disappearance of the huge crowds that were commonplace a half-century ago.

"One of the biggest things we did was stop selling standing-room," said longtime general manager Jim Campbell. Crowds often included up to four thousand standing-room-only patrons, who jammed the aisles and braved sore feet and several hours of jostling to catch a glimpse of the action. Occasionally the third deck was opened to accommodate overflow crowds. In the early sixties the Tigers dropped the discounted SRO tickets. "To the new breed of fan," said Campbell, "standing-room doesn't mean a damn thing." About this time the Tigers installed larger boxes, further reducing capacity. Then in 1978 all of the old green wooden chairs were ripped out and replaced with blue-and-orange plastic seats. Reacting to medical studies that showed the average American's behind had increased since the Second World War, the new seats were built several inches wider. This gave the individual fan a chance to breathe easy, but shrunk overall ballpark capacity by another fifteen hundred.

The broad beams also affected the number of people who could be seated comfortably in the bleachers, accounting for another thousand or so lost admissions. Today Tiger Stadium officially seats 52,416, guaranteeing that the record turnouts of the immediate postwar years will never be achieved, much less broken.

"I think there were eleven home runs hit that night, which was a record at the time," recalled third baseman George Kell, who'd been acquired from the Athletics for Barney McCosky midway through the 1946 season. "The Yankees hit six of those, I believe. It was unbelievable the way they were flying out. Even Dizzy Trout got into the act and hit a grand-slam. We'd fought back from about a seven-run deficit, but then New York scored a couple runs and had a one-run lead going into the bottom of the ninth."

The Tigers got a man on against Joe Page, "who was always tough," continued Kell. "He had that good fast ball. Evers got hold of one and drove it over DiMaggio's head in center field. It just bounced around out there, and by the time Rizzuto got the relay he'd circled the bases for an inside-the-park home run. There were probably fifty thousand people in Briggs Stadium that night, and the place was just going crazy."

In the stands that night were a couple of young fans. Fourteen-year-old Basil "Mickey" Briggs, nicknamed after Micky Cochrane, was the owner's grandson. His equally baseball-mad friend, Elliott Trumbull, occasionally let it slip that he was related to the old Revolutionary War poet for whom Trumbull Avenue had been named. (He wasn't.) The most serious name dropping they have done in the forty plus years since that wild night is of heroes like Hoot Evers, Vic Wertz, and Dizzy Trout.

"That game said it all," gushed Trumbull, today a Detroit-area public-relations executive. "It just symbolized what Mickey and I have always considered the best of times: a full ballpark yelling 'Ho-ooot! Ho-ooot!' for Hoot Evers, a great ball game in the middle of a pennant race, and a city where you could still walk around with no worries. The factories were working overtime, and you did your shopping at Hudson's downtown. You were proud to tell someone that you were from Detroit." That improbable evening still has such a hold on these two fans that every year they reunite on the home date nearest its anniversary to talk about the night it rained home runs.

In addition to the hard-hitting Evers and Kell (who edged Ted Williams for the 1949 batting title), the stars of the immediate post-war years included pitchers Fred Hutchinson and Virgil Trucks, shortstop Johnny Lipon, and outfielders Vic Wertz and Johnny Groth. Newhouser remained a force. In 1948 he won twenty-one games to once again lead the league. With this nucleus the team finished second three times in five years: to the Red Sox in 1946 and to the Yankees in 1947 and 1950.

Although Briggs was a staunch traditionalist, during this period he made one major concession to the changing times. In 1948, thirteen years after Cincinnati's Crosley Field hosted the first night game in the majors, he finally installed lights at Briggs Stadium. Ever the iconoclast, Briggs resisted the innovation until only the Tigers and Cubs played their entire home schedule in the daylight. But his son, Walter "Spike" Briggs Jr., campaigned for the change not long after joining the front office in 1936. According to some reports, the elder Briggs was ready to install lights during the 1942 season, but the attack on Pearl Harbor scrubbed the plan. Briggs diverted the steel he had ordered to the war effort, secretly pleased that the game would continue to be played in natural, not artificial, light. "Baseball belongs to the sun and the sun to baseball," he continued to argue after the war. "It's artificial without the sun. The people are entitled to see it played as it should be."

When he finally changed his mind, Briggs' only stipulation was that the lighting system be the finest available. On the night of May 10, 1948, the system was tested for the benefit of the press. Sitting in his wheelchair Briggs threw the switch to illuminate the park. The eight steel towers that rose 150 feet in the sky contained 1,458 giant incandescent bulbs—bright enough to allow grounds keeper Neil Conway to read a newspaper at second base.

Six weeks later, on June 15, fans began arriving at Briggs Stadium at 6:00 p.m. for the Tigers' inaugural night game. "There was a lot of excitement before the game," said George Kell. "Almost like a carnival. The funny thing is, I didn't realize the size of the crowd at first. In fact, I got a call from the front gate that some friends of mine from Arkansas were in town and wanted to watch the game. I told them they shouldn't have a problem getting seats, but they were told that the game was sold out. I went out on the field and looked around, and when I saw the size of the crowd, I got a chill. Just packed in there."

Unfortunately, nobody knew exactly when to turn on the lights and start the game. The chilly Tuesday evening forced the Detroit and Philadelphia players to huddle in their dugouts. Many in the crowd of 54,480 drank copious amounts of hot coffee. Everyone

On June 15, 1948, the Tigers inaugurated night baseball at Michigan and Trumbull with a 4–1 win over Philadelphia. The event was front page news for the city's three newspapers and inspired the *Free Press* to playfully put its own name in lights.

waited for the sky to fade to black so the lights could take full effect.

When the lights finally were flipped on at 9:29 p.m., a brief silence fell over the assemblage, followed by a collective Oooohh! Thanks to three outstanding fielding plays by Kell and Newhouser's two-hitter, the Tigers trimmed the Athletics, 4–1. Night baseball was off to a smashing start in the Motor City. "For some reason I can't explain, all the action looks faster under the lights," marveled Lyall Smith of the *Free Press*. "Runners appear to rip down the base lines and every ball that starts out from the bat seems headed for the stands."

The introduction of nighttime games substantially boosted the gate, with fourteen dates in 1948 averaging about 45,000 fans, including 56,586 for an August 9 contest with Cleveland. Attendance records were set three straight summers: 1,700,000 in 1948, 1,800,000 in 1949, and 1,951,474 in 1950, the last a figure that stood for nearly twenty years. The club regarded night games as special events, and restricted their number to fourteen each year until 1957, when seven were added to the schedule. Three more were added in 1960. Although the novelty of playing under the lights soon wore off, its convenience continued to make the games attractive. Evening crowds in Detroit averaged roughly 30,000 through the end of the decade, well above the league average.

The postwar era brought big changes to the broadcast booth at Briggs Stadium, both in terms of personnel and medium. Harry Heilmann, who had licked his problem with alcohol, battled crippling bouts of arthritis, and took elocution lessons to improve his speech, but found he couldn't beat cancer. The 1950 season was his last in the radio booth. He died the following July, on the eve of the All-Star Game in Detroit. Ty Tyson came out of retirement to pinch-hit for his longtime rival and friend, finally quitting for keeps after the 1952 campaign. But not before he had introduced the most pervasive, intrusive, influential, and controversial form of electronic communication to Tiger fans—television.

Radio technology begat television, whose development had been temporarily halted by the Second World War. Hundreds of thousands of people first witnessed video wedded to audio at the 1939

When your grandfather owns the Tigers you can use his ballpark as a playground. Mickey Briggs (right) and his pal, Elliott Trumbull, limber up their young arms sometime around 1950.

World's Fair in New York. Only a handful saw the first baseball game broadcast on August 26, 1939 between Cincinnati and Brooklyn at Ebbets Field. "Reception was fuzzy," *Life* magazine wrote of that historic telecast, "but no fuzziness can hide what it means to American sports. Within ten years, an audience of ten million sitting at home will see the World Series . . . ." *Life* wasn't far off the mark.

Hoot Evers is mobbed by teammates after his game-winning blast on "the night it rained home runs" at Briggs Stadium, June 23, 1950.

The 1947 World Series, the first to be televised and the new medium's first mass audience, attracted 3.9 million viewers—3.5 million of them in bars, where early sets were installed to test their popularity. Afterwards manufacturers rushed to put a set in every living room. The percentage of American TV households jumped from less than 1 percent to 50 percent in six years. Today nearly 99 percent of all U. S. homes have at least one television set.

The Tigers' first televised game was June 3, 1947, a sunny Tuesday afternoon affair at Briggs Stadium which the New York Yankees won, 3–0, behind Spec Shea's five-hitter. With only an estimated two thousand television sets in the Detroit area, the crowd of 17,114 watching at the stadium easily outnumbered viewers. Many of the sets were strategically placed inside bars and hotel lobbies. In one downtown saloon, patrons strained to make out the lilliputian figures on the eight-by-six-inch screen. Finally the proprietor brought out a set of field glasses. "They served to enlarge and clarify the picture on the small screen," reported Paul Chandler of the

Detroit News, "although the effect of patrons staring through binoculars at a wall 20 feet away may have been amusing to a stranger."

Tyson handled the first telecast. Along with a pair of cameramen and observer Paul Williams, they sat in the front portion of the second deck, directly behind home plate. They were protected from foul balls by a giant plexiglass screen. Unlike radio broadcasts, which required just an announcer and an engineer, early telecasts required a crew of twelve.

From the beginning writers complained about the opportunities for "mugging" that television suddenly provided. One local critic wrote in 1949:

> With television, naturally, it's going to be even worse than on the radio. For here, the managers and coaches not only can continue to enjoy the oral build-up as "master minds" but also can indulge their desire to "ham" it by doing some mugging for the camera. They can do their heavy thinking right in front of the lens. Already it has been necessary to caution some ball players against clowning for the television broadcast. Unless this tendency is curbed, we soon won't have athletes on the ball field, but actors. We may even expect them to insist on a professional makeup man to pretty them up before the game, with false eyelashes, marcelled hair, etc. In the near future, we may read that Right-Fielder Glutz lost Zilch's fly in the camera, instead of in the sun.

In 1948, the Tigers' first full season on television, WWJ aired twenty-six games. "These were primarily home telecasts," recalled WWJ veteran Fran Harris, "since there was still trouble hooking up audio and visual on remotes." By then there were nearly nine thousand television sets in the metropolitan area, including more than seven thousand in homes. Technology rapidly improved and TV sales boomed, though programming was fairly primitive. "Sports helped fill a lot of programming," said Harris, "though in the early years owners just couldn't understand that television would help rather than hurt attendance. They were afraid TV would clear out the bleachers and no one would come to the games."

The bleachers were cleared—but in places far from Detroit. During the Tigers' first three full seasons of television coverage (1948 through 1950), the team set new attendance marks each year, even as the number of televised home games reached thirty-five per season by 1950. However, the Tigers were careful not to air Sunday, holiday, or evening games, their most lucrative dates.*

Sports announcers continued to enjoy a status and following of their own. Van Patrick and Dizzy Trout became the first familiar local television announcers inside Detroit-area living rooms.

Long before most of the world heard of Howard Cosell, there was Patrick, a Texan who came to Briggs Stadium's broadcast booth via Buffalo and Cleveland. Loud, brash, and armed with an ego too large for any one ballpark to contain, the "Ol' Announcer" was America's busiest sportscaster, typically chalking up 150,000 miles on airplanes each year. It was common for him to cover three or four major sporting events on a weekend, including auto races, golf tournaments, and basketball games. Patrick, who had an interest in four radio stations and owned a house overlooking a Dearborn golf course, was the Tigers' play-by-play man from 1952 to 1959 and broadcast the Detroit Lions on radio or TV every week from 1950 to 1973. He also had daily radio and television shows in Detroit and covered Notre Dame football. He was the hardest working man in sportscasting, and until Cosell came along, one of the most vainglorious as well.

Trout, on the other hand, always gave the impression that he had just fallen off the back of a turnip truck. His malapropisms and fractured grammar reminded viewers of Dizzy Dean, who during this same period, became a national treasure through his colorful *Game of the Week* broadcasts. Patrick and Trout were a contentious pair, as Art Hill recalled in his delightful memoir, *I Don't Care If I Never Come Back.*

---

* Conversely, broadcasting major-league games helped kill hundreds of minor-league teams, whose sole source of revenue was the turnstile. Fans in these towns, given the choice between driving several miles to pay to watch the local Class B team or viewing for the first time big leaguers perform in the comfort of their living rooms, overwhelmingly opted to stay home. The results were catastrophic. In 1948 the Tigers had sixteen farm clubs, an all-time high. By 1964, the number of minor league affiliates had dwindled to five. The minors' collapse helped reinforce major league baseball's deep-seated fear of the consequences of "giving the game away." The immensely popular *Game of the Week* began telecasting on ABC in 1953, but this staple of Saturday afternoons in every town from Amarillo to Zeeland actually was banned in Detroit and all other major-league cities until 1965.

[Trout] had lived in Detroit for at least twenty years and played for the Tigers for fourteen, but he could pronounce neither the name of the city nor that of the team. He called them the "DEE-troit Taggers." He delighted me every time he referred to the player list as the "rooster." . . .

During breaks in the game, Trout used to entertain us with little anecdotes from baseball's past: odd incidents, unusual records and the like. We were supposed to believe he was ad-libbing these from his vast store of baseball lore. In fact, they were written for him, and he was usually reading them for the first time. This was evident because they contained modestly erudite words, not in Diz's normal vocabulary, which he often mispronounced and occasionally couldn't say at all. Sometimes, after taking two or three shots at a word, he would just skip it and go on. More than once, however, faced with a tough multi-syllable, he would simply abandon the whole project and, after a suitable pause, start talking about something else. So after an intriguing buildup we were left with no punch line because Diz had run into a word like "unpremeditated." ("One of the most unusual double plays ever made," he might say, "happened in a 1927 game between Beaumont and San Antonio in the Texas League. No fewer than six players, including all three outfielders, handled the ball on the play, which was completely unprem . . . unperdimate . . . unpredeminate . . ." Pause. "Well, the Tigers are coming to bat in the bottom of the fifth . . .")

Van Patrick used to get openly irritated at Diz Trout's outbursts, especially his unblushingly partisan comments about the opposing team or the umpiring. Patrick would huffily remind him that his conduct was unprofessional. It surely was, but it was also unpretentious and sincere and the perfect antidote to Patrick's consummate pomposity.

Trout was replaced by former New York Giants great Mel Ott in 1956. After Ott was killed in an auto accident after the 1958 season, George Kell joined Patrick in the booth. The former third sacker worked just one season with Patrick before a switch in beer sponsors forced him to find another partner. In 1960, after many years of being sponsored by Goebel Brewery, the Tigers sold the rights to their broadcasts to Stroh's. Patrick, so closely identified with Goebel's, was out. A crew-cut Southern gentleman with horn-rimmed glasses, Ernie Harwell, was in.

Nineteen fifty-one was a watershed year. Detroit, the oldest city between the Appalachians and the Rockies, celebrated its 250th anniversary. Thousands helped light a giant four-story birthday cake in Grand Circus Park. Urban renewal was the buzz word, as new high-speed expressways and the Civic Center were being built as quickly as old buildings and crumbling neighborhoods could be torn down. City fathers were able to convince Philadelphia to surrender that year's All-Star Game, which was held July 10 before 52,075 at Briggs Stadium. Unfortunately, an ailing Harry Heilmann died the night before the midsummer classic, which the Nationals won, 8–3, despite home runs by the Tigers' Hoot Evers and George Kell.

The year also marked the golden anniversaries of the Tigers and the American League, as well as the diamond anniversary of the National League. The country had changed dramatically in the last fifty years, and baseball was slowly following suit. In 1901 two out of every three people lived in the northeastern quadrant of the country, but now population shifts were moving the center of the country westward. The two major leagues, after having not experienced a franchise move in a half-century, saw five teams relocate between 1953 and 1958, including the California-bound Dodgers and Giants. With air travel supplanting trains (the Tigers took their first flight in 1957), road trips to distant cities consumed less time and dollars. An expansion of the schedule and the number of teams appeared inevitable. Talk circulated of locating a National League team in Detroit to take advantage of the metropolitan area's fanatical support of baseball.

At the same time that the game's geographical map was changing, so was its racial composition. After spending four long years of war to "save the world for democracy," the United States could no longer be so hypocritical in the abominable treatment of its own black citizens. When Brooklyn fielded Jackie Robinson in 1947, the

Even as his health declined, Walter Briggs regularly occupied his specially designed box seat. "No person in the stadium rejoices more over victory," observed the club's newsletter, "or is sadder in defeat than the sole owner of the Tigers." Briggs took a good deal of pride in the condition of his park, employing a force of more than four hundred stadium employees and timing his ground crew during rain delays.

The Tigers began television broadcasts of selected home games in 1947 with Ty Tyson calling the play-by-play from his second-deck perch directly behind the plate. Here a baseball is being thrown against a 91-by-79-inch sheet of plexiglass to test its ability to protect announcer and cameramen from foul balls.

majors' longstanding color barrier was broken. It served as a symbolic step for the civil rights movement, which was gathering steam in postwar America.

By the end of his first year as a Dodger, Robinson was called "Ty Cobb in Technicolor," a characterization that must have caused the real Georgia Peach and the Tigers' front office staff to flinch. The occasional black major leaguer began to appear at Michigan and

The Tigers' fortunes declined rapidly after 1950, although games against the Yankees continued to be a big draw. On this occasion the Briggs Stadium crowd joins Joe DiMaggio (lower right corner), Detroit first baseman Don Kolloway, and the jubilant Yankees bench in watching a John Mize home run sail into the seats.

Trumbull, but he was always wearing a visitor's uniform. Dizzy Trout, Bob Cain, and other bigoted pitchers relished dusting off pioneers like Cleveland's Larry Doby when they came to the plate. Once during the 1951 season, several Tigers pointed to the large number of black fans cheering for Doby in Briggs Stadium's bleachers and jokingly admonished Trout that his close barbering would start a race riot.

Walter Briggs, who'd already seen one during his lifetime, didn't live to see a second. On January 17, 1952, he died at his winter home in Miami, six weeks short of his seventy-fifth birthday. His passing produced a spate of glowing, affectionate obituaries. Tigers manager Red Rolfe, who would be fired midway through that summer's campaign, called Briggs "the last major league owner with the viewpoint of the fans."

The once-proud Tigers fell into disarray after Briggs' death. Rot had been seeping into the organizations for some time, but it had gone largely undetected. The disappointing fifth-place finish in 1951 was attributed by many to injuries. Most assumed the club would bounce back into contention. But even the apologists were shocked by the club's rapid on-field decline and front-office tumult. During the next nine years the Tigers employed seven different managers, five

Virgil "Fire" Trucks had a 5–19 record in 1952, the year the Tigers lost 104 games and finished in last place for the first time in their history. However, two of Trucks' victories were no-hitters, including a 1–0 gem on May 15 against Washington. Vic Wertz won the game with a ninth-inning home run, but only 2,215 were on hand that afternoon at Briggs Stadium to witness the dramatics. Most Detroiters were downtown watching a parade for the visiting General Douglas MacArthur.

During the 1950s, Harvey Kuenn cranked out singles and doubles in as machinelike a fashion as the city's auto plants.

general managers, and more ballplayers than at any time before or since. In 1952 alone, four deals with the lowly Browns and another with the Red Sox saw thirty-three players change clubs. The trades didn't help: that summer the Tigers lost their unique status as the only American League team never to finish last, falling into the basement with a 50–104 record. They moved up a couple of notches in 1953, then spent the rest of the decade in the middle of the pack. The mediocrity grew even more pronounced with the success of the Detroit Lions and Detroit Red Wings, franchises that enjoyed

Spike Briggs inside his office at Briggs Stadium.

their greatest successes between 1950 and 1957. During that time the Lions won three National Football League championships and the Wings took four Stanley Cups.

The biggest question mark concerned ownership, which remained muddled more than four years after Briggs' passing. Upon his death all of Briggs's holdings passed into trust, including the automobile division, which was sold to Chrysler in 1953. After a probate court ruled the Tigers were not a prudent investment, estate trustees ordered the club sold. Spike Briggs, who succeeded his father as Tigers president, tried to scrape together enough money to buy the team from the estate. The withdrawal of financial support from Henry Ford II, the young head of his grandfather's car company and an old drinking buddy, doomed his first attempt to form a syndicate. A group of interested buyers that included Briggs and Tigers executives Charlie Gehringer and Harry Sisson finally was formed and bid $3.5 million for the team in late 1955. Much to Spike's dismay, his four sisters, who frowned on his heavy boozing, refused to sell. In 1956 trustees solicited open bids.

Nearly thirty investors expressed interest in buying the Tigers, including the Detroit Lions. Mayor Albert Cobo created headlines when he suggested the city buy Briggs Stadium (which a board of assessors valued at slightly more than $2 million), but the city council, which included former Tigers shortstop Billy Rogell, negated that idea.

Ultimately, the major bidders sifted down to two syndicates. One was headed by Bill Veeck, the former maverick owner of the Cleveland Indians and St. Louis Browns. The other was comprised of eleven investors headed by Fred A. Knorr, owner of radio station WKMH, which in 1952 replaced WXYZ as the Tigers' flagship station. Knorr's most influential partner was Kalamazoo radio-television magnate John Fetzer, who was afraid his outstate stations would lose the rights to the Tigers' games once the club was sold.

Veeck, a true blue-collar hero who had lost a leg in the war, enjoyed the kind of popularity among working-class fans that Walter Briggs always liked to believe he had. Veeck's promotional gimmicks in Cleveland and St. Louis had endeared him to the populace, created record-level attendance, and injected some much-needed life into the ballpark. Black fans sang his praises because he was bold enough to field the American League's first black players. But he was persona non grata to Detroit's conservative baseball fraternity, which remembered the midget, Eddie Gaedel, that he had sent up to the plate in a 1951 game against the Tigers at Sportsman's Park. The thought of fireworks and large numbers of black fans suddenly appearing at staid Briggs Stadium also was discomfiting.

Veeck's personal style was an affront to buttoned-down traditionalists like Harry Salsinger. In a scathing piece published in the *Detroit News*, the aging but still-influential dean of local baseball writers attacked Veeck as a "medicine man" partial to open-throated sport shirts—surely a sign of a subversive looking to destroy the national pastime with his bag of carnival tricks.

During the early summer of 1956, as the Tigers stumbled toward a fifth-place finish despite the presence of four .300 hitters and a pair of twenty-game winners, eight potential buyers prepared bids. The Knorr syndicate was prepared to offer $4.5 million, but

The city's postwar freeway system carved up neighborhoods and helped expedite Detroiters' move to the suburbs. For opening day of the 1956 season, however, Tiger stars Harvey Kuenn and Frank Lary were transported along surface streets to the park.

then Fetzer caught wind of Veeck's comments as the old showman flapped his gums at one of his innumerable press conferences. Veeck told reporters that he had just been extended a $2.5-million line of credit from the National Bank of Detroit. Fetzer, who sat on the boards of several lending institutions, realized that in order to secure the loan Veeck must have had at least an equal amount of equity. Veeck's offer was probably going to be in the area of at least $5 million.

Fetzer quickly convened his group of investors and convinced them to up their ante to $5.5 million. The ground rules governing the competitive bidding stipulated that all offers were due by midnight, July 2. Fetzer's hunch paid off. When the sealed bids were opened the next day at a board meeting of the Detroit Baseball Company, Knorr's offer was highest. Veeck, whose $5.3-million bid

Spikes Briggs tries to absorb the news that John McHale has been named to replace him as the Tigers' general manager. Briggs' firing in April 1957 ended his family's active involvement with the Tigers. This shot by *Detroit Times* photographer Bernard Gold created considerable sympathy for Briggs, who appears to be crying over the news. According to sports editor Edgar Hayes (seated next to Briggs), in reality the deposed general manager was trying to rub a cinder out of his eye.

came in second, always maintained that he had been sandbagged by bank officials friendly to Briggs. "You know," he said, "every once in a while a guy will be taken by a bunch of river boat gamblers."

The sale, which involved cash, a $2-million loan from NBD (secured by a mortgage on Briggs Stadium) and a five-year, nine-hundred-thousand-dollar personal note with the Briggs family, was finalized on October 1, 1956. Knorr was named president, while Briggs was made general manager and executive vice-president.

In many ways Spike Briggs was a chip off the old block. He enjoyed pampering his players and basking in the limelight. He was stubborn or impulsive in his business decisions, depending on how much he'd had to drink, but most people genuinely liked him. Fetzer, who was now chairman of the board, was a quiet, disciplined man accustomed to conducting his affairs behind closed doors. It was inevitable the two would clash. Realizing this, Briggs kept an undated letter of resignation inside his desk.

In 1958 John Fetzer, the club's board chairman, was in the process of buying out his co-investors. He would soon become sole owner of the team.

The letter was used when Briggs, having fired Bucky Harris after five years as manager, ignored Fetzer's suggestion for a replacement. Fetzer wanted Al Lopez; Briggs hired farm system director Jack Tighe. Fetzer, already put off by Briggs' socializing with the players, called a meeting of the board, where it was agreed that Briggs would be given the heave-ho. Knorr, Briggs' friend, resigned rather than do the dirty work. On April 26, 1957, Fetzer and Knorr's successor, business associate Harvey Hansen, met with Briggs to pressure him to resign. It was a cruel blow. Briggs' entire life had been wrapped up in the club. Like his father, he loved the team and the attention that he derived from it. John McHale, a former Tigers first baseman who'd played in the first Goodfellows football game at Briggs Stadium two decades earlier, took over as general manager. Meanwhile, the dailies continued to repeat that Spike Briggs' dismissal "marked the end of an era."

Walter O. Briggs strove to make his stadium a refuge for the working man. That philosophy remained in place at the start of the

Briggs Stadium during the 1950s.

1957 season even as the new owners hiked the price of a box seat from $2.50 to $3.00 and from $1.75 to $2.00 for a reserved seat. General admission cost $1.25 and bleacher seats 75¢. For their money Detroit fans hoped to see players earning theirs. In Harvey Kuenn, Al Kaline, Jim Bunning, and Frank Lary, at least, they got full value for their ticket.

Kuenn was signed off the campus of the University of Wisconsin in 1952 for a fifty-two-thousand-dollar bonus and immediately became the Tigers' starting shortstop and lead-off batter. He hit .308 with a league-best 209 hits in 1953 and was the first Tiger named Rookie of the Year. Kuenn, who moved to center field in 1958, was a singles and doubles hitter who was tough to strike out. He hit at a .314 clip during his eight years in Detroit, leading the league in base hits four times, in doubles three times, and winning the batting championship in 1959.

Kaline joined the team in 1953, a scared, skinny eighteen-year-old off the Baltimore sandlots without an inning of minor-league experience. He'd grown up across the street from a factory where pick-up games were a regular lunch-hour feature. "They were always a man or two short," he said, "and I'd be standing under the trees to see if they were. They'd say, 'Come on, Al, play.'"

Kaline hit just .276 with four home runs in 1954, his first full season in right field, but the following year he batted .340 to become, at twenty years of age, the youngest batting champion since Ty Cobb in 1907. It was just the beginning of a brilliant twenty-two-year career in Detroit that culminated in his selection to the Hall of Fame during his first year of eligibility.

The "K-K Kids," as the alliterative-crazy sports publications of the era invariably called them, were about as different as any two teammates could be. Kaline was initially intimidated by his big-league surroundings, and preferred to clam up whenever a reporter approached. Kuenn was full of simple good cheer, called everyone "Slug" and never appeared rattled. Kaline, a Methodist whose father worked in a broomstick factory, didn't smoke or drink. Kuenn kept a six-inch chaw of tobacco jammed into the upper recesses of his left jaw and drank at a championship level. But when the two donned their uniforms and trotted onto the manicured lawn of Briggs Stadium, they were almost indistinguishable in their all-out play and conveyor-like production of hits, runs, and thrills.

The pitching staff featured a pair of future politicians. Jim Bunning, a lanky righthander from Kentucky, led the loop with twenty wins in 1957 and 201 strikeouts in 1959 and 1960. The future U. S. senator won 118 games for the Tigers between 1955 and 1963, including a no-hitter against the Red Sox.

Frank Lary hailed from Tuscaloosa, Alabama, where he later served a term on the Tuscaloosa County Board of Revenue. The slightly built righthander specialized in beating the Yankees, in one two-year stretch winning thirteen of fourteen decisions against them. Nicknamed "Taters" and "Mule," he was more of a work-horse, three times leading the American League in innings and complete games.

"The thing I remember most about baseball and Detroit was the fans," said Lary, whose twenty-one wins in 1956 topped the league. "They were the best fans I ever played under. Me, being from the south, may have helped. There were a lot of southern people working in those plants up there then. I felt like I was playing at home with the Tigers. I really enjoyed the fans."

During this period of outstanding individual performances the team became fascinatingly average, finishing 78–76 in 1957, 77–77 in 1958, and 76–78 in 1959. Although the Tigers continued to draw slightly better than the league average, hovering in the one-million range during the decade, ticket sales fell short of the level established during the postwar years. This was particularly true of day games, where crowds shrank in half in just ten years. By 1956, an average of only 11,088 fans chose to watch a game at Briggs Stadium in the sunlight, about one-third the size of the typical evening crowd.

This was a reflection of the great changes occurring in postwar America. There was a greater selection of leisure activities available, including television. The number of television sets in use leaped from less than 4 million in 1950 to nearly 46 million in 1960. Any of a growing number of personal recreational activities—golf, bowling, tennis, boating, camping—began to replace a day at the ballpark, especially now that it was no longer so close to home.

The rush to open spaces north and west of the city had actually started in the 1920s, but was slowed for nearly two decades by the Depression and war. Although urban renewal and the striking down of illegal housing covenants allowed blacks to break out of their east side ghetto and enter into traditionally white neighborhoods after the war, it was prosperity, not racism, that initially fueled white Detroiters' flight to suburbia. Unlike such cities as Boston, Washington, and New York, where workers lived in high-rise flats and tenement buildings, Detroit was a city of single-family homes. Because raw land is cheaper to develop and there were no natural barriers to impede growth, suburban sprawl was inevitable as Detroit households—most headed by someone drawing union wages from the flourishing auto industry—continued their quest for bigger houses with attached garages and spacious backyards. Subdivisions, factories, schools, and bowling alleys sprang up in the meadows and cornfields surrounding the city. Meanwhile, Detroit's population peaked at about two million in the early 1950s, then began a long, slow slide.

This migration was viewed as progress. However, the larger picture wasn't apparent at the time. In 1954 the J. L. Hudson Company opened Northland, the country's first suburban mall, on 161 acres of land in Southfield. Not coincidentally, that year the company's flagship store—a downtown fixture since Ty Cobb's days—posted its first annual loss. The Woodward Avenue store never again finished in the black and finally closed in 1983, another victim of Detroit's changing social and economic climate.

Freeways sliced and diced nineteenth-century neighborhoods. In July 1951 a two-mile section of the Edsel Ford Expressway running from the western city limits east to Livernois opened to traffic. The *Detroit News*, which called it the "most modern and most costly highway in the world," determined that commuters saved three minutes and missed eight traffic lights by not traveling on adjacent Michigan Avenue. Soon the Lodge and Fisher freeways fed the ever-widening web of interstate highways.

The freeway system proved a mixed bag for the Tigers and Briggs Stadium. It provided outstate fans with expeditious access to Michigan and Trumbull and helped transform the Tigers into a truly regional team. But the drawbacks were congestion and, paradoxically, a shrinking fan base in the immediate area.

For all his prescience when planning Navin Field, Frank Navin never imagined the mind-bending level of future traffic. When the last streetcar line shut down in 1955, more people than ever came to the park in automobiles. In an attempt to have fans avoid rush-hour traffic, afternoon game starting times were moved up until they finally reached 1:30 p.m. in 1958, a two-hour difference since the war. The club could do nothing about the lack of adequate parking, however. Throughout its history the club never operated a parking lot (except for players and stadium employees), leaving motorists to decide between a variety of privately owned lots in the neighborhood. Even then, many were nothing more than an enterprising neighbor's front lawn several blocks from the park.

The new high-speed roads further isolated the stadium from downtown and the surrounding neighborhoods, which continued to deteriorate as people and businesses moved away. For however many paying customers the Tigers may have gained because of the freeways, they likely lost a corresponding number from the immediate area.

While the 1950s were a decade of transition outside Briggs Stadium, changes also occurred inside its four gray walls. In 1953 the bullpens were relocated from center field to their familiar spots in the outfield corners. This was done to save time, as the trend toward heavy substitution, especially of pitchers, increased the average length of a game from less than two hours before the war to about two hours and thirty minutes. The following year a new rule prohibited players from leaving their gloves on the field when they went in to bat. The small thrill of watching Vic Wertz or Johnny Lipon nonchalantly flip his glove onto the grass after the last out of an inning, to be picked up again when he jogged back onto the field to take his position, was gone.

So, too, was the "keyhole," the dirt path connecting the mound to the batter's box. Memories are fuzzy on exactly when this quaint carryover from the game's cricket origins (the "alley" connected the two bases, or wickets, and was also where the bowler delivered the ball to the batsman) was finally filled in with grass at Briggs Stadium, but it appears to have been about 1955. The keyhole was symbolic, not functional, but its passing was just one more sign that the times were changing inside America's ballparks.

The most obvious and ongoing change was in the racial composition of the players. By the mid-1950s about one hundred black and Latin players were in the big leagues. The number increased every season, except in Detroit, where the growing black population (it would approach a half-million by the end of the decade) continued to be represented by a lily-white team.

Social experimentation never interested Walter Briggs. To the end of his days he was convinced that the Tigers could compete with an all-white lineup. As proof, he pointed to the Yankees, at once the most successful and most transparently racist organization in the majors, who won five straight World Series between 1949 and 1953, despite the absence of a single black on the roster. It wasn't until August 27, 1953—nineteen months after Briggs' death—that the Detroit organization finally signed a black prospect, Claude Agee, to a minor-league contract. It was the last club in the majors to do so. Five years later, on June 6, 1958, the Tigers became the second-to-

The "Sunday Punch," Charlie Maxwell, with several young admirers at Briggs Stadium.

last big-league club to desegregate. Only the Red Sox waited longer.

That spring the Tigers passed over a black prospect named Maury Wills in favor of starting Coot Veal at shortstop. Wills, the man who just four years later shattered Ty Cobb's single-season stolen-base record, was lost on waivers to the Dodgers' Spokane farm team.

Manager Jimmy Dykes rushes out to congratulate Frank Lary after the Tigers' Yankee-killer defeated New York in the first game of a Sunday doubleheader on May 3, 1959. Accompanying Lary off the field are catcher Lou Berberet and second baseman Frank Bolling.

Instead the Tigers picked Ozzie Virgil to be their first black player. In terms of talent, temperament, or impact, the twenty-five-year-old third baseman was no Jackie Robinson (or Coot Veal, for that matter) and not even African American (he was born in the Dominican Republic). But the front office evidently thought he pos-

sessed the proper amount of melanin to stifle the increasingly stri-
dent demands for integration from a local coalition of preachers,
union representatives, and other civil rights activists called the
Briggs Stadium Boycott Committee. (Among its officers was
schoolteacher Nettie Stearnes, the wife of former Negro-league
great Turkey Stearnes).

Tigers president Harvey Hansen, pointing out that a dozen blacks
were being developed in the farm system, initially responded to
threats of a boycott by declaring the club would not be pressured into
hastily fielding an unqualified black. "We will not use Negroes as a
gate attraction," he said, shortly before the decision was made to call
up Virgil from the Charleston farm team. During his first home start,
Virgil had five hits in five at-bats against Washington. The crowd
swelled to about twice its normal size with curious blacks, most of
whom sat in their traditional spot in the lower-deck bleachers.

Despite Virgil's dramatic Detroit debut, he was never embraced
by white fans, who pointed to his meager batting average (.228 in
three Tiger seasons), or by black patrons, who accepted his explanation to the press that he was "not a Negro."

"Nobody thought Virgil was black," said Willie Horton, who was.
At the time the future Tigers star, who startled scouts by rattling the
outfield seats at Michigan and Trumbull while still in high school, lived
in one of the city's housing projects. To Horton and other blacks, it
wasn't until the following summer, when the Tigers acquired the fad-
ing Larry Doby, that the Tigers truly broke their color barrier.

The city's blacks, which by the end of the 1950s accounted for
30 percent of the population, hungered for players to identify with.
"It was a special treat to be at the ballpark when Larry Doby and
Luke Easter came to town with the Cleveland Indians," Jim Bell, a
black Detroiter, once recalled for a reporter. "It was like a sea of
happy black faces out there in the bleachers when the Indians came
to bat. And even though the loyalist would be pulling for the home
team, there was a special look of pride on everyone's face when the
black players took the field. That rubbed off on me.

"As I grew, I also anticipated the day when as a Tiger fan, I
would be both loyal to my home team and proud of my black brothers who I knew would be on the team. Someone in the Tiger organization let me down."

There has always been speculation over the extent of Walter Briggs' racism. As with the unofficial color barrier that kept blacks from the major leagues for the first half of this century, no documents provide conclusive proof of Briggs' separatist policies. However, to hear many older blacks describe their apathy toward the team, there's no arguing their effect. "Briggs," said longtime player-coach Gates Brown in 1980. "The name doesn't set well in the black community. Say that name some places and you might get jumped on." Four years later, veteran sportswriter Al Dunmore wrote that most blacks over the age of forty considered the Tigers "an organization steeped in racism."

Subsequent regimes have attempted to rectify past mistakes. But the lack of black patronage at Michigan and Trumbull to this day is directly attributable to the Jim Crow policies Detroit's self-described "number one fan" employed at a critical juncture in the city's and the team's histories.

The Tigers concluded the less-than-fabulous 1950s with a fourth-place finish in 1959. Harvey Kuenn won his only batting title with a .353 mark, while Al Kaline finished second at .327. Don Mossi, Jim Bunning, and Paul Foytack all won seventeen games, and Frank Bolling played seventy-two consecutive errorless games at second base, one short of the major league record.

Under Bill Norman, who replaced Jack Tighe halfway through the previous season, the Tigers opened the 1959 campaign with fifteen losses in their first seventeen games. Detroit fans were pleased when he was replaced by old pro Jimmy Dykes, who had played and managed for the venerable Connie Mack in Philadelphia. On May 3, an excited Sunday afternoon crowd at Briggs Stadium watched the last-place Tigers sweep a doubleheader from the hated Yankees, launching a two-month comeback that put them within a half-game of the top before finally fizzling.

Dykes' managerial debut was notable in one other respect. It cemented the legend of Charlie Maxwell, the Tigers' "Sunday Punch." Maxwell, the thirty-two-year-old pride of Paw Paw, Michigan, joined the Tigers as a journeyman outfielder in 1955. The following season he hit .326 and established a club record for left-handers with twenty-eight home runs. He also established a reputation as someone whose play on Sunday seemed divinely inspired. In the twin killings of the Yankees, Maxwell homered in his last at-bat of the opening game and again in his first plate appearance of the nightcap. He walked his next time up, then pounded the ball into the seats his next two trips. By the time the Yankees finally got Maxwell out, he had homered in four consecutive official at-bats, tying a big-league record.

Maxwell followed up with home runs on five of the next eight Sundays. Each round tripper either tied the score or won the game. Maxwell cooled down after that, but by the time of his All-Star Game selection in July he was already being ballyhooed by the media as "The Sabbath Smasher."

"I really can't explain it except to say that it was one of those oddities that creates a lot of interest in the game," said Maxwell. "For example, my roommate was Frank Lary, and all he had to do was throw his glove on the mound to beat the Yankees. Then the next game he'd pitch against Kansas City and he'd get beat. So it was just one of those things." In 1959 Maxwell earned career highs in homers (31) and RBIs (95), with 12 homers and 33 runs batted in delivered on the Sabbath. Not bad for someone who admits today that he didn't go to church during the season.

The 1960 season featured several more bold moves by the Tigers, who the previous summer reinstated the fifty-cent Ladies' Day games after a sixteen-year hiatus. (During the war years male fans had complained of "screeching.") Under Fetzer, who was now the major shareholder, and new president Bill DeWitt, the club no longer appeared quite as moss-backed. Kids making a clean grab of a foul ball were given a Tigers contract. Also, the Olde English D on the home uniform was scrapped. In its place "Detroit" was written in script across the front of the blouse, a la the Brooklyn Dodgers, DeWitt's former employer. The experiment was short-lived, however. Fans disliked the new look, and after just one season the Tigers returned to their traditional home whites, from which they never again strayed.

Another new approach was to make headline-grabbing trades with Cleveland. As spring training ended, DeWitt and Indians general manager Frank "Trader" Lane engineered a momentous swap: batting champion Harvey Kuenn for home run champ Rocco Domenico Colavito or, as the newspapers liked to put it, "140 singles for 42 home runs." Outraged Cleveland fans unkindly characterized it hamburger for steak.

The handsome, dark-featured right fielder was an owner's delight. The twenty-six-year-old slugger was guaranteed to fill the seats with baseballs and fans alike. Strangely, at the time only four of Rocky's 129 career home runs were hit at Briggs Stadium. That didn't affect his enchantment with the place. "It's the nicest looking park in the league," Colavito said of his new surroundings. "It's green and it's beautiful. It has atmosphere. A guy feels like playing here."

Rocky homered his first at-bat in front of the home crowd, then smashed another the following day. He finished the season with thirty-five, the most by a Tiger since Hank Greenberg in 1946. (Kuenn, meanwhile, hit .308 for Cleveland and was dealt to San Francisco after the season.)

The new faces and uniforms had no effect on performance or attendance, as the Tigers stumbled home in sixth place, their worst record in six years. Thirty-one of their eighty-three losses were by one run, the inevitable result of a woeful .239 team batting average that was the club's worst since the 1904 edition swatted the dead ball around Bennett Park at a .231 clip. DeWitt resorted to gimmickry, on August 2 trading Dykes to Cleveland for Joe Gordon, still the only mid-season managerial swap in big-league history. By the end of the season Gordon himself was history.

For sentimentalists, the biggest change of the season was the ballpark's name, which for several years had remained the last link connecting the Briggs era to the new regime. Its severing wasn't totally unexpected. Upon his leaving in 1957, Spike Briggs asked that the family name be removed from the stadium. "The Briggs name is an honored one," Harvey Hansen had replied. "We can't do that." But DeWitt, who confessed to a reporter that he'd found "too much Briggs influence built into this club," had a different view, as did Fetzer.

On April 22, 1960—opening day in Detroit—club directors met before the game and voted unanimously to change the park's name to Tiger Stadium. DeWitt explained the reasoning. "It's in line with club policy to emphasize the name 'Tigers' in every way. I didn't suggest the change personally. The owners of the club have been thinking about it for two or three years. We believe Tiger Stadium is a more significant name. That's true of Yankee Stadium."

Down in Florida, Spike Briggs responded by saying that he was "awfully sorry the owners of the Tigers removed a memorial to my dad." However, he concluded, "I guess it's their business. They own it."

There was a minor glitch. The name change was to officially take place October 2, the last day of the season. But to spare the Lions the expense of reprinting tickets and promotional materials for the upcoming football season, the switch was delayed until January 1, 1961.

The changeover cost the Tigers twenty thousand dollars. Over the winter stationary was ordered and the old electric sign was taken down and a new one reading "TIGER STADIUM" erected in its place. And with that the Briggs name, for so long an integral part of the city's sporting, manufacturing, and social life, was officially expunged. The memories the name continues to evoke in many Detroiters, both good and bad, have proved much harder to erase.

Gridiron heroes: Buddy Parker is carried off the torn Briggs Stadium turf following the Lions' 17–16 victory over Cleveland in the 1953 NFL title game.

CHAPTER FIVE

Goalposts in the Outfield

Football at Michigan and Trumbull

MICHIGAN AND TRUMBULL may be a place for summer, but football fans fondly remember the corner as a place for autumn as well. Beginning in 1938 and continuing through Thanksgiving Day 1974, the Detroit Lions rented the ball park for most of their home games. Prior to that, the Tigers and Panthers—two of several unsuccessful attempts to establish a National Football League franchise in the city during the 1920s—played at Navin Field. The sights, sounds, and smells of a fall or early winter afternoon there—whistles piercing the chilled air, snowflakes pirouetting against a marbled sky, the faint perfume of wet wool, hot chocolate, and cigar smoke—were not those of sitting shirtless in the bleachers on a sun-splashed afternoon in July. But to generations of Detroiters, the memories are as vivid and the nostalgia as strong.

Who can forget the 1962 Thanksgiving Day massacre of Green Bay, when Vince Lombardi's undefeated Packers were humbled in front of a national television audience? Or the 1970 Turkey Day

Jimmy Conzelman was the owner, business manager, coach, and quarterback of the Detroit Panthers, which in 1925 became the second NFL team to play its home schedule at Michigan and Trumbull. After two seasons at Navin Field, the club was sold and moved. "We simply were ahead of our time in Detroit," Conzelman later reflected. "The town wasn't quite ready for pro football."

classic, when Mike Lucci and Charlie Sanders combined to shut up the haughty Oakland Raiders? Older fans still talk about the 1953 championship game against Cleveland, when Bobby Layne marched his team down the field in the final minutes for the winning touchdown, and the 1957 title game, when the joyous crowd carried local heroes Joe Schmidt and Tobin Rote off the field. There are even a few old-timers around who know what it was like when Jim Thorpe and his Canton Bulldogs came to town in 1926 to take on Jimmy Conzelman's Panthers.

For those who loved their football played outside in the elements, it was one long, glorious pigskin parade at Michigan and Trumbull. Counting regular season, exhibition, and championship games, some 11 million people paid to watch the city's professional football teams perform there between 1921 and 1974. This was a welcome demonstration of fan support and a healthy infusion of capital as the fledgling pro game struggled for acceptance by an initially skeptical and disinterested sporting public.

Professional football was a risky proposition in 1920, the year the American Professional Football Association was founded inside the showroom of a Hupmobile dealership in Canton, Ohio. Over the next dozen years the loosely organized affiliation of mostly midwestern clubs sounded more professional than it really was. Clubs made up their own schedules, statistics were sporadically kept, and the awarding of championships often was arbitrary and almost always hotly debated. The APFA, which changed its name to the National Football League in 1922, included a franchise in Detroit, the Heralds.

The Detroit Heralds, formed as a semi-pro team during the First World War, were headed by John Roesink, a downtown merchant who later owned the Detroit Stars of the Negro National League. The sixteen-man roster was a mix of former high school and collegiate stars and over-age sandlotters, including end Tillie Voss, from the University of Detroit, and Clarence "Steamer" Horning, an All-American tackle-punter from Colgate who also took an occasional turn running the ball. Players typically made between fifty and one hundred dollars a game and worked full- or part-time jobs to supplement their salary during the season.

The Heralds had known considerable success on the semi-pro circuit, winning the city and state championships in 1915 and then inaugurating "downtown football" at Navin Field in 1916 with a full slate of games against the Columbus Panhandles, Dayton Cadets, and other independent teams.* On November 11, 1917, they drew sixteen thousand rooters to Navin's lot for a benefit game against the

---

* From the beginning, Michigan and Trumbull regularly accomodated high school and college teams. In 1899, for example, a game between the Universities of Michigan and Virginia drew several thousand fans to Bennett Park. Outlining the gridiron on the baseball grounds proved awkward. When viewed from above, the south sideline almost formed a triangle with Michigan and Trumbull Avenues. The center of the gridiron was out beyond second base, and the goalposts were placed near Trumbull and the left-field trees. The arrangement "made every slightest pass or turn perfectly visible to everybody that had a long-range telescope," one newspaper wryly noted, but the bad sight lines and gale-force winds couldn't stop the Wolverines or the many fans sporting huge yellow chrysanthemums in their lapels and canes trailing maize and blue streamers. Michigan trampled Virginia 38–0; afterward a special train that consisted of ten jammed coaches left for Ann Arbor hailing the conquering heroes.

officers of Camp Custer. When they didn't lease spacious Navin Field, the Heralds played home games at cramped Mack Park, the six-thousand-seat wooden facility Roesink owned on the east side. This was more typical of the playing venues of the era: a minor-league baseball park or simply a lumpy sandlot with circus bleachers and a rope along the sidelines to keep the fans at bay. The latter was dangerous stuff. Once a hard-charging Herald collided with a mounted policeman, requiring treatment for the player and the horse.

This was the age of smash-mouth, single-platoon football, where toothless men in high-top cleats and flimsy leather helmets (assuming they wore headgear) pushed, wrestled, scratched, and slugged each other for sixty minutes in a slowly moving whirlwind of pebbles and dust. Offensive strategy revolved around an endless succession of line plunges and third-down punts, so points—and excitement—were at a premium. In the APFA's inaugural season the Heralds were involved in four shutouts, dropping three of them. Their sole victory was a 6–0 whitewashing of the Columbus Panhandles on October 24, 1920. Emblematic of the pro game's low status was the fact that the Heralds' tussle with their traditional rival had to be played at Mack Park because Frank Navin had reserved his field for an amateur hurling match.

The Heralds dropped out of the league after one season. Their place was taken by the Detroit Tigers, a new organization that retained John Roesink as business manager and Bill Marshall as coach. The Tigers' nickname, an attempt to capitalize on the baseball team's cachet, also reflected a change of venue. The football Tigers played their entire home schedule at Navin Field, beginning with a game against the Dayton Triangles on October 9, 1921. "Never before has so much interest been manifested in the 'pro' sport here as at the present time," observed the *Detroit Free Press*. "The announcement of the formation of a regular league which will be conducted as a major baseball organization, with stringent rules and a championship of the legitimate order for the contesting teams to strive for, has given the game added impetus. . . . That it is destined to become as popular as baseball is the belief of those who are interested in its promotion on the present basis."

The Sunday afternoon contest between the Tigers and Triangles marked the first NFL presence at Michigan and

Trumbull. The Tigers wore natty new uniforms of orange and black, the goalposts were decorated, and a jazz orchestra entertained the fans. Detroit won, 10–7, as Tillie Voss—one of five former Heralds on the squad—returned a blocked kick sixty-six yards for a touchdown for the decisive points. The *Free Press* reported that the game "was played under fine weather conditions and a good sized crowd was on hand to cheer the home team, something that has been lacking in past games here."

The Akron Pros, enticed by a large guarantee, visited Navin Field the following Sunday. The defending league champions featured some of the most notable names in early NFL history, including a pair of black players: wingback Fritz Pollard and end Paul Robeson, the future singer, actor, and activist. The game was a bust for the Tigers, who were soundly beaten, 20–0, in front of a meager crowd. They never recovered from the financial loss and folded at the end of the season with a 1–7–1 record.

It's doubtful that even a winning team could have prevented either Detroit entry from dropping out of the pro ranks. In 1920–21 the country was in the midst of a severe post-war recession, an economic downturn that hit Detroit especially hard. Another contributing factor was the public apathy toward professional football. The fan base was geared toward prep and college ball. Local sports pages, which were filled with the happenings of the University of Detroit and University of Michigan elevens, paid little attention to the play-for-pay pro game, which was largely considered a pale, corrupt imitation of its pure and more spirited amateur cousin. During the 1920s, Detroit's football fans were accustomed to spending their autumn Sunday afternoons at Belle Isle, Clark Park, and Corrigan Field watching local sandlot teams like the Detroit Mystics, Square Deal Millers, Wyandotte Arrows, and Royal Oak Independents battle each other for little more than the love of competition.

Baseball also cut into the Heralds' and Tigers' gate. The immensely popular playoffs of the Detroit Amateur Baseball Federation occupied the several diamonds at Northwestern Field through the early fall. Other Detroiters flocked to the various establishments offering electronic re-creations of major-league games. John Roesink, understanding the great public interest in the 1921 World Series between the Giants and Yankees, advertised that the score would be regularly given to fans attending the football Tigers' season opener at Navin Field. Despite pro football's attempts to ride the coattails of the national pastime, recognition and respectability were a long time coming. The *Sporting News* didn't cover the NFL until 1942, assuming readers would rather read off-season news of baseball players.

After a three-season hiatus, the NFL returned to Detroit in 1925. Jimmy Conzelman, a twenty-seven-year-old St. Louis native who bounced around the country as a player and coach before settling in Chicago as a realtor, was contacted by league president Joe Carr about placing a franchise in the country's fourth-largest city. Considering Detroit a potential box-office bonanza, Carr offered to lower the franchise fee from one thousand dollars to just fifty.

Conzelman, aided by several of his Chicago friends, went to work creating Detroit's third NFL team, the Panthers. He met with Frank Navin and arranged to rent Navin Field for one thousand dollars a game. A born promoter, he interested local theatrical agents in his idea to hire Notre Dame's "Four Horsemen." Conzelman planned to send the storied backfield on a twenty-two-week vaudeville tour before and after the season. He even worked out a routine for the boys, including a song, monologue, and clog dance.

Recalled Conzelman: "I was scheduled to be the piano player and the agents decided to get me a week's booking in Cicero so that one of us would have some real experience. Either Cicero wasn't ready for me or I wasn't ready for Cicero. I was terrible and the Cicero people let me know it."

To compound matters one of the Four Horsemen took a job with the recreation department in Davenport, Iowa. "That was the end of our vaudeville tour because the agents couldn't see an act called 'The Three Horsemen and Conzelman' going over," he said. "I still think these Four Horsemen might have given Detroit its first great professional football team."

However, the team Conzelman fielded in 1925 more than held its own. During their first full season of football at Michigan and Trumbull the Panthers compiled an 8–2–2 record, thanks to the heroics of coach-quarterback Conzelman and such now-forgotten stars as tackle-place kicker Gus Sonnenberg and fullback Dinger Doane. Since NFL teams drew up their own schedules, all but one of the Panthers' contests were played at Navin Field. The only team to win in Detroit was the Rock Island Independents, which

Jim Thorpe and his Canton Bulldogs played the Detroit Panthers at Navin Field in 1926. Other famous visitors that autumn included George Halas of the Chicago Bears, Curly Lambeau of the Green Bay Packers, and Ernie Nevers of the Duluth Eskimos.

tripped the Panthers, 6–3, on November 26, the last scheduled game of the season.

Conzelman decided he needed to draw ten thousand spectators per game to break even, but attendance, hampered by several rainy dates, averaged only about three thousand. Conzelman knew about the crowds Red Grange was attracting at the time on his post-colle-

giate barnstorming tour with the Chicago Bears. Figuring that
Detroit fans would be anxious to see "the Galloping Ghost" because
of the famous 1924 game in which the University of Illinois star had
scored four touchdowns in eleven minutes against the University of
Michigan, he booked the Bears for a December 12 game at Navin
Field.

"Once we broke the news, the tickets began to move like mad,"
recalled Conzelman. Visions of twenty thousand or more cheering
fans packed into Navin Field danced in his head. "I figured we
would make about $20,000 clear on the game. That meant we could
wipe out all our debts and have a few dollars left for the beginning
of the next season."

But the Wednesday before the game, Conzelman was told that
Grange had hurt his arm and probably wouldn't play. Being an honest fellow, Conzelman informed the newspapers.

"A few hours before the game was about to start," he said, "I
looked out the window and saw a long line at the box office. I
remember thinking to myself, 'What a great sports town. Grange
isn't going to play but they're still lining up to buy tickets.' Then I
got the news from the ticket man. They were lining up to get
refunds."

More than ten thousand people demanded and received their
money back. The Panthers defeated the Bears, 21–0, in front of just
four thousand fans. A box-office bust, the Panthers played one more
season at Navin Field, averaging about fifteen hundred fans for nine
home dates, before Conzelman sold the franchise back to the
league. "We were simply ahead of our time in Detroit," he later
reflected. "The town wasn't quite ready for pro football."

Two years later a syndicate of twenty local investors pooled ten
thousand dollars to back another attempt to launch pro football in
Detroit. The syndicate bought the Cleveland Bulldogs and moved
them lock, stock, and jockstrap to the Motor City. Dubbed the
Wolverines, the franchise owed its nickname, as well as its quarterback, to the University of Michigan. Two-time All-American quarterback Bennie Friedman, two years removed from U-of-M's gridiron, had popularized the forward pass, regularly drawing gasps
from the crowd by daring to throw the ball on first down. Sobered
by Jimmy Conzelman's experience with trying to fill Navin Field,
the Detroit Wolverines scheduled most of their games at the
University of Detroit's Dinan Field. Although the crowds were no

larger there, the sight lines and rent were better than what Navin Field offered. When the Wolverines were sold to Tim Mara of New York at the end of their losing 1928 campaign, each investor got back $350 of his original $500 investment.

The Great Depression dashed the fortunes of individual NFL teams. But hard times ultimately proved beneficial to the league in general and to Detroit in particular. The widely scattered small-town teams that characterized the infant NFL—Racine, Kenosha, Pottsville and the like—proved utterly incapable of supporting a pro team. They either broke up or, like the Portsmouth Spartans, were sold intact to big-city investors.

The Spartans, the pride of an Ohio steel-mill town located ninety miles south of Columbus along the Kentucky border, spent most of the early 1930s forlornly chasing the powerful Chicago Bears and Green Bay Packers for the top spot in the NFL. But even a competitive team couldn't expect to draw well when the local mills and shoe factory closed down. The Spartans attracted nine to ten thousand fans on Fridays to watch practice for free, and then draw two thousand paid customers for that Sunday's league game. "They had the enthusiasm," recalled the team's top player, halfback Earl "Dutch" Clark, "but not the price."

On March 24, 1934, the Spartans were sold to a syndicate of Detroit investors headed by George A. Richards. They paid a $15,000 franchise fee plus $7,952 to pay off Portsmouth's old debts. Richards, who owned radio station WJR, was egotistical, controversial, flamboyant, and knew little about football. He also was confidence personified. "I can assure the fans of Detroit that we will have a high-class team," he declared. "And by that I mean a winning team."

The new owner was correct on all accounts. The Detroit Lions (nicknamed to maintain the jungle-cat theme begun by the baseball Tigers) immediately became a high-class, winning team. Playing at Dinan Field (where rent was four hundred dollars a game), the Lions defeated their first ten opponents, the first seven by shutout. Games were broadcast on Richards' powerful station, spreading the appeal of what many called "post-graduate football."

Despite the Depression, the NFL took off in popularity. In 1933 owners emulated the major leagues by splitting the league into two divisions and arranging a balanced schedule that culminated in an annual championship game. The football itself, once a fat bladder, gradually reached its modern streamlined shape that season. This modification, when coupled with a new rule allowing passing from any point behind the line of scrimmage, opened the game considerably. Other innovations in the 1930s, such as a college draft, an annual all-star game, colorful uniforms, and regular halftime entertainment, helped the NFL survive the Depression and two rival pro leagues, both of which folded.

Richards' most enduring contribution to the new NFL was to create the Lions' annual Thanksgiving Day game. Thanks to Richards' contacts in the radio industry, ninety-four NBC affiliates coast-to-coast agreed to broadcast the 1934 game. Outfitted in striking silver-and-blue uniforms, the new team hosted Bronko Nagurski and the Chicago Bears that first Turkey Day before a standing-room-only crowd of twenty-six thousand. In a showdown for first place, the Lions lost an exciting match, 19–16, and fell just short of claiming the Western Division championship.

However, during their inaugural season the Lions "collected not only the customers' money, but their whole-hearted loyalty as well," reported *Detroit Times* sports editor Bud Shaver. "Until the Lions put up their game stand against the Bears, professional football was still just a new enterprise which had most of Detroit's best wishes, but little else.

"In their last home game the Lions won them over," continued Shaver. "They became Detroit's own team, just as the Tigers and Red Wings are Detroit's own. The capture of the fans' loyalty and interest in that one game was worth a great deal more to George A. Richards and his associates than all the coins which clinked into the cash register."

The following season coach George "Potsy" Clark's troops regrouped and edged Green Bay for the divisional title. On December 15, 1935, the Lions defeated the New York Giants, 26–7, for their first NFL championship. A crowd of twelve thousand sat in the freezing rain at Dinan Field and cheered as Dutch Clark, Ace Gutowsky, Ernie Caddell, and Buddy Parker churned up the mud for 235 rushing yards and a touchdown apiece. The victory came just two months after some of these same fans had watched the Tigers win their first World Series at Navin Field. Newspapers were already calling Detroit "the City of Champions," a title that was cemented four months later when the Red Wings captured their first Stanley Cup, completing an unprecedented sweep of champi-

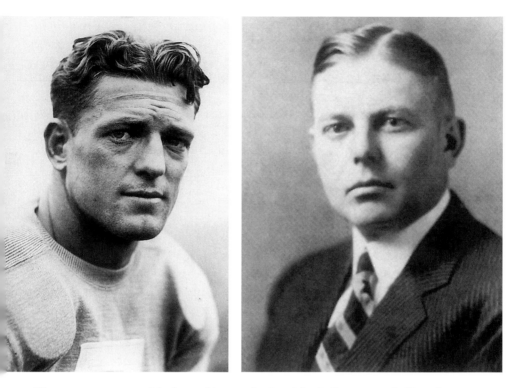

The two men responsible for making professional football a success in Detroit during the 1930s were Dutch Clark (left) and radio magnate George A. Richards.

onships. Thanks to the combined talents of George Richards and Dutch Clark, professional football finally found a permanent home in Detroit.

While no more championships were immediately forthcoming, the Lions continued to draw well at the University of Detroit. Temporary bleachers boosted seating capacity to twenty-five thousand, but the club soon recognized that a larger venue was needed. On July 3, 1938, Bud Shaver (who had left the *Times* to become the Lions' vice president of public relations) announced "Public support to the Lions has been so generous that University of Detroit Stadium no longer can provide adequate accommodations . . . The Lions are moving into Briggs Stadium this season to give every football fan the opportunity to see the best football players in the world."

By allowing the Lions inside his just-completed, newly renamed sports palace, Walter Briggs hoped to establish Briggs Stadium's reputation as the country's premier, all-purpose facility. At the time, only New York's Yankee Stadium and three other parks had baseball and football teams as co-tenants.

The Lions played their first game at Briggs Stadium on October 18, 1938. A crowd of 42,855 showed up on a warm Sunday afternoon to watch the Washington Redskins, featuring quarterback Sammy Baugh, win a lackluster affair by the baseball-like score of 7–5. A field goal and a safety produced a 5–0 Detroit lead after two quarters, which made halftime festivities—an acrobat, four whooping kids in Indian headdress, and the Wayne University marching band—all the merrier. But in the third quarter, former University of Detroit standout Andy Farkas scored on a short run to give Washington the winning margin. Washington owner George Marshall later pronounced Briggs Stadium "perfect" for the sport. "It is perfect as far as the gridiron's location in relation to the stands is concerned and it is perfect for spectators. Football here will be enjoyable in any kind of weather."

Not all fans shared Marshall's enthusiasm. Briggs Stadium, like all parks originally designed for baseball, could not be configured precisely for football. The gridiron stretched from the first base line to left field. After the game some of the fans that had paid 55¢ for one of the ten thousand unreserved seats complained that the coaches and players standing along the sideline had obstructed their view. Those who could afford it quickly bought one of the nineteen thousand lower-deck reserved seats at $1.10 apiece. The more affluent paid $2.20 for reserved seats with superior sight lines. These included all seats in the upper deck, as well as those located in the lower-deck third-base grandstand and left-field pavilion between the goal lines.

The Lions' first game at the corner almost doubled the previous attendance high for a pro football game in the city, but sportswriters correctly predicted that the caliber of competition, not the amenities, would determine the level of attendance at the team's new venue. The following Sunday, a game with the woeful Chicago Cardinals drew little more than seventeen thousand people. One month later, however, 45,139 turned out to watch the Lions lose to

Green Bay, 28–7, in a showdown for first place. It was at the time the largest crowd ever to watch a football game in the city. All told, the second-place Lions attracted 181,251 fans in six dates at Briggs Stadium, an average of 30,209 per game.

Briggs rented the stadium for 15 percent of the gross receipts. He also kept the concession and parking revenues. This was standard for the time; if the Lions had any complaints about the arrangement they were kept out of the newspapers. While Briggs occasionally opened his stadium to concerts and prizefights during this period, there was never any doubt that he was first and foremost a baseball man. As late as 1950, conflicting schedules often forced the Lions to play league games at the University of Detroit. In 1940 Briggs booted the football team out of his stadium for the entire season. The rent receipts were welcome, but apparently he just didn't like the damage the cleats inflicted on his meticulously manicured turf. That year, George Richards sold the Lions to a syndicate headed by Chicago department store owner Fred Mandel. The $225,000 sale price meant the franchise had appreciated tenfold in value in just seven years.

At the same time that Walter Briggs grumbled over his torn turf, he retained a soft spot for those less well-off members of the community. Over the years the Old Newsboys Goodfellow Fund of Detroit, a charitable organization launched in 1914 by James J. Brady, has cared for tens of thousands of the city's needy children—not only at Christmas, but year-round. Beginning in 1938 and continuing for the next three decades, the corner of Michigan and Trumbull was the site of one of the Goodfellows' biggest fundraisers and one of the city's finest sports traditions: the annual high school football championship game between the Public School League and the Catholic League.

The first Goodfellow Game pitted unbeaten Catholic Central against a powerful Hamtramck squad. Unfortunately for the ten bands and two thousand ROTC members scheduled to perform in a pregame extravaganza, a heavy snowstorm buried the city the night before the game. The stadium's ground crew worked from six in the morning to just before kickoff to ready the field. Despite being outweighed by a considerable margin, Catholic Central (a thirty-five-point underdog in many Hamtramck bars) upset the PSL representative, 19–13, on a pair of interception returns for touchdowns. One was by center John McHale, who later played parts of five seasons for the Tigers.

Briggs, who sold papers as a youth, was a major supporter of the game, donating the use of his stadium and selling refreshments at half-price. From the 1940s through the early 1960s, the Goodfellow Game typically attracted crowds of thirty thousand and more. Attendance fell off in the mid-1960s, however, and the series was finally discontinued after the 1967 clash between Divine Child and Denby. All told, the event raised nearly one million dollars in thirty years. Sixty percent of that went to the Goodfellow Fund and the rest was divided among the PSL and the Catholic League.

Catholic Central's John McHale played center and linebacker in the first Goodfellow Game in 1938. The prep star returned to Briggs Stadium in the 1940s as a part-time first baseman for the Tigers; he later became the club's general manager.

After a one-season hiatus, the Lions returned to Briggs Stadium in 1941. On November 30, tailback Byron "Whizzer" White—destined to become a U. S. Supreme Court justice—ended the Lions' 4–6–1 season and his football career by accounting for two touchdowns in a 21–3 win over the Chicago Cardinals at Briggs Stadium. The following Sunday, the Japanese attacked the U. S. fleet at Pearl Harbor.

Football, like baseball, continued during the war as a morale booster, although the first wartime edition of the Lions hardly qualified. The 1942 club lost all eleven games and became the league's first winless team since the 1929 Dayton Triangles. The Lions were shut out five times, never scored more than seven points in any game, and scored a grand total of thirty-eight points for the entire season. The Lions concluded the season with a 15–3 loss to Washington on November 29, as just 6,044 fans rattled around Briggs Stadium—the second-lowest home turnout in franchise history. Only a 1934 game with Pittsburgh at Dinan Field attracted fewer fans.

It wasn't until September 20, 1943, that the Lions won again. The victims were the same as on that last prewar Sunday afternoon, the Chicago Cardinals. An enthusiastic fan buttonholed Fred Mandel after the Lions' 35–17 win in their home opener. "You got a great ball club!" he yelled. "I wouldn't say it's a great club," responded Mandel, "but it's a great improvement."

It certainly was. The club's five touchdowns that afternoon equaled its entire 1942 output. The Lions quickly reverted to form. Their final record of 3–6–1 included a 0–0 deadlock with the New York Giants at Briggs Stadium on November 7. The teams managed a combined nine first downs in the muck during the rain-swept snoozer, with the Giants' Carl Kinscherf punting fourteen times. More than fifty years later, it remains the last scoreless tie in NFL history.

The war ended three weeks before the 1945 NFL campaign started, but travel restrictions limited the Lions to just four home games. They won all but the last, a Thanksgiving Day battle with the Cleveland Rams for first place. With Bob Waterfield finding end Jim Benton ten times for a record 303 yards, the Rams clinched the Western Division title with a 28–21 victory. The Lions wound up 7–3, their best record in a decade.

Decimated by injuries, the Lions stumbled through a 1–10 season in 1946, the first of three consecutive last-place finishes. In early 1948 Fred Mandel sold the team to a syndicate headed by brewery executive Edwin J. Anderson and electrical engineer Lyle Fife. The board of directors quickly moved the club in a new direction. Alvin "Bo" McMillan was named head coach and general manager. The team's first black players, Bob Mann and Mel Groomes, were

Bill Callihan attempts to haul in a pass against the Chicago Bears in 1945, the first season of peace at Michigan and Trumbull in four years. Only eight players from the 1941 squad returned from military service to play for the Lions.

signed. Now that Briggs Stadium was finally equipped with lights, the Lions began playing occasional Saturday- and Monday-night games, using a league-mandated white football for better visibility.

However, the half-filled ballpark proved Detroit fans wanted more than novelty. "In those days, baseball and hockey were the big sports in Detroit," recalled quarterback Bobby Layne, who joined the club in 1950. "Football players were recognized around town by

On Sundays in September and early October, the Briggs Stadium lawn where outfielders lazily drifted under fly balls earlier in the week was transformed by chalk and sideline markers into a no-man's land of blitzes, fullback plunges, and blind-side hits.

very few people. We didn't average but twenty or maybe twenty-two thousand a game. Early in the season we'd have to play our games at [the University of Detroit] because the Tigers were still playing baseball at Briggs Stadium, and we had to work out at a place called Jayne Play field, which was a public playground out in Hamtramck, a tough part of town. We'd go out to practice and Bo would try to

Bobby Layne and Buddy Parker, architects of the Lions' never-say-die offense of the championship fifties. Parker is credited with inventing the two-minute offense; Layne is said to have never truly lost a game in his life. "Time just ran out on him," said teammate Yale Lary.

clear the neighborhood kids off the field and they'd tell him, 'Go screw yourself!' Oh, lor-dee! Bo couldn't do a thing about it. Those kids stayed out there while we practiced."

Layne, more than anyone else, was responsible for filling Briggs Stadium and making Detroit a football town in the 1950s. It was a toss-up as to what wobbled more: Layne's passes or the team that

Jack Christiansen, leader of the Lions' famous secondary, "Chris's Crew," returns a punt for a touchdown against Green Bay in the 1951 Thanksgiving Day game at Briggs Stadium. The turkey-day tradition, which began in 1934 at Dinan Field, has continued to its present-day location at the Pontiac Silverdome.

loyally followed him in and out of his favorite downtown watering holes. But it's undeniable that the blonde-haired, squinty-eyed, slightly paunchy product of Texas's hard-scrabble gridirons was a true leader of men.

"Bobby had an affinity for chewing your rear end out," said Lou Creekmur, a Pro Bowl tackle eight of the ten years he played in Detroit. "If you ever missed a block, not only did you know about it, but all the other guys on the offensive team and everybody on the bench knew about it. On top of that, the fifty thousand fans up in the stadium all knew about it, too, because he told you right then, out there in front of the whole crowd. And it was so embarrassing that we all made a pact that we would never miss a block that would ever disturb Bobby Layne."

After the 1950 season the unpopular McMillan was canned by team directors and replaced by assistant coach Raymond "Buddy" Parker. The tall, thin, and leather-faced Parker, who had played half-back on the Lions' 1935 championship team, became the Lions' eighth head coach in the twelve years since moving into Briggs Stadium. He was a moody, chain-smoking tactical genius and a per-ceptive judge of men and talent. Through draft picks and trades he assembled the nucleus of what would become the NFL's dominant team of the 1950s. These included defensive back Jack Christiansen, tackle Thurman McGraw, end Cloyce Box, halfback Bob "Hunchy" Hoernschemeyer, and a pair of Heisman Trophy winners, Southern Methodist halfback Doak Walker and Notre Dame end Leon Hart. Layne paid this rollicking group his highest compliment. "Every son of a bitch on that team," he said, "was all football."

Although the improved Lions won only half of their games in 1950, their sudden competitiveness foreshadowed their primacy over the next seven autumns. Between 1951 and 1957 they captured four divisional titles and missed two others on the last day of the season. They played six postseason games and won five: Western Division playoffs against the Rams in 1952 and the 49ers in 1957, and NFL championships against the Browns in 1952, 1953, and 1957. The only blemish was a loss to Cleveland in the 1954 title game. A corresponding rise in attendance occurred, which doubled between 1950 and 1953 to an average of fifty thousand a game. It remained at that level until the Lions left Michigan and Trumbull more than twenty years later.★

The Lions' loss in San Francisco on the final Sunday of the 1951 season allowed Los Angeles to slip past them for the confer-ence title. But the following season Detroit—bolstered by rookie defensive backs Yale Lary and Jimmy David—returned to the NFL championship game for the first time in seventeen years.

★ The largest Lions crowd at the corner was on September 28, 1964, when Green Bay beat Detroit, 14–10, in front of 59,203 fans. The largest Thanksgiving Day crowd was on November 27, 1969, when 57,906 gathered to watch the Lions lose to Minnesota, 27–0.

The Lions looked anything but glory-bound during the early part of the season. They lost two of their first three games, including a 28–0 thrashing to San Francisco in front of the home folks that saw Layne benched and Doak Walker injured for the balance of the regular season. The following Sunday the defending champion Rams came to town, building a thirteen-point lead before Layne rallied the Lions to a last-minute 24–16 victory. Detroit lost just one of their final eight games as Los Angeles rebounded to win their last eight straight. The clubs' identical 9–3 records meant a playoff would be held to determine which team would face Cleveland for the title game.

The tiebreaker was played on December 21 before 47,645 fans at fog-wrapped Briggs Stadium. An unlikely hero emerged from the gloom: veteran fullback Pat Harder, a hard-nosed castoff from the Chicago Cardinals who was just one of many Lions with a reputation for clothesline tackles and sharpened elbows. "When somebody would slug him on the first play of a game his eyes would light up," remembered Parker. "It was as if he were saying, 'Oh, it's going to be like that, is it?'"

On this afternoon Harder set a new postseason record by scoring nineteen points. In the first quarter he took a pitch out twelve yards for a touchdown, then kicked the extra point for a 7–0 Lions lead. In the second stanza he ran four yards for another touchdown and added the conversion to increase the advantage to 14–0. The Rams retaliated just before halftime when Norm Van Brocklin found Tom Fears on a fifteen-yard scoring pass, but a third-quarter option pass from Walker to Leon Hart and a forty-three-yard field goal by Harder produced a commanding 24–7 lead. Midway through the final quarter the Rams struck back with a pair of touchdowns to make it a three-point game, 24–21. However, Los Angeles's quick-strike offense was short-circuited for good when Lavern Torgeson intercepted a pass in the last minute of play, and set up a short Hoernschemeyer touchdown run with just thirty seconds left. Harder converted and the Lions waltzed off the spongy turf 31–21 victors in the first postseason football game played at Michigan and Trumbull.

The following week the Lions beat the Browns in Cleveland. Walker, who hadn't scored all season, broke off a brilliant sixty-seven-yard touchdown run in the third quarter to ice the Lions' 17–7 victory. "It was the happiest I've ever been in football," said Layne.

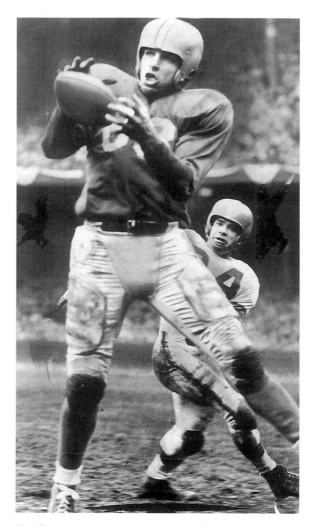

Jim Doran grabs the winning touchdown pass against Cleveland during the 1953 title game.

Many stories about Layne have been told over the years, some of them true. Every Monday he ritually brought the team into the Stadium Bar, across the street from Briggs Stadium, for fun, drinks, entertainment, and a little football talk. Layne belted out such songs as "Ida Red" between shots of scotch while 330–pound middle guard Les Bingaman performed a tippy-toe dance. Even those who didn't drink, such as Doak Walker, valued the camaraderie developed there.

Defensive stalwarts for Detroit, safety and punter Yale Lary (left) and middle linebacker Joe Schmidt, are among several Lions from the 1950s to be enshrined at the Pro Football Hall of Fame.

"The biggest thing about our success was the tightness of the group," said Layne. "You showed up whether you drank or not. We had one-hundred percent attendance. The worst thing that could happen was if a couple of players went somewhere and two others somewhere else. Pretty soon those two are blaming the other two for something that went wrong. We'd meet, go over Sunday's game, and iron out any differences we had. We all left there friends and, if we had a loss, by Tuesday we'd have it behind us and be ready for the next game. Nobody was blamin' anybody else."

The best yarns told of Layne's ability to pull a game out of the fire. "Bobby never lost a game in his life," insisted Yale Lary. "Time just ran out on him." In 1953 the Lions defended their championship with a succession of narrow victories; six of their ten wins were decided by ten points or less. While Layne earned cudos for engineering several last-minute scoring drives, the patent belonged to Parker, who originated the concept of the "two-minute offense."

"I had noticed how so many teams let down the two minutes before halftime," Parker explained. "It seemed you could get things done then that you couldn't in the other fifty-six minutes of play. So we drilled on it every day. But the theory wasn't much without execution and I had that big guy as quarterback."

Parker was at his best December 27, 1953, in the title game rematch against Cleveland. It was the first NFL championship game ever played at Michigan and Trumbull. Seated in the packed stands was a cadre of Lions wives wearing green-dyed jockstraps on their heads for good luck.

The Browns, playing in their eighth straight championship game, finished the regular season with an 11–1 record and were four-point favorites. The passing combination of Otto Graham to Dante Lavelli was especially feared. "Here possibly are the two best teams ever to meet for the championship," proclaimed NFL commissioner Bert Bell.

On this cool Sunday afternoon the game lived up to the hype. The teams battled on the torn turf to a 10–10 tie after three quarters. In the final stanza Lou Groza kicked a fifteen-yard field goal to give Cleveland a 13–10 lead. With less than five minutes left he widened the advantage to 16–10 with a forty-three-yard field goal.

After Groza kicked off into the end zone, Layne assembled his troops on the Detroit twenty yardline. Only four minutes remained to play. This was the time of the game when Layne excelled. "Jest give me the time boys," he drawled in the huddle, "and I'll get you downfield and back into that All-Star Game at Chicago. Jest block."

It took Layne "jest" two minutes to move eighty yards through the gloom. He hit Jim Doran—a defensive end filling in for injured Leon Hart—three times on the drive. The last was a thirty-three-yard touchdown strike that knotted the game at 16–16. "The winning pass play was an amazingly smooth operation," reported the *New York Times*, "but it shocked the 54,577 spectators from their seats. Layne lofted a soft pass into the end zone and it was just a matter of whether the speeding Doran would catch up to it. He did. The former Iowa State end broke loose behind Ken Konz, Brownie halfback, and cradled the ball into his arms as he sped past the final money stripe."

Doak Walker's place kick gave Detroit a 17–16 lead and, after the Lions' defense hounded Graham into another interception in the waning moments, its second straight NFL championship. Jubilant players picked up Buddy Parker and carried him off the field. "What a season!" he exclaimed, perhaps unnecessarily.

In 1954 the Lions captured a third straight division title with a 9–2–1 record. Layne's chubby face even made the cover of *Time*, with sold-out Briggs Stadium in the background. He was the first pro footballer so honored by the magazine. The Lions were favorites to make history as the first team to capture three consecutive NFL titles, but the Browns spoiled the party, winning big, 56–10, in Cleveland. During his eighth try, Cleveland coach Paul Brown finally bested his nemesis, Buddy Parker.

Injuries to Layne caused the Lions to drop to last place in 1955 and to lose a season-ending showdown for the conference crown in Chicago in 1956. In 1957 Buddy Parker abruptly quit during training camp, announcing to a stunned "Meet the Lions" banquet at the Statler Hotel that he could no longer discipline his players. George Wilson, an assistant coach for eight years, took over the team.

Parker's sensational outburst was just one of the elements that helped make the 1957 campaign the most dramatic season of football ever played at the corner. It featured the heroics of Tobin Rote, who was acquired before the season as insurance for the oft-injured Layne. The rugged Rote fit right in with the Lions. With his close-cropped hair and hard, seamed face, the six-foot, three-inch, 215-pound Texan looked like he might have shared a foxhole with John Wayne in *The Sands of Iwo Jima*. He served as a one-man gang at Green Bay in 1956, leading the league in touchdown passes and rushing for eleven more. All in all, the twenty-nine-year-old Rote was too good to be a mere backup. When the regular season began he and Layne were alternating starting assignments.

The Lions lost the opener in Baltimore, but rebounded to win the next two. Game four was a rematch with the undefeated Colts.

Baltimore's young wizard, Johnny Unitas, tossed four touchdown passes as the Colts amassed a 27–3 lead. The gray, overcast weather matched the mood of the fans huddled in Briggs Stadium.

Late in the third quarter, Rote replaced Layne and hit rookie end Steve Junker with a scoring pass to make it 27–10. That's the way it stood when Layne re-entered with just eight minutes to play.

Almost immediately, Layne found Howard "Hopalong" Cassady for a touchdown, slicing the lead to ten points. With two minutes to play, Layne heaved a bomb that Cassady gathered in at the Colts' one-yardline. John Henry Johnson, the heavy-duty veteran fullback picked up from the 49ers, smashed over on the next play. Suddenly it was just 27–24, and the crowd was in an uproar.

Baltimore tried to run out the clock after the ensuing kickoff, but Yale Lary forced Lenny Moore to fumble and pounced on the loose ball at the Colts' 29. Layne didn't waste any time. He arched a long pass downfield, and once again it was Cassady on the receiving end. Touchdown, Detroit! The Lions miraculously pulled the game out, 31–27, wiping out a twenty-four-point deficit in less than twenty minutes. The victory tied the Lions with the Colts for first with 3–1 records. Even *Detroit News* sportswriter Doc Greene, who had seen his share of heroics in his day, asked: "What'll they do for an encore?"

What the Lions did was split their next six games. Going into the final home game of the season against Cleveland, Detroit and San Francisco were tied for second at 6–4, one game behind the surprising Colts. With 55,814 people on hand, the Lions led Cleveland 3–0 in the second quarter when Layne was gang-tackled going back to pass. Layne's foot caught in the turf, snapping his right ankle as he fell. Rote came in and carved out a 20–7 win. While Layne was being operated on, San Francisco beat the Colts on a last-second touchdown pass by rookie John Brodie, creating a three-way tie for first between the Lions, 49ers, and Colts. Only one game remained in the wildest race in NFL history.

The Lions traveled to Chicago and, behind Rote's three touchdown passes, came from behind to win, 21–13. San Francisco also won; only an upset of the Colts in Los Angeles prevented a complicated round-robin playoff. As it was, Detroit flew to San Francisco for a special playoff to determine the Western Conference crown. Losing 27–7 early in the third quarter, and with jubilant 49ers fans standing in line to buy tickets for the following week's championship game against Cleveland, the Lions stormed back to win, 31–27, in one of the greatest postseason comebacks ever. Layne, on crutches, witnessed the improbable rally on the sidelines. Standing next to him was Alex Karras, a myopic tackle from Iowa and the Lions' number-one draft pick. "I don't believe it," repeated Karras. "You better," shouted Layne. "You better believe it." One week later, on a cold, sunny Sunday afternoon in Detroit, the sky-high Lions blew the Browns off the Briggs Stadium grass. It was still a game when rookie fullback Jimmy Brown ran twenty-nine yards for a score on the first play of the second quarter, slicing Detroit's lead to 17–7. But midway through the quarter, the Lions' offense ignored George Wilson's instructions to go for a field goal. "This is our money," Rote said in the huddle, "and we can play with it." Rote, holding the ball for Jim Martin, received the snap, jumped up from his knee, rolled to his right, and lobbed the ball to Steve Junker for an easy touchdown and a 24–7 lead. By the end of the day Rote had thrown four touchdowns and run for a fifth as Detroit drubbed the Browns, 59–14.

Paul Brown, on the receiving end of the second-worst championship game shellacking ever, was gracious in defeat. He shrugged over the bounces of the ball, praised the Lions' effort, and gave an assist to their twelfth man—the 55,263 delirious fans that filled nearly every seat in Briggs Stadium. "We couldn't hear our own signals," he said. "That crowd noise was terrific. There's something about this ball park that makes the crowd noise drown our signals. Finally we just gave up trying to defeat the confusion."

In the Lions' locker room Steve Junker was still stunned by it all. "I just hope next season can be like this season," he said. "It couldn't be much better, could it?"

As it turned out, no. It was the end of an era. The next season Layne was traded to Pittsburgh following a poor performance against lowly Green Bay that caused fickle Detroit fans to howl for his scalp. Rote took over in the huddle, but no one could replace Layne's unique brand of leadership. Rote turned out to be just the first of a long line of signal callers who attempted to fill Layne's shoes over the next

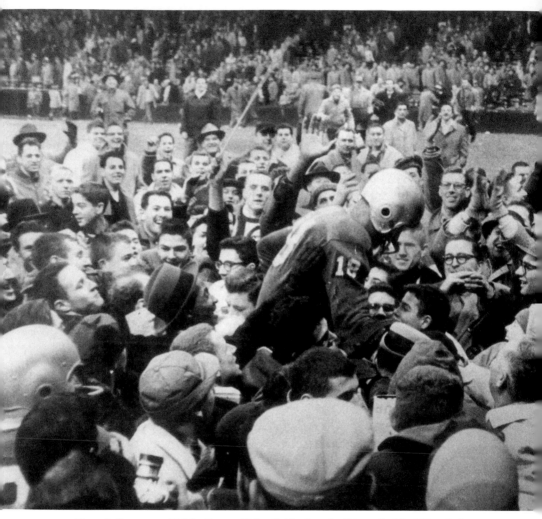

Detroit fans carry Tobin Rote off the field after the Lions, behind Rote's four touchdown passes, routed the Browns, 59–14, in the 1957 championship game at Briggs Stadium.

decade. The litany of names—Jim Ninowski, Milt Plum, Earl Morrall, Karl Sweetan—sounded like a bad mantra to spoiled fans, who saw league primacy pass to the Packers in the 1960s.

The Lions experienced a transitional period after Layne left. Within a couple of seasons many of the old favorites quit. "When Bobby was traded the ball players in Detroit changed," explained

Jimmy David. "I just went ahead and retired a year later in 1959. The fun of playing was gone. The concept of all for one and one for all was gone."

Young blood, in the persons of new young players, such as full-back Nick Pietrosante (who set a club rushing record with 872 yards in 1960), linebacker Wayne Walker, defensive back Dick LeBeau, and ends Jim Gibbons and Gail Cogdill, took their place. The defense, featuring middle linebacker Joe Schmidt, cornerback Dick "Night Train" Lane, and the original "Fearsome Foursome" of Alex Karras, Roger Brown, Sam Williams and Darris McCord, re-established itself as one of the game's best. The three-hundred-pound Brown, an unheralded fourth-round draft pick from Maryland, was particularly devastating. He astonished fans one afternoon in Detroit when he picked up a Chicago lineman and threw him at the quarterback, knocking him down for a safety.

Karras, who refused to wear contact lens despite his terrible vision, was still intense and noncommunicative hours after the game. Playing "by feel," as he described it, the squat but nimble lineman was dubbed "The Mad Duck" for his explosive forays into the enemy backfield. Karras, who like Brown was a four-time Pro Bowl selection, was among the best pass rushers of his time. "To me, football is a contest of embarrassments," explained Karras, who often included "milk-drinking quarterbacks" in his frequently hilar-ious soliloquies about life, football, and anything else his fertile imagination could conjure up. "The quarterback is out there to embarrass me in front of my friends, my teammates, my coaches, my wife, my daughter, and my three boys. The quarterback doesn't leave me any choice. I've got to embarrass him."

As the NFL moved into a decade of expansion and war with the upstart American Football League, the Lions continued to sell out most of their home games. The club finished second three straight years, including 1961 when all five of their losses came at what was now called Tiger Stadium. One was a 49–0 drubbing by San Francisco, which surprised the proud Detroit defense by rotating three quarterbacks in an offensive formation known as the shotgun.

The inaugural Runner-up Bowl, a contrived postseason clash of second-place finishers from both conferences, was held in Miami after the 1960 season. The Lions won this consolation game three straight times before it was discontinued. Their success inspired all sorts of fantasies over just how far the team could have gone if today's convoluted playoff system had existed then.

The 1962 squad arguably was not only the Lions' finest, it may have been the best team never to have played for a championship. That year Detroit finished second at 11–3, setting a team record for victories that stood for three decades until the 1992 club, benefitting from an expanded schedule, racked up a dozen wins. The three losses were by a total of eight points: 9–7 to Green Bay, 17–14 to New York, and 3–0 to Chicago in a meaningless finale. All were agonizingly close losses to strong teams. The Packers and Bears were destined to win the next two NFL titles, beating the powerful Giants each time.

The toughest defeat to swallow came in the fourth week of the season at Green Bay. Both teams were undefeated. In a bitterly contested game played on a muddy field, the Lions put the defending champions on the ropes, nursing a 7–6 lead with less than two minutes to play. On third down Milt Plum, the veteran quarterback acquired before the season from Cleveland, threw an ill-advised pass intended for Terry Barr. Barr slipped and Herb Adderly intercepted, returning it deep into Detroit territory. This set up Paul Hornung's game-winning field goal with twenty-seven seconds left and created acrimony between the offensive and defensive units that poisoned the clubhouse for years to come. "It still ticks me off," admitted Joe Schmidt thirty years later. "We never should have thrown the fucking ball. We should have run Nick Pietrosante. Yale Lary could have punted the ball all the way to Milwaukee. Green Bay had only one time out left. At least we should have made them earn it."

By the time the two teams met again on Thanksgiving Day, the Lions had fallen to the Giants, which accounted for their 8–2 record. The Packers came into the game undefeated at 10–0. In fact, reaching back into the previous season, coach Vince Lombardi's shock troops had lost only once in their last eighteen outings, and that by a single point. Their 37–0 rout of New York in the 1961 title game was their first of five eventual championships in seven years. Their aura of invincibility was underscored by the wire services' All-Pro selections, which included eleven Packers, and magazine cover stories that proclaimed them the greatest congregation of football players ever to buckle a chinstrap.

Roger Brown tackles Bart Starr for a safety in the Lions' Thanksgiving Day massacre of the Packers in 1962, the most famous football game ever played at the corner.

They may have been at that. But not on this overcast afternoon. Ever since the loss in Green Bay the Lions had been pointing to the rematch in Detroit. "The people can help us," Wayne Walker told the press. "When we come out on the field, they can let loose, make noise, let us know they're for us."

On the Packers' first pass play, Bart Starr was swarmed under by several blitzing Lions for a fifteen-yard loss. It set the tone for the afternoon. Before 57,598 wildly screaming fans and 32 million disbelieving television viewers, the revenge-minded Lions practically

Broadcaster Van Patrick dubbed the Lions' defensive line "The Fearsome Foursome," half of which—end Sam Williams (number 88) and tackle Roger Brown—is pressuring Baltimore quarterback Johnny Unitas in this action shot taken at Tiger Stadium in the mid-1960s.

chased the Packers out of Tiger Stadium and back to Wisconsin. By the it was over, Starr had been sacked eleven times and lost 110 yards attempting to pass. Jimmy Taylor, the league's leading ground gainer, was held to a mere forty-seven yards. Roger Brown was credited with six sacks, including a safety and a jarring hit that knocked the ball out of Starr's hands. Sam Williams picked up the fumble and ran it in for a touchdown. Detroit built up a 26–0 lead early in the third quarter before coasting home, 26–14. The relatively close final score doesn't adequately convey the sense of mayhem and dominance visited upon the Packers, however.

"We just got up for it like I've never, ever seen a team get up for anything before," explained Walker. "Everything we did that day was just perfect. If we blitzed, they didn't pick it up. If we looped linemen, they didn't pick it up. If we didn't blitz and played a zone, Bart Starr couldn't read it. We just killed them physically." Green Bay rebounded from the mauling to finish the season at 13–1 and beat New York for the title. But the Thanksgiving Day massacre remains the best remembered game in Lions history and one that few Packer fans are likely to forget, as well.

From such a high point the rest of the decade rolled downhill. In 1965 George Wilson was replaced as coach by Harry Gilmer, a onetime backup to Bobby Layne and, like Layne, a dyed-in-the-wool Texan. Gilmer spoke in a nearly indecipherable drawl, spit chewing tobacco into potted plants, and wore cowboy boots and a wide-brimmed Stetson hat on the sidelines on Sundays. Unlike Wilson, Gilmer made no attempt to get close to his players. They in turn ripped him privately and publicly. The team was in chaos, and its record reflected that fact. Detroit won a grand total of nine games during the 1965 and 1966 seasons under Gilmer.

One of the Lions troublemakers was Joe Don Looney, whose front-page escapades made him into a minor folk hero at Tiger Stadium. In the second quarter of a 1966 game with Atlanta, Looney took the field to a thunderous ovation. He responded by quickly ripping off a pair of brilliant runs, including a twenty-four-yard touchdown. Later in the quarter, Gilmer motioned to Looney on the sideline and told him to deliver a play to Milt Plum.

"If you want a messenger," his indignant fullback retorted, "call Western Union."

Milt Plum and head coach Harry Gilmer were two of the most unpopular figures at Tiger Stadium during the 1960s. Years after he left the Lions in 1967, Plum remained notorious for one ill-advised pass against Green Bay. Gilmer was best remembered for being on the receiving end of snowballs thrown by restless fans.

As the losses and insubordination mounted, Tiger Stadium became a dangerous place for Gilmer. One October Sunday, as the Packers pounded the Lions, 31–7, hundreds of fans lifted their voices and sang: "Goodbye, Harry, goodbye, Harry, we hate to see you go." Six weeks later, the Gilmer regime came to a sorry end as Detroit fans pelted the coach with snowballs during a loss to Minnesota. "At least they didn't have rocks in them," said Gilmer, who was fired a month later.

Gilmer was replaced by assistant coach Joe Schmidt, who had retired from playing a year earlier. William Clay Ford, sole owner of the club after buying out his fellow shareholders for $4.5 million in 1964, signed the popular Schmidt to a five-year deal in January 1967. Under his leadership the club began its long, slow climb out of the basement. Several good drafts produced halfback Mel Farr, defensive back Lem Barney, quarterback Greg Landry, tight end Charlie Sanders, and Heisman Trophy winner Steve Owens, whose 1,035 rushing yards in 1971 made him the first Lion to top the thousand-yard mark. The defense jelled around the line-backing corps of Wayne Walker, Mike Lucci, and Paul Naumoff.

In 1966 the NFL and rival American Football League ended a bitter and costly six-year war. The first Super Bowl, which pitted the champions from each league, was played that season. The following year the NFL realigned into four divisions, placing Detroit with Minnesota, Green Bay, and Chicago in the Central Division of the Western Conference. In 1970 the two leagues officially merged and formed two separate conferences of three divisions each. A fourth wild-card team from each conference was added to the playoff mix. For the first time since the Lions joined the NFL, it was no longer necessary for the team to win a divisional crown to qualify for the championship. Second place would do nicely, assuming it had the best record among all the runner-ups.

The Lions shot out of the gate in 1970 with five wins in six games, and then faltered with three straight losses. At 5–4, the Lions needed to win the rest of their games for a chance at the playoffs. They won their next three home games against San Francisco, Oakland, and St. Louis—all division leaders. The Oakland win, their first on Thanksgiving Day since the 1962 defeat of Green Bay, was particularly sweet. The haughty Raiders zoomed to a 14–0 lead in the first seven minutes and enjoyed themselves immensely on the sidelines. "Those bastards are laughing at us," declared an angry Mike Lucci.

The defense tightened and held George Blanda, who was in the midst of a storybook season as a kicker and backup quarterback, to zilch after he relieved Daryle Lamonica in the final quarter. Meanwhile Greg Landry breathed new life into the offense, tossing three touchdown passes. Charlie Sanders made acrobatic catches of two of them. Mel Farr's eleven-yard scamper sewed up a satisfying 28–14 victory. Afterwards Sanders scolded Detroit's fickle fans. "I felt good because the fans got to me," he said. "The booing—that was the main thing that fired us up. The people put us down. We figured then we'd try to see if we could win it for ourselves. It proved what Joe Schmidt had been telling us—we've got a helluva team."

The art of pass coverage. *Detroit News* photographer Drayton "Doc" Holcomb captures Lem Barney, Mike Weger, and San Francisco's Gene Washington in an airborne ballet during a 1970 game at Tiger Stadium.

A five-game winning streak at the end of the 1970 season put the Lions in the playoffs for the first time since 1957. Fans celebrated the clinching win over Green Bay by pulling down the goalposts.

The Lions beat Los Angeles on the coast, then returned home to whitewash the Packers in the season finale. Highlights of the 20–0 triumph, which clinched a wild-card berth in the playoffs, could have been packaged as "The Lem Barney Show." The Lions' cornerback returned a kickoff seventy-four yards to set up a field goal, hauled back a punt sixty-five yards to set up a touchdown, and returned an interception forty-nine yards for a score. After the game

Lions fans tore down the goalposts for the first time since 1957, the last year the team played in the postseason. The final-game crowd established a new season attendance record at the stadium of 401,200, which worked out to an unprecedented 57,314 paid admissions per game.

The bubble burst in Dallas, when the Cowboys won the opening-round playoff game by the unlikely score of 5–0. Armchair quarterbacking had barely subsided when, a few weeks later, William Clay Ford dropped a bombshell. On February 1, 1971, he announced that the Lions were leaving Detroit.

Despite three decades of coexistence with the Tigers, the Lions long desired their own facilities—for convenience's sake, as well as for the huge profits to be made from expanding capacity and controlling concessions and parking.

Tiger Stadium was already considered antiquated by many in the Lions' and Tigers' organizations. But the Lions, who felt like second-class citizens even as they won championships, experienced a special urgency to move. The baseball season forced them to practice at Cranbrook School, their training site, until the Tigers finished their home schedule. Whenever bad weather forced the ground crew to drain or repair the field, the Lions boarded buses to nearby Wayne State University or a local high-school field to run plays. A lack of space meant the Lions' corporate offices were located off-site. Jamming forty-five oversized footballers into a locker room that proved a tight squeeze for half that many baseball players was like trying to park a locomotive in a one-car garage.

Serious talk circulated since 1948 about building a massive, multipurpose stadium at the State Fairgrounds on Eight Mile Road to lure the Olympic Games to town. After the games ended, the thinking went, several of the city's professional and collegiate teams, including the Lions, would move in. The notion of a municipally funded facility lost favor as the city struggled with more pressing needs for its tax dollars. After the final variation of the Olympic stadium idea died in 1969, Mayor Jerry Cavanaugh and Governor Bill Milliken backed a plan to build a riverfront stadium near the spot where the Joe Louis Arena now stands. The proposed domed stadium, to be built with a combination of private and public funds, would seat seventy thousand for football and fifty-five thousand for baseball.

The Lions refused. They wanted their new home near Tiger Stadium—either on Michigan Avenue or north of the Fisher

Steve Owens, the Lions' first thousand-yard rusher, leaves the field
on Thanksgiving Day 1974. The injured fullback's final day as a pro
coincided with the Lions' last game at the corner.

Freeway. Cavanaugh, worried about repercussions at the ballot box,
balked over the idea of relocating hundreds of Corktown residents.
He and the commission set up to study the stadium project essentially told Ford that it was the riverfront or nothing.

Ford chose neither. He picked Pontiac.

Emboldened by two decades of steady sellouts, Ford earlier
informed the *Wall Street Journal*, "Football has grown to a stage
where it no longer has to be a stepchild of baseball. Our fans want
a football-only stadium, and we're going to give them one."

Civic leaders, who touted a riverfront stadium as a key to revi-
talizing the downtown area in the wake of the 1967 riot, attempted

to get Ford to change his mind. Henry Ford II, who would be instrumental in getting the giant Renaissance Center built on the river, worked on his younger brother, but to no avail. On December 11, 1972, Pontiac voters passed a bond issue to finance construction of the $55.7-million stadium. The following September, ground was broken at the 132-acre site near the intersection of Opdyke Road and M-59. When it was completed in 1975 Pontiac residents began dropping an annual subsidy of about $800,00 into the giant pit, roughly ten taxpayer dollars for every seat.

The last four lame-duck seasons at Michigan and Trumbull saw the Lions come in second to the Minnesota Vikings each year except 1972, when Green Bay finished ahead of Detroit. These were dreary years of unfulfilled expectations and tragedy, including the sudden deaths of Chuck Hughes and Don McCafferty.

Hughes' death on October 24, 1971 was the greatest single tragedy ever to occur at the corner of Michigan and Trumbull. On that raw and dreary Sunday, a steady, melancholy rain fell all afternoon. The Lions were playing the Chicago Bears in a see-saw game they lost, 28–23.

Fans cheered when the twenty-eight-year-old flanker made a tumbling grab of a Greg Landry pass to give the Lions a clutch first down on the Bears' 37-yard line in the waning minutes of the game. It was Hughes' first reception of the year and only the fifteenth catch of his unremarkable five-year pro career. As the clock ticked off the final two minutes of play, Landry went back to pass twice and threw incomplete each time. On third down, Hughes flanked out to his right. The Chicago cornerback covering him later remarked that Hughes' eyes "looked kind of strange" as they faced each other across the line of scrimmage. Hughes ran a down-and-in, but Landry passed instead to Charlie Sanders, who dropped the ball near the Chicago goal line. A collective groan went up in the stands. Most eyes were on Sanders when Hughes, returning to the huddle, collapsed on the Bears' 15-yard line. Lying face down in the arca of deep left field, Hughes twitched uncontrollably on the soggy turf. Four trainers and doctors raced out. Over fifty-four thousand people in the stands quietly watched as they beat their fists on Chuck Hughes' chest. The marbled sky hung low over the left-field stands and a cold drizzle continued to fall. The stadium clock showed sixty-two seconds left in the game.

An autopsy revealed that Hughes had died of acute coronary thrombosis, or hardening of the arteries. Later it was reported that Hughes had complained of pain throughout the season, but doctors concluded that even if the problem had been correctly diagnosed, Chuck Hughes, with the heart of a sixty-year-old man, probably would have died soon anyway.

Joe Schmidt, who retained his own premonitions about fate ("getting the ziggy" is how he described getting fired) resigned as coach following the 1972 season. Don McCafferty, who had won the Super Bowl in 1971 with Baltimore, replaced him. After taking the club to a 6–7–1 record in 1973, McCafferty unexpectedly suffered a fatal heart attack the following July. Assistant coach Rick Forzano took over and stood on the sidelines for the Lions' last season at Tiger Stadium.

The Lions ended nearly four decades of play at Tiger Stadium on November 28, 1974. A crowd of 53,314 showed up on Thanksgiving Day, the second largest draw of the season, but still a slightly disappointing number, considering the occasion. Outfitted in stocking caps and long underwear, patrons sipped from thermoses, blew their noses, and stamped their feet—as much to jumpstart their circulation as get the home team going.

On this late fall football afternoon the Denver Broncos slipped past the boys in blue and silver, 31–27. There was a certain amount of nostalgia, but there also was anticipation and excitement over the future, especially among the players, who no longer had to worry about postage-stamp-sized weight rooms, bus rides to high school practice fields, and arctic Sundays when one's toes felt as if they had been lopped off with an axe. Imagine spiking a football in a climate-controlled end zone in December!

On the sidelines that afternoon a young assistant coach was finishing up his first year in the pro ranks. Jerry Glanville, a native Detroiter who for years watched the Lions from the center-field bleachers, went on to a colorful career as an NFL head coach with Houston and Atlanta. When he brought his teams to the Silverdome he detected a difference in the crowd's composition.

"I think what happened at Tiger Stadium is that we sold tickets in twos and fours, to people who cared enough to buy them," said Glanville. After moving to the Silverdome, however, the atmosphere "went corporate, and people started buying 200 tickets to entertain.

Perennial Pro Bowl tight end Charlie Sanders, who
played the first seven of his ten NFL seasons in the
open air of Tiger Stadium, inspects the Lions' $56-mil-
lion domed facility in Pontiac.

And people started sitting there who cared, but didn't really care
because it was the event. When we were at Tiger Stadium, it was love."

On August 23, 1975, nearly eighty thousand people gathered
under the Silverdome's inflatable roof and watched the Lions beat
Kansas City, 27–24, in a preseason game that was the first indoor
game ever played in the state. On October 6, the *Monday Night
Football* crew was on hand to broadcast the first regular season
game. Dallas demolished home boys, 36–10, but indoor football was
on its way in Detroit . . . er, Pontiac.

Despite the comfortable surroundings, the Lions' new home doesn't set too well with many hard-core traditionalists, who loyally turn out at the Silverdome but still listen with faint hope when, every so often, somebody with a desk and a title but no sense of reality makes noise about the team returning to the open air of Tiger Stadium. It'll never happen. Those days are gone for good. Memories are all that's left.

In recalling the Lions' golden era for a reporter, Jack Christiansen described the elemental difference between the game as played at Michigan and Trumbull and today's indoor variety.

"I can remember picking up a handful of snow, or mud, and throwing it in the receiver's eyes," said the old Lion, flashing back perhaps to some cold, steel-gray afternoon at Briggs Stadium, with snowflakes spinning crazily in the raw wind and players' panting breaths hanging in the air like cartoon balloons. "They'd holler and bitch, but we'd get away with it. You can't do that today. For one thing, you can't pick up a handful of AstroTurf."

The fan phenomenon known as "the wave" works its way around Tiger Stadium in 1984.

CHAPTER SIX

Modern Love

Tiger Stadium, 1961–1997

U NLIKE PREVIOUS OWNERS of the Detroit Tigers, John Fetzer was a man of the twentieth-century. He was born in Decatur, Indiana on March 25, 1901, just a month before the Tigers opened major-league play with their astounding ten-run, ninth-inning rally against Milwaukee at Bennett Park.

Fetzer's own story was just as remarkable. His father died when he was two years old. His hard-scrabble life saw the family move from town to town as his mother plied her trade as a milliner. Throughout his life Fetzer's guiding force was this unobtrusively spiritual woman, who warned him time and again that "possessions can blight a life." On her death bed she told her son "Pray, John, pray."

Fetzer, a true broadcasting pioneer, first began tinkering with wireless sets at the age of nine. Even then the Detroit Tigers were a part of his life. His brother-in-law, who worked for the Wabash Railroad in Lafayette, Indiana, translated telegraphic game accounts for Tiger fans gathered outside the depot, chalking the results on a large scoreboard. As a young man Fetzer used bedsprings for antennas and operated ham radios. In between studying engineering at Purdue and examining several countries' broadcasting systems firsthand in Europe, he helped build several rudimentary radio stations in the Midwest. In 1930 he opened a five-hundred-watt station in Kalamazoo, WKZO. The Depression-era station was cash poor, so Fetzer swapped air time for groceries. Despite the difficulties, the little station began to prosper.

As he grew older Fetzer's six-foot, one-inch, broad-shouldered frame became a familiar sight in Washington. He played an integral part in the successful fight against public control of the airwaves and also was involved in a lengthy, landmark lawsuit over a directional antenna he helped develop. During the Second World War, President Roosevelt appointed him the U. S. Censor for Radio. Fetzer monitored shortwave transmissions both at home and abroad and created guidelines for what was broadcast. He traveled to Europe at the close of the war to help restore broadcasting in repatriated countries, rolling into Berlin shortly after the Russians' arrival.

After the war Fetzer helped formulate national broadcast policy and authored the television code of ethics. He also built a personal fortune by purchasing a variety of Midwestern radio-TV stations, including several in Michigan that he organized into the statewide Detroit Tigers radio and television networks.

Fetzer's upbringing created an unusual but logical philosophy about the proper place of material wealth, even as he became a millionaire many times over. "Money is not an end in itself," he said. "It's been amply shown that money does not bring happiness. And money cannot be a clock of what a person is actually worth. If it is, then I think you're on the wrong track. Anybody that has possessions, anybody who is very honest, will say 'I don't own anything—my possessions all own me.'"

By 1956 one of the possessions that owned Fetzer was a one-third share of the Tigers. It quickly became evident to him that, with ten other investors to answer to, there were far too many balls in the ball bag. During the fall of 1960 he bought out Kenyon Brown, one of the other two principal shareholders, and became president of the club. After Fred Knorr was tragically scalded to death in Florida several weeks later, he negotiated a deal with Knorr's estate. On November 14, 1961, sixty-year-old John Fetzer finally became the sole owner of the team he once followed as a child on the old Wabash line.

Almost from the beginning Detroiters characterized Fetzer as "old gray John." Fans and players believed he was an invisible, colorless, aloof skinflint with an obsession for the bottom line. The reality was that Fetzer was a caring, thoughtful, highly principled person who shunned the public spotlight. His gray-flannel image belied an active, open mind. He was more than a man of the world—he was a creature of the universe, exploring such mysteries as telekinesis, Buddhism, and biofeedback at an age when most men are content to spend their mental energy tabulating golf scores. Through his charitable foundation he donated millions of dollars to paranormal research. He believed in unidentified flying objects and meditation, though he never brought up either subject with his fellow owners. At the age of seventy Fetzer spelled out his unconventional beliefs in a self-published book, *America's Agony*, which blended social commentary and parapsychology. Fetzer believed divine intelligence was found swirling somewhere out in space—a kind of low-frequency radio wave that humans, constructed of transistor-like cells, could tune into.

The Tigers' owner was an important man, but not self-important. He lived simply and, because he had no children, considered loyal employees his family and treated them accordingly. One example was Jim Campbell, an Ohio State graduate who joined the Tigers' organization in 1949 as the twenty-five-year-old business manager of their Thomasville, Georgia, farm club. The day he reported for work the park burned down. Despite this ominous beginning, Campbell moved quickly up the ranks, thanks in large part to Fetzer, who promoted him to vice president in 1959. Three years later Fetzer named Campbell general manager and, in 1978, president of the club.

During this period the portly, cigar-chomping, straight-shooting executive turned the Tigers into consistent winners on the field and at the gate, though the players consistently criticized him for his Old World ways. "He ran the club like it was the 1940s and 1950s," complained one Tiger when Campbell finally left the club in 1992. Campbell didn't care. His devotion to the job gained him the praise of peers although it cost him his wife of fifteen years. "She accused me of loving baseball more than her," he once said. "Damned if she wasn't right."

Because of Fetzer's integrity, intelligence, and wide-ranging experience, the Detroit owner's views—at least on more conventional topics —became as eagerly sought within baseball circles as they were inside the broadcasting industry. Fetzer negotiated the first national television contract in 1965, which spread the wealth equally among all owners. By the late 1970s each owner's take had grown from $300,000 to about $1 million a season, but that was peanuts compared to what was down the road. By the early 1990s long-term deals signed with CBS and ESPN brought each club $14 million a year.

The contracts provided a monetary windfall for the owners and helped fuel their spending frenzy. Paradoxically, the visionary Fetzer would become renowned as a dinosaur, unwilling to participate in the free-agent sweepstakes that television money created. Through Campbell he ran a tight ship, as any sensible businessman should. If he wasn't out to profit from baseball, neither was he interested in wrecking the franchise by spending more than he took in. The guaranteed, multi-year, multimillion-dollar contracts—particularly for .220-hitting shortstops and journeyman relievers—would only destroy the game, he warned, keep tickets out of the hands of the average working stiff and cause division, jealousy, and selfishness among the players. Despite his concerns, he loved the national pastime with a quiet passion until the very end. "To me," Fetzer would say many times before his death in 1991, "baseball is the fulfillment of an obligation of public interest."

In 1961, the Tigers' first summer at the renamed Tiger Stadium, public interest in baseball was near an all-time high. Nineteen sixty-one is best remembered by most baseball fans for the home-run duel between the Yankees' Mickey Mantle and Roger Maris, as they chased Babe Ruth's season record of sixty. Others remember it as the beginning of baseball's expansion era, with the American League adding two teams to the old eight-team circuit and eight games to the traditional 154-game schedule.

But not in Detroit, where fans recalled with frustration a summer where the heavy-hitting Tigers remained in the race until late September. Under new manager Bob Scheffing they eventually fin-

Al Kaline snags a Mickey Mantle blast against the right-field screen late in the 1961 pennant race. Despite winning 101 games, the Tigers finished eight games behind the Yankees.

Al Kaline is flanked by Rocky Colavito (left) and Norm Cash. The trio of long-ball bashers was unsurpassed in baseball. In their four seasons together, 1960 through 1963, they hit a collective 353 home runs.

ished second despite tying a franchise record with 101 victories. The balanced Tigers attack led the circuit in scoring and batting and finished second in slugging and stolen bases. Al Kaline hit .324 with a league-high forty-one doubles, Rocky Colavito smacked forty-five home runs and drove in 140 runs, and Frank Lary finished 23–9. For the first time, a Detroit pennant contender featured black regulars: rookie second baseman Jake Wood, who led the loop in triples and strikeouts, and veteran center fielder Billy Bruton, who conveniently shaved two years off his age after coming over from Milwaukee.

The biggest story of the summer was Norman Dalton Cash, a twenty-six-year-old first sacker who had spent two seasons with the White Sox prior to joining Detroit in 1960. Stormin' Norman reminded local sports fans of another blond, hard-partying, Texas good ol' boy from the city's recent sporting past, Bobby Layne. As with Layne, the booze contributed to an early demise. One night in 1986 Cash knocked back several vodka tonics inside a northern Michigan bar, and then fell off a dock. They found his body the next morning face-up in fifteen feet of cold water, his eyeglasses still on and the toes of his cowboy boots pointing heavenward.

Cash battled demons his entire adult life, but that didn't obscure the joy he delivered during his fifteen seasons at the corner of Michigan and Trumbull. His 373 home runs, which still rank him second on the Tigers' career list, are only a part of the story. Cash, a gamer and a showman, regularly doffed his cap to the crowd, flipped balls into the stand, and fielded his position with flair and grace. He was a master at running down foul flies hit high over his head. He strode to the plate in his familiar bandy-legged way, spitting tobacco juice and whirling three bats over his head. More often than not he made the umpire and catcher smile as he set himself in the box. Once he offered the ump a pair of novelty sunglasses with battery-operated wiper blades. On another occasion near the end of his career, as Nolan Ryan was halfway through tossing a no-hitter at Tiger Stadium, he came to the plate brandishing a table leg.

"Normy was one of the top five ballplayers, as far as human goodness was concerned," said Jimmy Butsicaris, owner of downtown's premier sports bar, the Lindell A.C. "He'd think nothing of taking a few balls down to Children's Hospital and autographing them for kids. When it came time to speak at some charity dinner, Norm was always there. He wasn't like a lot of these other guys, where the first thing out of their mouths was 'How much?' Ol' Normy just said, 'Where and when?' when it came to giving to other people."

In 1961 Cash set a club record for lefthanders with forty-one home runs, including the first ball ever hit by a Detroit player completely out of Tiger Stadium. He also knocked in 132 runs and hit .361 to capture the batting championship—the Tigers' last to date. (Kaline finished a distant second.) The free-swinging power hitter, who in retirement confessed to hollowing out his bats, admitted he

Two local broadcasting legends, George Kell and Ernie Harwell, teamed up in 1960.

was an improbable batting champion. He called the entire season "a freak. Even at the time I realized that. Everything I hit seemed to drop in, even when I didn't make contact. I never thought I'd do it again."

And he didn't. In 1962 his average plummeted 118 points to .243, still the biggest drop ever experienced by a batting champion. But that summer he hit three more balls over the right-field roof, part of a season total of thirty-nine. Colavito, who led the league in total bases, chipped in with thirty-seven. Jim Bunning won nineteen games while Cash's drinking buddy, Hank Aguirre, finished 16–8 and led the majors with a 2.21 ERA. Despite ripping a club-record 209 home runs, the Tigers—hobbled by Kaline's shoulder injury—

dropped to fourth. The following season they fell two more notches, costing Bob Scheffing his job and causing Bunning and Colavito
to be traded.

During the early 1960s Detroit's farm system, rebuilt under
Fetzer and Campbell, finally began to pay dividends. Jug-eared, pot-
bellied Mickey Lolich, a self-styled "working-class pitcher," earned
five victories with his left arm in 1963. They were the first of an
eventual 207 games he won during his thirteen-year career in
Detroit. On the receiving end of most of them was Bill Freehan, a
Detroit native and ex-Michigan end who spent his first full season
at Tiger Stadium in 1963. The muscular six-foot, three-inch, 205-
pound catcher—an All-Star in eleven of his fifteen Tiger seasons—
was a powerful hitter and excellent defensive player.

Willie Horton, who played parts of the 1963 and 1964 seasons
before bursting on the scene with twenty-nine homers and 104 RBI
in 1965, was the Tigers' first legitimate black star. One of sixteen
children raised in a Detroit housing project, Horton raised eyebrows
with tremendous clouts at Northwestern High School, near
Olympia Stadium, where the bouncing ball stopped traffic on
Grand River. At sixteen he played a sandlot game at Briggs Stadium
and knocked a ball into the upper deck in deep right-center. On
weekends clubhouse manager Jack Hand let him shine players'
shoes and clean the locker room. "I thought the players were God,"
Horton once recalled, "and I couldn't believe I could get that close
to them."

The stocky, moody left fielder, whose parents were killed in a car
accident shortly after he joined the Tigers, clubbed 262 round-trippers
during his fifteen seasons with the Tigers. Both black and white fans
joined together to scream from their seats, "Hit the ball, Wil-liiee!"

Other notable farmhands included infielders Dick McAuliffe,
Ray Oyler, and Tom Matchick; outfielders Jim Northrup, Gates
Brown, and Mickey Stanley; and pitchers Pat Dobson and John
Hiller. Blended in with veterans like Cash and Kaline and such key
additions as pitchers Denny McLain and Earl Wilson (acquired
from the White Sox and Red Sox, respectively), the team soon was
positioned to contend for the pennant after two decades of disappointment.

The Tigers' gate sagged to little more than eight hundred thousand during the transitional seasons of 1963 and 1964 before

Willie Horton, a muscular, moody product of Detroit's sandlots, joined the Tigers in 1963 and stayed fifteen seasons.

rebounding to an average of 1.2 million in 1965–67. These numbers—a good showing at a time when one million fans served as the benchmark for a financially successful season—weren't as large as they might have been. One factor was suburbanization, which continued to pick up steam during the decade. Middle-class white families, many of whom saw their neighborhoods carved to pieces by the freeway system, followed the freshly paved concrete paths out to subdivisions in Livonia, Warren, Lincoln Park, and Southfield. Racial animosity played a role in the movement, but it was not nearly as great a factor as it would become. In fact, Detroit enjoyed a reputation in the national press as a progressive, harmonious community—America's "model city," as one publication termed it. Overblown as this image was, it was true that Detroit had a large black middle class that, thanks to the auto industry, enjoyed higher wages and a better standard of living than nearly any other place in the country.

For a few years during the 1960s, Tiger Stadium hosted Bat Day, a promotion that gave every fan fourteen and younger a free Louisville Slugger. The promotion was discontinued, however, when structural engineers warned that the pounding of tens of thousands of bats on the concrete floors could damage the stadium.

This all changed during the muggy, early morning hours of Sunday, July 23, 1967, when police raided a blind pig above a printing shop at the corner of Clairmount and Twelfth Streets. A crowd gathered as police led scores of black men into custody. Good-natured at first, the mob quickly turned ugly as several in the grow-

Ray Oyler retired with the lowest batting average of any player with at least one thousand big-league at-bats, but his glovework forced All-Star shortstop Dick McAuliffe to move to second base in 1967. After four seasons in Detroit, Oyler was lost to Seattle in the expansion draft in 1969. He closed out his career with California, leaving behind a .175 career average.

ing throng began hurling epithets and then rocks. Police, who one year earlier had gained national acclaim for handling a three-day disturbance on Kercheval without firing a shot, decided not to use force to disperse the throng. It was a fateful decision. Within hours looters broke into storefronts, carted away merchandise, and torched buildings. A few blocks away, the Tigers and Yankees squared off at the stadium, unaware of the growing conflagration.

Ernie Harwell and Ray Lane were covering the game on radio. "We didn't know it was a riot at that time," said Lane. "We weren't

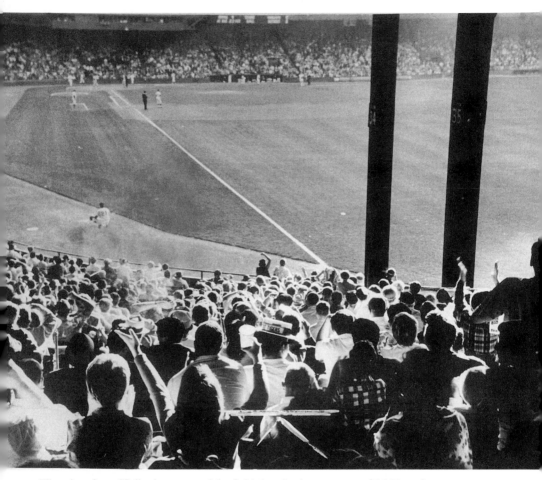

The view from Kaline's corner, right field, late in the summer of 1967 as the Tigers battled Chicago, Minnesota, and Boston down to the wire for the pennant.

allowed to say anything about the smoke coming in over the left field stands. Jim Campbell and WJR told us not to mention it."

Players were ordered to stay home. Horton, who lived downtown, entered the embattled neighborhoods and pleaded for calm, but to no avail. Four days of rioting resulted in 43 deaths, 682 injuries, and 7,231 arrests. There were 682 fires and 1,700 stores looted. Other American cities experienced similar violent outbreaks during the 1960s, but none were as terrible as the one that ripped apart Detroit.

The 1967 riot, at that time the bloodiest in American history, left deep scars on the Detroit community. Bill Freehan, shown during a home-plate collision with Cleveland's Tony Horton the following summer, thought 1968's "Year of the Tiger" had a therapeutic effect on the city. "A baseball team and a world championship can't cure such social ills," he said. "But I honestly think that pride in our team helped the healing process and gave everyone a focal point to look at and feel like it belonged to everyone who lived there."

By Tuesday, July 25, thousands of policemen, army paratroopers, and National Guardsmen patrolled the streets. The Tigers canceled that night's game with the Orioles and then decided to move the final two games of the series to Baltimore. "I thought that was out of line," said Jim Northrup. "It was too dangerous to play ball in Detroit, but we had to go on the road and leave behind our wives and kids. Back then, baseball players didn't question things. You just did what you were told." Mickey Lolich wound up missing a pitching turn. As a member of the Michigan Air National Guard he was assigned to riot duty, guarding police headquarters downtown.

Even as the embers of the riot cooled in Detroit, the pennant race turned into a torrid affair. Four teams battled for the top spot all the way through the final days. On September 27, Minnesota led the league, a game in front of Boston and Chicago and a game and a half ahead of the Tigers. A doubleheader loss to Kansas City dropped the White Sox out of contention; meanwhile, the Tigers were scheduled to finish the season with four single games against California at Tiger Stadium. But three straight days of rain and cold forced a pair of doubleheaders.

Saturday, September 30, arrived crisp and clear. The standings showed the Twins on top, a game ahead of the Red Sox and Tigers. Detroit held its destiny in its hands: a sweep of the Angels would give the Tigers the pennant. Three wins would create a special one-game playoff with either Minnesota or Boston, who were ending their seasons with a two-game set at Fenway Park.

In the first game, Lolich tossed his third straight shutout, 5–0, as the scoreboard showed the Red Sox had defeated the Twins. A Tigers win in the second game would have created a virtual three-way tie for first. Instead, the Angels rallied for six runs in the eighth inning against Hank Aguirre to pull out an 8–6 victory.

With the riot fresh in most Detroiters' minds, only 20,421 watched Saturday's games, but nearly twice that number filled Tiger Stadium on Sunday, October 1, for the climactic doubleheader. The Tigers grabbed the opener, 6–4, as Joe Sparma won his sixteenth game and Eddie Mathews, the longtime National League slugger, acquired August 17 for the stretch drive, banged out his sixth game-winning hit as a Tiger. The victory placed Detroit a half-game behind Boston, which that afternoon capped its remarkable Impossible Dream season by beating the Twins. The Tigers needed to win the nightcap to force a playoff with the Red Sox, who started the year as 100-to-1 shots to win the pennant.

As Red Sox players gathered around clubhouse radios and WJBK-Channel 2 broke into regular programming to televise the final game commercial-free, Detroit manager Mayo Smith pulled out all the stops. Denny McLain, who had not pitched for two weeks due to a mysteriously injured foot (some rumored it was the result of a warning by a loan shark to repay a debt), carried a 3–1 lead into the second and then unraveled. The Angels chased McLain in the third and carved out a 4–3 lead. By the fifth the advantage had grown to 8–3 off a succession of pitchers. In all, Smith used eight of them.

Don Shapiro, a long-suffering Tigers fan, squirmed in his seat as The Great Race played out in the cool autumn dusk. No admirer of the Detroit skipper, Shapiro maintained that Mayo Smith was a nice guy who had no business managing a big-league team.

"That last game, he did everything wrong," he recollected for Roger Angell. "He let our pitcher stay in, and I was standing up on my seat screaming, 'Take him out! Take him out!' I was blind with rage. I can still see what happened next—that pitch coming in to the Angels' [Jim] Fregosi, and Fregosi getting ready to hit it—and I can see the man coming around third to put them ahead."

But what remains burned into the collective memory of Shapiro and everybody else watching or listening in Detroit was the drama's final moments, as Dick McAuliffe walked to the plate in the ninth with runners on first and second and one out. The All-Star second baseman, who had averaged twenty-one home runs over the last four seasons, represented the tying run. The Tigers had battled back to score a pair of runs in the eighth to make it 8–5. George Brunet, a low-ball pitcher, stood on the mound, a surrealistic figure bathed in mist and the electric lights. Thousands in the pleading crowd stood, afraid to breathe; some fell to their knees and prayed, afraid to watch. High up in his private suite in right field, invisible to the world, John Fetzer surveyed the scene through one-way glass.

McAuliffe, who had not batted into a double play all season, guessed a downstairs fast ball. "Sure enough, there it was," he said. "It was too low."

He swung. The ball bounced to second baseman Bobby Knoop, who tossed it to shortstop Jim Fregosi, who in turn relayed it to first to nip the hard-charging McAuliffe for the season-ending double play. It was 7:42 P.M. and the long, draining summer of disappointment and strife had officially ended.

A dam of emotion broke. Some people jumped onto the field, ripped up chunks of turf and battled security guards. Others broke chairs and tossed them onto the diamond. Eddie Mathews fired a ball at a photographer. Pete Waldmeir, covering the games for the *Detroit News,* accurately described the ending as "kind of bush." Don Shapiro went home and broke all of the flower pots in his basement. None of it changed the outcome.

For a long time the Tigers' heavy-hearted owner watched Detroiters loot his stadium. Finally he sat down and wrote a letter to himself that he later placed inside a desk drawer. He titled it "A True Confession—By Fetzer."

> On this infamous evening of October 1, 1967, there is no happiness in that section of Mudville near the corner of Michigan and Trumbull. The heroes have fallen and I am ill. I have been here alone for hours but a few tears cannot wash away the hurt. As I tuned in on the waves of reflection, the brilliant lights of Tiger Stadium began to fade and I watched hundreds of fans give vent to their frustrations. They destroyed scores of stadium seats and piled the rubble on the dugouts. Still others clawed at home plate and the pitcher's mound, while a bedlam of confusion turned many more hundreds into a near mob scene with the elements of combat everywhere on the playing field. In stony silence I thought of how desperately hard I had fought to build a winner in Detroit. It seemed that my long-sought goal was near fruition. I thought a pennant would have meant more to Detroit than all of the man-made remedies put together. I thought that 1967 would be a crowning year of glory for our city and that the world would soon forget our stormy past.

But it was not to be, concluded the Tigers' owner, who ended his sad note: "John Fetzer has just died. This is his ghost speaking."

The Tigers, convinced to a man they had blown the pennant, came to spring training a resolute group. "I was so upset that we didn't

On August 22, 1968, Dick McAuliffe, enraged by a brushback pitch, charged the mound and tangled with Chicago's Tommy John, who tried to tackle the onrushing Tiger. McAuliffe was fined $250 and suspended for five games, but John's punishment was worse: a severe shoulder injury that nearly cost him his career.

win," said McAuliffe. "I was frustrated and angry. We had the best team. But we didn't win."

The disappointment of 1967 set the stage for "the Year of the Tiger," as the championship season of 1968 was dubbed. After dropping their opener, the Tigers strung together nine straight wins, several of them of the comeback variety. Everyone contributed, from front-line players to third-string shortstops. William Brown, a chunky reserve outfielder nicknamed "Gates" because of his prison past, hit .370 and became baseball's most feared pinch hitter. Earl Wilson, who led the league with twenty-two victories in 1967, slipped to thirteen but produced some timely home runs. Right fielder Jim Northrup hit four grand slams, three in one week, and finished third in the league with ninety RBIs. Ray Oyler at shortstop and Mickey Stanley in center field gobbled up everything in sight. McAuliffe, who moved from short to second the year before to make room for Oyler, led the loop in runs scored. As a team Detroit was tops in scoring, home runs, fielding, and attendance, drawing 2,031,847 to Tiger Stadium. It was the first two-million gate in team history.*

Last-licks victories became the leitmotiv of the 1968 club, which had its own media-inspired slogan: "Sock it to 'em, Tigers." It appeared everywhere: in songs and on signs, commercials, and bumper stickers. Reflecting the cultural diversity of the area's fan base, it was spoken or written in a multitude of languages, including Hungarian (*Verd neg oket Tigerish*), Yiddish (*Dalaing iss tze zay Tigers*), Polish (*Die che eem tygrysy*), and Japanese (*Bonzai, Tigers*). Soon the team was outdistancing the field, so that by the All-Star break the only question seemed to be how many games the Tigers, and Denny McLain, would win.

The answer to the first was 103, a new club record. The answer to the second was 31, making McLain baseball's first 30-game winner since Dizzy Dean in 1934. Dean was present at Tiger Stadium on September 14, when the Tigers delivered McLain's historic win in characteristic fashion, rallying for two ninth-inning runs against

---

* That summer the Tigers opened their doors to the Detroit Cougars, a professional soccer team that included local businessman Ralph Wilson as part owner. Unfortunately, most of the fifteen hundred or so who showed up for the match thought they had bought tickets to a baseball game, Wilson said. "Millions like it in Europe, Asia, or wherever they play it. They don't like it in Detroit."

Oakland. For the season the right-handed fastballer was 31–6 with a 1.96 ERA and 280 strikeouts while pitching a league-high 336 innings.

McLain enjoyed as storybook a season as could be imagined. As a fielder he started a triple play against Baltimore and, as a batter, failed to advance a runner in sacrifice situations only twice all summer. He was the unanimous choice for the Cy Young Award as the league's top pitcher and also captured the MVP plaque.

The twenty-four-year-old McLain was cocky, flamboyant, and great copy. He played his giant Hammond X-77 organ in clubs, drank twenty-five bottles of Pepsi a day, and rearranged the facts of a story to fit the man or the moment. He appeared on the cover of national magazines and was a guest on several top television shows. Impish and impulsive, he breezily bent the rules as only a spoiled superstar could. One July Sunday he won his sixteenth game in the first game of a doubleheader against Oakland, and then climbed into the organ loft during the nightcap to entertain Tiger Stadium fans with his version of "Satin Doll." A few days later he almost missed his regular turn, racing from a recording studio on Livernois where he had just finished cutting an album for Capitol Records (*Denny McLain at the Organ: The Detroit Tigers' Superstar Swings with Today's Hits*) to Tiger Stadium, where he overpowered Cleveland for his twenty-third win.

McLain even served up a home run on a platter to an aging idol. On September 19, he had a 6–1 lead over the Yankees when Mickey Mantle struggled up to the plate in the eighth inning. The game was over, the pennant was clinched, the day was gray and dismal, and the only thing keeping the remnants of a small midweek crowd at Tiger Stadium was the chance to see The Mick hit one more out of the park before ending his eighteen-year career. Fans gave him a nice round of applause, and then groaned as McLain quickly got two strikes on him. At this point catcher Jim Price told Mantle that McLain was going to groove one for him. Where would he like it? Mantle, who needed one more home run to move into third place on the all-time home-run list, motioned to McLain to throw the next pitch chest high.

"It was obvious," said Al Kaline. "They all thought it was the last time he was going to appear at Tiger Stadium, which it was. He wanted to know where Mickey wanted it. Mickey thought he was

A Baltimore loss in Boston gave the Tigers the '68 pennant on the evening of September 14. But club officials, fearing a celebration that might result in a forfeit, decided against posting the final score until the Tigers had finished their own game with New York. Don Wert's single in the bottom of the ninth gave the Tigers yet another come-from-behind victory and touched off the city's first pennant celebration in twenty-three years. The postgame festivities included a fireworks display sponsored by Hudson's, a longtime civic booster.

kidding. Denny threw the ball right there and he took it. So he finally found out that Denny was serious and he threw one right there and Mickey hit it in the upper deck."

Mantle grinned as he circled the bases, Detroit fans stood and cheered, and the organist played "East Side, West Side, All Around the Town." Players filled the top steps of the Detroit dugout, clapping and laughing. "Thanks, Denny," Mantle said with a nod as he rounded third base and headed home.

"I remember Mayo Smith telling him in the dugout, 'Denny,

The turning point of the '68 World Series. In the fifth inning of the fifth game, with St. Louis leading by a run, Lou Brock tried to score standing up on a single to left but was muscled off the plate by Bill Freehan. The Tigers rallied to win the game, 5–4. Detroit captured the final two contests in St. Louis and won the Series.

you can't do that, you got to deny that you did that, we're not sup-posed to do this in baseball, you're supposed to go out and try to get guys out and play to win all the time,'" said Kaline. "But he def-initely grooved it for Mantle." These juvenile escapades hinted at a troubling dark side—suspicions later borne out by several shady post-baseball business deals, a series of bankruptcies, and two stints in prison—one for racketeering and the second for embezzlement.

Mayo Smith went into the World Series against the St. Louis Cardinals with a dilemma: what should he do about Kaline? Detroit's favorite and oldest Tiger had missed five weeks with a broken hand. After his return Smith alternated him at first base with Norm Cash and in the outfield, afraid to break up the winning trio of Horton, Stanley, and Northrup. He decided to put Kaline in the outfield and move Stanley, perhaps the finest natural athlete on the team, to shortstop. This put Kaline's bat in the lineup and sacrificed little defense. Stanley, who had never played the position before Smith hastily started him in a few regular-season games after the pennant was clinched, made one of the most daring moves in World Series history pay off by committing just two harmless errors against the Cardinals. Kaline, meanwhile, batted .379 and contributed one of the series' key hits.

McLain faced Bob Gibson in the eagerly anticipated opener in St. Louis. The expected pitchers' duel never materialized, as McLain was chased in the sixth. Gibson, who hurled an amazing thirteen shutouts with an even more astounding 1.12 ERA, blew the ball past seventeen Tigers to shatter the series' single-game record for strikeouts. The Cardinals literally won in a breeze, 4–0. Detroit rebounded to win game two, 8–1, Mickey Lolich pitching a six-hitter and smacking what turned out to be the only home run of his sixteen-year career.

The middle three games were set for Tiger Stadium. On October 5, the first of three straight capacity crowds officially listed as 53,634 showed up for the Tigers' first World Series game at the corner in twenty-three years. Orlando Cepeda and Tim McCarver both belted three-run homers as St. Louis rolled to a 7–3 victory. Left fielder Lou Brock continued his history of excelling in the postseason by swiping three more bases for a total of six in just three games.

The following afternoon, a rainy Sunday, Brock led off the game with a long home run into the right-center-field upper deck off McLain. St. Louis bolted to a 4–0 lead before rain caused a one-hour and fourteen-minute delay at the top of the third. The Tigers embarrassed themselves trying to drag out the game in hopes of having it canceled, but ultimately the full nine was played. Gibson mowed down ten more Tigers in a 10–1 walloping and even chipped in a home run. Brock generated a double, triple, and home run and stole another base, tying his own series record of seven.

The two teams gathered the next day, the Cardinals only one victory from their third championship in five years. Brock got things going out of the gate by doubling off Lolich and then coming home on Curt Flood's single. Cepeda then belted a two-run homer. Before anyone in Detroit knew what had happened, the Cardinals enjoyed a 3–0 lead.

The Tigers clawed back. Freehan, maligned all week for his poor throws, finally nailed Brock as he tried to steal in the third. The next inning triples by Stanley and Horton produced two runs. Then came the series' turning point. At the top of the fifth, Brock doubled with one out. Julian Javier singled to left, where Horton charged the ball and unleashed a strike home. Brock failed to slide and umpire Doug Harvey called him out as Freehan's left foot blocked Brock off the plate. That kept the score at 3–2 as Detroit came to bat in the seventh.

With one out, Smith decided to let Lolich bat for himself. The .114 hitter responded with a bloop single to right, causing the Tiger Stadium crowd and St. Louis bullpen to stir. Joe Hoerner relieved starter Nelson Briles, and promptly surrendered a single to McAuliffe. He then walked Stanley. This brought up Kaline, who faced the biggest moment of his career.

Kaline swung and missed Hoerner's first offering, and then took a ball. "The third pitch was low and away, but I was counting on that and I got a good cut at it," said Kaline, who lined the ball over the second baseman's head into right center. Lolich and McAuliffe scored the tying and go-ahead runs. Moments later, Cash's single brought in Stanley with the insurance run in a rousing 5–3 victory. Lolich sewed up his second win by getting Brock to bounce back to the mound with two on and two out in the ninth.

Once given up for dead, the rejuvenated Tigers were loose as they took the field for game six in St. Louis. With McLain's high fast ball finally living up to its advance billing, Detroit socked it to 'em, 13–1, scoring ten runs in the third. This made it Lolich vs. Gibson in the deciding seventh game. Lolich, his arm tired, worked careful-ly and craftily. Twice he picked runners off first base. Gibson, gun-ning for his eighth straight complete-game win spanning three

World Series, appeared invincible. The game remained scoreless until the seventh, when Curt Flood misjudged a fly ball off Northrup's bat and it sailed over his head. Two runs scored on the triple. Before the inning was over the Tigers added two more for a 4–0 lead. It was 4–1 in the bottom of the ninth when, with two outs, Lolich induced Tim McCarver to lift a foul fly. Freehan ripped his mask off and camped under it. Freehan always relished recalling the moment he squeezed his mitt shut on McCarver's pop-up. "When you grow up in the city like I did, and used to hitch-hike down to Briggs Stadium and sit in the bleachers, the culmination of all that was almost overwhelming."

So was the public response back in Detroit. Tens of thousands of people fled their television sets and transistor radios and took to the streets. This time it wasn't an orgy of looting and violence, but rather an outpouring of communal pride and the chance to get in on a citywide party. The Tigers were champs! And the way they had done it! Those comeback kids! Detroiters alternately laughed in relief and shook their heads in disbelief: *How 'bout them Tigers!* Blacks and whites hugged, mugged, and tugged the confetti out of their hair as the Motor City went bonkers. Fifty thousand people ran onto the landing strip at Metropolitan Airport and forced the plane bringing the victorious Tigers home from St. Louis to detour to Willow Run. There five thousand fans jammed the runway. Elsewhere, members of both races rejoiced up and down major avenues and side streets. Future *Free Press* reporter Bill McGraw remembered some yelling, "Willie Horton, save our city!" That was a pretty tall order for anybody, even a fellow who'd hit thirty-six home runs during the season and batted .304 against the Cardinals.

In a sense, the Tigers' championship season represented the end of an era. The following year both leagues divided into Eastern and Western divisions, doubling the number of pennant races and creating a preliminary round of playoffs. No longer would the teams with the best record in each circuit automatically face each other in the World Series. By the time the Tigers made it back into the fall classic sixteen years later, baseball had undergone a string of other minor corruptions, including the designated hitter rule (adopted by the American League in 1973); World Series played entirely at night (the better to appease prime-time advertisers); the widespread acceptance of artificial turf and domed stadiums (most of which looked exactly alike); and an on-going series of labor disputes.

From 1969 through 1993, a span of twenty-five seasons, Detroit shared the Eastern Division with Baltimore, Boston, Cleveland, Milwaukee (which replaced Washington in 1972), New York and, beginning in 1977, the expansion Toronto Blue Jays. The Year of the Tiger proved just that; the squad that had won it all in 1968 finished second in 1969, fourth in 1970 (costing Mayo Smith his job), and second in 1971 under new manager Billy Martin.

Denny McLain generated the most excitement at Michigan and Trumbull during this period, winning a second Cy Young Award with his 24–9 record in 1969, before he was suspended three separate times in 1970. The first suspension was for his alleged participation in a bookmaking operation in 1967 (the year of his mysterious foot injury); the second came after he doused two sportswriters with buckets of water; and the third was for carrying a pistol. That winter Jim Campbell, tired of the constant controversy, sent McLain to Washington in a multi-player swap that brought Joe Coleman, Aurelio Rodriquez, and Eddie Brinkman to Detroit. The businesslike Lolich emerged as the ace of the staff in McLain's absence, leading the majors with twenty-five wins, 376 innings, and a club-record 308 strikeouts in 1971. That summer the stadium hosted the All-Star Game for the third time in its history. On the evening of July 13, a crowd of 53,559 was entertained by a record-tying six home runs, each hit by a future Hall of Famer: Johnny Bench, Hank Aaron, Roberto Clemente, Frank Robinson, Harmon Killebrew, and Reggie Jackson. The home-run barrage matched the number hit in the 1951 game, the last time the midsummer classic was held at the corner. Jackson's wind-aided blast was the most impressive, banging off the light tower atop the right-field roof. Lolich pitched the final two innings to earn a save in the American League's 6-4 victory, the junior circuit's first win since 1962.

Coleman, who averaged twenty-one victories his first three summers at Tiger Stadium, and Brinkman, who finally ended the revolving door at shortstop, were key members of the 1972 team that battled Boston for the divisional flag. The rest of the roster was a patchwork quilt of holdovers from the 1968 team and late-season addi-

On July 1, 1970, the Tigers' largest home crowd in nine years—53,863 people—gave Denny McLain a raucous hero's welcome after his return from serving a half-year suspension for gambling. He left the game in the sixth inning after surrendering five runs to the Yankees. "I thought I was going to cry when I heard those cheers," said McLain, who won just three of eight decisions and was traded to Washington shortly after the season ended.

tions, including gentle giant Frank Howard and southpaw Woodie Fryman.

Because a players' strike over the issue of salary arbitration delayed the opening of the season two weeks, teams played an unequal number of games in 1972. The season came down to the last series of the season between Boston and Detroit at Tiger

Tiger Stadium fans whoop it up after the Tigers beat Boston to clinch the 1972 Eastern Division crown.

Stadium. The Red Sox led the Tigers by a half-game. Whichever team won at least two of the three games would advance into the playoffs.

The Tigers won the opener, 4–1, as Kaline collected three hits and Lolich fanned fifteen (one shy of the club record he had set three years earlier at Tiger Stadium against California). Lolich's twenty-second victory put the Tigers a half-game up and needing to win just one of the remaining two games.

The next day 50,653 rooters screamed their lungs out, banged the old wooden chairs up and down, and generally did anything in their power to implore Woody Fryman to unknit the Sox. "I remember walking off the mound in the eighth with a 3–1 lead," said Fryman, who had compiled a 10–3 record with a 2.05 ERA after coming over from Philadelphia, "and the Tiger Stadium fans gave me a standing ovation. It was the greatest moment of my career."

Protecting the left side of the infield that game, as it had all season, was as fine a pair of glove men as baseball has ever seen. Aurelio Rodriquez was the proverbial vacuum cleaner at third and had a laser beam for a throwing arm. He also displayed good power at the plate. For nine seasons he was the hero of Detroit's growing Hispanic community, centered on Bagley just blocks from the park.

Eddie Brinkman was an inspiration to every skinny accountant wrapped inside Walter Mitty dreams. Back in high school in Cincinnati, the slightly built, bespectacled shortstop had been the home run hitter on a team that included Pete Rose. The pitching got a little tougher in the majors, as Brinkman's puny .224 career average attested, but he compensated with a solid-gold glove. In 1972 Brinkman set five fielding records, including seventy-two consecutive errorless games. His most notable contribution to Tigers lore came during a live interview on camera inside the Tiger Stadium clubhouse after the clincher against the Red Sox. "We really beat those fuckers!" Brinkman joyously announced to hundreds of thousands of fans watching in their living rooms.

Unfortunately for Detroit's chances, a bad back caused Brinkman to miss most of the playoff against the Oakland Athletics. The A's, a swashbuckling, mustachioed group garbed in gold-and-green uniforms, were on the brink of stringing together three straight world titles with a lineup that included Reggie Jackson, Joe Rudi, Sal Bando, Campy Campaneris, Vida Blue, and Jim "Catfish" Hunter.

After dropping the first two games on the coast, 3–2 and 5–0, the Tigers regrouped at home. On October 10, Joe Coleman set a playoff record with fourteen strikeouts in a 3–0 shutout. The next day the Tigers knotted matters with a comeback reminiscent of the '68 season. Trailing 3–1 in the bottom of the tenth, they loaded the bases with nobody out. Then Gene Tenace, a catcher playing second base because of some lineup juggling, dropped the ball on a sure double

Tempestuous Billy Martin took over the club in 1971. He lasted just long enough to win a division title in 1972 before he was fired near the end of the 1973 season.

play, making it 3–2. A walk to Norm Cash forced in the tying run and then Jim Northrup's single scored Kaline with the winning run.

The 4–3 triumph put the Tigers just one win from entering the World Series against Sparky Anderson's Cincinnati Reds. Although Detroit had led the loop in attendance, only 78,771 attended the first two games at Tiger Stadium. But now some fifty thousand filled the seats for the showdown, primed for a pennant party.

The Tigers struck first, McAuliffe scoring on a ground out in the opening frame. The A's tied it in the second off Fryman, as Reggie Jackson stole home on a delayed steal. In the fourth they went ahead to stay. In a controversial play George Hendrick was ruled safe on an infield grounder when the umpire said the throw pulled Cash off the bag. With two outs, Hendrick then scored on Tenace's only hit of the series. Toward the end, when it became apparent that the Tigers weren't going to touch Vida Blue, fans began tossing firecrackers, toilet paper, and smoke bombs onto the field. This delayed play but not the outcome. The A's won 2–1, and advanced to the World Series, where they beat Anderson's Big Red Machine.

For the ten years following their half-pennant in 1972 the Tigers were not particularly fun to watch. Billy Martin was canned toward the end of the 1973 season. Ralph Houk presided over the team for the next five summers, which included last-place finishes in 1974 and 1975. The 1975 squad lost 102 times, including a near-record nineteen in a row. On June 18, Boston's Fred Lynn put on the most sensational one-man show ever seen at the corner. He hit a single, a triple, and three home runs, driving in ten runs in a 15–1 rout. The performance aided Lynn's selections as that year's MVP and top rookie. (Lynn became a Tiger at the end of the 1988 season and stayed through 1989, but he never remotely approached that kind of production in a Detroit uniform.) Through 1982 the team finished as high as fourth only once. Houk was replaced by Les Moss, who in turn gave way to Sparky Anderson (who had been fired by Cincinnati) one-third of the way through the 1979 schedule.

The team's competitive inertia contributed to the fans' increasingly unruly behavior, particularly the bleacher creatures. Mike Emmerich, a college student home for the summer, was in the cheap seats one boisterous June night in 1980. "Sitting in the bleachers had become the 'in' thing to do," he recalled. "I remember some guy was on crutches and he was making his way down the aisle when someone just grabbed them from him and started beating him with them. I guess they thought it would be great entertainment.

"Other people were throwing batteries at Milwaukee's Gorman Thomas in center field. You know how outfielders usually trot out to their positions and toss the ball back and forth for a couple of minutes? Well, on this night Thomas would wait just before the batter stepped up to the plate before he ran out to his position. That's how crazy it was.

In 1974 the Tigers took a chance on a raw Detroit youngster named Ron LeFlore, a recent parolee from Jackson State Prison. The charismatic center fielder responded with three .300 seasons and gave the team its greatest stolen-base threat since the 1930s.

"I was there because the tickets were cheap. I had no intention of beating up somcone."

Thomas's outfield mate, Sixto Lezcano, was another favorite target of the bleacherites' abuse. On June 17, 1980, Jim Campbell announced that the bleachers would be closed indefinitely because of rowdyism. He reopened them on June 30 after adding tighter security and a more restrictive beer sales policy.

In the dozen years between playoff appearances there were several local heroes to hoist a beverage to at the old ball yard. Ron LeFlore, a Detroit boy who had served time for armed robbery, left Jackson State Prison for Tiger Stadium and became the Tigers' greatest base-stealing sensation since Ty Cobb. From 1974 to 1979, he averaged forty-nine steals (including a league-best 68 in 1978) and had three .300 seasons. Rusty Staub, a red-haired National League veteran and the only gourmet chef in baseball, was the league's premier designated hitter for three seasons, averaging 106 RBIs between 1976 and 1978. Left fielder Steve Kemp and first baseman Jason Thompson, a pair of businesslike sluggers, each provided five seasons of power before moving on to other teams. Alan Trammell and Lou Whitaker, who would turn out to be the game's longest-running keystone combination, debuted together at the end of the 1977 season.

The biggest breath of fresh air during this transition period was a gangly, curly-mopped pitcher from Massachusetts who dazzled America during its bicentennial summer of 1976. On May 15 of that year, Mark Fidrych won his first big-league game, a two-hit 2–1 verdict over Cleveland on a drizzly Saturday afternoon at Tiger Stadium. Fans loved his antics, which included talking to the ball, dropping to his knees to landscape the mound, and enthusiastically egging on his teammates. "I used to throw any ball that someone got a hit off me back to the ump," he once explained, "so it could rub up against the other balls. Then maybe the next time it would come back out as a pop fly." He exhibited a pure uninhibited joy in his game, redolent of after-school afternoons spent in playgrounds and backyards. The baseball world fell in love with The Bird.

At the end of June Fidrych had earned a sparkling 10–1 record. His defining moment was a Monday night game against the powerful Yankees. As 47,855 fans at Tiger Stadium and a national TV audience of millions watched, Fidrych sweet-talked his fast balls and sliders into a 5–1 triumph. The old green park rocked with the chant, "Let's go, Bird! Let's go, Bird!" Afterwards fans stayed on their feet, chanted "We want the Bird!" and refused to leave until Fidrych obliged them with a curtain call. The sky was the limit for the high-flying Bird, who appeared on the cover of such diverse publications as *Rolling Stone* and *Sports Illustrated*. Tigers broadcaster Ernie Harwell considered him the most genuine player he ever

Mark "The Bird" Fidrych makes a curtain call.

knew, as well as his favorite. On July 3, Fidrych shut out Baltimore, and then woke up the next morning to help America celebrate its two hundredth birthday. Baseball didn't get any better than this. The Bird started the All-Star Game and finished the season 19–9 with a league-best 2.34 ERA.

Fidrych was only twenty-two during his second season in 1977, too young to have his career cut short, but that's exactly what happened. He tore up his knee shagging an innocent fly ball during spring training. A week after he left the disabled list, something in his pitching shoulder popped. The Bird's ailing wing never healed properly. He wound up winning only half of his twenty decisions over the next four seasons. Detroit finally waived him in 1981. He tried to come back with a Boston farm team, but the magic was gone. When reporters looked him up on the tenth anniversary of his first and only great big-league season, they found him raising pigs in Massachusetts. A corner of his farmhouse was filled with boxes of stuffed birds given him by fans.

The innocence of Bird Mania played out against the backdrop of seismic socioeconomic change in the Motor City. In less than a generation Detroit had come to illustrate all the ills that afflicted Rust Belt cities: poverty, unemployment, drugs, violence. The 1967 riot proved the pivotal event in Detroit's long history. Practically overnight the gradual exodus of white families and businesses to the suburbs became a headlong race for the exits. The phenomenon that came to be known as "white flight" turned the city on its head. In 1973, Detroit for the first time had more black than white residents. It also elected its first black mayor, Coleman A. Young, a profane, charismatic civil-rights firebrand who spent a contentious two decades in office.

During his tenure Young watched much of the black middle class abandon Detroit, leaving behind a dispiriting landscape of poverty and crime that his police chief called "one big ghetto all the way to its borders." Contributing mightily to this urban moonscape was the shocking evaporation of well-paying factory jobs as the auto industry—damaged in the 1970s by higher fuel prices and foreign competition—closed plants, laid off tens of thousands of workers, and automated as many manufacturing jobs as possible. Between 1978 and 1988 fifty thousand Detroit auto workers lost their jobs. No longer could an unskilled person walk in off the street and find a job welding fenders at Chrysler, General Motors or Ford. The once-mighty UAW lost a third of its national membership and banned Japanese cars from its parking lots. However, when Mazda opened a plant in suburban Flat Rock, one hundred thousand people swallowed their pride and applied for the two thousand available positions.

An empty Tiger Stadium during the 1981 strike.

Despite such occasional achievements as the Renaissance Center and General Motors Poletown plant, the Motor City's manufacturing and retail base largely disintegrated during the 1970s and 1980s, as the closing of such landmarks as downtown Hudson's, Dodge Main, and the giant Uniroyal plant made painfully clear. Even Motown Records, the symbol of a vibrant and upbeat Detroit, relocated to Los Angeles. People in Sun Belt cities derisively referred to migrating Detroiters as "black taggers" because of their black Michigan license plates. By 1990 the city's population dropped to one million, half of what it had been when Al Kaline broke in with the Tigers. Four of every five Detroiters were black, and most hovered around the poverty line. Coleman Young, backed by studies that showed the metropolitan area to be the most racially segregated in the country, accused the prosperous suburbs that ringed the core city of intentional neglect. "It occurs to me that people outside Detroit like to think of the metropolitan area as a doughnut, with the suburbs as the sweet meat and the city as the hole in the goddamn middle," he observed.

The national media plumbed the depths of that hole, whether touting Detroit's image as Murder City in the 1970s (when it had the nation's highest homicide rate) or playing up the Devil's Night debacles of the late 1980s, when fire buffs from around the world descended on Detroit to watch hundreds of houses burned up during an annual ritual of mindless arson. Violence became so endemic the Michigan State Police were brought in to patrol the city's freeways. Even Jim Campbell scrambled under a table to avoid a gunfight outside his downtown apartment that put three bullet holes in his wall.

Fans hoping to find diversion during this period were increasingly disappointed, as dollars began to dominate the sports pages. Because spiraling payroll costs have had a direct and significant impact on the future of baseball and of Tiger Stadium, it is impossible to avoid at least a cursory look at baseball's labor-management issues in this narrative.

As long as professional baseball had been played, management enjoyed the upper hand when dealing with labor. Under the guidance of Marvin Miller, however, the fledgling players association gained strength during the militant 1960s. The first Basic Agreement was hammered out by owners and players in 1968, a year in which the Tigers paid World Series MVP Mickey Lolich thirty thousand dollars and Gates Brown, the game's premier pinch-hitter, eighteen thousand dollars(owners had just lifted the minimum salary from seven thousand to ten thousand dollars). Both players received raises in 1969, but that offered no guarantee that even a slight fall-off in performance or a bad season at the gate wouldn't result in a substantial pay cut when negotiations rolled around for the next year's salary. If a player didn't like the offer, he had no recourse. The reserve clause in his contract silenced his complaints. He could try to reach a happy compromise, demand a trade, sit out the season without pay, or, like most players, sign for what he was being offered.

One year Hank Aguirre refused to sign a contract unless he received a raise. The pitcher told Jim Campbell he didn't care how small a raise it was; it was a matter of principle. Campbell obligingly tacked one cent onto Aguirre's contract and both went away happy. A few years later the Tigers attempted to make Al Kaline the team's first $100,000-a-year player. At that time big salaries, when paid, reflected seniority, not performance. But the eighteen-year veteran, who was coming off a .278 season in 1970, said no, he didn't deserve that amount. He would play at his previous season's salary of $93,000 until his performance warranted a boost to six figures. Kaline's gesture, while noble in the eyes of fans, reporters, and management, did nothing to advance the cause of his younger, poorer-paid brethren, some of whom regularly outperformed the aging star on the field.

The first Basic Agreement largely addressed such concerns as player pensions and working conditions. Owners contested the larger issue of arbitration, locking out the players during spring training in 1973 because of it, but it was finally adopted later that year. This procedure allowed a player unhappy with his club's offer to make a counter-proposal. The dispute was heard by an impartial arbitrator, who then chose one or the other figure; no compromise was permitted. The spread between what a player was offered and what he wanted was usually small, approximately ten or fifteen thousand dollars. The system worked well enough at first—the average player's salary rose from $19,000 in 1967 to $51,000 in 1976 as a result—but then the numbers started ballooning.

Perhaps the most important date in baseball history was December 23, 1975, when a three-man arbitration panel voted 2–1 to grant players the right of free agency. Owners were outraged, but after they were defeated in court they had no choice but to accept the new world order. The 1976 Basic Agreement allowed a player to sell his services on the open market after he completed his sixth full major league season.

Owners of richer clubs paid huge sums of money in hopes of buying a championship. More conservative owners, notably those in small markets and those whose roots in baseball stretched back several decades, preached fiscal restraint and stayed out of the bidding. Finishing the season on top with a couple of well-paid mercenaries draining the coffers was not nearly as important as finishing the season in fourth place in the black. The Tigers occasionally dipped into the market, but their tastes ran toward players such as journeyman second baseman Tito Fuentes, who received a mere fraction of what higher-priced stars commanded. Fuentes, memorable for the gold jewelry that jangled on his wrists and around his neck, was the team's first free-agent signing, hitting .309 in 1977 before moving on to another team.

The Detroit front office's philosophical distaste for arbitration and free agency was understandable. Ever since the days of Walter O. Briggs the club maintained one of the highest payrolls in baseball. The largesse was directly attributable to a traditionally healthy gate and increasingly higher broadcast revenues. The Tigers were often generous but always cautious. John Fetzer had charged Jim Campbell with making a profit, and the general manager wasn't about to blow the bottom line and risk dissension in the clubhouse by wildly throwing around wads of cash. Unlike the new breed of owners creeping into the game, both were staunch believers in developing a strong farm system, having seen it pay off at least once with the 1968 world champions.

From the fans' perspective, the reserve clause had a positive effect, even if they rarely thought about it. The legal ball-and-chain kept many of their favorites at Michigan and Trumbull for years and years. The longevity of such storied Tigers as Ty Cobb and Al Kaline (twenty-two seasons each in a Detroit uniform), Charlie Gehringer (nineteen), Tommy Bridges (sixteen), Sam Crawford, Harry Heilmann, Hal Newhouser, Mickey Stanley, Bill Freehan, Willie Horton, Norm Cash (fifteen), Dizzy Trout and Dick McAuliffe (fourteen) had as much to do with the restrictive natures of their contracts as any loyalty they may have felt for the Detroit organization. In the absence of free agency, it was inevitable a bond would be forged with the community they represented for so long on the field.

The Tigers' already conservative attitude toward the game's radically changing economic structure was cemented by their sour experience with Steve Kemp, the club's top pick in the 1976 winter draft. The stone-faced, heavy-hitting outfielder was signed off the Southern Cal campus for a $50,000 bonus and quickly moved into the Tigers' starting lineup. In his third season, 1979, he hit .318 with twenty-six homers and 105 RBI. The Tigers offered their All-Star $150,000 for 1980, but Kemp elected to go to arbitration, where he was awarded the $210,000 he asked for. He hit .293 with twenty-one homers and 101 RBIs and made the All-Star team a second time in 1980, after which he again took the Tigers to arbitration. Again he emerged victorious, this time receiving $600,000, a stunning amount of money. It was by far and away the most ever paid a professional athlete in Detroit and, at that point, the second-highest award ever won by a major leaguer in arbitration.

Kemp's agent, the aggressive, cocksure Dick Moss, coupled with his client's blatantly money-grubbing attitude, sickened Fetzer, Campbell, and assistant general manager Bill Lajoie and set the tone for future dealings. Of greater importance, Kemp's award established another ever-climbing benchmark that was used to settle other arbitration cases and boosted already skyrocketing inflation of the free-agent market. The potent combination of free agency and arbitration was responsible for raising the players' average salary from $51,000 in 1976 to about $1.2 million in 1994. To put this jump in perspective, a mechanic making $12,000 in 1976 would now be changing spark plugs for more than a quarter of a million dollars a year if he had received the same rate of increase.

Moss, who had once been Marvin Miller's right-hand man, ignored management's screams. He spoke of players like Mark Fidrych, who had been responsible for selling a lot of tickets but whose career

Steve Kemp, traded to Chicago for Chet Lemon prior to the 1982 season, smiles upon his return to Tiger Stadium in a White Sox uniform.

was over before he was able to see the benefits of his popularity reflected in his paycheck. In 1976 Fidrych's pitching turns accounted for about 60 percent of the Tigers' home attendance. The *Wall*

Street Journal estimated the Bird personally accounted for roughly one million dollars of the team's revenues. For this he was paid sixteen thousand dollars and drove a Dodge Colt to the park. "He never got paid what he should have," Moss explained. "You have to pay special players like Fidrych . . . what they're worth *today*. You can't assume they're going to be able to keep going on in the future."

Initially, it was easy to side with the players, particularly in a strong union town like Detroit. To blue-collar fans, pleas of poverty from any boss were always viewed with skepticism. Strikes and walkouts had long been a regular feature of the car industry, particularly when it came time for the United Auto Workers to negotiate a new national contract with the Big Three automakers.

But the disastrous 1981 baseball strike occurred when the federal government was bailing Chrysler out of bankruptcy and the other two automakers were cutting jobs left and right. These were days of uncertainty and double-digit unemployment. When players walked out on June 12 to protest proposed changes to free agency, they were making an average $196,000 a year. "A lot of people work harder and make a lot less money," said one Tigers fan. "I go with the owners."

Play resumed in early August. The season, which was split into two halves and involved an extra round of playoffs, was a travesty to purists. The Tigers finished fourth in the first half with a 31–26 record, second in the second half (29–23), and fourth overall (60–49). That winter Kemp, who had hit .277 and led the team with forty-nine RBIs, aroused public ire by taking the Tigers to arbitration a third straight time. The Tigers refused to meet Kemp's asking price, a rumored $6 million for five years. Noting that he was in the option year of his contract, meaning that at the end of the season he would be a free agent who could be lost with no compensation (the very issue that created the strike), the Tigers shipped him to the White Sox for center fielder Chet Lemon.

Afterwards Kemp was asked if Detroit's salary philosophy hurt the fans. "I'm glad to be on a team where the front office is concerned about building a winner," he responded. "If we struggle, it'll go out, change things, pay free agents. That's obviously not the Tiger way; they're bottom line . . . I can't say what they do is wrong, because they draw their 1.7 million to the park whatever happens. They make their profit and don't go one penny over the budget. But they keep finishing fifth, and in that town they'd draw 2.5 million if they won."

Kemp's words proved prophetic, but not before several old-line owners, unable or unwilling to keep pace with what a discouraged Bill Veeck termed "the high cost of mediocrity," sold their franchises. Their number included old gray John Fetzer. At the end of the 1983 season, the eighty-two-year-old owner sold the club for $53 million to Tom Monaghan, the boyish-looking founder and owner of Domino's Pizza.

Fetzer undoubtedly saw much of himself in his hand-picked successor. For one thing, they shared the same birthday. Monaghan, too, lost his father at an early age, forcing him into a succession of orphanages and foster homes while his mother scrounged for work. Like Fetzer, Monaghan invented himself through hard work, vision, perseverance, and faith.

Unlike Fetzer, the man who had parlayed a single pizza shop in Ypsilanti, Michigan into a $1.4-billion-a-year international chain of over two thousand stores enjoyed spending his money. He paid a record $1 million for one of only seven Duesenbergs in the world, owned an $8-million Bugatti, and planned to build a giant multi-million-dollar skyscraper based on the designs of his hero, architect Frank Lloyd Wright. After he bought the Tigers he constructed a helicopter pad on the roof of the Brooks Lumber Yard, the better to make a grand entrance or exit on game days. He wore six-hundred-dollar shoes, forty-two-dollar socks, and twelve-thousand-dollar watches. "I'd like him to be less ostentatious," admitted Fetzer.

Monaghan represented the new breed of corporate owners: no background in baseball but equipped with deep pockets and a giant ego. Although he spoke openly and sincerely, Monaghan often came across as half-baked as a six-minute pizza. Here was a rosary-reciting Catholic who admitted to being able to rattle off a Hail Mary in eleven seconds (the Lord's Prayer took thirteen) and to secretly lusting after actress Debbie Reynolds. After an initial blush of on-field success and acceptance by the community, he revealed himself a socially inept public figure and no friend of the city.

By 1983, most of the pieces were in place for the Tigers to make a run at the top. In addition to Alan Trammell, Lou Whitaker, and Chet Lemon, the roster now included third baseman Tom Brookens, outfielder Kirk Gibson, catcher Lance Parrish, and pitchers Jack Morris, Dan Petry, and Milt Wilcox. That final season of the Fetzer regime saw the Tigers finish second to Baltimore with a

Soon after the 1983 season ended, John Fetzer sold the team to Domino's Pizza magnate Tom Monaghan, whose schoolboy dream had been to play shortstop for the Tigers.

92–70 mark, their best record in fifteen years. Temperamental Jack Morris, who emerged as the winningest pitcher of the 1980s, had his first twenty-win season, while Petry notched nineteen. Parrish, the chiseled All-Star backstop who had hit thirty-two homers in 1982, followed that up with twenty-seven home runs and 114 RBIs in 1983. He was generally regarded as the best all-around catcher in the game.

The nucleus of the club was the double-play combination of Trammell and Whitaker. In the field the pair meshed like pork and beans and at the plate were just as explosive. The two were first teamed in 1976 at the Instructional League in St. Petersburg. They broke into the bigs together on the same day, September 9, 1977. Whitaker, a quiet, slender product of New York City, batted leadoff, followed by Trammell, a ruddy-faced native of San Diego. In 1983 they hit .320 and .319, respectively (the first second base-shortstop combo to hit .300 in a quarter-century) and joined Parrish as the Tigers' first-ever trio of Gold Glove winners. In 1988 the perennial All-Stars became the longest-running middle-infield pair in history, and they still had several years to go. As they matured their power numbers went up, with both players moving from single digits in home runs to as many as twenty-eight in a season. By the end of 1995, their nineteenth big-league season together, their consistency and longevity produced a combined 4,689 base hits, 448 home runs, and 373 stolen bases. Between them they scored 2,601 runs and knocked in 2,071 more. All of this offensive production was in addition to their steadily brilliant defensive play.

Nobody had a better view of Tram and Sweet Lou than Parrish, the Tigers' everyday backstop for eight seasons. "I've seen them regularly make difficult plays look routine," he said. "They get to balls that other people wouldn't, and then turn on a dime and throw and know that the other guy is going to be there. They both have strong and accurate arms.

"As a catcher, when I see a ball go to a certain place on the infield, I almost stop running down to first to back it up because I think there isn't going to be a play. But so many times I've seen Lou go behind second base and grab a ball and think he's got no chance. Then he turns and throws almost like he was set up. I was always amazed at how strong of an arm he had when he was off-balance. And Alan is the same way, going in the hole and making the difficult plays look routine.

"I can honestly say I enjoyed sitting behind the plate and watching those two play. There are times you sit behind the plate and get frustrated watching what goes on. Watching those two day in and day out was pure pleasure."

Riding heard over this group of young stars was Sparky Anderson, who'd been broomed out of Cincinnati despite leading them to four pennants and back-to-back World Series wins in 1975–76. Anderson, notable for his fractured grammar, snow-white hair, and a face as brown and rutted as the Oregon Trail, was extremely popular with the press and the fans—even after he pronounced that, in his heart, he knew that "the 1984 Tigers would be the best baseball team Detroit has ever seen." Given the skipper's track record with predictions, this could likely mean a plunge to the cellar.

For once Sparky was right. The only things missing were a first baseman and a reliever. Bill Lajoie, who became general manager following Jim Campbell's promotion to president, immediately went to work. He traded John Wockenfuss and Glenn Wilson to

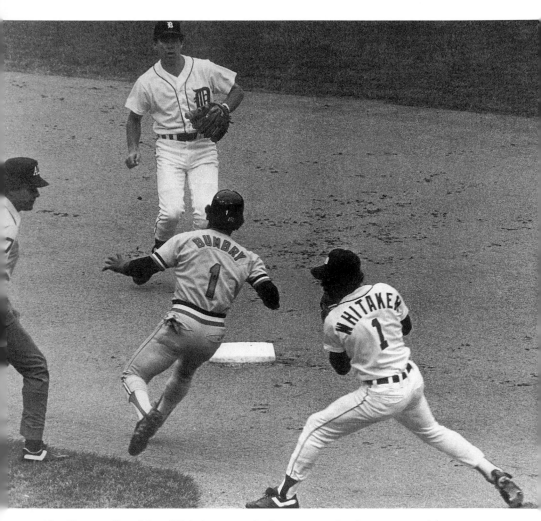

Alan Trammell and Lou Whitaker were the longest-running keystone combination in baseball history, playing together from 1977 to 1995.

Philadelphia for reliever Willie Hernandez and first baseman Dave Bergman. He also outbid twenty other teams for free agent Darrell Evans, the longtime Atlanta Braves slugger. Although Evans' sixteen home runs fell far short of expectations, his eight-hundred-thousand-dollar signing was an important symbol that, under the new regime, the Tigers were finally changing their stripes. In his first Tiger Stadium at-bat, Evans smashed a three-run homer. Of greater importance was his clubhouse manner. Depending on the situation, the thirty-seven-year-old Evans could be counted on for a pat on the back or a verbal kick in the butt. Whenever he heard someone griping too loud or too long he let out a baby's wail, "Waaaaaaaaaa!" On the same day that Evans learned his father had died of cancer, he was comforting a rookie shortstop, Doug Baker, who had just been informed that he was being sent to the minors.

Nineteen eighty-four turned out to be as dreamy a season as 1968. The Tigers shot out to a record 35–5 start, then cruised home to the Eastern Division title with a 104–58 record, fifteen games ahead of Toronto. These were the most wins ever recorded by a Detroit club. Surprisingly, although the Tigers led the loop in scoring, home runs, and pitching, nobody scored or drove in one hundred runs and no pitcher reached twenty wins. This was a tribute to Anderson's masterful platooning of subs like Marty Castillo, Rusty Kuntz, Barbaro Garbey, Johnny Grubb, and Ruppert Jones.

If one moment of drama defines the season, it was Dave Bergman's heart-stopping at-bat against second-place Toronto on June 4. Before a full house at Tiger Stadium and a national television audience, Bergman confronted the Blue Jays' Roy Lee Howell with two on, two out, and the score tied in the bottom of the tenth inning. At the time Toronto was only three and a half games behind in the standings; a victory would move Detroit's toughest rival one game closer to the top and momentarily halt the Tigers' momentum. Howell got two strikes on Bergman, but then the Tiger started fouling off pitch after pitch, increasing the tension to an almost unbearable level. After seven minutes of battling, Bergman finally ended the suspense. He got around on Howell's thirteenth delivery and drove it into the upper deck in right field for a game-winning three-run home run. The ballpark erupted and the Tigers never looked back.

Morris won nineteen games and Petry eighteen, but the monster on the mound in 1984 was moody left-handed screwballer, Hernandez. He led the loop with eighty appearances, was successful in all but one of thirty-three save situations, and had a 1.92 ERA. For this he was named the MVP and Cy Young Award winner. Not to be forgotten was his righthanded counterpart, Aurelio Lopez, who was 10–1 with fourteen saves. Their contributions were instrumental in the Tigers having the league's lowest ERA for the first time in forty years.

More than 2.7 million people visited the ballpark in 1984, shattering the old 1968 mark. A new craze was imported from the West Coast—the "wave," where sections of fans abruptly stood up, waved their arms, and then sat down. Sometimes the wave moved clockwise; at other times, counterclockwise. There were variations, such as the slow-motion wave and the double-time wave. It was good, clean fun, especially since the team's winning ways attracted a considerable number of nonbaseball types who just wanted to be where the action was.

The postseason began in Kansas City, where the Tigers met the winner of the American League West. The Tigers rolled to 8–1 and 5–3 victories, the last an eleven-inning affair decided by Johnny Grubb's two-run double. On October 5 Detroit wrapped up a best-of-five series with a 1–0 win before a capacity crowd of 52,168 at Michigan and Trumbull. Castillo brought Chet Lemon home with a groundout in the second inning, while Milt Wilcox and Hernandez combined for the shutout.

Four days later the Tigers were in San Diego to battle the Padres, an uninspiring franchise with no tradition and ugly brown and yellow uniforms. Jack Morris won the World Series opener, 3–2, behind Larry Herndon's two-run blast in the fifth. A key play was when Kirk Gibson nailed Kurt Bevacqua trying to stretch a double into a triple in the seventh. In the next game Bevacqua redeemed himself by smacking a three-run shot that gave the Padres a 5–3 win. Gibson seethed in right field as Bevacqua rounded the bases, blowing kisses to the crowd.

On October 12 the Tigers were home—to stay, as it turned out. Capacity crowds attended all three games. Detroit won game three, 5–2, on a Friday evening, and then returned the following afternoon to win again, 4–2, behind Morris's second win and Trammell's pair of two-run homers. The Tigers took a commanding 3–1 series edge and paved the way for Kirk Gibson to become a household name across America.

Gibson grew up in Waterford and traveled as a boy to Tiger Stadium to root for Cash, Kaline, and company. That the twenty-seven-year-old player was now completing his sixth big league season and tramping the same ground as his Tiger heros was a wonderment to Gibson. He had only taken up the game seriously as a senior at Michigan State University. The All-Big Ten flanker could

World Series MVP Alan Trammell watches one of his two two-run homers head for the Tiger Stadium seats in game four, a 4–2 triumph.

have gone into the NFL, but he saw a longer career in baseball. He'd been burdened from the outset by his personality ("I was a self-centered, egotistical jerk," is how he later described himself) and by Sparky Anderson's prediction that he would be "the next Mickey Mantle."

In the beginning Gibson played more like the next Bronko Nagurski, bowling over infielders and catching fly balls with his head. He was often rude, profane and occasionally violent in his dealings with the public. Once in 1983, at a bar near Tiger Stadium, he grabbed a heckler by his shirt and snarled, "Listen, you son of a bitch. You can get on me at the ballpark. I get paid to put up with assholes like you at the park. But not here in public. So say another fucking word, and I'll rip your head off your shoulders." Then he slapped his antagonist across the face.

Kirk Gibson on the loose. The former Michigan State football star transferred his power and desire to Tiger Stadium's diamond in 1979, but it took a while for fans to warm up to him.

Gibson had matured, if not exactly mellowed, by 1984, a season in which he posted typically versatile numbers: twenty-seven home runs, twenty-nine steals, a .282 average. The six-foot, three-inch, 215-pound Tiger played with a fury that inspired teammates and cowed opponents. The sign on Gibby's locker said it all: "Please do not annoy, torment, pester, plague, molest, worry, badger, harry, harass, heckle, persecute, irk, bullyrag, vex, disquiet, grate, beset, bother, tease, nettle, tantalize, or ruffle the animal." Marveled Darrell Evans, who'd been in professional ball for two decades, "I've never seen a player with his intensity."

It was on display for the world to see on a misty Sunday afternoon at Tiger Stadium. In the first inning he banged a tremendous two-run homer to right and helped Detroit build a quick 3–0 lead. The Padres fought back and tied, but in the fifth Gibson singled, proceeded to second on a fly ball, then moved to third on a pair of walks. Kuntz lifted a fly to shallow right field. Second baseman Alan Wiggins, his back to the plate, snared it but didn't think Gibson would break for home. He was wrong. Gibson, using his great speed, roared across the plate ahead of Wiggins' hurried, off-balance throw.

Gibson's dash gave the Tigers a 4–3 lead. Parrish then made it 5–3 with a home run in the seventh. The following inning Gibson came to the plate with runners on second and third and one of baseball's most intimidating relievers on the mound, Goose Gossage. The safe strategy would have been to walk Gibson to load the bases, but Gossage talked his manager out of it.

Gossage came in with a fastball on his second pitch; Detroit's be-whiskered warrior whacked it high and deep into the right upper deck. The tremendous blast sealed an 8–4 victory and capped a wondrous year. The Tigers joined the 1887 Detroit Wolverines and 1927 Yankees as one of the handful of teams to remain in first place every day of the season. And Sparky Anderson became the first manager ever to pilot World Series winners in both leagues.

Gibson, rubbing it in, pumped his fists and blew kisses all the way around the bases, and then nearly broke the wrists of several high-fiving teammates. A conga line of pretzel vendors, their boxes on their heads, danced through the aisles as the apoplectic crowd sang "Goosebusters," the rousing parody of a popular summer song. "It was the ultimate scene of an impossibly delirious, delightful summer," reported the *Free Press*, "a mind-boggling six months when Tiger Stadium truly became the epicenter of the baseball cosmos."

It got wilder outside the old concrete walls, as the crowd boiled into the streets and started the usual post-championship ritual of yelling, waving pennants and signs, exchanging beers and high-fives with happy strangers, blowing horns, and setting off firecrackers. Even the normally reserved audience at Orchestra Hall exploded into cheers when the final score was announced just before the start of Stravinsky's *A Soldier's Tale*.

Outside Tiger Stadium, a few bottles were thrown and a Detroit police car was overturned and set on fire. One of the rowdies was an inebriated seventeen-year-old dropout from Lincoln Park named Kenneth "Bubba" Helms. Bubba, who later admitted to drinking a fifth of Jim Beam with his friends and smoking "a few bad ones," became something of an international celebrity when an Associated Press photographer posed him by the burning police car, holding a Tigers pennant. Helms had no interest in baseball, but had ventured downtown to participate in the expected celebration. By the end of the evening Helms had been chased by cops, gotten into a fistfight over a piece of souvenir sod ripped from the field, drank several more bottles of beer, then passed out face down in the mud on a neighbor's lawn. "It was one big party," he recalled. "It was great."

But not so great for Detroit's image. The photograph "was used virtually across the board," said the AP photo editor in New York. "It seemed to be the picture that was used of events happening outside the stadium." It appeared in publications across the U.S., Canada, Europe, and Asia, accompanied by copy taking Detroit to task for its violent celebration of the Tigers' victory.

The dynasty many predicted for the Tigers after their remarkable 1984 season never materialized. The following April players received their championship rings on opening day, then beat Cleveland for the first of six straight victories to start the season. For the rest of the summer they managed to win just one more game than they lost, finishing a distant third at 84–77. This despite Darrell Evans' forty home runs, which made him the first Tiger since Hank Greenberg to lead the league in that category. The dive of 1985 was

Kirk Gibson deposits Goose Gossage's fastball deep into the upper deck to seal the Tigers' win in the fifth and final game of the 1984 World Series.

a mystery to the players, press, and nearly 2.3 million fans who came out to the park. How to explain the dismal 17–25 record at home against the weaker Western Division? "I spent the whole year thinking it would all turn around the next day," said Lance Parrish. "It never did."

Contributing to the sour taste was the wrangling between Bill Lajoie and Gibson, who became a free agent after the season. Detroit's favorite Goosebuster had made $685,000 during the last year of his contract. His World Series heroics, coupled with his twenty-nine home runs and thirty steals in 1985, motivated him to demand a five-year, $8-million contract. The negotiations turned bitter—Gibson stated he would "vomit" rather than accept the Tigers' counterproposal. But as time ran out to re-sign with Detroit and with no other clubs expressing interest, Gibson agreed at the last minute to $4 million for three years, making him the Tigers' first million-dollar-a-year player.

Attendance dropped by four hundred thousand in 1986 as the Tigers again finished third. Parrish, hobbled by a bad back, played only ninety-one games but still managed to crunch twenty-two homers. Jack Morris finished 21–8 with a league-high six shutouts. That winter the battery mates became the latest stars to test their worth in the marketplace. Morris, accompanied by agent Dick Moss, hit the road in search of the best offer. Television viewers in Detroit were treated to the sight of their top pitcher, garbed in a floor-length fur coat, peddling his flesh in Minnesota. Then it was on to see Yankees owner George Steinbrenner. When no one bit, Morris, grumbling, went to arbitration and won $1.85 million from the Tigers.

At the same time Lajoie offered Parrish a one-year contract for $1.2 million. Parrish, whose back injury concerned the Tigers, added hurt feelings to what was ailing him. After ten seasons and 212 home runs in a Detroit uniform, he signed a contract with Philadelphia worth one-third less. For the rest of his checkered career, the gentlemanly, well-liked backstop moaned that his decision to leave was the biggest mistake he ever made.

Parrish's departure was the beginning of a strange, exciting season in 1987. After their first eighteen games the Tigers were ten games out of first place. By mid-May they were 11–19. Then they caught fire, going 87–37—a blazing .702 winning percentage—the rest of the way. Between August 12 and September 24 Detroit and Toronto were never more than a game and a half apart. Jack Morris once again won twenty-one games. Grizzled Doyle Alexander, a late-season pickup from Atlanta, won nine straight down the stretch with a 1.53 ERA. Matt Nokes took over behind the plate and enjoyed the one great season of his career: thirty-two home runs and eighty-nine RBIs. Trammell moved into the clean-up spot and had his finest offensive year: a .343 average, twenty-eight home runs, and 105 RBIs. During the closing days of the season he was greeted with chants of "M-V-P" whenever he came to bat at Tiger Stadium. Trammell finished second to Toronto's George Bell in the official balloting by sportswriters, but after the smoke cleared on the 1987 season it was the Tigers, not the Jays, who were sitting on the top of the Amcrican League East standings.

On September 27, Gibson's thirteenth-inning home run dramatically salvaged the last game of a four-game series in Toronto. This put the Tigers two and a half games back with seven to play. While Detroit split four games with Baltimore, Toronto was swept three straight by Milwaukee. The pennant race boiled down to a final three-game weekend set between the Tigers and the Blue Jays at Tiger Stadium.

On Friday, October 2, thousands of fans lined up to buy tickets for a possible Monday playoff, which would occur if the Tigers won two of the three games. That evening Detroit won, 4–3, and pulled even in the standings. On Saturday Detroit won again, 3–2 in twelve innings, on Trammell's hit. Detroit moved up a game in front with one to go. Toronto, losers of six straight and on the verge of a historic collapse, needed a victory that final Sunday to force a special one-game tiebreaker.

Frank Tanana, a Detroit boy who had made his name as a speedballer before joining the Tigers in 1985, responded to the cries of 51,005 screaming fans. His left arm spun mostly junk now—curve, slider, change up, an occasional fast ball—but it was enough to frustrate the Jays, 1–0. Larry Herndon's solo home run off Jimmie Key, which barely dropped into the seats in the second inning, gave Tanana his fifteenth victory and put the cork on Detroit's gutsy comeback. As the Tigers celebrated, Lou Whitaker impulsively uprooted second base and inscribed the following before presenting the bag to his double-play partner:

2B This year's MVP
Alan Trammell
Congratulations
Louis Rodman Whitaker

"That was not common for Lou to do something like that," said Trammell, who years later still had the base hanging on his living

Frank Tanana, a product of Catholic Central High School, came back to his home town in 1985 after years of mowing down batters in California, Boston, and Texas. His repertoire as a Tiger was limited to slow and slower, but he reached double digits in victories each summer for the rest of the decade. His biggest moment was a 1–0 blanking of the Blue Jays on the final day of the 1987 season, which clinched the Tigers' Eastern Division crown.

room wall. "But it meant a lot. I'll remember that forever. While we were jumping in the pile, he's grabbing the bag to give to me. That's the highlight I'll remember."

The Tigers finished with the most wins (98) and home runs (225) in the majors. Their 896 runs were the most in the majors in thirty-four years and made them the favorite to go all the way. Anderson and his one-time pitching coach, Roger Craig, who had guided San Francisco to a half-pennant in the National League, chortled over butting heads in the World Series.

But first there was the little matter of the American League Championship Series. The underdog Minnesota Twins, playing in the Hubert H. Humphrey Metrodome, proved that there really is no place like home, no matter how sterile, ugly, and plastic it may be. Their mediocre 85–77 record included an outstanding 56–25 mark inside the dome, which during the postseason (when they won all six of their home games) amplified the cheering and mechanical noise making to temple-bursting levels. Experts compared the volume to that of standing behind a power lawn mower for three hours. Against this wall of sound the Twins unexpectedly won the first two games, handing Doyle Alexander his first loss as a Tiger, 8–5, and then beating Morris, 6–3.

The Tigers tried to regroup at home. On October 10, Pat Sheridan's two-run blast in the eighth sent 49,730 Detroit fans home happy, but the 7–6 victory was followed by a 5–3 loss in game four. The key moment came when Darrell Evans, on third base with one out and representing the tying run, was picked off. For several seconds the embarrassed veteran knelt in the dirt, hands on his hips, pleading his case with the umpire. Alexander was pounded again in the fifth game, a 9–5 loss that sent the shell-shocked Tigers home for the year. In a nice touch of class, the 47,448 people on hand got on their feet and gave Evans a long ovation as he walked to the plate. "It was something I didn't expect," said Evans, who left the team after one more season. "You can't pay enough money to have these things happen to you."

The Tigers soon suffered another big loss. A labor arbitrator ruled that owners had conspired to restrict the movement of free agents, which accounted for the mysterious lack of interest in Lance Parrish, Jack Morris, and Kirk Gibson a couple of years earlier. His ruling freed several players from their contracts, including Gibson, who demonstrated a prematurely balding head for business by signing a three-year contract with Los Angeles worth $4.5 million. "Hey," said Gibson, who went on to capture the National League's MVP award and a World Series ring with the Dodgers, "that's modern baseball."

That it was, although under Fetzer and Campbell the Tigers had preferred to operate as baseball's version of the Flat Earth Society. For years the organization's marketing strategy could be summarized in three words: *Open the gates.* It worked well enough, especially when salaries were low and the Tigers fielded competitive teams. Now, with payroll expenses climbing halfway to the moon, the Tigers began to shop around for fresh approaches to selling tickets and new ways to produce ancillary income.

In late 1987 Jeff Odenwald was hired as the club's first vice-president of marketing. He immediately began to pull the Tigers out of their 1950s mind set. The number of promotional days jumped from just two in 1987 to thirty-four in 1989. Park patrons were regularly handed water bottles, refrigerator magnets, picnic cooler bags, notebook binders, tankard mugs, equipments bags, umbrellas, caps, digital watches, and other corporate-sponsored freebies. On October 1, 1988, as the Tigers ended a frustrating summer one game behind the Red Sox, the club held its first Fan Appreciation Day. Odenwald also sold sponsorships for the park's electronic scoreboard. Now fans could try to answer the "Milk Duds Tiger Trivia Quiz," follow the fortunes of minor-league teams with the "John Deere Farm Report," and sigh over memories of Reno Bertoia and Bill Tuttle during the "Unocal Where Are They Now?" segment. In 1989, a year in which the Tigers lost 103 games and Sparky Anderson had a nervous breakdown, the club aired its first television commercials.

The changes didn't end there. The park's ham-fisted security officers were replaced by polite, well-trained college students. Fans rejoiced when three employees in the ticket office were fired after an investigation revealed that they had been involved in a long-running ticket scam. For the first time in years, choice seats were available to the public instead of reserved for scalpers and insiders. In 1992 the ticket office began accepting credit-card orders, the same year smoking was banned throughout the stadium, except on the first- and third-floor concourses.

Lance Parrish, baseball's best all-around backstop of the 1980s, left Detroit in a salary dispute after the 1986 season. The popular catcher later admitted it was the biggest mistake he ever made. His strong-armed and strong-willed battery-mate, Jack Morris, was the winningest pitcher of the decade. Unlike Parrish, he had absolutely no regrets about leaving town in the 1990 offseason.

A panoramic view from the bleachers during the 1987 playoffs.

These were welcomed and long-overdue changes. But whatever goodwill Monaghan initially enjoyed dissipated rapidly after a series of public relations disasters, most notably the fiasco over a new stadium and the firing of Ernie Harwell.

The ballpark was in and out of the news for years. On January 12, 1972, Fetzer announced the club had signed a forty-year lease for a planned $126-million domed stadium. The facility, to be shared with the Lions, would be built in the general vicinity of where Joe Louis Arena now stands. There was considerable glee in the Tigers' organization. One night Jim Campbell took baseball commissioner Bowie Kuhn to a window high up in the Pontchartrain Hotel and pointed to the intersection below. "That's

Baseball's first "stadium hug" took place on April 20, 1988, when more than a thousand fans encircled the aging ballpark before a game with Boston.

where the home plate of the new Tiger Stadium is going to be," Campbell proudly said. But the dream of a new downtown stadium faded after a bond issue failed, lawsuits were filed, and William Clay Ford decided to move his Lions to a football-only facility in Pontiac.

Although Fetzer insisted the Tigers would not leave Detroit, in 1976 he warned that, without much-needed renovation, Tiger Stadium would last only another ten years. The park had become a dangerous eyesore. The outside walls were peeling, the rest rooms, scoreboard, and players' facilities were antiquated, and the concrete-and-steel foundation—subject to decades of cold, ice, and rock salt—was in danger of turning into crumb cake. Fetzer complained of spending five hundred thousand dollars a year on maintenance (though this was what Walter Briggs had spent a quarter-century earlier). In the fall of 1977 the Tigers' owner sold the park, estimated to be worth $8 million, to the City of Detroit for one dollar. In return he agreed to rent it back from the city for the next thirty years. The carefully worded lease, later described as "ironclad," included an option for an additional thirty years.

It was the first time the property at Michigan and Trumbull fell into public hands. The arrangement enabled the Tigers to fix up the park and assured their fans that the team would stay put. The city issued bonds for $8.5 million, which were repaid through a fifty-cents surcharge on every ticket.

The first phase of the renovation, financed by the bond issue and a $5-million federal grant, took place between 1977 and 1981. The foundation and decking were reinforced and the electrical and plumbing systems overhauled. New luxury boxes (one for the owner, the other for the media) and broadcast booths were hung from the facing of the upper deck behind home plate, while a third-deck press box was built to replace the one destroyed by fire a year earlier.

Sentimentalists mourned the demolition of the old hand-operated scoreboard above the center-field bleachers, which was replaced with a computerized version that displayed graphics and pictures of the players. Unfortunately, out-of-town scores were shown only briefly and irregularly. The distinctively colored, canoe-green wooden chairs that filled the park for generations were replaced with bright orange-and-blue plastic seats. Though these items quickly added some pizzazz to the stadium's interior, many fans missed being able to employ the old chairs as impromptu noisemakers during late-inning rallies and hankered for the days when one could look up at any time during the game and immediately spot the score of the Boston–New York game.

The second phase of renovation, financed by selling an additional $3.6 million in bonds, took place in 1982–83. By then the park exterior, which was painted annually during the Briggs years, had become a disgrace. Rather than paying up to $500,000 to have the peeling, blistered walls prepped and painted, the club paid about $2 million to cover them with beige metal siding. Blue-glazed, graffiti-proof masonry was installed at ground level to foil urban

Detroit's ballpark has been the site of various political and religious rallies through the years, including presidential hopeful Eugene McCarthy in 1968 and the Jehovah's Witnesses in 1970. On June 28, 1990, some forty-nine thousand people filled Tiger Stadium to hear African National Congress leader Nelson Mandela address the issue of apartheid in South Africa.

artists and sloganeers. Two new lavatories were installed and the clubhouses were renovated. These additional changes were paid off by tacking a ninety-cents surcharge on each ticket.

The price tag for the two-phase facelift, which reduced seating capacity to 52,806, was $18.1 million. In a sense, it was disappointing. The thirty-seven new mezzanine-level private boxes, escalators, and other luxury items proposed to the city in 1978 by the Detroit architectural firm of Rosetti Associates never materialized because actual costs far exceeded the original estimates. Had these sweeping changes been implemented, they would have boosted club revenues and might have stifled future charges of the stadium being too antiquated.

Tom Monaghan gave conflicting signals regarding his views on Tiger Stadium. Upon buying the club in 1983 he said, "As long as I own this team, we will not build a new stadium. I like the old stadium, and we'll do all we can to keep it. We'll keep fixing it up and making it look as good as possible."

Over the next several years he waffled, speaking one moment of the park as "a shrine" worth preserving and then saying that any decision on its future was up to Jim Campbell and the landlord, Mayor Young, neither of whom favored keeping the stadium. "It's obvious the damned thing is falling down," Young said early in 1988.

That remark came just days after Monaghan's chief stadium aide, John McDevitt, announced that his study revealed that renovating the stadium and adding an inflatable roof would cost upwards of $100 million—a prohibitive amount, even for a man whom *Fortune* estimated was a billionaire.

A group of concerned citizens recently organized as the Tiger Stadium Fan Club argued that the price tag was absurd. Regardless, renovation or replacement was certain to involve public money. Therefore, the "public has a right to this information before any decision is made about the future of the ballpark." It evolved that there was no feasibility study; the $100-million figure had basically been pulled out of McDevitt's hat. Thus began a long, drawn-out battle between those who wanted to build a modern sports/entertainment complex—largely at taxpayers' expense—and those who saw a retrofitted relic hosting professional baseball well into the twenty-first century.

Sparky Anderson replaced Les Moss as manager in June 1979 and stayed sixteen and a half seasons. He left Detroit at the end of the 1995 campaign as the team's all-time leader in victories and as the third winningest manager in baseball history, behind only Connie Mack and John McGraw. Anderson is best remembered for his fractured grammar and his "My way or the highway" philosophy, which kept the Detroit clubhouse the least volatile in baseball during his tenure.

No one who listened to Monaghan's love for Frank Lloyd Wright or strolled through his impressive classic car collection dared doubt his passion for the past. After becoming owner he had hired a full-time curator to create a Detroit Tigers museum. That it was housed inside his corporate headquarters rather than inside Tiger Stadium or at some place in the surrounding neighborhood, was small but revealing. Although Monaghan appreciated the historic aspects of Tiger Stadium, talking wistfully of restoring the green wooden seats and ripping off the siding and growing ivy on the outside walls, it was clear through his actions that he was no booster of Detroit. The scenes of Murder City mayhem that had flickered across his television set all those years in Ann Arbor, capped by the image of beer-bellied Bubba Helms clutching a Tigers pennant while a police car burned in the background, probably told him all he really wanted to know about his immediate fan base. To Monaghan, the best of all possible worlds would have been to renovate Tiger Stadium—and then move it fifty miles west to Ann Arbor.

As the debate heated up, that's exactly where Monaghan found his new club president. On January 8, 1990, he promoted Jim Campbell to chairman and chief executive officer to make room for Bo Schembechler, an old friend to whom he had once impulsively given a pizza franchise and now promised a ten-year deal worth $220,000 a year, a $200,000 condominium, two Cadillacs, and country club memberships. The University of Michigan's famous, fire-breathing, recently retired head football coach was a popular, but illogical choice to succeed Campbell. He soon proved himself temperamentally unsuited to handle the delicate issue of a new stadium.

Schembechler endured a good deal of grief during his two and a half years with Monaghan. Late in 1990 Ernie Harwell, the Tigers' longtime radio voice, announced he had been let go, effective at the end of the 1991 season. The final decision had been station WJR's, not Schembechler's, yet Bo took the public pounding. In response Schembechler assumed his usual bulldog stance, which only fueled the public animosity toward him and his boss. The 1991 opener was filled with protests inside and outside the stadium and led to a rare less-than-capacity crowd. Scores of ballpark patrons wore fans bearing Harwell's image in front of their faces, a gift from a local radio station that had joined in the public howl over the club's treatment of the Hall-of-Fame announcer.

Harwell, born in Atlanta in 1917, joined the Tigers' broadcasting crew in 1960, replacing Van Patrick. He'd been recommended to John Fetzer by George Kell, who worked with Harwell in Baltimore

Ernie Harwell's firing and rumors of the Tigers abandoning Tiger Stadium led to an opening-day boycott in 1991. Bleachers were set up on Michigan Avenue across from the park, where protesters danced, ate hot dogs, and listened to organ music.

before moving into the Tigers' booth in 1959. Harwell could look back on a full and interesting life. He had been the paper boy for *Gone With The Wind* author Margaret Mitchell; was a correspondent for *The Sporting News* when he was sixteen; covered the Pacific theater as a Marine during the Second World War; and served as the television announcer for the Brooklyn Dodgers when Bobby Thomson hit "the shot heard 'round the world" in the third game of the 1951 Giants-Dodgers playoff. Along the way Harwell was a patent-holding inventor, had scores of his songs recorded by name acts, and wrote several popular books. His greatest claim to fame was as the omnipresent voice of the Tigers, good enough to be elected to the Baseball Hall of Fame in 1981. His signature phrase—"He stood there like the house by the side of the road" for a batter who watches a strike sail by—was a classic.

Even great announcers occasionally slip up. Once Harwell informed the world that catcher Bill Freehan, vigorously arguing a call, was "beating his meat," instead of his mitt, at home plate. Another time Harwell, who thought the second game of a double-header had been rained out, announced that fact and then left for home. It wasn't until he turned on his car radio and heard his partner, Paul Carey, plead for him to return to Tiger Stadium that he realized that he had made a mistake. Management, forced to refund tickets to hundreds of fans who took Harwell's word as gospel, was not amused.

Harwell, a born-again Christian, in the 1960s was instrumental in bringing the Baseball Chapel—Sunday bible study meetings—into major-league parks. To the players who sat on stools inside the cramped Tiger Stadium clubhouse, no better man ever walked the earth, as attested by the worried Detroit pitcher who plopped down in the seat next to Ernie during a wild and woolly airplane ride. "Why'd you do that?" someone asked after the plane had landed safely. "I figured if anything was going to happen," the pitcher responded, "I wanted to go where he was going."

Harwell began his American League broadcasting career with the Baltimore Orioles. His play-by-play of the Orioles' 1954 opener was the first time he set foot in Briggs Stadium, a park rather unfriendly to the electronic media. Due to the influence of longtime *Detroit News* sports editor Harry Salsinger, only print journalists were allowed in the press box. And reaching the precariously perched third-deck broadcast booth was only slightly less treacherous than scaling Mount Everest. "The roof was peaked and had a hatch," he recalled. "Toughest part of the job was dropping down that hatch into the booth. Radio announcers didn't eat in the press room then. They lowered groceries down through the hatch, which was a cold hot dog and a warm coke. And that was your repast for the afternoon."

Through 1964, the Tigers' announcers split broadcasting duties whenever a game was also televised, exchanging TV and radio booths in the bottom of the fifth inning. The following season, as an incentive to lure Kell back to the fold after a year of retirement, Fetzer hired separate radio and TV crews. Kell worked each season's fifty or so telecasts with several partners, before Al Kaline began his current reign as color man in 1976. Although Kaline was almost unbearably rough his first few summers, Detroit fans forgave his grammatical mistakes and awkward transitions. He still calls third basemen "third basemans," but his confidence and candor grew so that he became an absolute asset to the broadcast. When Kell was inducted into the National Baseball Hall of Fame in 1983, he and Kaline became the first Hall-of-Fame broadcasting duo in baseball.

Harwell, devoting himself exclusively to radio in 1965, worked two seasons with Gene Osborn and six years with Ray Lane. In 1973 he teamed up with Paul Carey, a longtime WJR hand who had first visited Navin Field as a youngster in 1936 and cried all the way home after the Yankees beat Tommy Bridges. For nineteen summers Carey's basso profunda was the perfect complement to Harwell's mellifluous voice, until ball club and WJR executives became convinced that a change to a more up-tempo broadcast was in order. The illogical decision to let Harwell go and retire Carey was one of several made during the final years of the Monaghan regime. "Y'know, Mom," a gloomy young fan lamented in one editorial cartoon, "we'll never be able to see the Tigers as well on radio without Ernie and Paul."*

Like a good soldier, Schembechler unquestioningly defended the company line on the matter of announcers and, of greater importance, on the issue of Tiger Stadium. He rejected any renovation plans out of hand and proceeded full steam ahead in trying to get a new park built at public expense. For Monaghan had let it be known that he could not afford to build it himself. The city and Wayne County governments would be expected to share in the cost.

* A pair of young, eager, sound-alike outsiders—Rick Rizzs and Bob Rathbun—were imported for 1992; by the following season the club had been sold to Mike Ilitch and Harwell was squeezed back into the booth for what amounted to a summer-long swan song before assuming other community relations duties for the new owner. Rizzs and Rathbun understandably resented the awkward presence of a third person—a living legend, no less—but in the long run it didn't matter. Rizzs and Rathbun never caught the audience's fancy. In December 1994 they were fired after three years on the job. WJR sports director Frank Beckmann was named play-by-play man and Larry Sorenson was hired to provide color. Both announcers had grown up in the area and were already familiar to listeners. Harwell resumed his local television duties, first on cable station PASS, then as the replacement for George Kell, who retired after the 1996 season.

In return they would enjoy the spin-off effects of a state-of-the-art baseball emporium in their backyard, though scores of studies remained inconclusive about what those benefits were. If not, he hinted, the team would have to consider moving out of Detroit, perhaps out of Michigan. Schembechler announced that his dream was that the Tigers would be playing inside a new stadium *somewhere* in 1995.

In an infamous speech given to the Economic Club of Detroit on April 22, 1991, Schembechler drove home the club's position as if he were reading the riot act to a group of nineteen-year-olds at halftime. "It's unfair," he said, "for you to think that you can shackle us to a rusted girder in Tiger Stadium and expect us to compete and win, because it's not going to happen."

Doing battle with Monaghan and Schembechler at every turn was the Tiger Stadium Fan Club, which yielded a clout disproportionate to its original size. Appropriately, it was founded inside a pizzeria (Buddy's, not Domino's) on September 2, 1987 by five longtime fans, including Frank Rashid, an English professor at Marygrove College who had grown up near Twelfth Street. Unconvinced of the need, either structurally, economically or morally, of abandoning the stadium, members decided to twist the Tigers' tails at every turn. The nonprofit organization soon grew to eleven thousand members. It called for independent assessments of the park, succeeded in getting Tiger Stadium listed in the National Register of Historic Places (a designation that prevents federal funds from being used to demolish it), arranged boycotts of Domino's Pizza, and distributed leaflets. It conducted its own renovation study, the Cochrane Plan, a $26-million proposal to modernize the stadium through the addition of luxury suites and the expansion of existing rest-rooms, concession areas, and offices.

The question the fan club continually asked was why must taxpayers support the construction of a multimillion-dollar facility that was to be owned by a private enterprise. It wasn't the fans who had put the Tigers in their current precarious financial state. Now ordinary citizens were being asked to bail the club out, diverting dollars that could be put to better public use.

Like other major-league owners, Monaghan, who made a tidy $8-million profit his first season as owner (and who reportedly did not lose money during any of the nine seasons he owned the club), saw greater riches in building a stadium filled with luxury suites, four-star restaurants, a stadium club, and other "fan amenities," and surrounded by parking lots that the club controlled. In keeping with his bunker mentality, the site he eventually favored—the Briggs community a few blocks north of Tiger Stadium—would have the new park completely encircled by a massive, well-lit, fenced parking lot. "What we want," said Schembechler, was a place "where people can feel safe and secure. That's what people need today if they're going to drive in." Assuming five dollars per car, a fifteen-thousand-car lot could produce upwards of $6 million a year. The suites, attractive to corporations for entertaining clients, could easily exceed that amount.

The new park itself would feature steep cantilevered grand-stands. This style, common to the multipurpose stadiums built during the last thirty years, would do away with the aggravating posts that hold up Tiger Stadium's second deck, but would also place fans far from the action. Depending on one's definition of "obstructed view," Tiger Stadium has between 2,500 and 10,000 seats where sight lines are at least partially blocked. Because these are the last sold, theoretically they become a problem only when the crowd nears capacity size. The trade-off is that Detroit fans are closer to the field than in any other major-league park. Another concern was that any new stadium would drastically reduce the number of cheap seats; Tiger Stadium boasts 10,000 bleacher seats, the most in base-ball.

The Briggs site excited few people. Early plans called for an "enterprise zone" of shops, restaurants, offices, and a nine-hole golf course, but developers and local officials warned the acres of asphalt would be no economic catalyst. "If you put all the parking right around the stadium at the Briggs site," said stadium consultant Philip Bess, "people would drive in, spend their money inside the stadium, then leave and drive home. It would be a publicly funded fortress for the Tigers that would benefit Detroit not a dime."

Wayne County executives preferred a downtown site near the burgeoning theater district. Parking and freeway access would be a problem, but most developers felt that a new stadium on Woodward Avenue would be far more likely to stimulate growth. Schembechler angrily denounced the plan, as well as a scaled-back version of the Briggs plan, and talked of the team being forced to leave town.

Throughout this quandary a groundswell of support formed for the aging edifice. The Tiger Stadium Fan Club organized a couple of group embraces of the park (the first such "stadium hugs" in the game's history) and in 1991 helped get it listed on the National Trust for Historic Preservation's annual list of most important endangered historic places. It was the first time a ballpark had ever been included with Walden Pond, Independence Hall, Antietam National Battlefield, and other historic sites. All this helped raise public consciousness about one of the city's few remaining landmarks. That year Royal Oak playwright Kim Carney produced "The Last, Best Detroit Tigers Fan," a one-act play where an ancient fan chains himself to the soon-to-be-demolished Tiger Stadium after the club is sold to a Japanese investor and moved to Novi. At one point a young member of the demolition crew tries to get the old-timer to change his mind before the wrecking ball starts to swing:

YOUNG MAN: This place is history!

OLD MAN: You're darn right, it is. American history. Why, I remember before the Great War, and then later during the Depression, we used to—.

YOUNG MAN: That's not what I meant. I meant the place is history. Vanished. Not there anymore.

OLD MAN: Is that what history means to you? Hell, son, history's always there!

YOUNG MAN: Okay, old man, okay, okay—.

OLD MAN: Don't "okay" me! Let me tell you, this place has seen near on a hundred years worth of action. Seen changes you wouldn't believe. Seen Detroit rise up, then crumble down around it. Sure would be nice if it was around to see the city rise up again.

With all the public squabbling over Tiger Stadium's future, it was easy to forget at times that there were games still being played inside the ballpark. During the 1990s the team took on a beefier, more lethal look. Tony Phillips, a peppery jack-of-all-trades acquired from Oakland, and Mickey Tettleton, a big silent catcher previously with Baltimore, were switch-hitters who regularly placed at or near the top in runs scored, walks, and on-base percentage. Third baseman Travis Fryman, whose ramrod posture and terse speech suggested his military school background, arrived in 1990 and quickly represented the American League in the All-Star Game. Whitaker and Trammell continued to hold down the fort up the middle, although by 1993 young Chris Gomez had been groomed as the everyday shortstop and Whitaker was in the lineup only against right-handed starters.

The biggest addition, literally and figuratively, was a six-foot, three-inch, 230-pound first baseman who had been given up on by Toronto. Detroit fans may have recognized Cecil Fielder as the big, slow guy who was thrown out on a botched steal attempt in the exciting final game of the 1987 season against the Blue Jays at Tiger Stadium. In 1990 the congenial twenty-six-year-old, who played the previous season in Japan, took the country by storm, smacking fifty-one homers. He added forty-four the next, leading the loop for a second straight year. His 133 and 132 RBIs, respectively, also were best. In 1992 Big Daddy (who also was a surprisingly agile glove man) knocked in 124 more to join Babe Ruth as the only men ever to lead the majors in runs batted in three straight seasons. Fielder's reputation as a big, slow player remained intact, as nobody in the history of the game has ever played as long (1,097 games) before recording his first stolen base.

This fullback-sized lineup was fun to watch if you had the time. The Tigers finished first or second in home runs and scoring four straight seasons, 1990 through 1993. In 1992 they piled up 899 runs, more than any major-league team since the 1953 Brooklyn Dodgers. The following April they scored twenty runs twice in four days at home. "If they're punishable," Anderson said one day after his shock troops bombed Boston at Michigan and Trumbull, "we'll punish them."

On the flip side, the staff's ERA was typically ranked at or near the bottom, due in part to a notable defection. After the 1990 season, Jack Morris had turned up his nose at $3 million a year with Detroit and signed with Minnesota. Like Gibson, he immediately led his new employer to a World Series title.

Win or lose, games took forever to play. The home run trots, base traffic, and pitching changes added up to interminably long games. During the 1990s, no big-league team took longer to play an average game than Detroit. On September 14, 1993, for example, the Tigers took four hours and twelve minutes to lose a nine-inning contest, 15–8, to Toronto at Tiger Stadium. It fell just six minutes short of the major league record.

Nobody personified this one-dimensional team better than Rob Deer, a strapping, sensitive right fielder who came over from Milwaukee in 1991. Deer ran well for a big man and had good range and an above-average throwing arm. But his batting style—or lack of one—exasperated observers. No matter what the situation, Deer could be counted on to swing for the downs, even when a simple ground ball was all he needed to bring the runner in from third. "I just swing hard and if it goes out, it goes out," he explained. In 1991 Deer's indiscriminate swishes at the plate produced a woeful .179 average with twenty-five home runs and 175 strikeouts in just 448 at-bats. Only the fact that Sparky Anderson sat him down for much of the final month prevented him from breaking the all-time single-season record for striking out. Nonetheless, he figured in a couple of historic K's as the free-swinging Tigers set an American League record with 1,185 strikeouts. He was victim numbers 1,000 and 1,149, the latter breaking Seattle's 1986 mark. Deer was one of seven Detroit regulars to whiff at least ninety times. The following season Deer upped his average to .247 with thirty-two round-trippers, although injuries limited him to 110 games. His first five hits that season were home runs, an oddity unmatched by anyone in big- league history. Once again the Tigers led the majors in avoiding the ball, this time Deer contributing 131 strikeouts. Deer was sent packing to Boston the following August, but not before he had fanned the breeze 120 more times in ninety games. He left behind an incredible legacy. In two and a half summers he struck out more times than Charlie Gehringer had in nineteen seasons.

The constant whiffing may have provided a welcome breeze on muggy nights at the corner but did nothing to move the team up the standings. Except for 1991, when the team surprised everybody by staying in the chase until swooning in late August, it was a struggle to play .500 ball. Between 1990 and 1993 the Tigers won 323 games and lost 325.

If the Tigers couldn't restore the roar, perhaps they could stifle the snore. The promotion department issued everything but pillows. In the 1960s, the club discontinued Free Bat Day because it feared the vibration from the constant pounding of the bats on the floor would cause the stadium to crumble. In 1992 Monaghan reinstated the giveaway for a game against the Texas Rangers. Some forty-two thousand fans obligingly took wood to concrete, with no visible adverse effects.

Monaghan could be excused for idly dreaming that he could finally be rid of his biggest headache, if only the dammed place would fall down. By then the Tigers' owner, weary of the abuse he was receiving and experiencing a spiritual crisis, started selling off his baubles. He wanted to get back to basics, he explained, to concentrate his efforts on Christian philanthropy and pizza, two areas of interest that had suffered during his high-profile years as the Tigers' owner. "None of the things I have bought, and I mean none of them, have ever really made me happy," he said. "Most of the time I was buying things to get attention, to have people notice me. That's the sin of pride, the worst sin of all. And I'm the guiltiest person. So anything I've got that gives me pleasure only for selfish reasons, I'm selling." Monaghan's decision to peddle the Tigers was cemented in the spring of 1992, when voters approved a ballot initiative that prevented municipal funds from being used for a stadium project. The initiative's sponsor was the Common Ground Coalition, a group of individual activists and organizations that included the Tiger Stadium Fan Club.

On August 26, 1992, the baseball owner who once dreamed of playing shortstop for the Tigers sold the club to Mike Ilitch, a fellow pizza baron who'd come close to fulfilling the very same dream. Before leaving the scene, however, Monaghan managed to pull off one last embarrassing public relations gaffe. He severed Jim Campbell's forty-three-year relationship with the Tigers by phone and fired Schembechler via a faxed message. (Bo got even. He filed a lawsuit and eventually settled out-of-court.) With this kind of public image, it would have been next to impossible for any buyer of the team not to be greeted with open arms.

Ilitch had for some time been regarded as a civic savior. At a time when businesses were fleeing Detroit, he moved his corporate headquarters from Farmington Hills to downtown Detroit and ren-

Unlike the man who sold him the Detroit Tigers, Little Caesar's owner Mike Ilitch actually played shortstop for the Tigers—or at least, for their farm team.

ovated the Fox Theater, an Art Deco movie palace on Woodward Avenue that had fallen into disrepair. A community activist for years, he sponsored hundreds of athletic teams, built his downtown hockey franchise into a powerhouse, and developed the Woodward Avenue strip into a thriving entertainment district.

With his dyed jet-black curls, lopsided Mediterranean features, and uneasy smile, the sixty-three-year-old head of Little Caesar's had the slightly zany look of a lobotomized Roman emperor not terribly unlike the caricature that was his corporate logo. ("Jeez, we can

Television monitors were installed throughout the stadium in the 1990s, so fans could keep tabs on sluggers like Cecil Fielder while standing in line to buy a hot dog or beer.

never get him to take a good picture," one of his public relations people confided.) There was nothing little about Little Caesar's. At the time Ilitch paid Monaghan $85 million for the Tigers his company had almost four thousand outlets and his personal worth was estimated at $280 million.

Ilitch was a Detroit boy through and through. He grew up near Clinton Elementary School, on Chalfonte between Roselawn and

Greenlawn, and was a smooth-fielding shortstop at Cooley High. According to a pal, Vince Magi, Ilitch "was the best infielder in the city" in the years immediately following the Second World War. "He had quick hands, good arm. He really knew the game and knew what was going on all the time. He was a smart ballplayer and a competitor."

For some reason never made clear, Ilitch turned down a minor-league offer from the Tigers for five thousand dollars (some say the hard-nosed prospect held out for twice that amount) and enlisted in the Marine Corps instead. After his tour of duty ended in 1952 Ilitch accepted a bonus of three thousand dollars from the Tigers to play at Jamestown, New York, in the PONY League. Ilitch, charitably described by Jim Campbell as "a good, journeyman local prospect," got as high as the Class B Tampa Smokers before a bum knee convinced him it was time to give it up. He married in 1955 and bounced around, taking a college class or two, selling cookware and then aluminum awnings. By 1959 he had saved ten thousand dollars, enough for him and his wife Marian to open a pizzeria in Garden City. Who knew then that fast food, not a slow bat, would ultimately bring him to the corner of Michigan and Trumbull?

As the ninth principal owner of the Tigers since they started playing ball at Michigan and Trumbull, Ilitch came across as a sincere steward of the team's tradition. He did all the right things, signing the regulars to big contracts, bringing back a pair of old favorites, Ernie Harwell and Kirk Gibson, and vowing to study the stadium issue for a year before making any decision.

People visited Tiger Stadium to experience the new surroundings. During the winter of 1992–93 Ilitch spent a reported $8 million to spruce up the park. The players' parking lot alongside Michigan Avenue was turned into a food court called Tiger Plaza. Fans washed down nachos and a Caesar salad with a $3.50 cup of Ingelnook Navalle pink wine while a three-piece band played Dixieland pop—surely an experience that George Vanderbeck could never have imagined when he first built Bennett Park. Jim Campbell sniffed that the place "looked like an amusement park."

Ilitch appeared intent on changing everything. He increased the number of day games from twenty-seven to thirty-five and started night games a half-hour earlier—at 7:05 p.m. Rock music, once anathema to old-school types like Jim Campbell, blared on the public address system. John Fogarty's "Down on the Corner" became a standard selection.*

There were three Fan Appreciation weekends and a giveaway or discount for every home game. On Mondays kids ran the bases after the game; on Fridays genuine Zambelli fireworks lit up the sky after the final out. Local celebrities led the crowd in renditions of "Take Me Out to the Ball Game" in the seventh-inning stretch; four Couch Potatoes were chosen each game to sit on a couch in right field and receive free food and drinks. The team's logo and uniforms were redesigned.

The park became the site of popular summer concerts for the first time since Pat Boone crooned at Briggs Stadium in the 1950s. British rocker Rod Stewart performed one drizzly night in 1993, followed a year later by the Eagles. "I always wanted to play center field at Tiger Stadium," the Eagles' Glenn Frey, a native of Royal Oak, told the crowd of 36,500. "I just thought I'd have a glove instead of a guitar."

Earlier, Frey explained that the group had vacillated "back and forth about different venues for Detroit. Ultimately we decided on Tiger Stadium because it's such a historic place and it's not going to be there forever." The Tiger Stadium Fan Club, sniffing opportunity, tried in vain to enlist the Eagles in its preservation movement. Nonetheless, "the fact that the Eagles chose Tiger Stadium reflects not only Glenn Frey's affection," said fan club board member Bill Dow, "but also that it continues to be a very viable facility."

Not everyone agreed. Many people long associated with Tiger Stadium supported the construction of a new park.

"I'm sure there has to be a new ballpark," said Al Kaline. "Everybody hates to leave a great stadium like Tiger Stadium, except maybe the players because of the small clubhouses. Mr. Ilitch, regardless of the money he has, can't afford to spend the kind of money he has and not have it coming back in. You can't lose the

---

* Those who longed nostalgically for the return of organ music to Michigan and Trumbull probably did not remember that when it was introduced to the ballpark in 1966, many fans hated the piped-in intrusion. By the 1970s supplementary music was played over the scratchy public address system, though both the sound quality and song selection were widely criticized. "I could care less," responded Jim Campbell in 1984. "I'm a baseball man, not a stage-show manager." The last Tiger Stadium organist, Steve Schlesing, was fired after the 1990 season and replaced by a more blaring assault on the senses: cranked-up rock anthems distributed over a state-of-the-art sound system.

BLOCKBUSTER ENTERTAINMENT   DETROIT NEWSPAPERS

Present...

ROD STEWART
A night to remember

TICKETS ON SALE THIS SATURDAY!

WITH SPECIAL GUEST
PATTY SMYTH

TIGER STADIUM • SATURDAY, SEPT. 25
Tickets at Joe Louis Arena Box Office, and all TICKETMASTER.
CHARGE BY PHONE (313) 645-6666

The Ilitch regime opened the park to rock concerts, including performances by the Eagles, Rod Stewart, and Kiss.

kind of money he's going to lose. If you're going to get star players, you have to spend." Kaline, who considered Tiger Stadium one of the three best ballparks he'd ever seen (along with Fenway Park and Wrigley Field), favored a park like Camden Yards, which opened to universal acclaim in 1993 in his hometown of Baltimore: neo-classic styling with no artificial turf and no dome. "That's my opinion. Mr. Ilitch is going to do what he thinks is best. He knows more about marketing than I do."

Ilitch, who made his millions through savvy promotion, put everything up for sale at Tiger Stadium from the opening pitch to the power alleys. Rotating signs behind the plate shilled nearly every imaginable product, from Jensen Car Audio Systems and Bud Light beer to Scotts Turf Builder and Thorn Apple Valley Bun-Sized Smoked Sausages. Budweiser and Coca-Cola ads plastered the outfield walls and giant signs hung from the right- and left-field upper decks pitched potato chips, pizza, dairy products, and banking services. Even some of the posts were painted with advertisements for Health Alliance Plan. Depending on how one viewed such things, the wall-to-wall hucksterism was either merely intrusive or downright odious.

The new regime considered such a marketing plan elemental to survival. In 1993, Ilitch's first full season at the switch, the Tigers drew 1,970,791 fans, their sixth-best showing ever. But the days where ticket revenue alone made a franchise profitable were long gone. That year the club received an estimated $10.3 million from local stations WDIV and PASS for broadcast rights. Another $14 million poured in as its share of the national TV package. It wasn't enough to offset the team's operating costs, which in 1994 reached an estimated $55 million—about $20 million more than the club took in.

Fan club members generally gave Ilitch high marks until he came out in favor of a new stadium. The Tigers' multimillion-dollar losses, sure to increase, convinced Ilitch of the need for a park along the lines of the ones opening to great fanfare in Cleveland, Chicago, Baltimore, and Texas. His announced vision was a breathtakingly expensive project called Foxtown, which would feature an open-air, forty-seven-thousand-seat stadium on an eighty-acre site north of the theater district. Ilitch offered to put a sizable chunk of his pizza dough—$175 million—toward building the stadium if the city, state, and county came through with the estimated $230 million needed to acquire the land, build the infrastructure, and improve street and freeway access. These were estimates; nobody knew exactly what the final costs would be. More significantly, nobody knew what the benefits would be, except that a multimillionaire would own and operate a facility built primarily with taxpayers' dollars.

Always viewed as a knight of the community, Ilitch wasn't prepared for the vollies aimed his way. "It's hard to buck a millionaire team owner who wants a new stadium, one created according to his vision, located near his corporate headquarters, a monument to his civic leadership and a token of his prestige among fellow club owners," wrote Nicki McWhirter of the *Detroit News*. "One knows how hard Mike Ilitch has lobbied, promising a near rebirth of downtown prosperity at very reasonable taxpayer cost—as millionaires adjudge reasonable cost." Stung by the criticism, Ilitch took his proposal off the table. In the spring of 1994 he announced he now wanted to lease a publicly built ballpark. While waiting for a positive response from a largely disinterested state legislature, the Tigers limped through another lame-duck season at Michigan and Trumbull.

Critics charged that Ilitch's top advisors—several of whom were named Ilitch—lost sight of the primary focus of a day at the ballpark: the game. The new regime operated on the assumption that the modern fan craved diversion more than competition. Beach parties in the bleachers, celebrity singalongs, Friday night fireworks—the only things missing were hula hoops on the umpires and string bikinis on the usherettes. "My grandfather's probably rolling in his grave," said Mickey Briggs one evening, wincing at the ear-splitting air-raid sirens that wailed after a home run.

"I maintain the fans have to have their money's worth before they sit in the seat, before they watch the ballgame," responded Ilitch. "That's the way I'm designing my stadium. They've got to have a blast, and it's all got to revolve around the family."

But what of the fuddy-duddies for whom a day at the park once meant quiet discussions of strategy and fantasy trades between pitches? They believed the game had sold its soul. One of the most revealing items about modern baseball was that it was increasingly being referred to by players, owners, and social commentators as an industry. For the 1994 season the *industry* adopted a convoluted three-division, wild-card playoff system in each league. It was a quick way to recoup some of the $7 million per club that the new, drastically cut national television contracts—the result of plunging ratings—cost it. The possibility of crowning a cardboard champion concerned few people.

The threat of another work stoppage did, however. Because owners and players allowed their collective bargaining agreement to expire on the final day of 1993, the probability of a strike hung like a rotting awning over the upcoming season. Owners disclosed that a new Basic Agreement would have to contain provisions for a salary cap similar to those employed by pro football and basketball. This would have been laughable if the consequences weren't so serious. In the three labor negotiations since free agency was granted in 1976, the owners had tried without success to do collectively what they couldn't do individually: put a lid on salaries. The results? A fifty-day strike in 1981, a two-day strike in 1985, a spring-training lockout in 1990, and—if the owners were to be believed—a spreading pool of red ink.

Ilitch responded to the pressure to field a championship team by signing stars like Cecil Fielder to long-term, megabucks contracts. Fielder's five-year, $36-million deal helped inflate the Tigers' payroll from $22 million in 1991 (seventeenth in the majors) to a staggering $42.7 million in 1994, the highest in major-league history. He participated in the bidding wars for free agents. Tim Belcher, as ordinary a pitcher as ever toed the slab, was ardently pursued by Joe Klein, Ilitch's new general manager. After Belcher's best offer was an unguaranteed $2.1-million deal from Cleveland, Klein signed him to a *guaranteed* deal worth $3.4 million. Belcher won seven, lost fifteen, and recorded a 5.89 ERA his only summer with Detroit. This meant each of Belcher's victories cost the Tigers a cool half million dollars.

To be more precise, it cost the fans that amount. Detroit's bloated payroll costs were passed on to the public in the form of higher prices for tickets and concessions. The price of watching a game at the old ballpark increased dramatically under Ilitch. According to the April 1994 issue of *Team Marketing Report*, the cost of taking a family of four to Tiger Stadium was $103.45, eighth highest among twenty-eight teams. Since Ilitch bought the team the price of box seats rose from $12.50 to $15; reserved seats from $10 to $12; grandstand seats from $7 to $8; and bleachers from $4 to $5.

The best chairs were appropriated for a premium seating area called the Tiger Den. This included the first seventeen rows of the lower deck, and the first four rows of the upper deck, between first and third—a total of 3,750 seats. Tickets that once cost $12.50 now sold

Following a loss to Milwaukee at Tiger Stadium on August 11, 1994, the Tigers and every big-league city went on strike. Left in the cold were the fans as the rest of the season went down the drain.

for $20 on a season-ticket basis, with most of the buyers corporate types. The Tiger Den, which featured waiter service and preferred parking, stratified what had long been a democratic mix of fans. It was impossible to buy a seat on a single-game basis, as in the past, or to move to an empty chair on a slow night, as long was customary.

"On weekday afternoons and late-season nights, customers in the Tiger Den are often outnumbered by stadium employees, whose main function is to make sure those good seats stay empty," observed Tom Faulkner in a wry, perceptive essay on the sociology of Tiger Stadium.

Inside the Den, everything tells you you're special: padded seats and wooden armrests with brass plates stamped "reserved;" a wait staff to fetch your food and drink [and] an army of solicitous ushers defending your turf.

It's the exact opposite of the bleachers, where you're told in similar terms that you're on the economy plan: metal benches; no-frills food; a security staff deployed to keep you from getting out of the bleachers, and out of control inside them. Bleacherites must settle for beer (until recently, the low-alcohol type), but the Den-izens can choose from a variety of brews, wine or cocktails. After all, drunks in ties are different from drunks in T-shirts, right? . . .

Speaking of idiocy, consider the implications of the "Chicken Dance." "All right, all you Bleacher Creatures!" the hearty PA announcer thunders. "You didn't think you'd get out of here without dancing, did you?" While a polka plays, the scoreboard TV shows pictures of bleacher bums boogying. Few fans dance in other parts of the park. In the Tiger Den, they point at the bleachers and laugh and cluck like chickens. Trinkets are flung out for the bleacherites to fight over—a spectacle also shown on the big screen. OK, it's nothing but good clean fun at the ballpark. But why aren't the folks in the Tiger Den ever called on to entertain the rest of us?

Under the new three-division format, Detroit became part of the American League East, which also included New York, Baltimore, Toronto, and Boston. The folly of such restructuring was apparent when fans glanced at the standings after the games of August 11, 1994. Texas, ten games under .500, led the Western Division. Ten of fourteen American League teams had better records, including the Tigers, who were mired in the basement of the Eastern Division. That Thursday afternoon, after sitting through a three-hour rain delay, the soggy remnants of a Tiger Stadium crowd of 18,857 watched Milwaukee score six runs in the eighth inning to beat the Tigers, 10–5. The puddled stands seemed portentous. At midnight, as predicted, players struck rather than have the owners' salary cap forced on them. The walkout scratched the Tigers' Friday night contest with California and plunged the national pastime into its eighth work stoppage in twenty-two years.

The public, already numb from years of hearing and reading about threats, lawsuits, strikes, and contractual mumbo jumbo, displayed scant sympathy for the owners, who had raked in record broadcasting and merchandising revenues, only to blow them; or for the players, who saw eye-popping salaries triple over the last seven years to an average $1.2 million each. It was inconceivable to ordinary working folks that the two sides couldn't figure out a way to divide the riches equitably. Those who could least afford it were most affected: vendors, parking lot operators, and area businesses. The lack of game-day traffic shut down two popular watering holes, Hoot Robinson's and the Irish Saloon.

Not everybody mourned the sudden inactivity at Michigan and Trumbull, though. "I don't have to chase drunks off my lawn," said Tom Cieszkowski, who lived across the street from Tiger Stadium. "Nobody urinates on my wall. It's been kind of nice." Still, admitted Cieszkowski, "I do miss the sounds of the cheering and the lights being turned off at night. There was something romantic about that."

Players and owners behaved as if they were in a schoolyard spat. Neither side was willing to budge on the central issue of a salary cap, and the final fifty-two days and 669 games of the regular season were wiped out. On September 14, owners canceled the World Series for the first time since 1904. The Tigers, fielding the most expensive lineup in baseball history, officially ended the season in last place with a 53–62 record, eighteen games behind division leader New York. For all of Ilitch's promotional gimmicks and good intentions, they also finished dead last in the American League in average attendance, drawing a mere 20,820 a game, ten thousand under the major-league average.

"We all know this is a miserable situation," said Ilitch. "I don't think there is any question the fans are turned off. I don't know what we'll do to win them back." To make matters worse for Detroit fans, Ilitch voted with other National Hockey League owners to lock out skaters after they too refused to agree to a salary cap. The NHL season, scheduled to begin October 1, was put on hold. Unlike the Tigers, Ilitch's Red Wings—consistently rated the most valuable franchise in the league—were a championship contender and a money-making machine. Every game not played at Joe Louis Arena cost Ilitch an estimated six hundred thousand in ticket sales alone, not including revenue from parking, concessions, and merchandise sales. To the relief of Ilitch's accountants, hockey players and owners hammered out a labor agreement and began playing games in early January.★

The baseball strike dragged on through the winter and into the new year. The owners abandoned the idea of a salary cap in favor of a league-imposed tax on teams that spent more than an agreed-upon amount on salaries. The tax would then be used to support small-market clubs. The players union accepted the concept in principle, but could not reach an agreement with the owners over the tax rate and at what salary level it should kick in.

Meanwhile, some belt tightening became necessary. Cecil Fielder, who also had a grand home in Texas, put his Grosse Pointe Farms mansion on the market, listing the seven-bedroom, ten-bath, 8,800-square-foot mansion at $1.3 million. The price included such amenities as a pool, heated garage, carriage house, maid's quarters, and three walk-in safes. The latter presumably were useless, now that Fielder—whose base annual salary was $7.2 million—was losing $19,726 a day. Others on the verge of clipping store coupons were Mike Henneman, the $4.5-million-a-year reliever who was out $12,329 each day; Travis Fryman ($3.75 million/$10,274); Tony Phillips and Lou Whitaker ($3.5 million/$9,589); and Mike Moore ($3 million/$8,219).

As spring training approached, the Tigers joined other big-league clubs in announcing that they would use replacement players to start the 1995 season. After mulling things over, Sparky Anderson announced on the eve of opening camp that his personal integrity was on the line managing ersatz Tigers. "I'm not going to tarnish this game by accepting this," he said. "I'm looking forward to opening day, and I'm looking forward to regular players. I'm not looking forward to no replacement thing. That's not for me." He packed up his double negatives and flew back home to California on unpaid leave.

While the front office grumbled over Anderson's remarks, scores of wannabes assembled under the wing of interim manager Tom Runnells, who had managed the Triple-a Toledo Mudhens the year before.

★ Some inadvertent cross-marketing involving Ilitch's two downtown teams occurred at Tiger Stadium on June 17, 1995. That evening Detroit's wackiest sports tradition made its first recorded appearance at the corner when someone—presumably a hockey fan unable to get a ticket to the opener of the Stanley Cup Finals at nearby Joe Louis Arena—heaved an octopus onto the field in the fourth inning of a game against Baltimore.

Who were these guys? There was thirty-year-old second base-man Paul Blair III, whose father had once starred for Baltimore. Blair was working as a dispatcher for a courier service when he heeded the call. Bryan Clutterbuck, a Detroit native who injured his right arm six years earlier pitching for the Milwaukee Brewers, left his job as a garbage man in Royal Oak for another chance at the show. "Sanitation engineer?" he snorted when a reporter delicately asked about his former line of work. "I don't go for those big words. What the heck, I was a garbage man. Long johns, sweatshirt with a hood over my head, driving the truck in below-zero temps, that was me."

Clutterbuck should have been hired to haul away the debris that was once the national pastime. The game was an absolute mess. Baltimore refused to field a replacement team, while Toronto announced that Canadian labor laws would force it to move its reg-ular-season home to a 6,200-seat park in Dunedin, Florida. Everything from advertising campaigns to broadcasting schedules collapsed into a state of confusion. Topps, the Brooklyn-based base-ball-card manufacturer, laid off two hundred workers. The bottom of the collectibles market fell out.

Because of the uncertainty, the Tiger Stadium issue was con-signed to a back burner. "It is not so much anti-Detroit," explained one outstate legislator, "as anti-baseball at the moment." Governor John Engler, careful not to offend the unionized members of his constituency, turned down the Tigers' request to throw out the cer-emonial first pitch on opening day at Tiger Stadium, which was scheduled for April 3 against Kansas City.

While striking players snickered and advertisers fretted, owners maintained that they were dead serious about starting the season with substitutes. The Tigers announced a 50-percent reduction in ticket prices for games played by replacements and a season-long reduction for bleacher seats regardless of who played. About twen-ty-two thousand tickets were sold for opening day.

On the Friday before the regular season opener, however, a fed-eral court ruled on an unfair labor practices suit filed with the National Labor Relations Board. The judge issued an injunction against the owners, who in their union-busting enthusiasm had uni-laterally attempted to eliminate salary arbitration, free agent bid-ding, and anti-collusion provisions. The union immediately voted to end its strike and offered to return to work. The owners huddled to discuss their next move. Because it was well-known they lacked a majority of hard-liners among them to carry a vote needed to lock out the players, the court's decision effectively ended the 234-day work stoppage as soon as it was announced.

The fill-ins were left in the lurch. The replacement Tigers arrived at Tiger Stadium the day after the injunction, understanding even as they soaked in the surroundings that the final piece of their dream had probably been snatched from them. The owners' vote to junk the replacement process and welcome back the "real" players made it official. "It would have been a nice ending of this process to have played a game there with those kids," admitted Tom Runnells. Instead, Runnells was reassigned to Toledo and the ersatz Tigers were released, just hours short of a midnight deadline that would have paid each of them a twenty-five-thousand-dollar bonus. They were allowed, however, to keep the home whites that had hung so briefly inside the Detroit clubhouse. Appropriately enough, the charade ended on April 1—April Fool's Day.

What was accomplished? Absolutely nothing. The strike cost major-league baseball more than one billion dollars and alienated millions of fans. No new collective bargaining agreement was reached. There was no guarantee that yet another season wouldn't be splintered by labor strife. If not for the courts, the two sides would have continued throwing spitballs at each other into a second, possibly a third season.*

* The players' strike that wiped out the balance of the 1994 season and delayed the start of the Tigers' centennial season at Michigan and Trumbull was just the latest in a long line of labor disputes that plagued major league baseball and played havoc with fans' emotions. What follows is a chronology of the national pastime's contract-related work stoppages, including the season, action, issue involved, and length of the dispute. "Games lost" refers to the number of regular season games the Tigers were forced to cancel; home dates lost are in parentheses.

Season(s)	Action	Issue(s)	Days	Games Lost
1972	Strike	Pensions	14	6 (4)
1973	Lockout	Arbitration	12	None
1976	Lockout	Free agency	17	None
1980	Strike	Free agent compensation	8	None
1981	Strike	Free agent compensation	50	53(26)
1985	Strike	Salary cap, arbitration	2	None
1990	Lockout	Salary cap, arbitration	32	None
1994–95	Strike	Salary cap	234	63 (31)*

* Includes 16 games, including 8 home contests, lost at beginning of 1995 season.

A scene from the Tigers' poorly attended, undisciplined 1995 home opener: Travis Fryman patiently waits as security guards remove a fan who jumped the outfield fence, ran across the diamond, and slid face first across home plate.

Major leaguers were instructed to report to training. Lou Whitaker, grown fat and bored from months of watching the O. J. Simpson double-murder trial on television, pulled up to the Tigers' Lakeland camp in his Rolls Royce. "This was supposed to be opening day in Detroit," he mused, the bright Florida sun reflecting off the limousine's gold hood ornament. "I'd be up there right now, freezing my little tail off." Asked about the fans' disappointment over the strike and their possible reaction to the resumption of play, Whitaker responded, "People don't turn on baseball that quickly. Not the real fans, anyway. Some, it may take them a little while to get over their crushed feelings. It's just like a man and a woman. Maybe we'll send a few flowers."

"Fans are funny," Sparky Anderson observed when the strike began. "They'll forgive anybody for anything."

Well, maybe. On May 2, 1995, the Tigers returned from a West Coast trip and opened against Cleveland in front of a rowdy house. Its size was officially announced as 39,398 but ten thousand must have come disguised as empty seats. Unlike National League clubs, which use actual turnstile counts in determining crowd size, American League clubs count all tickets sold for at least fifty cents as game attendance. The Tigers, tabulating scads of unused, heavily discounted tickets, released disingenuous numbers all season. The turnout was the smallest for an opener since 1972, another strike-shortened season.

Restless fans interrupted play from the beginning, swatting a dozen beach balls onto the field in the first inning alone. A banner reading "Greed" hung in the bleachers; ushers tore down another adorning the upper deck behind third base. Outside the stadium apathy reigned. A solitary picket walked Trumbull while downtown restaurants and street vendors reported lukewarm business. The nine televisions inside a Dearborn Heights bar were all tuned to music videos or golf instead of the game's local broadcast.

Cleveland scored four runs in the first inning. As the score mounted, Tiger Stadium took on the look of a Brazilian soccer arena. Patrons began hurling the free magnetized schedules they had been given onto the field. These were followed by batteries, coins, snuff tins, cigarette lighters, wadded-up clothes, even a chrome napkin holder. "I was all right 'til they started throwing beer bottles, whiskey bottles, Coke bottles," said Cleveland center fielder Kenny Lofton, who fled to the infield for safety in the fifth inning. Umpires halted play to point out offenders to security guards. Cleveland general manager John Hart, who'd already had a drunk fall on him as he sat in the stands, phoned the American League office to complain about the growing unrest. In the sixth inning boozy adventurers began scaling the outfield fences in twos and threes, and zig-zagged across the grass while orange-jacketed security guards huffed and puffed after them. One voyager made it all the way from center field to home, capping his frolic by sliding face-first into the plate as Travis Fryman impassively watched from the batter's box. The final numbers for the afternoon read Cleveland 11, Detroit 1; thirty-four people were arrested on charges ranging from disorderly conduct to carrying a concealed weapon. It was late and it was ugly, but the one hundredth season of baseball at Michigan and Trumbull was finally underway.

Some observers later contended that baseball's acrimony contributed to the circus, highlights of which had made all of the national news and sports programs. "The fans who bothered to show up," wrote Doron Levin of the *Free Press*, "whether they realized it, were not just rowdy, they were acting out collective contempt for the national pastime. Running across the field and tossing trash—mere attention-getters in some contexts—symbolized the ritual desecration of hallowed ground, Tiger Stadium."

Others weren't willing to attach noble motives to the hooliganism. "There are a million ways to protest without making our city look stupid," responded Kirk Gibson. "That's pure ignorance. I think the protest is an excuse. I tell you what—it doesn't make me proud of this place." The club immediately beefed up security and for the rest of the season cut off beer sales in the bleachers after the fifth inning.

On the field, the Tigers managed to pare their payroll to about $36 million by not re-signing Tim Belcher and their two top catchers, Mickey Tettleton and Chad Kreuter, and trading Tony Phillips to California for the younger (and cheaper) Chad Curtis. The speedy center fielder, a Michigan native who had once dreamed of playing at Tiger Stadium alongside Alan Trammell, probably never imagined how bad a team he'd be sharing with his boyhood hero. The Tigers, a dozen of whom hadn't been with the team a year earlier, stumbled through a truncated schedule of 144 games, losing far more games than they won. To save more money the Tigers dealt their top starter, David Wells, and top reliever, Mike Henneman, after the All-Star break for a pair of prospects.

There were a couple of historic moments at the park. On May 28, the Tigers and White Sox combined for a big-league record twelve home runs. Despite hitting a club-record seven of them, the Tigers fell, 14–12. On June 18, the Tigers beat Baltimore, 10–8, to give Anderson the 2,158th managerial win of his career, putting him third behind Connie Mack and John McGraw on the all-time list. Few people saw either game. Season attendance, officially placed at

As the ongoing debate over a new stadium continued throughout 1995, the Ilitch organization stepped up its public relations campaign, including the opening of an information office on Woodward.

1,050,555, extended the Tigers' league record of consecutive million-plus seasons to thirty-five. However, attendance on a per-game basis was the lowest since the back-to-back last-place finishes of 1974–75. In terms of people actually inside the park, Tiger Stadium was emptier than at any time since the mid-1960s.

Marketing-wise, the club strained to restore the game's ruptured symmetry. Family Value Nights offered four reserved seats, hot dogs, and soft drinks for twenty-four dollars. Kids' Row, featuring a new mascot (a costumed Tiger named Paws) and carnival games, was introduced behind the family section in the lower left-field stands.

New club president John McHale, Jr., who had been hired over the winter primarily to serve as the point man on the stadium issue, had deep Detroit roots. Fifty years earlier his father played prep football and pro baseball at Michigan and Trumbull, then briefly served as the Tigers' general manager. With 1995 a transitional year, McHale reached into the past to sell the team. Trammell and Gibson, old favorites made free agents by the strike, were signed at the last moment to one-year contracts, although Gibson, troubled by a sore shoulder and sick of all the losing, abruptly retired in early August. An advertising campaign centered not on the current group of players, but on Ty Cobb and Al Kaline—players from a less ambiguous era. Their names, along with those of other Hall of Famers who spent all or most of their careers at the corner, were painted on the facing of the third deck in right, as were the club's three retired uniform numbers: 2 (Charlie Gehringer), 5 (Hank Greenberg), and 6 (Kaline). One Saturday evening in July the club hosted a salute to the Negro leagues, dressing players in reproduction uniforms worn by the Detroit Stars, the city's black professional team of the 1920s. In the final home stand of the season Trammell and Whitaker were reunited in the lineup, giving fans one last look at the longest-running pair of teammates—nineteen seasons—in baseball history. The Tigers, never a sentimental organization, seemed awash in nostalgia. But the club still resisted marketing its greatest asset—Tiger Stadium.

To the dismay of preservationists like Jack Walter, the intentional neglect of one of Detroit's oldest, most storied plots of common ground remained unofficial club policy. Historic preservation, viewed by the Tigers as irritating and irrelevant, really "is about keeping us in active contact with our past—the good and the bad—so that we will never forget it, and learn from it," said Walter, president of the National Trust for Historic Preservation. "In the long run this is why it is vital that we preserve historic places like Tiger Stadium—for what they teach us about ourselves, as well as about the game. When we preserve our past, we preserve what unites us, not what divides us, which is why cities that do preserve the best of their heritage and culture have more soul and community spirit than those that do not."

The Ilitch organization remained adamant that a new stadium was central to the club's fortunes. McHale, a Denver lawyer who was instrumental in getting the Mile High City an expansion franchise, the Colorado Rockies, and a new stadium, Coors Field, brought his seven-point system for judging a baseball franchise to Detroit. Among those points were "respect for the franchise's heritage and tradition" and "being part of the community." But, hedged McHale, "It's not possible to fulfill those criteria without a new park."

On September 20, 1995, the Tigers took a giant step in that direction when board members of the Michigan Strategic Fund voted to kick in $55 million to help fund a new stadium. After months of negotiations between the club, the city, and the state, the project was drastically reduced in size and scope from Ilitch's original Foxtown proposal. The still-to-be-determined site was whittled down from eighty acres to between twenty and thirty, the planned entertainment and retail shops were dropped, and the overall cost of the project was slashed from more than $400 million to a more modest $230 million. The Tigers' share dropped from an estimated $175 million to about $145 million. The city's $40-million share would come from the sale of bonds issued by the Downtown Development Authority.

Thanks for the memories. In the final home game of the Tigers' one hundredth summer at Michigan and Trumbull, Alan Trammell and Lou Whitaker bowed out together after an unprecedented nineteen seasons as teammates. Earlier, responding to rumors that he might be traded to a contender for its stretch drive, Trammell said, "I don't want to look at the bottom of my baseball card and see any team other than the Tigers. Trammell later signed a contract to play the 1996 season, his twentieth in Detroit.

The governor avoided putting the state-aid package to a legislative vote by unilaterally earmarking tax revenues from Indian casinos into the Strategic Fund. Under the plan, $25 million of the state's contribution would be used for land acquisition. The balance, $30 million, would be used for environmental cleanup, building demolition, and road repairs. A thirty-seven-page document outlined a series of conditions and deadlines that the club and the city would have to meet in order to receive the $55-million grant.

The news came on a raw, windy Thursday. That afternoon Alan Trammell, Lou Whitaker, and Sparky Anderson tugged on the home whites for what everybody assumed would be the last time. "These years in Detroit have been the fondest of my life," Anderson said after the home finale, which was interrupted several times by long ovations for the departing trio. "But if you live in the past, you've got nothing to look forward to. This is a normal process—seasons end, careers end. We just passed through and took up time. That's it. Sorry, I ain't a goodbye person."

The day after the Tigers closed out a sad-sack season with three straight shutout losses in Baltimore, Anderson officially confirmed what had been rumored all summer: he was stepping down as manager after a club-record seventeen years. Coach Dick Tracewski also ended his thirty-year association with the team. Three weeks later Joe Klein was fired as general manager. The *Chicago Tribune* noted the exodus of players and executives, commenting that "the dinosaurs are leaving Jurassic Park, also known as Tiger Stadium."

On October 28, 1995, Ilitch and McHale joined Detroit Mayor Dennis Archer inside a conference room at the City-County Building to announce that the details of a new downtown stadium had been ironed out. To the surprise of most people, the site selected was not east of Woodward Avenue. Speculation for a proposed casino had recently driven up prices in the area, so Ilitch settled on a parcel of land a couple of blocks west of Woodward behind the Fox Theater. The twenty-five-acre site was primarily occupied by weed-choked lots, boarded-up buildings, and a few struggling businesses. Fewer than one hundred people lived in the thirteen-block area. Acquiring the various lots posed few problems, especially since the city could proceed with demolition as it battled recalcitrant property owners in court over what they should be paid.

A variety of issues were resolved. The stadium would be owned by the Development Authority, and the Tigers would sign a thirty-five-year lease. The team, which would be responsible for any cost overruns and all but $250,000 of the stadium's projected $6.5-million annual operating costs, would receive all ticket, parking, and concession revenue from baseball games. The city would share in revenue from concerts and other non-baseball events held there. The Tigers planned to move their offices into a renovated building at 1922 Cass.

It was announced that the forty-two-thousand-seat park would be an open-air, grass-field facility featuring traditional architecture and no obstructed views—something similar to Baltimore's Camden Yards. The middle of three decks would contain sixty-five luxury boxes and fifty-two-hundred club seats. The stadium would also include four thousand bleacher seats. In addition to more rest areas than Tiger Stadium, the new park would offer spacious picnic, concession, and retail areas, with between fifteen hundred and two thousand parking spaces reserved for luxury-box and club-seat ticket holders. The paucity of parking spaces was a bonus for those who envisioned the park as an economic catalyst for area shops and restaurants. It meant thousands of fans would stroll through downtown streets from a variety of outlying parking lots or take the People Mover, an electrified elevated train, to the stadium's entrance. The city quickly announced a $1.1-million spruce up of adjacent Grand Circus Park, which would become the gateway to the rejuvenated neighborhood. Archer enthusiastically called the planned stadium "a grand slam." The city council quickly approved the project and overturned the 1992 referendum prohibiting public funds from being used for a new stadium. The council also voted to issue $40 million in Downtown Development Authority bonds.

Two young men, Buddy Bell and Randy Smith, were brought aboard as manager and general manager, respectively, to oversee an unfledged team through what McHale admitted would be at least two or three years of learning-by-losing in lame-duck Tiger Stadium. The club's philosophy was that its return to competitiveness and profitability would coincide with its move into a new stadium, which—assuming a twenty-four-month construction cycle, would be 1998 if everything went according to schedule; 1999 if there were delays. McHale conceded that after factoring in debt service, the annual attendance at a new ballpark probably would have to approach three million fans in order for the Tigers—a club that had drawn as many as two million in a season only five times—to post a profit. Left unresolved was what to do with Tiger Stadium after the team moved into a new park. The Tigers were committed to contributing $2 million toward the maintenance or demolition of their former home, although the decision to turn the vinyl-sided

Tony Clark, who took over Cecil Fielder's job at first base in 1996, was one of
several young players being groomed to open the new downtown stadium.

cathedral at Michigan and Trumbull into a mall, museum, or vacant
lot didn't need to be made immediately.

Ilitch's quest for private financing and the issuing of municipal
bonds were stalled by the Tiger Stadium Fan Club, which managed
to collect enough signatures to force a referendum on the issue of

using public money for a new ballpark. At the same time the club filed suit to halt the state's proposed $55-million contribution toward the project.

The vote was scheduled for March 19, 1996, the day of the state Republican primary. While the fan club was ready to spend eleven thousand dollars on leaflets and a few strategically placed radio spots, the new stadium's backers unleashed a sophisticated six-hundred-thousand-dollar campaign that included phone banks, sound trucks, and a tidal wave of radio and television commercials. The Sunday before Detroiters went to the ballot box, Ilitch and Dennis Archer made a series of joint appearances at local churches, driving home the message that a new stadium was in the city's best interests. The mayor's earlier criticism of fan club members as being "outsiders" (most were white suburbanites) played well to his overwhelmingly black constituency. Even Coleman Young, no fan of Archer, voiced his support, a message from the ailing former mayor piped live to the congregation via a telephone hookup.

Among players in spring training, the question of a new park was a no-brainer.

"We need a new ballpark—we really do," said Alan Trammell, probably the most tradition-conscious ballplayer ever to tug on a Detroit uniform. "That's not to take anything away from the memories and the moments—hell, I've got great memories of Tiger Stadium. Who better? I've played almost as long as anybody that's ever played there.

"I'm not trying to downgrade the Tiger Stadium Fan Club. I think their feelings and emotions are real, and they have a special feeling for this ballpark, which I do. And I agree with them on that. But I just think that with the new ballparks I've seen, the people in Michigan and Detroit would like what would be built.

"This new ballpark is not really for us. It's for the new generation, like my kids. They want the new parks. Sometimes we—the older crowd, so to speak—need to recognize that. We have the memories of Tiger Stadium, and they're valid, but the new ball park is not for us in my estimation. It's for the new generation. The things that I did and liked are not what the kids like now. They want the modern conveniences. They want the scoreboards with all that stuff."

On primary day, the scoreboard showed that 81 percent of Detroit's voters agreed with Archer, Ilitch, Young, and Trammell. They overwhelmingly approved the ballot proposal permitting the use of city funds for a new stadium. Players were thrilled by the news.

"Those of us who work there—the players and the front office—realize that times are changing and it's time for a new stadium," said pitcher John Doherty. "I think it will bring a lot of revenue to the city, and that in the long run it will help the city more than hurt it.

"It's time for a new stadium. I don't know how else to put it."

Two days later in Lansing, Ingham Circuit Judge James Giddings dismissed the fan club's lawsuit challenging the state's contribution from the Strategic Fund. "They are essentially private funds," ruled Giddings, which meant their distribution was not subject to legislative appropriation. Team and city officials were ecstatic. They had cleared the last major hurdle.

With a new stadium now a certainty, the Tigers proceeded to stink out the old one. Not only did the 1996 season disintegrate into the worst in the franchise's history, it went down as one of the most god-awful ever recorded in the annals of big-league baseball. With cost-cutting now the dominant theme in the front office, the club headed north from spring training with a roster dominated by rookies and discount-price castoffs.

The pitching staff was abysmal. On April 24, Minnesota pounded seven pitchers in a 24–11 rout at Tiger Stadium. No Tiger team has given up more runs in a game. "It's probably not the last time it will happen," admitted Buddy Bell. The skipper was right. The next afternoon the Twins smoked the home nine, 11–1. By the end of the year a total of twenty-seven different pitchers had been used and abused. The staff set team records for hits, runs, and walks allowed. It also surrendered more home runs and grand slams than any team in major-league history. Its 6.38 ERA was the highest in league history and second-worst of all-time. Omar Olivares' seven victories made him the "ace" and was the first time a Tiger hurler led the team with fewer than ten wins.

In a year of unprecedented bashing, the Tigers finished last in batting. On May 3–4, Ken Hill and Roger Pavlik of Texas threw consecutive one-hitters at Tiger Stadium, the first time a major-league team accomplished such a feat in seventy-nine years. Hoping to trim a still bloated payroll by several million dollars, at mid-season the club traded Cecil Fielder to the Yankees for outfielder Ruben Sierra and $1 million. While Fielder helped New York win the World Series, the lackadaisical Sierra contributed to the Tigers' woeful defense, which ranked last in fielding percentage.

By June the losing, which at one point included a skid of 39 losses in 44 outings, reached epic proportions and positioned the Tigers to replace the 1962 New York Mets as the worst team of the century. "I still think the game has been moving too fast for them," Bell said of his young charges. "Either they're thinking too much or not enough." As the losses continued to mount, the team became material for Jay Leno and David Letterman jokes on national television. Even worse, Cleveland fans—unable to get tickets at sold-out Jacobs Field—descended en masse on Tiger Stadium one weekend, accounting for the season's largest series turnout. Detroit players looked up into the packed stands to find three-quarters of the crowd rooting against them. "I'd rather they were cheering for us," observed Bell, "but it's kind of nice to see some people in the stands." The club, which had advertised the availability of tickets on Cleveland radio, carefully reminded patrons in mid-game announcements of the Indians' next visit to Michigan and Trumbull.

Season attendance was less than 1.2 million—second worst in the majors and the lowest for a full season since 1975—but only roughly half that number actually entered the park. For example, the Tigers sold 24,372 tickets for a May contest against Kansas City. These included 15,000 heavily discounted pasteboards purchased by a local TV station for a giveaway promotion. The turnstile count, however, was 7,204. The lack of patronage affected not only the Tigers' bottom line but also those of area businesses. Many struggling retailers simply gave up. "It's not a great neighborhood, and it's an old, broken-down stadium. Who wants to go there?" explained Allan Simpson, editor of *Baseball America* magazine. "People want a fun atmosphere, a vibrant stadium and neighborhood where they feel safe." At no time was the apathy more evident than on Fan Appreciation Night, when only 6,604 showed up, most more intent on winning a VCR or a year's supply of free hot dogs than cheering for the likes of Clint Sodowsky, Todd Van Poppel, and Andujar Cedeno.

Outfielder Curtis Pride, the first deaf player in the majors since 1945, was physically unable to hear what little cheering occurred during this endless summer. But the crowds were so thin there was precious little vibration for him to feel, either, making it seem like he was playing in a graveyard most nights. "It's frustrating because we like to have a lot of people to kind of pump us up," said Pride, who joined left fielder Bobby Higginson as the team's sole .300 hitters. "I don't blame them for not coming out, the way we're losing."

The few people on hand witnessed several record performances during the year. On September 18, Boston's Roger Clemens matched his own big-league record by striking out twenty Tigers. "We're not having fun," Travis Fryman told the home-plate ump after whiffing for the third time. The next game produced another loss and another low. Tony Clark, a former basketball standout who had become the first baseman of the future, struck out in the first inning against Boston's Tom Gordon. This broke the league record of 1,185 set by the 1991 edition of the Tigers. By the end of the summer the team had swished 1,268 times, most in major-league history.

The most notable of the many negative marks the boys of '96 established was the franchise record for defeats. They tied the 1952 squad's record of 104 on September 24 with a 6–4 loss to Toronto at Tiger Stadium, then eclipsed it the following night when they dropped a 4–1 verdict to the Blue Jays. They finished with 109 losses, including their last seventeen home games. The finale, a 7–5 loss to Milwaukee, featured several standing ovations from the home folks for Alan Trammell, who had returned for one last, bittersweet season. To the crowd's joy, the former All-Star shortstop—now a balding, struggling role player—lined a single in the bottom of the tenth inning. A few seconds later a double play ended the game and Trammell's twenty-year career. Mercifully, it also brought the curtain down on a long, suffocating season.

If Detroiters largely ignored the Tigers' bummer of a summer, a news conference held in the mayor's office toward the end of the season snapped them to attention. On morning of August 21, 1996, members of the Ilitch and Ford families joined representatives of the city and Wayne County in announcing that, after months of wearying and secret negotiations, a $505-million deal had been worked out for side-by-side downtown stadiums—one for the Tigers and the other for the Lions. The Lions' projected stadium would be domed and have a seating capacity of between 65,000 and 75,000, including upwards of 120 private suites and 8,500 club-level seats. The $245-million price tag would be paid by owner William Clay Ford ($50 million), the county ($20 million), the Downtown Development Authority ($45 million), a tourism tax ($80 million), and corporate pledges ($50 million). The figures included $20 million for parking structures; the team also was committed to building a $20-million state-of-the-art practice facility in Allen Park. The look and cost of the Tigers' new quarters had not changed—it would remain an open-air facility of 42,000 seats budgeted at $240 million—but the location had. The twin stadiums would be built next to each other on forty acres of land east of Woodward Avenue and south of I-75.

Project supporters hailed it as an example of what could happen when public- and private-sector leaders dared to dream big. "My children and grandchildren will grow up here," William Clay Ford Jr., vice-chairman of the Lions, said. "There's nothing more important to the health of our region than a vibrant city of Detroit." Wayne County voters evidently agreed. On November 5 they approved a proposal calling for new lodging and car rental taxes. Its passage—crucial to the project going forward—meant that out-of-town visitors would fund a large share of the project's cost, an attractive alternative to increased local taxes.

As heartening as the widespread support for the twin stadiums was Detroit's continuing boom in development activity. Since 1994 the city saw some $5.5 billion in new investments, the result of a healthy economy, a new attitude in city hall, and renewed commitment from corporate giants, particularly the Big Three automakers. Among the many highlights were General Motors' purchase of the Renaissance Center for its world headquarters, the opening of the new Museum of African American History (the country's largest), the renovation of Music Hall, and a flurry of new housing development. Other high-profile developments, including a Hard Rock Cafe and several casinos, were about to move from the drawing board to the bricks-and-mortar stage. A ten-year federal grant made stretches of Detroit eligible for $100 million in aid, spurring commercial activity in the so-called empowerment zone. The long-vacant Hudson's building, an eyesore that had for so many years symbolized the death of Detroit, was finally scheduled to be demolished.

"For twenty years we had a disease of inactivity in Detroit, and that was contagious," said developer Charles Mady. "But so is renovation. One good project gives life to another." Crime, crumbling roads, a poor public school system, and municipal red tape were still major concerns, but for the first time in decades the mood regarding the city's future was upbeat. The new stadiums were widely viewed as one of the centerpieces of a new Detroit. While urban economists remained largely unconvinced of the economic benefits of public-subsidized sports facilities, civic boosters spoke of such intangibles as increased community pride and a better national image. "While professional football teams in other cities are picking up stakes and breaking bonds, the Detroit Lions are coming home and reaffirming ties to our community," said Mayor Archer. "This signifies hope, progress, and opportunity."

Exactly when the Lions would start construction was unclear. If unable to negotiate a buy out from its lease with the city of Pontiac, the team was obligated to play in the Silverdome through the 2004 season. But the Tigers hoped to be in their new digs within a couple of years, assuming financing, land acquisition, and construction proceeded smoothly.

They didn't. Ilitch's attempt to negotiate a loan of $145 million from a local consortium of a dozen banks ultimately failed, the result of Detroit lenders' traditional conservatism. It wasn't until March 1998 that the club was able to announce that it had secured a loan from Sumitomo Bank Ltd., a Japanese bank with a history of bankrolling stadium projects. With the Stadium Authority experiencing delays in gaining title to several parcels of land, the projected opening of the new park was pushed back to April 2000. One could hardly blame Mike Ilitch for wanting to get the first spadeful of dirt out of the ground. *Financial World* judged that, at about $85 million, the Tigers had the least value of any big-league team. But the magazine estimated that that figure would balloon to more than $200 million after the first season in a new park.

Meanwhile, management continued its fiscal mission, going so far as to charge members of the media for their press-box dinners.

Randy Smith got rid of several players with top-heavy salaries and ignored the free agent market. As a result, the Tigers started the 1997 season with the league's lowest payroll—$16,454,500—of which $6.4 million was paid to one player, Travis Fryman. In less than three years, the Tigers' outlay for player salaries had been slashed by $26 million.

Elsewhere, payrolls skyrocketed. Two years after the end of the players' strike, the average big leaguer's salary had jumped 17.6 percent to $1.38 million a year. An unprecedented 197 players made $2 million or more. The cost-conscious Tigers were paying crowd-pleasing Bobby Higginson, a cocky Philadelphian who'd hit .320 with twenty-six home runs in 1996, a comparative pittance: $350,000. Several other Tigers made $150,000. Before the season players and owners finally hammered out a labor agreement that provided for revenue sharing and luxury taxes, gimmicks designed to help small-market clubs compete with their big-market cousins. The handouts and penalties weren't nearly large enough to bridge the ever-widening gulf between the financial haves and have-nots, so cash-strapped owners continued to approach the public for help in constructing stadiums to remain competitive. Their pleas all had familiar refrain: build it and they will come; don't build it and we may leave. Detroit players, knowing a new revenue-churning stadium was the best bet for improving their own and the team's fortunes, couldn't help but look hopefully two or three years down the road for their 42,000-seat ship to come in.

But the stadium issue wasn't all about money. Higginson, along with Tony Clark, center fielder Brian Hunter, and pitcher Justin Thompson, was one of the young stars being counted on to help fill Detroit's new park when it opened. He spoke of the excitement of playing before a packed house. "There would be more electricity," he said. "If you can get 30,000 or 35,000 people at a ballgame, it's just going to elevate the way that everybody plays. It's just going to make them play better.

"I don't think there's anything negative at all to a new stadium. We're not going to have Tiger Stadium anymore, but times have changed and you need to move on. If you get a new stadium, maybe they can build memories in the new stadium. The Tiger Stadium memories are always going to be there. Nobody is ever going to take them away."

Sparky Anderson, as integral a part of the corner's lore as George Vanderbeck, Ty Cobb, Goose Goslin, Bobby Layne, Willie Horton, and Ballpark Franks, previously addressed the issue of memory serving as mortar. "Baseball is great history," he had reflected in early 1995, not long before the Tigers embarked on their one hundredth season at Michigan and Trumbull. "It's not players and it's not owners and it's not managers, it's history. And that's what people live by. If you really think about it, we live by history." In the spring of 1997, as preparations were made to break ground on a new ballpark and the lush grass at Michigan and Trumbull welcomed a second century of players, Tiger Stadium was unarguably that—history, in every sense of the word.

Tiger Stadium stands nearly empty during a game played late in the 1997 season.

An Empty Feeling

NCE IT BECAME OFFICIAL that a new baseball park would be built in Detroit, the Tigers' marketing department moved quickly to promote the notion of scarcity.

"Reserve your seats now for the new Tiger Stadium," read the bold-faced headline of a quarter-page newspaper ad that appeared at the end of 1996. "Did you know both Chicago and Cleveland tripled their season ticket base upon moving into their new stadiums?" the copy breathlessly continued. "Baltimore had to establish a waiting list because demand was so high! We anticipate a similar reaction for the new Tiger Stadium." Another ad that appeared over the winter pictured a 1997 season ticket ("Order this now") alongside an empty chair, identified in the copy as a prime seat location in the new Tiger Stadium ("Get this later").

Fans felt little urgency. Faced with another lackluster year at the gate, the club slashed the price of its upper-deck box and reserved seats by five and four dollars, respectively. At the same time it increased bleacher tickets for adults from \$2.50 to \$4.00. The club also offered service clubs, community groups, and other organizations a significant fund-raising opportunity. For every ticket they sold, they kept four dollars. "You've been there," said marketing director Mike Dietz, alluding to the sea of empty seats over the last few seasons. "We won't oversubscribe this offer."

Not even the historic introduction of inter-league play encouraged activity at the box office. On June 16, 1997, when the Tigers hosted the Florida Marlins in the first of six home dates against National League clubs, less than twenty-four thousand curiosity seekers turned out on a Monday night to watch Detroit lose, 7–3. Attendance for the next two games against the future World Series champions averaged about 13,500. They were the two smallest crowds for an interleague game in any of the twenty-eight big-league parks. For the second year in a row, the Tigers finished next to last in attendance among all major league teams.

On the field, Buddy Bell's rebuilding Tigers accomplished a minor miracle. They improved their record by twenty-six games, from 53–109 to 79–83, while moving from the cellar to third place in the American League West. The Tigers had been bad so long that mediocre now looked good, but at least they seemed to be moving in a positive direction. In addition to shaving a run and a half off the team ERA, they rose from last to first in team fielding. This was due in part to the brilliant defensive play of shortstop Deivi Cruz, who surprised observers by easily making the jump from the Midwest League to the majors, and Bobby Higginson, who for the second straight year led the league in outfield assists. Higginson, with 27 home runs and 101 runs batted in, joined budding superstar Tony Clark (32, 117) and reliable Travis Fryman (22, 102) as the first trio of Tigers since 1961 to knock in one hundred runs apiece. Justin Thompson won fifteen games and was selected to the All-Star team.

One of the biggest stories of the summer was Brian Hunter, an unheralded outfielder obtained in a nine-player trade with Houston. Although bothered by an assortment of minor aches and pains, the banged-up twenty-six-year-old played the full schedule in center field, the first Tiger in thirty-five years to play every game. His seventy-four stolen bases made him the first Detroit player since Ty Cobb in 1917 to lead the major leagues in that category. "To be mentioned with Ty Cobb in anything is amazing," Hunter said before the last game of the season. On that Sunday afternoon, 38,171 people—the largest crowd since opening day—poured through the turnstiles to watch the home nine battle the New York Yankees. The total included about nine thousand walk-up sales—a practically unheard-of number for the Tigers during the gray nineties. For a day, at least, it was just like old times.

One month later, on October 29, 1997, two thousand people were on hand as ground was ceremoniously broken on the new stadium in a parking lot across the street from the Fox Theater. It was a crisp Wednesday morning, bright with sun and optimism. Seventy-six-year-old Hal Newhouser threw out the first pitch to an eleven-year-old Little Leaguer named Brandon Glenn. The choice of batterymates symbolized the Tigers' intention to blend the best of the past with the future. Architectural drawings reflected a park with the intimate, fan-friendly environment of Wrigley Field, but equipped with the modern conveniences players and customers desired. Seats would be wider than in Tiger Stadium, with the upper rows closer to the action than in any of the other new stadiums. There would be several "family bathrooms," complete with diaper-changing tables, batting and pitching cages for fans, and a restaurant in right field. There also would be eighty luxury suites, all on one level. The players' creature comforts included plush locker rooms and spacious, well-equipped fitness facilities. The club was exploring the possibility of moving the center-field flagpole from the old stadium to the new.

Ilitch initially resisted selling the name of his facility to a corporate sponsor, a decision that figured to cost him as much as fifty million dollars. "It will not be a stadium or a field," he announced at the groundbreaking, "it will be a ballpark." His preference was Tiger Park. However, by the following March the possibility of going over budget had him seriously considering selling the naming rights to raise some cash.

For all of the good feeling surrounding the new park and all of the money spent in its design and construction, the one element that could not be manufactured was a century's worth of tradition. It will be many years before the Tigers' new home can inspire the nostalgia evident in one visitor to Tiger Stadium during the lame-duck season of 1997.

In late August, the Philadelphia Phillies came to town for a weekend series. "It's going to be very special," Phillies first baseman Rico Brogna told a reporter, "because a dream came true literally when I first set foot in Tiger Stadium."

Brogna had played nine games as a rookie for the Tigers in 1992. The first time he reported to the park he walked onto the field and took a long, loving look around. The place was empty except for a smattering of players and stadium employees. But Brogna could sense the presence of generations of players who'd passed through this vinyl-sided storehouse of memories. Some had been giants in baggy flannels, others were one-game wonders in double knits. On that day the wide-eyed rookie joined their ranks, performing a pre-game ritual common to players of all abilities and from all eras: languidly snapping the ball back and forth across the grass and feeling the warmth of the afternoon sun on his face as the old park slowly stirred to life around him.

"I remember thinking, 'This is baseball. Old-time stadium, fresh-cut grass, a beautiful August day,'" said Brogna.

"That's always what I hoped baseball would be like."

APPENDIX A

Standings and Attendance at Michigan and Trumbull

	Season Record				Home Record					Home Attendance	
Season	Won	Lost	Pct.	GB	GP	Won	Lost	Tied	Pct.	Attendance	Avg.
1896	80	59	.576	10.5	72	51	20	1	.718	122,148[a]	1,697
1897	70	66	.514	28.5	77	46	30	1	.605	101,500[b]	1,318
1898	50	87	.365	37	70	32	38	0	.457	78,950	1,128
1899	64	60	.516	12	61	35	26	0	.574	94,259[c]	1,545
1900	71	65	.522	11.5	74	49	24	1	.671	147,075[d]	1,988
1901	74	61	.548	8.5	70	42	27	1	.609	259,430[e]	3,706
1902	52	83	.385	30.5	68	35	**33**	0	.515	189,469[f]	2,786
1903	65	71	.478	25	65	37	28	0	.544	224,523[g]	3,454
1904	62	90	.408	32	79	34	40	**5**	.459	177,796	2,251
1905	79	74	.516	15.5	76	45	30	1	.600	193,384[h]	2,545
1906	71	78	.477	21	78	42	34	**2**	.553	174,043	2,231
*1907	**92**	58	**.613**	—	79	50	27	2	.649	297,079	3,760
*1908	**90**	63	**.588**	—	78	44	33	1	.571	436,199	5,592
*1909	**98**	54	**.645**	—	78	57	19	2	**.750**	490,490	6,288

| | Season Record | | | | | Home Record | | | | Home Attendance | |
Season	Won	Lost	Pct.	GB	GP	Won	Lost	Tied	Pct.	Attendance	Avg.
1910	86	68	.558	18	78	46	31	1	.597	391,288	5,017
1911	89	65	.578	13.5	76	51	25	0	.671	484,988	6,381
1912	69	84	.451	36.5	76	37	39	0	.487	402,870	5,301
1913	66	87	.431	30	76	34	42	0	.447	398,502	5,243
1914	80	73	.523	19.5	78	42	35	1	.545	416,225	5,336
1915	100	54	.649	2.5	76	50	26	0	.658	476,105	6,265
1916	87	67	.565	4	77	**49**	28	0	**.636**	616,772	8,010
1917	78	75	.510	21.5	76	34	41	1	.453	457,289	6,017
1918	55	71	.437	20	58	28	29	1	.491	203,719	3,512
1919	80	60	.571	8	70	46	24	0	.657	**643,805**	**9,197**
1920	61	93	.396	37	78	32	46	0	.410	579,650	7,431
1921	71	82	.464	27	77	37	40	0	.481	661,527	8,591
1922	79	75	.513	15	77	43	34	0	.558	861,206	11,184
1923	83	71	.539	16	77	45	32	0	.584	911,377	11,836
1924	86	68	.558	6	78	45	33	0	.577	1,015,136	13,015
1925	81	73	.526	16.5	77	43	34	0	.558	820,766	10,659
1926	79	75	.513	12	81	39	41	1	.488	711,914	8,789
1927	82	71	.536	27.5	78	44	32	2	.579	773,716	9,919
1928	68	86	.442	33	77	36	41	0	.468	474,323	6,160
1929	70	84	.455	36	77	38	39	0	.494	869,318	11,290
1930	75	79	.487	27	78	45	33	0	.577	649,450	8,326
1931	61	93	.396	47	77	36	41	0	.468	434,056	5,637
1932	76	75	.503	29.5	78	42	34	2	.553	397,157	5,092
1933	75	79	.487	25	78	43	35	0	.551	320,972	4,115
*1934	101	53	**.656**	—	80	**54**	26	0	.675	**919,161**	**11,490**
*1935	**93**	58	**.616**	—	79	53	25	1	**.679**	1,034,929	13,100
1936	83	71	.539	9.5	77	44	33	0	.571	875,948	11,376
1937	89	65	.578	13	77	49	28	0	.636	**1,072,276**	**13,926**
1938	84	70	.545	16	79	48	31	0	.608	799,557	10,121
1939	81	73	.526	16.5	78	42	35	1	.545	836,279	10,722
*1940	**90**	64	**.584**	—	79	50	29	0	.633	**1,112,693**	**14,085**
1941	75	79	.487	26	77	43	34	0	.558	684,915	8,895
1942	73	81	.474	30	77	43	34	0	.558	580,087	7,534
1943	78	76	.506	20	77	45	32	0	.584	606,287	7,874
1944	88	66	.571	1	78	43	34	1	.558	**923,176**	**11,836**

	Season Record					Home Record				Home Attendance	
Season	Won	Lost	Pct.	GB	GP	Won	Lost	Tied	Pct.	Attendance	Avg.
★1945	**88**	65	.575	—	76	50	26	0	.658	**1,280,341**	**16,847**
1946	92	62	.597	12	79	48	30	1	.615	1,722,590	21,805
1947	85	69	.552	12	80	46	31	3	.597	1,398,093	17,476
1948	78	76	.506	18.5	77	39	38	0	.506	1,743,035	22,637
1949	87	67	.565	10	78	50	27	1	.649	1,821,204	23,349
1950	95	59	.617	3	81	50	30	1	.625	1,951,474	24,092
1951	73	81	.474	25	77	36	41	0	.468	1,132,641	14,710
1952	50	**104**	.325	45	77	32	**45**	0	.416	1,026,846	13,336
1953	60	94	.390	40.5	79	30	47	2	.390	884,658	11,198
1954	68	86	.442	43	77	35	42	0	.455	1,079,842	14,024
1955	79	75	.513	17	77	46	31	0	.597	1,181,838	15,349
1956	82	72	.532	15	78	37	40	1	.481	1,051,182	13,477
1957	78	76	.506	20	77	45	32	0	.584	1,272,346	16,524
1958	77	77	.500	15	77	43	34	0	.558	1,098,924	14,272
1959	76	78	.494	18	77	41	36	0	.532	1,221,221	15,860
1960	71	83	.461	6	77	40	37	0	.519	1,167,669	15,165
1961	101	61	.623	8	82	50	31	1	.617	1,600,710	19,521
1962	85	76	.528	10.5	82	49	33	0	.598	1,207,881	14,730
1963	79	83	.488	25.5	81	47	34	0	.580	821,952	10,148
1964	85	77	.525	14	82	46	35	1	.568	816,139	9,953
1965	89	73	.549	13	81	47	34	0	.580	1,029,645	12,712
1966	88	74	.543	10	81	42	39	0	.519	1,124,293	13,880
1967	91	71	.562	1	82	52	29	1	**.642**	1,447,143	17,648
★1968	**103**	59	**.636**	—	81	56	25	0	**.691**	**2,031,847**	**25,085**
1969	90	72	.556	19	81	46	35	0	.568	1,577,481	19,475
1970	79	83	.488	29	81	42	39	0	.519	1,501,293	18,534
1971	91	71	.562	12	81	**54**	27	0	.667	1,591,073	19,643
+1972	86	70	.551	—	78	44	34	0	.564	**1,892,386**	**24,261**
1973	85	77	.525	12	81	47	34	0	.580	**1,724,146**	**21,286**
1974	72	90	.444	19	81	36	45	0	.444	1,243,080	15,347
1975	57	**102**	.358	37.5	80	31	**49**	0	.388	1,058,836	13,235
1976	74	87	.460	24	80	36	44	0	.450	1,467,020	18,338
1977	74	88	.457	26	81	39	42	0	.481	1,359,856	16,788
1978	86	76	.531	13.5	81	47	34	0	.580	1,714,893	21,172
1979	85	76	.528	18	80	46	34	0	.575	1,630,929	20,387

	Season Record					Home Record					Home Attendance	
Season	Won	Lost	Pct.	GB	GP	Won	Lost	Tied	Pct.	Attendance	Avg.
1980	84	78	.519	19	82	43	38	1	.531	1,785,293	21,772
1981	60	49	.550	2	55	32	23	0	.582	1,149,144	20,894
1982	83	79	.512	12	81	47	34	0	.580	1,636,058	20,198
1983	92	70	.568	6	81	48	33	0	.593	1,829,636	22,588
*1984	**104**	58	**.642**	—	82	**53**	29	0	**.654**	**2,704,794**	**32,985**
1985	84	77	.522	15	81	44	37	0	.543	2,286,609	28,230
1986	87	75	.537	8.5	81	49	32	0	.605	1,899,437	23,450
+1987	98	64	**.605**	—	81	54	27	0	.667	2,061,830	25,455
1988	88	74	.543	1	81	50	31	0	.617	2,081,162	25,693
1989	59	**103**	.364	30	81	38	43	0	.469	1,543,656	19,057
1990	79	83	.488	9	81	39	42	0	.481	1,495,785	18,466
1991	84	78	.519	7	81	49	32	0	.605	1,641,661	20,267
1992	75	87	.463	21	80	38	42	0	.475	1,423,963	17,800
1993	85	77	.525	10	81	44	37	0	.543	1,970,791	24,331
1994	53	62	.461	18	58	34	24	0	.586	1,184,783	20,427
1995	60	84	.417	26	72	35	37	0	.486	1,050,555	14,591
1996	53	**109**	.327	39	81	27	**54**	0	.333	1,142,623	14,160
1997	79	83	.488	19	81	42	39	0	.519	1,365,157	16,854
Totals	7978	7514	.515		7813	4362	3409	42	.558	104,631,228	13,392

a Includes 1 game (3,483) at Athletic Park

b Includes 2 games (1,500) at Athletic Park

c Includes 9 games (20,400) at River Rouge Park

d Includes 11 games (40,700) at Burns Park

e Includes 13 games (67,400) at Burns Park

f Includes 10 games (43,250) at Burns Park

g Includes 3 games (13,662) in Grand Rapids and Toledo

h Includes 2 games (10,702) in Columbus

* Won American League pennant

+ Won American League Eastern Division

Bold indicates led league.

Postseason

Year		**Home Record** GP	Won	Lost	**Home Attendance** Attendance	Avg.
1907	World Series	2	0	2	18,676	9,338
	Lost to Chicago, 4 games to 0 (1 tie).					
1908	World Series	3	0	3	29,929	9,976
	Lost to Chicago, 4 games to 0.					
1909	World Series	4	2	2	63,410	15,853
	Lost to Pittsburgh, 4 games to 3.					
1934	World Series	4	1	3	171,409	42,852
	Lost to St. Louis, 4 games to 3.					
1935	World Series	3	2	1	142,553	47,518
	Defeated Chicago, 4 games to 2.					
1940	World Series	3	2	1	162,159	54,053
	Lost to Cincinnati, 4 games to 3.					
1945	World Series	3	1	2	163,773	54,591
	Defeated Chicago, 4 games to 3.					
1968	World Series	3	1	2	160,902	53,634
	Defeated St. Louis, 4 games to 3.					
1972	A. L. Championship Series	3	2	1	129,047	43,016
	Lost to Oakland, 3 games to 2.					
1984	A. L. Championship Series	1	1	0	52,168	52,168
	Defeated Kansas City, 3 games to 0.					
1984	World Series	3	3	0	156,001	52,000
	Defeated San Diego, 4 games to 1.					
1987	A. L. Championship Series	3	1	2	149,117	49,706
	Lost to Minnesota, 4 games to 1.					
Totals		35	16	19	1,399,144	39,976

APPENDIX B

Opening Day at Michigan and Trumbull

At Bennett Park (1896–1911)

1896 (Tuesday, April 28) Playing on a muddy field in a park that was barely ready in time for its inaugural, the Tigers nonetheless gave the largest opening-day crowd in the Western League something to cheer about with a 17–2 thumping of Columbus. The afternoon's tone was set at the top of the first when a Columbus outfielder was knocked cold after colliding with a fan, allowing George Stallings to circle the bases for the first home run hit at Michigan and Trumbull. Pitcher John Fifield scattered seven hits and also contributed a home run and a triple to the cause.

			R	H	E	Pitchers
Detroit	430 008 200	—	17	15	2	Fifield (9)
Columbus	000 000 101	—	2	7	6	Jones (9)

Winning Pitcher: Fifield   Losing Pitcher: Jones
Home Runs: (DET) Stallings, Fifield
Attendance: 6,000   Time: 2:20   Weather: Cool, wet

1897 (Monday, May 3) Indianapolis pulled out a 5–4 victory when they scratched out a run off Tommy Thomas in the bottom of the tenth, but the real story of Detroit's home opener was the riot that followed. Left fielder Burnett, still upset over a bad call an inning earlier, charged Umpire Ebright after the game and sucker punched him several times in front of the Indianapolis bench. It took a phalanx of police and bat-wielding players to protect the battered arbiter from the mob of angry cranks that threw punches, epithets, and seat cushions at him before he was finally spirited away in a horse-drawn bus.

	R	H	E	Pitchers
Detroit 000 120 001 0 —	4	8	2	Thomas (9.1)
Indianapolis 000 200 110 1 —	5	7	3	Wolters (10)

Winning Pitcher: Wolters   Losing Pitcher: Thomas
Attendance: 3,500   Time: 2:15   Weather: Wet, cloudy, high 40s

1898 (Friday, April 29) The Tigers fell to 1–6 for the season when Indianapolis broke a 5–5 deadlock with a pair of runs off starter George "Rube" Waddell in the seventh. Waddell, an eccentric southpaw with a passion for chasing fire engines and drinking beer, soon wore out his welcome in Detroit, splitting eight decisions before moving on to another town. The Tigers, batting first as was their custom, scored once in the top of the ninth but the rally fell short. The 7–6 defeat was one of twenty-one games the Tigers lost by a single run in 1898.

	R	H	E	Pitchers
Detroit 110 021 001 —	6	9	4	Waddell (6.1),
				Underwood (1.2)
Indianapolis 040 010 20x —	7	6	2	Phillips (9)

Winning Pitcher: Phillips   Losing Pitcher: Waddell
Attendance: 2,700   Time: 2:00   Weather: 63 degrees

1899 (Thursday, April 27) Detroit opened Western League play on a warm afternoon with a tough loss to ex-Tiger Rube Waddell and his new employer, the Columbus Senators. Trailing 4–1 in the bottom of the ninth, Egan notched a one-out single. The scatter-armed Waddell hit the next two batters and filled the bases. A wild pitch scored one run, making it 4–2, and a sacrifice fly scored a second. Then Waddell reared back and fired a pitch to Slater, who took a called third strike to end the game with Columbus ahead, 4–3.

	R	H	E	Pitchers
Columbus 022 000 000 —	4	11	2	Waddell (9)
Detroit 010 000 002 —	3	8	1	Thomas (9)

Winning Pitcher: Waddell (1–0)   Losing Pitcher: Thomas (0–1)
Attendance: 4,500   Time: 2:20   Weather: 80 degrees

1900 (Thursday, April 19) Detroit's debut in Ban Johnson's new American League was anything but grand, as the home team suffered the indignity of being no-hit by Buffalo's Doc Amole, 8–0. The lefthander was far from perfect, walking two, hitting two, and tossing a wild pitch. But he befuddled Detroit batters with an assortment of curves and fastballs. He struck out four and his fielders took care of the rest. The Tigers committed seven errors, including three by shortstop Kid Elberfeld, which led to half of Buffalo's runs.

	R	H	E	Pitchers
Buffalo 001 001 303 —	8	7	1	Amole (9)
Detroit 000 000 000 —	0	0	7	Cronin (9)

Winning Pitcher: Amole (1–0)   Losing Pitcher: Cronin (0–1)
Attendance: 5,000   Time: 1:40   Weather: 64 degrees

1901 (Thursday, April 25) In what was labeled "the grandest and greatest finish ever seen at Bennett Park," the Tigers overcame a 13–4 deficit in their last at-bat to shock Milwaukee. The key play came when third baseman Jimmy Burke fumbled Kid Gleason's grounder on what should have been the final out of the game. Instead of killing the rally and allowing the visitors to escape with a narrow 13–12 victory, this put the winning run on base. Pop Dillon then delivered his fourth two-base hit of the day to knock in the tying and winning runs, climaxing an incredible 10–run comeback.

	R	H	E	Pitchers
Milwaukee 025 000 330 —	13	16	4	Hawley (6),
				Dowling (2),
				Husting (0.2)

Detroit   000 210 01(10) — 14   19   7   Miller (2.1),
                                                    Frisk (6.2)
Winning Pitcher: Frisk (1–0)   Losing Pitcher: Husting (0–1)
Attendance: 10,023   Time: 2:35   Weather: Wet, 68 degrees

1902 (Thursday, May 1) The Tigers captured first place at 4–2 with
a 4–1 decision over Cleveland. Detroit's all-purpose Roscoe Miller
scattered nine hits and delivered the key hit of the game. With runners on second and third and the score tied at a run apiece in the
seventh, Miller drove Earl Moore's pitch over the Cleveland left
fielder's head for a two-run double.

		R	H	E	Pitchers
Cleveland	000 001 000 —	1	9	0	Moore (8)
Detroit	100 000 21x —	4	7	2	Miller (9)

Winning Pitcher: Miller   Losing Pitcher: Moore
Attendance: 14,183   Time: 1:40   Weather: 54 degrees

1903 (Wednesday, April 22) The Tigers broke a 2–2 deadlock by
scoring twice off Cleveland ace Addie Joss in the bottom of the
eighth inning. Sam Crawford, playing his first game after jumping
to Detroit from the National League, led off the frame with a walk,
went to third on a hit-and-run single by Kid Elberfeld, and then
scored when the Indians' right fielder threw the ball into the grand-
stands. Doc Gessler knocked in Elberfeld for the insurance run in a
4–2 triumph. George Mullin pitched a seven-hitter for Detroit.

		R	H	E	Pitchers
Cleveland	101 000 000 —	2	7	2	Joss (8)
Detroit	000 020 02x —	4	8	2	Mullin (9)

Winning Pitcher: Mullin (1–0)   Losing Pitcher: Joss (0–1)
Attendance: 16,482   Time: 1:33   Weather: 38 degrees

1904 (Friday, April 22) After splitting a six-game road trip to open
the campaign, the Tigers remained at 3–3 for the season after a tie
with St. Louis. The visitors moved ahead, 4–3, with a run in the
ninth, but Detroit countered with its own run to produce the final
4–4 deadlock. Umpire Silk O'Loughlin called play after twelve
innings due to darkness. George Mullin and Barney Pelty each went
the distance in what remains the only unresolved home opener in
Tiger history.

		R	H	E	Pitchers
St. Louis	000 030 001 000 —	4	14	4	Pelty (12)
Detroit	000 002 101 000 —	4	11	1	Mullin (12)

No pitchers of record.
Attendance: 15,996   Time: 2:35   Weather: 45 degrees

1905 (Wednesday, April 19) Detroit evened its season record to 1–1 with a 3–0 win against the visiting White Sox, as Wild Bill Donovan blanked Chicago on five hits. In the third inning Jack Sullivan singled and came around to score the Tigers' first run on an overthrow from the Chicago outfield. In the sixth Bill Coughlin scored on a sacrifice fly by Piano Legs Hickman. The following inning Sullivan knocked in Germany Schaefer for the Tigers' final tally.

		R	H	E	Pitchers
Chicago	000 000 000 —	0	5	2	Patterson (3), Owen (5)
Detroit	001 001 10x —	3	7	1	Donovan (9)

Winning Pitcher: Donovan (1–0)   Losing Pitcher: Patterson (0–1)
Attendance: 9,412   Time: 1:32   Weather: 54 degrees

1906 (Tuesday, April 17) The White Sox used a thirteen-hit attack to beat George Mullin and the Tigers on an otherwise pleasant afternoon for baseball. Trailing 2 0, Detroit tied the score with single runs in the sixth and seventh innings. But Chicago rallied for two in the eighth and another in the ninth to earn its 5–3 win. Frank Owen surrendered six hits in going all the way; half were by Germany Schaefer, who led the Tigers with a single and a pair of doubles.

		R	H	E	Pitchers
Chicago	100 001 021 —	5	13	4	Owen (9)
Detroit	000 001 101 —	3	6	0	Mullin (9)

Winning Pitcher: Owen (1–0)   Losing Pitcher: Mullin (0–1)
Attendance: 13,875   Time: 2:20   Weather: 65 degrees

1907 (Thursday, April 11) On a wintry afternoon, George Mullin chilled the already frozen Cleveland bats with a three-hit shutout performance. Ty Cobb, starting in right field in his first opening day appearance, had two singles, a stolen base, and scored both Detroit runs off Cleveland's Glenn Liebhardt—one in the fourth and another in the eighth. Helping the cause was a pair of Germanys—second baseman Schaefer and backstop Schmidt—who also had two hits apiece.

	R	H	E	Pitchers
Cleveland 000 000 000 —	0	3	3	Liebhardt (8)
Detroit 000 100 01x —	2	9	1	Mullin (9)

Winning Pitcher: Mullin (1–0)   Losing Pitcher: Liebhardt (0–1)
Attendance: 6,322   Time: 1:45   Weather: Windy, upper 30s

1908 (Friday, April 17) Detroit dropped a wild twelve-inning affair to Cleveland, 12–8. Germany Schaefer paced Detroit with four singles and a double, while Ty Cobb added three in a losing cause. The Tigers overcame an early five-run deficit against Bill Latimore, finally chasing the Naps' starter with two runs in the ninth to knot the game at 6–6. Cleveland scored twice in the eleventh, but Detroit matched it with two of its own. In the twelfth Cleveland slugged out a four-spot for the win. George Mullin surrendered twenty hits, as the Tigers fell to 1–2 for the season.

	R	H	E	Pitchers
Cleveland 012 101 001 024 —	12	20	3	Latimore (8.1), Joss (3.1)
Detroit 000 003 102 020 —	8	12	1	Mullin (12)

Winning Pitcher: Joss   Losing Pitcher: Mullin
Attendance: 14,051   Time: 2:52   Weather: 54 degrees

1909 (Wednesday, April 14) George Mullin, en route to a league-leading twenty-nine-win season, needed just eighty-two minutes to twirl a one-hit masterpiece against the White Sox. Gavvy Cravath's leadoff single in the eighth spoiled Mullin's bid for a no-hitter, so the Tigers' ace settled for his second opening day shutout in three years. Frank Smith held Detroit to four hits, but the Tigers bunched three of them in the fifth for both runs. Newly acquired third baseman George Moriarty doubled, and then came home when Germany Schaefer's single got away from the outfielder. Matty McIntyre plated Schaefer with a base hit.

	R	**H**	**E**	**Pitchers**
Chicago 000 000 000 —	0	1	2	Smith (8)
Detroit 000 020 00x —	2	4	0	Mullin (9)

Winning Pitcher: Mullin (1–0)   Losing Pitcher: Smith (0–1)
Attendance: 11,514   Time: 1:22   Weather: 47 degrees

1910 (Thursday, April 14) In its season opener with Cleveland, Detroit blew a 4–0 lead, rallied to tie the game in the ninth, then lost it in the tenth when the Naps solved George Mullin for four runs and a 9–7 victory. Addie Joss went all the way for Cleveland, allowing ten hits, including four by Sam Crawford and two apiece by Ty Cobb and Donie Bush.

	R	**H**	**E**	**Pitchers**
Cleveland 000 022 100 4 —	9	14	2	Joss (10)
Detroit 201 100 001 2 —	7	10	1	Mullin (10)

Winning Pitcher: Joss (1–0)   Losing Pitcher: Mullin (0–1)
Attendance: 14,203   Time: 2:22   Weather: 70 degrees

1911 (Thursday, April 13) After being rained out the previous day, the Tigers waited until the last minute before deciding to play, which resulted in one of the smallest opening day crowds in club history. Fittingly, the White Sox started spitballer Ed Walsh, who was outdueled by George Mullin. Sam Crawford's RBI triple and Ty Cobb's homer—the first in a Tigers home opener since 1896—gave Detroit a 2–0 lead. But Chicago rallied to make it a one-run game in the sixth. In the eighth Crawford sewed up the 4–2 win by doubling in Donie Bush and then scoring from second on a wild pitch.

	R	**H**	**E**	**Pitchers**
Chicago 000 001 001 —	2	6	1	Walsh (8)
Detroit 101 000 02x —	4	8	2	Mullin (9)

Winning Pitcher: Mullin (1–0)   Losing Pitcher: Walsh (0–1)
Home Runs: (DET) Cobb
Attendance: 5,107   Time: 1:50   Weather: Wet, 50 degrees

At Navin Field (1912–1937)

1912 (Saturday, April 20) Navin Field's inaugural game, delayed two days by rain, proved a nail-biter. George Mullin, starting his ninth home opener in ten years, went the distance for Detroit and knocked in Donie Bush with a two-out single in the eleventh for a 6–5 victory, moving the Tigers to 4–3 for the season. Mullin was in trouble all day long, but continued to work out of jams. Ty Cobb and Sam Crawford pulled off a pair of double steals in the first inning, with Cobb swiping home for the Tigers' first run. Detroit, trailing 5–3 in the eighth, tied the game on a single by Jim Delahanty.

		R	H	E	Pitchers
Cleveland	102 020 000 00 —	5	12	1	Gregg (10.2)
Detroit	201 000 020 01 —	6	12	5	Mullin (11)

Winning Pitcher: Mullin (1–1) Losing Pitcher: Gregg (0–1)
Attendance: 24,384 Time: 2:32 Weather: Hazy, 50 degrees

1913 (Thursday, April 17) The Tigers improved their record to 2–4 for the season as they jumped on Pacific Coast League call-up Walter Leverenz for four runs in the first two innings. Donie Bush led off the home half of the first with a triple and scored on Sam Crawford's fly ball. Four hits and two St. Louis errors in the second frame produced three more Detroit runs. In his debut as a Tiger, Mark Hall shut out the Browns for six innings before tiring and allowing two runs in the seventh and another in the eighth.

		R	H	E	Pitchers
St. Louis	000 000 210 —	3	4	4	Leverenz (2), Stone (6)
Detroit	130 000 00x —	4	6	2	Hall (9)

Winning Pitcher: Hall (1–0) Losing Pitcher: Leverenz (0–1)
Attendance: 16,579 Time: 2:00 Weather: 65 degrees

1914 (Tuesday, April 14) After exchanging goose eggs for twelve innings, the Tigers and Browns scored all their runs in the thirteenth. Detroit finally prevailed, 3–2, on a sacrifice fly by Bobby Veach. Starter Jean Dubuc faltered in the top of the thirteenth, surrendering two St. Louis runs. Ty Cobb, whose wild throw allowed one of those runs, vindicated himself with a two- run triple off St. Louis starter Carl Weilman into the roped-off area in right-center field. He then scored the winning run when Veach flied to center off reliever Bill James.

		R	H	E	Pitchers
St. Louis	000 000 000 000 2 —	2	8	0	Weilman (12.1), James (0.1)
Detroit	000 000 000 000 3 —	3	8	5	Dubuc (12.1), Dauss (0.2)

Winning Pitcher: Dauss (1–0)   Losing Pitcher: Weilman (0–1)
Attendance: 20,143   Time: 3:00   Weather: 52 degrees

1915 (Wednesday, April 14) Sloppy defense doomed the Tigers to an opening day 5–1 loss to the Indians. Five Detroit errors led to three Cleveland runs off starter Harry Coveleski, who gave way to new-comer Bernie Boland. The Tigers' offense was spearheaded by Sam Crawford and Bobby Veach, each of whom gathered two hits off Cleveland southpaw Willie Mitchell. Despite the inauspicious beginning, the Tigers went on to a spectacular near-miss of the pennant, becoming the first team to win 100 games but still finish second.

		R	H	E	Pitchers
Cleveland	100 001 300 —	5	8	2	Mitchell (9)
Detroit	000 100 000 —	1	6	5	H.Coveleski (7), Boland (2)

Winning Pitcher: Mitchell (1–0)   Losing Pitcher: Coveleski (0–1)
Attendance: 19,893   Time: 2:03   Weather: 69 degrees

1916 (Thursday, April 20) Although the heart of the Tigers' offense, Ty Cobb and Sam Crawford, missed the opener because of colds contracted on a road trip, Detroit evened its season record at 4–4 with an exciting last-licks victory that took just ninety-five minutes to play. Chicago's Oscar Felsch broke up a scoreless pitching duel between Mel Wolfgang and Harry Coveleski with a solo home run in the eighth. But in the bottom of the ninth, Harry Heilmann drilled a two-base hit to knock in Ossie Vitt and Bobby Veach for a 2–1 triumph.

			R	**H**	**E**	**Pitchers**
Chicago	000 000 010	—	1	6	0	Wolfgang (8)
Detroit	000 000 002	—	2	9	0	H.Coveleski (8),
						Boland (1)

Winning Pitcher: Boland   Losing Pitcher: Wolfgang
Home Run: (CHI) Felsch
Attendance: 20,760 Time: 1:35 Weather: 50 degrees

1917 (Wednesday, April 11) The customary flag-raising ceremonies had increased significance this year—for the first time in major-league history a baseball season opened with the country formally at war. Detroit starter Bill James was touched for four runs in the first on three hits, three walks and two errors. The Tigers, behind Bobby Veach's home run and double and a pair of two-baggers by Ty Cobb, fought back but couldn't overcome the early deficit. Stan Coveleski, younger brother of the Tigers' Harry, picked up the 6–4 win for Cleveland.

			R	**H**	**E**	**Pitchers**
Cleveland	400 101 000	—	6	8	0	S. Coveleski (9)
Detroit	200 100 001	—	4	8	4	James(1),
						Couch (6), Jones (2)

Winning Pitcher: S. Coveleski (1–0)   Losing Pitcher: James (0–1)
Home Run: (DET) Veach
Attendance: 25,884 Time: 1:49 Weather: 50 degrees

1918 (Wednesday, April 24) Detroit pushed its record to 2–1 by knocking off the Indians, 5–2, in a rematch of the season opener in Cleveland. Eric Erickson got his revenge, scattering ten hits for his first major league win. The Tigers built up an early four-run lead, tallying twice in the first and third innings off Cleveland ace Jim Bagby. Ty Cobb (playing his first game of the season due to a lingering cold), Leo Dressen, Bobby Veach and Pep Young each had two hits to propel the Tigers' eleven-hit attack.

			R	**H**	**E**	**Pitchers**
Cleveland	000 020 000	—	2	10	1	Bagby (4),
						Lambeth (4)
Detroit	202 010 00x	—	5	11	2	Erickson (9)

Winning Pitcher: Erickson (1–1)   Losing Pitcher: Bagby (1–1)
Attendance: 15,624 Time: N/A Weather: 45 degrees

1919 (Friday, April 25) Snow, rain and icy winds pushed the Tigers' season opener back two days and kept the crowd to only about nine thousand hardy fans, including a couple thousand convalescent veterans. Trailing 1–0, the Tigers rallied for three runs in the third inning off Cleveland's Stan Coveleski. Donie Bush singled with the bases loaded to drive in the first two runs, and then later scored on Ty Cobb's two-base hit. That proved to be all that Detroit starter Howard Ehmke needed to record a complete game, 4–2 win.

		R	**H**	**E**	**Pitchers**
Cleveland	010 000 001 —	2	8	3	S. Coveleski (7),
					Coumbe (1)
Detroit	003 000 10x —	4	11	2	Ehmke (9)

Winning Pitcher: Ehmke (1–0) Losing Pitcher: S. Coveleski (0–1)
Attendance: 9,000 Time: 1:48 Weather: Windy, 38 degrees

1920 (Thursday, April 22) Whispers in the Navin Field press box rumored that Chicago had thrown the previous fall's World Series to Cincinnati, but a public disclosure of the fix was still several months off. Meanwhile, it was business as usual for the defending American League champions, who easily disposed of the Tigers, 8–2, behind Red Faber's seven-hitter. Shoeless Joe Jackson, one of eight Black Sox destined to be thrown out of baseball, stroked two singles and two doubles, as the Tigers fell to 0–6 for the season.

		R	**H**	**E**	**Pitchers**
Chicago	110 040 101 —	8	8	1	Faber (9)
Detroit	000 010 100 —	2	7	3	Leonard (5),
					Oldham (2),
					Ayers (2)

Winning Pitcher: Faber Losing Pitcher: Leonard (0–1)
Attendance: 25,216 Time: 2:02 Weather: Rainy, windy, 53 degrees

1921 (Thursday, April 14) A steady drizzle turned the field into soupy mud, but twenty-three thousand wet fans happily witnessed the Tigers pull out a ninth-inning victory during Ty Cobb's managerial debut. Trailing 5–1, the Cobbmen rallied for four runs in the seventh inning off Big Ed Morris to knot the score. In the ninth Morris walked the bases full with one out, the last an intentional pass in order to pitch to Harry Heilmann. However, Heilmann lined a single into the right-center field overflow to score Pep Young for a 6–5 win.

		R	**H**	**E**	**Pitchers**
Chicago	002 021 000 —	5	8	0	Kerr (6.2),
					Morris (1.2)
Detroit	000 100 401 —	6	10	0	Leonard (5),
					Sutherland (4)

Winning Pitcher: Sutherland (1–0)   Losing Pitcher: Morris (0–1)
Attendance: 23,000   Time: 2:20   Weather: Rain, 58 degrees

1922 (Thursday, April 20) The Tigers remained winless, dropping their home opener to Cleveland for a sixth straight loss. Howard Ehmke let a one-run lead slip away by surrendering back-to-back doubles with two outs in the ninth. Detroit built a three-run cushion in the second inning on a run-scoring double by Lu Blue and a two-run single by Ehmke, but Cleveland hurler Jim Bagby was stingy after that. Ty Cobb, who tore ligaments in his right knee during spring training, ended his first game of the season hitless.

		R	**H**	**E**	**Pitchers**
Cleveland	001 002 002 —	5	7	0	Bagby (8),
					Morton (1)
Detroit	030 100 000 —	4	8	0	Ehmke (9)

Winning Pitcher: Bagby (2–0)   Losing Pitcher: Ehmke (0–2)
Save: Morton
Attendance: 23,000   Time: 2:03   Weather: 44 degrees

1923 (Thursday, April 26) With the American League office delaying Detroit's opener for a week so that expansion of Navin Field could be completed, the Tigers won four of six games in St. Louis and Cleveland before returning home to a record crowd. The Browns didn't cooperate, however, scoring a run in the ninth off reliever Ray Francis to pull out a 4–3 victory. The Tigers scored their three markers in the third on successive hits by Fred Haney, Ty Cobb, Bobby Veach and Harry Heilmann, capped by a steal of home by Veach.

		R	**H**	**E**	**Pitchers**
St. Louis	000 021 001 —	4	8	0	Shocker (9)
Detroit	003 000 000 —	3	11	0	Collins (6.1),
					Francis (2.2)

Winning Pitcher: Shocker   Losing Pitcher: Francis (2–1)
Home Run: (STL) Williams
Attendance: 36,000   Time: 2:19   Weather: 68 degrees

1924 (Tuesday, April 15) Dazzling fielding by both sides was the highlight of the Tigers' 4–3 opening day win over the Indians. Trailing 3–1 in the bottom of the sixth, the Tigers rallied for three runs against southpaw Joe Schaute. Lu Blue led off with a home run, the Tigers' first round-tripper in a home opener since 1917. Ty Cobb walked and scored on a hit by Harry Heilmann. Heilmann eventually scored what was the winning run on a sacrifice fly by Topper Rigney. George Dauss scattered eleven hits for the win.

	R	H	E	Pitchers
Cleveland 000 102 000 —	3	11	0	Shaute (8)
Detroit 000 103 00x —	4	8	0	Dauss (9)

Winning Pitcher: Dauss (1–0)   Losing Pitcher: Shaute (0–1)
Home Run: (DET) Blue
Attendance: 35,000   Time: 2:00   Weather: 42 degrees

1925 (Tuesday, April 14) On a warm, sunny afternoon, Dutch Leonard held the White Sox to three hits (including a solo home run by Earl Sheely) before tiring in the seventh and asking manager Ty Cobb to take him out. Rookie Jesse Doyle took over and, despite some tense moments in the top of the ninth, got the last eight outs to preserve the Tigers' 4–3 win. The Tigers scored two runs off Chicago's Sloppy Thurston in the second inning on a single by Harry Heilmann, a double by Red Wingo and two groundouts to shortstop.

	R	H	E	Pitchers
Chicago 010 000 101 —	3	5	2	Thurston (9)
Detroit 020 001 10x —	4	10	0	Leonard (6.1),
				Doyle (2.2)

Winning Pitcher: Leonard (1–0)   Losing Pitcher: Thurston (0–1)
Save: Doyle
Home Run: (CHI) Sheely
Attendance: 34,000   Time: 2:20   Weather: Sunny, 72 degrees

1926 (Tuesday, April 13) For the sixth straight home opener, the Tigers produced a one-run affair, this time dropping a 2–1 decision to the Indians. George Uhle gave up nine hits and seven walks, but Detroit failed to capitalize on its chances. The Indians scored single runs in the third and fourth innings; Detroit countered with a tally in the sixth. Lu Blue walked, went to third on a double by Jackie

Tavener, and scored on a groundout. In his final home opener as a Tiger, Ty Cobb lined into a double play as a pinch hitter.

		R	H	E	Pitchers
Cleveland	001 100 000 —	2	8	1	Uhle (9)
Detroit	000 001 000 —	1	9	0	Whitehill (8),
					Barfoot (1)

Winning Pitcher: Uhle (1–0)   Losing Pitcher: Whitehill (0–1)
Attendance: 36,565   Time: 2:00   Weather: 58 degrees

1927 (Wednesday, April 20) Detroit ace Earl Whitehill spun a four-hit shutout, and the Tigers romped to a 7–0 win over the St. Louis Browns. Bob Fothergill got the large crowd on its feet with a three-run home run in the fifth inning. Other contributors to the Tigers' thirteen-hit attack were Jackie Tavener, who racked up three hits, and Heinie Manush, Harry Heilmann and Lu Blue, each with two hits. The victory, which upped Detroit to 3–1 for the season, marked the first radio broadcast of a Tigers game. Ty Tyson of station WWJ did the honors.

		R	H	E	Pitchers
St. Louis	000 000 000 —	0	4	1	Zachary (6),
					Wingard (2)
Detroit	000 132 10x —	7	13	0	Whitehill (9)

Winning Pitcher: Whitehill   Losing Pitcher: Zachary
Home Run: (DET) Fothergill (2 on)
Attendance: 33,971   Time: 1:58   Weather: 56 degrees

1928 (Wednesday, April 11) Detroit scored a run in the first on three singles and had St. Louis starter Sam Gray on the ropes with the bullpen working. But then Marty McManus smashed a ball to the left side that was stopped by veteran shortstop Wally Gerber, who turned it into an inning-ending double play. Despite four St. Louis errors, the Tigers never threatened again. The Browns bunched their scoring in the middle innings, tallying single runs in the fourth and fifth and adding two more in the sixth for a 4–1 win.

		R	H	E	Pitchers
St. Louis	000 112 000 —	4	6	4	Gray (8.1),
					Blaeholder (0.2)
Detroit	100 000 000 —	1	6	2	Billings (7),
					Stoner (2)

Winning Pitcher: Gray (1–0)   Losing Pitcher: Billings (0–1)
Attendance: 33,000   Time: 2:03   Weather: 48 degrees

1929 (Wednesday, April 24) After starting the season with an eight-game road trip, the Tigers moved to 4–5 for the year with a narrow 7–6 victory over Cleveland. Harry Heilmann was the hero of the Tigers' offense this drizzly afternoon, smacking two singles and a home run and sending three teammates across the plate. Although Detroit enjoyed a 6–0 lead after three innings, the Indians battled back to within a run. The issue remained in doubt until center fielder Harry Rice made a diving catch to end the game with the tying run on third base.

	R	H	E	Pitchers
Cleveland 000 302 001 —	6	14	2	Miljus (5), Harder(2), Holloway (1)
Detroit 051 001 00x —	7	14	1	Sorrell (5.1), Stoner (3.2)

Winning Pitcher: Sorrell (1–1)   Losing Pitcher: Miljus
Save: Stoner
Home Run: (DET) Heilmann
Attendance: 30,000   Time: 2:10   Weather: Drizzle, 60 degrees

1930 (Tuesday, April 15) Icy rain couldn't freeze the Tigers' and Browns' bats, as the greatest hitting season in major league history (nine teams would hit .300 or better) started off with a bang. Detroit and St. Louis combined for twenty-four hits and four home runs, including a two-run shot by George Uhle, who pitched into the seventh inning to get credit for the Tigers' 6–3 win. Roy Johnson, Charlie Gehringer and Liz Funk contributed two hits apiece to the cause, while Whitlow Wyatt was untouchable in three innings of relief.

	R	H	E	Pitchers
St. Louis 000 001 200 —	3	12	0	Gray (5), Holhouser (1), Kimsey (2)
Detroit 220 010 01x —	6	12	0	Uhle (6), Wyatt (3)

Winning Pitcher: Uhle (1–0)   Losing Pitcher: Gray (0–1)
Save: Wyatt
Home Runs: (DET) Uhle (1 on) (STL) Gullic, Kress, Schulte
Attendance: 26,125   Time: 2:32   Weather: Sleeting, 38 degrees

1931 (Thursday, April 23) Curveballer Tommy Bridges shut out the St. Louis Browns, 1–0, allowing four hits in a game that took just ninety-four minutes to play. The Tigers scored the only run of the afternoon in the fourth inning when Charlie Gehringer doubled and came home on a single by Dale Alexander. The Browns' only threat came in the sixth when, with runners on first and third and one out, third baseman Marty McManus snared a line drive and threw to Alexander at first base to complete a double play. Detroit improved to 3–5 for the season.

			R	H	E	Pitchers
St. Louis	000 000 000	—	0	4	0	Stewart (8)
Detroit	000 100 00x	—	1	5	0	Bridges (9)

Winning Pitcher: Bridges (1–1)   Losing Pitcher: Stewart (2–1)
Attendance: 20,520   Time: 1:34   Weather: Overcast, windy, 45 degrees

1932 (Wednesday, April 13) After the previous afternoon's contest was cancelled because of cold, the Tigers took the field with their fingers evidently still numb. Cleveland scored five unearned runs, including the winner in the top of the eleventh inning, as they capitalized on five errors in a 6–5 victory. Wes Ferrell managed to go all the way for Cleveland, despite giving up fourteen hits. Four were from Roy Johnson, who hit a leadoff homer in the first and later added three singles. The arctic-like wind and hard times kept the crowd to only ten thousand fans.

			R	H	E	Pitchers
Cleveland	010 021 100 01	—	6	11	1	Ferrell (11)
Detroit	120 100 100 00	—	5	14	5	Sorrell (8),
						Hogsett (3)

Winning Pitcher: Ferrell (1–0)   Losing Pitcher: Hogsett (0–1)
Home Run: (DET) Johnson
Attendance: 10,000   Time: 2:47   Weather: Windy, 30s

1933 (Wednesday, April 12) For the second home opener in a row, the Tigers dropped an extra-inning affair to Cleveland. This time the Indians broke open a 1–1 tie in the thirteenth inning with three unearned runs off Tommy Bridges, after Gee Walker dropped an easy fly ball in the outfield. Bridges, who had given up only two hits in the first eleven innings, deserved a better fate. Walker's miscue was just one of five the Tigers committed this afternoon. Clint Brown went the distance for Cleveland, surrendering just seven hits, two of them to Bridges.

	R	H	E	Pitchers
Cleveland 000 001 000 000 3 —	4	7	0	Brown (13)
Detroit 001 000 000 000 0 —	1	7	5	Bridges (13)

Winning Pitcher: Brown (1–0)   Losing Pitcher: Bridges (0–1)
Attendance: 19,000   Time: 2:49   Weather: 50s

1934 (Tuesday, April 24) Detroit came home after winning three of four on the road under new player-manager Mickey Cochrane. The fiery catcher had his troops put on an exhibition of aggressive base-ball, including double steals and a couple of attempts at swiping home. The blustery weather produced football-style cheers and, with beer sold in the park for the first time, several arrests for public drunkeness. Losing 2–0 to Chicago in the sixth, Detroit sent eleven men to the plate, getting RBI hits from six different batters.

	R	H	E	Pitchers
Chicago 000 101 001 —	3	9	3	Heving (5.2), Gallivan (2.1)
Detroit 000 006 01x —	7	11	0	Marberry (9)

Winning Pitcher: Marberry (2–0)   Losing Pitcher: Heving (0–1)
Attendance: 24,000   Time: 2:12   Weather: Snow flurries, 36 degrees

1935 (Wednesday, April 17) Goose Goslin had a single, double and home run and drove in four runs. But it wasn't quite enough as Chicago's forty-two-year-old Sad Sam Jones spoiled the defending American League champions' home opener, which had been delayed a day by cold weather. Trailing 7–4 in the bottom of the eighth, Detroit scored twice before ex-Tiger Whitlow Wyatt extinguished the fire for the White Stockings. Schoolboy Rowe struggled but went all the way for Detroit, principally because manager Mickey Cochrane wanted to keep his bat in the lineup.

		R	**H**	**E**	**Pitchers**
Chicago	020 200 030 —	7	10	3	Jones (7),
					Wyatt (2)
Detroit	000 103 020 —	6	7	0	Rowe (9)

Winning Pitcher: Jones (1–0) Losing Pitcher: Rowe (0–1)
Save: Wyatt
Home Run: (DET) Goslin
Attendance: 24,000 Time: 2:11 Weather: 38 degrees

1936 (Friday, April 17) After splitting two games in Cleveland, the defending world champions lost their home opener to the White Sox, 5–3. The Tigers scored twice in the first on an RBI triple by Hank Greenberg and a single by Al Simmons, the veteran outfielder obtained in the offseason from the Chisox. Detroit had a chance to blow the game open in the fifth, but rookie center fielder Mike Kreevich stabbed Ray Hayworth's line drive with the bases loaded. Chicago then rallied for three seventh-inning runs off starter Eldon Auker.

		R	**H**	**E**	**Pitchers**
Chicago	000 101 300 —	5	8	1	Whitehead (9)
Detroit	200 010 000 —	3	7	2	Auker (6.1),
					Lawson (2.2)

Winning Pitcher: Whitehead (1–0) Losing Pitcher: Auker (0–1)
Attendance: 32,175 Time: 1:58 Weather: Snow flurries, 37 degrees

1937 (Tuesday, April 20) In the season opener against Cleveland, the Tigers' colorful center fielder, Gee Walker, hit for the cycle in reverse order. He blasted a solo home run off Mel Harder in the first inning, then added a triple, double and single in his next three at-bats. Eldon Auker spread nine Cleveland hits in his route-going performance. Thirty-six-year-old Goose Goslin, appearing in his seventeenth American League opener, made a spectacular catch with two on in the eighth to preserve the 4–3 victory.

		R	**H**	**E**	**Pitchers**
Cleveland	011 100 000 —	3	9	2	Harder (7),
					Brown (1)
Detroit	110 200 00x —	4	8	2	Auker (9)

Winning Pitcher: Auker (1–0)   Losing Pitcher: Harder (0–1)
Home Run: (DET) Walker
Attendance: 38,200   Time: 2:20   Weather: 55 degrees

At Briggs Stadium (1938–1960)

1938 (Friday, April 22) A record crowd of 54,500 crammed into Walter Briggs' enlarged ballpark, which over the winter became the first in the majors to be completely double-decked and enclosed. Unfortunately, Cleveland spoiled the inaugural with a 4–3 win. The Indians scored all their runs off starter Tommy Bridges, but Schoolboy Rowe was splendid in relief, allowing just one hit in five innings. All three Tiger runs came as the result of two Cleveland errors. The loss dropped Detroit to 1–3 for the season.

		R	**H**	**E**	**Pitchers**
Cleveland	020 020 000 —	4	6	2	Harder (9)
Detroit	000 200 010 —	3	8	0	Bridges (4),
					Rowe (5)

Winning Pitcher: Harder (1–0)   Losing Pitcher: Bridges (0–1)
Attendance: 54,500   Time: 2:28   Weather: 53 degrees

1939 (Tuesday, April 18) The Tigers' home opener against the White Sox began during a steady drizzle that didn't let up until the seventh inning. Detroit batters reached John Rigney and Bill Dietrich for twelve singles as the field conditions went from bad to worse. Hank Greenberg led the Tigers' pop-gun offense with a pair of hits and two runs batted in. The home team tallied twice in the second inning, three times in the seventh and added a run in the eighth to account for the 6–1 win. Tommy Bridges went the distance, scattering seven hits.

		R	**H**	**E**	**Pitchers**
Chicago	000 000 100 —	1	7	1	Rigney (7),
					Dietrich (1)
Detroit	002 000 31x —	6	12	0	Bridges (9)

Winning Pitcher: Bridges (1–0)   Losing Pitcher: Rigney (0–1)
Attendance: 47,000   Time: 2:34   Weather: Steady rain, 50 degrees

1940 (Tuesday, April 16) George Coffman, who spent the previous three seasons with Detroit, pitched what proved to be the last complete game of his career in the Browns' 5–1 victory. After the Tigers scored in the first inning on a walk, single and two groundouts, the slim righthander handcuffed the big Tiger bats the rest of the cold, windy afternoon, allowing only two runners as far as second. Meanwhile, the Browns chipped away at Detroit starter Bobo Newsom, acquired from St. Louis the previous season.

			R	H	E	Pitchers
St. Louis	000 021 110	—	5	10	0	Coffman (9)
Detroit	100 000 000	—	1	7	2	Newsom (7),
						Thomas (2)

Winning Pitcher: Coffman (1–0)   Losing Pitcher: Newsom (0–1)
Attendance: 49,417   Time: 2:19   Weather: Windy, 42 degrees

1941 (Friday, April 18) After dropping the only game of a rain-shortened series in St. Louis, Detroit evened its season record at 1–1 with a 4–2 triumph over the visiting Cleveland Indians. Charlie Gehringer unknotted a 1–1 tie with a solo home run off Jim Bagby, Jr., in the sixth inning. Birdie Tebbetts added a two-run shot in the following frame for the winning margin. Tommy Bridges pitched the first eight innings and got credit for the victory, while Al Benton pitched the final inning and picked up his first save of the season.

			R	H	E	Pitchers
Cleveland	000 001 001	—	2	6	0	Bagby (8)
Detroit	010 001 20x	—	4	6	1	Bridges (8),
						Benton (1)

Winning Pitcher: Bridges (1–0)   Losing Pitcher: Bagby (0–1)
Save: Benton
Home Runs: (CLE) Keltner (DET) Gehringer, Tebbetts (1 on)
Attendance: 42,165   Time: 1:59   Weather: Clear, 75 degrees

1942 (Tuesday, April 14) The Tigers' Al Benton was on the ropes early and often as the Cleveland Indians pounded out thirteen hits, including three doubles and a pair of home runs, in a 5–2 win. Ken Keltner put the Tribe on top with a bases-empty home run in the first, but the Tigers tied it on a second-inning single by Eric McNair. Detroit took a brief 2–1 lead on first baseman Les

Fleming's error in the third, but the Indians roughed up Benton and Roy Henshaw in the seventh to move ahead. Jim Bagby, Jr., and Joe Heving combined on a seven-hitter.

		R	**H**	**E**	**Pitchers**
Cleveland	100 100 210 —	5	13	1	Bagby (8), Heving (1)
Detroit	011 000 000 —	2	7	1	Benton (7), Henshaw (2)

Winning Pitcher: Bagby (1–0)   Losing Pitcher: Benton (0–1)
Save: Heving
Home Runs: (CLE) Keltner, Fleming
Attendance: 39,267   Time: 1:47   Weather: 66 degrees

1943 (Wednesday, April 28) The Tigers evened their record at 3–3 as Tommy Bridges shut down the St. Louis Browns until the eighth inning, when Johnny Gorsica closed off a rally to preserve a 4–2 victory. Nursing a one-run lead, Detroit broke the game open with three runs in the sixth off Steve Sundra. Bridges struck out six and contributed a couple of hits to square his record at 1–1 after losing a 1–0 heartbreaker in the opener in Cleveland. Rainy weather was responsible for the smallest crowd for a Detroit home opener since 1919.

		R	**H**	**E**	**Pitchers**
St. Louis	000 000 020 —	2	6	0	Sundra (6), Potter (2)
Detroit	000 103 00x —	4	9	0	Bridges (7.2), Gorsica (1.1)

Winning Pitcher: Bridges (1–1)   Losing Pitcher: Sundra (0–1)
Save: Gorsica
Attendance: 17,943   Time: 2:06   Weather: Rainy, 52 degrees

1944 (Tuesday, April 18) Poor fielding sabotaged Dizzy Trout, who surrendered six hits to St. Louis but still lost, 2–1. The Browns scratched out a run in the first on a couple of playable grounders and then added another on Vern Stephens' ninth-inning homer. The Tigers got one back on Pinky Higgins' blast, but George Caster, in relief of Jack Kramer, slammed the door. The game's significance wasn't evident until the final standings. Had the outcome been reversed, the Tigers would have won, rather than lost, the pennant by a game to the Browns.

		R	**H**	**E**	**Pitchers**
St. Louis	100 000 001	— 2	6	1	Kramer (8),
					Caster (1)
Detroit	000 000 001	— 1	6	2	Trout (9)

Winning Pitcher: Kramer (1–0)   Losing Pitcher: Trout (0–1)
Save: Caster
Home Runs: (STL) Stephens (DET) Higgins
Attendance: 26,034 Time: 2:04 Weather: 55 degrees

1945 (Friday, April 20) The Tigers fell to 2–2 as the Indians prevailed, 4–1. Cleveland starter Steve Gromek, a Hamtramck native, easily handled the home nine, much to the delight of a large contingent of Polish faithful in the stands. Stubby Overmire started for the Tigers and was pounded for four runs and eight hits before being removed in the third inning. Walt Wilson was outstanding in relief, allowing two hits and no runs in six and two-thirds innings, but Gromek was even better, scattering six hits.

		R	**H**	**E**	**Pitchers**
Cleveland	112 000 000	— 4	10	1	Gromek (9)
Detroit	000 001 000	— 1	6	3	Overmire (2.1),
					Wilson (6.2)

Winning Pitcher: Gromek (1–0)   Losing Pitcher: Overmire (0–1)
Attendance: 28,357 Time: 2:14 Weather: 56 degrees

1946 (Tuesday, April 16) For the first time since 1942, the baseball season opened without the country at war. The Tigers celebrated by defeating the St. Louis Browns, 2–1, before the largest home-opener crowd in eight years. Hal Newhouser, hero of the previous fall's World Series win over the Chicago Cubs, gave up a run in the first and then shut out the Browns the rest of the way. Meanwhile, Detroit tied the score in the second on a Pinky Higgins sacrifice fly, then went ahead for good when Hank Greenberg homered off Nelson Potter in the fourth.

		R	**H**	**E**	**Pitchers**
St. Louis	100 000 000	— 1	6	0	Potter (8)
Detroit	010 100 00x	— 2	6	0	Newhouser (9)

Winning Pitcher: Newhouser (1–0)   Losing Pitcher: Potter (0–1)
Home Run: (DET) Greenberg
Attendance: 52,118   Time: 2:05   Weather: 47 degrees

1947 (Friday, April 18) Roy Cullenbine and Pat Mullin hit solo
home runs in the sixth and seventh innings, respectively, to break up
the pitching battle between Cleveland's Red Embree and Detroit's
Virgil Trucks and hand the Tigers a 2–0 victory. Trucks was sensational, allowing only three hits, but center fielder Hoot Evers turned
in the play of the afternoon. With two outs in the ninth and two
Indians streaking for the plate, Evers made a spectacular game-end-
ing catch on pinch-hitter Jimmy Wasdell's line shot to the fence.

			R	**H**	**E**	**Pitchers**
Cleveland	000 000 000	—	0	3	0	Embree (8)
Detroit	000 001 10x	—	2	4	1	Trucks (9)

Winning Pitcher: Trucks (1–0)   Losing Pitcher: Embree (0–1)
Home Runs: (DET) Cullenbine, Mullin
Attendance: 46,111   Time: 2:10   Weather: 46 degrees

1948 (Friday, April 23) Coming off a season-opening three-game
sweep in Chicago, the Tigers faltered during their home opener and
lost to the Indians, 8–2. Fred Hutchinson was rocked for four home
runs, including a pair by Ken Keltner and a two-run shot by his old
Navy buddy, Cleveland starter Bob Lemon. The Tigers tied the
game at 1–1 in the third on an RBI double by Eddie Mayo, but
Cleveland went ahead for good the following inning. Vic Wertz
smacked one of the six hits off Lemon, a three-bagger in the seventh, and came home on a fly ball by George Kell.

			R	**H**	**E**	**Pitchers**
Cleveland	001 104 011	—	8	15	1	Lemon (9)
Detroit	001 000 100	—	2	6	0	Hutchinson (5.2),
						Gray (1.1),
						White (2)

Winning Pitcher: Lemon (1–0)   Losing Pitcher: Hutchinson (0–1)
Home Runs: (CLE) Doby, Keltner, Keltner (1 on), Lemon (1 on)
Attendance: 45,233   Time: 2:10   Weather: 68 degrees

1949 (Tuesday, April 19) The Tigers solved Chicago's Al Gettel and
Matt Surkont for seven hits, including three round-trippers, in a 5–1

opening-day win over the White Sox. Rookie center fielder Johnny Groth hit two home runs, including an inside-the-park shot down the right-field line. Catcher Aaron Robinson added a two-run blast to support a strong three-hit performance by Hal Newhouser.

		R	**H**	**E**	**Pitchers**
Chicago	000 100 000 —	1	3	1	Gettel (7),
					Surkont (1)
Detroit	020 010 11x —	5	7	0	Newhouser (9)

Winning Pitcher: Newhouser (1–0)　Losing Pitcher: Gettel (0–1)
Home Runs: (DET) Robinson (1 on), Groth 2
Attendance: 53,485　Time: 1:45　Weather: 50 degrees

1950 (Friday, April 21) After starting the year with two wins in Cleveland, the Tigers ran their record to 3–0 after a comeback win over the visiting Chicago White Sox. Trailing 1–0 in the seventh, and held to only three hits by Mickey Haefner, Detroit tied the game on Johnny Groth's one-out homer to left. In the eighth Detroit starter Virgil Trucks led off with a double. After retiring the next two batters, Haefner intentionally walked George Kell. The strategy backfired when Vic Wertz slammed a three-run homer for a 4–1 victory.

		R	**H**	**E**	**Pitchers**
Chicago	000 100 000 —	1	5	0	Haefner (8)
Detroit	000 000 13x —	4	6	0	Trucks (9)

Winning Pitcher: Trucks (1–0)　Losing Pitcher: Haefner (0–1)
Home Runs: (DET) Groth, Wertz
Attendance: 44,642　Time: 1:48　Weather: Gusty winds, low 40s

1951 (Tuesday, April 17) Detroit shortstop Johnny Lipon booted a ground ball in the ninth, allowing Larry Doby to score the winning run in Cleveland's 2–1 win. The unearned run settled a pitching duel between veterans Bob Lemon and Hal Newhouser. Newhouser survived a shaky first inning in which the Indians collected four singles but only one run. The Tigers tied the score in the third when Jerry Priddy, who had both of the hits off Lemon, led off with a double, was sacrificed to third, and then stole home on an aborted suicide squeeze.

		R	**H**	**E**	**Pitchers**
Cleveland	100 000 001 —	2	8	0	Lemon (9)
Detroit	001 000 000 —	1	2	1	Newhouser (9)

Winning Pitcher: Lemon (1–0)   Losing Pitcher: Newhouser (0–1)
Attendance: 43,470   Time: 2:16   Weather: 40 degrees

1952 (Tuesday, April 15) Detroit, destined to finish last for the first time ever, foreshadowed its fate with an uninspired 3–0 loss to the league's perennial cellar dwellers, St. Louis. Browns starter Ned Garver was in complete control, holding Detroit to six singles, walking one and fanning nine. Marty Marion's wind-blown double over Vic Wertz's head in right led to the Browns' first run. Garver accounted for the second with an RBI single off starter Dizzy Trout. A throwing error by reliever Marlin Stuart produced the Browns' final tally.

			R	H	E	Pitchers
St. Louis	000 110 001	—	3	6	0	Garver (9)
Detroit	000 000 000	—	0	6	1	Trout (8),
						Stuart (1)

Winning Pitcher: Garver (1–0)   Losing Pitcher: Trout (0–1)
Attendance: 43,112   Time: 2:10   Weather: Gale-force winds, low 50s

1953 (Thursday, April 16) A disappointingly small crowd watched the Tigers lose a slugfest to the Cleveland Indians, 11–8. Ray Boone set the tone by leading off the game with a home run off Art Houtteman. The Tigers' starter didn't last the third inning, giving up seven runs before being relieved by Ray Herbert. Walt Dropo paced the Tigers' attack with a double, triple and five RBI. Larry Doby matched that RBI total for the Indians with a two-run single, a sacrifice fly, and a mighty two-run blast that landed on the roof in right field.

			R	H	E	Pitchers
Cleveland	106 002 110	—	11	15	2	Garcia (4),
						Wilks (1),
						Hooper (4)
Detroit	210 050 000	—	8	10	0	Houtteman (2.2),
						Herbert (5.1),
						Jordan (1)

Winning Pitcher: Hooper (1–0)   Losing Pitcher: Herbert (0–1)
Home Runs: (CLE) Boone, Doby (1 on)
Attendance: 25,253   Time: 3:01   Weather: Windy, 39 degrees

1954 (Tuesday, April 13) Steve Gromek, aided by solo home runs from Ray Boone, Walt Dropo, and Frank Bolling, shut out the Baltimore Orioles—formerly the St. Louis Browns—during their American League debut. The loser was Don Larsen, who two years later made history by throwing a perfect game for the New York Yankees in the 1956 World Series. The game was notable in other respects. Harry Salsinger, longtime sports editor of the *Detroit News*, was hit in the eye by a foul ball in the press box and ultimately lost the vision in it. He never attended another Tigers game. It also marked the first time Ernie Harwell, then broadcasting for Baltimore, sat behind the microphone at Michigan and Trumbull.

	R	H	E	Pitchers
Baltimore 000 000 000 —	0	7	1	Larsen (8)
Detroit 000 101 10x —	3	9	0	Gromek (9)

Winning Pitcher: Gromek (1–0) Losing Pitcher: Larsen (0–1)
Home Runs: (DET) Boone, Dropo, Bolling
Attendance: 46,994 Time: 2:02 Weather: Upper 60s

1955 (Thursday, April 14) After beginning the season with a two-game split in Kansas City, the Tigers returned home for a bleak, wet opener whose start was delayed forty-five minutes by rain. Al Smith drove Billy Hoeft's first pitch of the game into center for a single, then stole second just before rain caused another forty-nine-minute delay. When play resumed, Hoeft struck out out the next two batters but then surrendered a single and three walks for a 2–0 Cleveland lead that was never headed. Al Kaline produced all three Detroit runs with a pair of triples.

	R	H	E	Pitchers
Cleveland 200 020 001 —	5	11	0	Garcia (9)
Detroit 100 020 000 —	3	6	1	Hoeft (0.2),
				Zuverink (4.1),
				Aber (3.2),
				Flowers (0.1)

Winning Pitcher: Garcia (1–0) Losing Pitcher: Hoeft (0–1)
Home Runs: (CLE) Smith (1 on), Hegan
Attendance: 42,684 Time: 2:26 Weather: 40s, showers

1956 (Tuesday, April 18) Kansas City won the game, 2–1, but the heroics belonged to Frank Lary, who pitched a six-hitter and legged out an inside-the-park home run in the fifth inning to give the Tigers a 1–0 lead. However, Gus Zernial's pinch-hit double to left-center in the seventh, aided by a poor relay throw from Bill Tuttle, scored two and gave Kansas City the edge for good. The game marked the American League debut of former Brooklyn pitcher Tommy LaSorda. The future Dodgers manager retired Earl Torgeson for the final out to pick up his only big-league save.

		R	H	E	Pitchers
Kansas City	000 000 200 —	2	6	0	Kellner (6), Gorman (2.2), LaSorda (0.1)
Detroit	000 010 000 —	1	8	1	Lary (9)

Winning Pitcher: Kellner (1–0)   Losing Pitcher: Lary (0–1)
Save: LaSorda
Home Run: (DET) Lary
Attendance: 40,037   Time: 2:37   Weather: 30s

1957 (Thursday, April 18) Rookie left fielder Roger Maris hit a grand slam homer in the top of the eleventh inning to cement an 8–3 Cleveland win. The Tigers, who opened the season with two losses in Kansas City, fell to 0–3 for the season. The small crowd was attributed to a combination of damp weather and television, which allowed Detroiters to watch the home opener from the comfort of their living rooms for the first time. "I'm not saying television killed us," said general manager Spike Briggs. "But we won't televise next year's opener."

		R	H	E	Pitchers
Cleveland	120 000 000 05 —	8	9	0	Lemon (5.1), Mossi (2.2), Narleski (3)
Detroit	000 102 000 00 —	3	11	2	Hoeft (1.2), Bunning (4.1) , Foytack (3.1), Aber (1), Crimian (0.2)

Winning Pitcher: Narleski (1–0) Losing Pitcher: Aber (0–1)
Home Runs: (CLE) Smith (1 on), Maris (3 on)
Attendance: 31,227 Time: 3:35 Weather: Drizzle, 48 degrees

1958 (Friday, April 18) Herb Score and Roger Maris were the stars of the Indians' third opening-day win over the Tigers in four years. Maris had four hits and three RBIs, while Score went the distance for his first win since being struck in the eye by a Gil McDougall line drive the previous May. The southpaw walked eight, struck out eight, and surrendered five hits. Tied 5–5 in the eighth inning, the Indians surged ahead on RBI singles by Minnie Minoso and Rocky Colavito. Detroit, which had opened the season in Chicago, fell to 2–2.

			R	**H**	**E**	**Pitchers**
Cleveland	021 011 020	—	7	16	4	Score (9)
Detroit	200 111 000	—	5	5	2	Hoeft (2.2),
						Valentinetti (1.1),
						Shaw (1.1),
						Morgan (2),
						Sleater (1.2)

Winning Pitcher: Score (1–1) Losing Pitcher: Morgan (0–1)
Home Runs: (CLE) Maris (DET) Kaline (1 on)
Attendance: 46,698 Time: 3:12 Weather: Sunny, 68 degrees

1959 (Friday, April 10) The light-hitting "Go-Go Sox," on their way to their first pennant in forty years, edged the Tigers on a rare round-tripper by Nellie Fox (his fifth hit) in the fourteenth inning. This was after Charlie Maxwell's pinch-hit, three-run homer in the eighth knotted the score at 7–7. The marathon session fell short of the major-league record for longest opening-day game. (Washington beat Philadelphia, 1–0, in fifteen innings in 1926.) The 43 players used missed by one the American League's two-team total, set by New York-Boston in 1956.

			R	**H**	**E**	**Pitchers**
Chicago	000 120 400 000 02	—	9	17	0	Pierce(5),
						Lown(1),
						Moore(2),

		R	H	E	Pitchers
					Shaw (0.2),
					Arias (0.1),
					Staley (4.2),
					Rudolph (0.1)
Detroit	100 030 030 000 00 —	7	14	1	Bunning (4.1),
					Morgan (2.1),
					Narleski (0.1),
					Susce (3),
					Mossi (4)

Winning Pitcher: Staley (1–0)　Losing Pitcher: Mossi (0–1)
Save: Rudolph
Home Runs: (CHI) Landis (1 on), Fox (1 on) (DET) Kaline, Maxwell (2 on)
Attendance: 38,322　Time: 4:25　Weather: Overcast, 36 degrees

1960 (Friday, April 22) In front of a near-record opening day crowd of 53,563, weak-hitting backstop Lew Berberet capped a perfect afternoon for baseball by smacking a two-out, bases-loaded single in the bottom of the ninth for a 6–5 win. It kept the Tigers, who had opened the year with two wins in Cleveland, the majors' only undefeated team. Rocky Colavito, acquired earlier in the week from the Indians for Harvey Kuenn, homered his first time up. Afterwards, appreciative fans gave "The Rock" a standing ovation when he took his position in right field.

		R	H	E	Pitchers
Chicago	010 310 000 —	5	7	0	Donovan (5),
					Garcia (0.2),
					Baumann (1.1),
					Shaw (1.2)
Detroit	020 021 001 —	6	10	1	Bunning (4),
					Aguirre (2),
					Sisler (2), Bruce (0),
					Morgan (1)

Winning Pitcher: Morgan (2–0)　Losing Pitcher: Shaw (0–1)
Home Runs: (DET) Colavito (1 on), Yost (1 on), Bilko
Attendance: 53,563　Time: 3:07　Weather: Sunny, 76 degrees

At Tiger Stadium (1961–1997)

1961 (Tuesday, April 11) The Tigers opened with a new name for their ballpark, a new manager in Bob Scheffing, and six fresh faces in the lineup. But the result was distressingly familiar— the Indians scored six times in the second to knock starter Jim Bunning out of the box. Jimmy Piersall had four hits for Cleveland. The troubled center fielder, again the target of objects thrown from unruly fans, pocketed several golf balls and gave a tossed hairbrush to balding coach Luke Appling. Detroit second baseman Jake Wood homered in his first big-league game.

		R	H	E	Pitchers
Cleveland	060 100 020 —	9	18	1	Perry (9)
Detroit	002 000 300 —	5	7	1	Bunning (1.2),
					Regan (3.1),
					Donohue (2),
					Fischer (2)

Winning Pitcher: Perry (1–0)   Losing Pitcher: Bunning (0–1)
Home Runs: (CLE) Phillips (1 on) (DET) Wood (1 on)
Attendance: 41,643   Time: 2:48   Weather: Clear, 50 degrees

1962 (Friday, April 13) Friday the thirteenth worked its black magic on Yankee killer Frank Lary, who boosted his career record against New York to 28–10 with a 5–3 win. Lary pitched seven strong innings but was forced to leave the game when he pulled a leg muscle running a triple in the seventh. The three-base hit tied the score at 3–3; Luis Arroyo then walked the next three batters to give Detroit the victory. The win, which improved Detroit to 1–1 for the year, proved costly. Lary's leg injury caused him to alter his pitching motion, leading to a series of arm and shoulder problems that ended his Tigers career two years later.

		R	H	E	Pitchers
New York	020 100 000 —	3	9	1	Stafford (6),
					Arroyo (0.1),
					Coates (1.2)
Detroit	000 002 30x —	5	7	1	Lary (7),
					Bunning (2)

Winning Pitcher: Lary (1–0)   Losing Pitcher: Arroyo (0–1)
Save: Bunning
Home Run: (NY) Howard

Attendance: 29,411   Time: 2:46   Weather: Snow, freezing rain, 36 degrees

1963 (Tuesday, April 10) The Tigers blew an early four-run lead and bowed to Chicago, thanks to a costly error by first baseman Norm Cash and some sterling relief pitching by knuckleballer Hoyt Wilhelm. Detroit was ahead 5–3 in the seventh when the White Sox rallied with four unearned runs. With one out and two on, Cash fumbled a routine grounder by Joe Cunningham. One out later, Pete Ward lifted Jim Bunning's first pitch into the upper right-fields seats for a 7–5 lead. Wilhelm retired the last nine Tigers in a row to seal the win.

		R	**H**	**E**	**Pitchers**
Chicago	003 000 400 —	7	10	1	Herbert (1.1), Joyce (0.2), Baumann (4), Pizarro (0), Wilhelm (3)
Detroit	040 010 000 —	5	13	1	Bunning (7.2), Egan (0.1), Dustal (1)

Winning Pitcher: Baumann (1–0)   Losing Pitcher: Bunning (0–1)
Save: Wilhelm
Home Runs: (CHI) Ward (2 on) (DET) Triandos
Attendance: 37,781   Time: 2:53   Weather: Clear, 40s

1964 (Tuesday, April 14) Gusts of up to thirty miles per hour resulted in several wind-blown extra-base hits, but the Tigers benefitted from most of them in a 7–3 win over Kansas City. Starter Phil Regan, employing a new overhand curveball, finally faltered in the ninth and was relieved by Mickey Lolich and Dave Wickersham, who retired Gino Cimoli with the bases loaded for the final out. Veteran Jerry Lumpe, acquired from the Athletics to play second base, paced the Tigers' offense with a single, a double, and a triple.

		R	**H**	**E**	**Pitchers**
Kansas City	000 000 102 —	3	5	0	Pena (5), Handrahan (1.1), O'Donoghue (1.2)
Detroit	110 110 21x —	7	12	0	Regan (8.1), Lolich (0.1), Wickersham (0.1)

Winning Pitcher: Regan (1–0)   Losing Pitcher: Pena (0–1)
Save: Wickersham
Home Runs: (KC) Gentile, Jiminez (DET) Cash, Bruton (1 on)
Attendance: 35,733   Time: 2:47   Weather: 60s, gusty winds

1965 (Wednesday, April 21) The Tigers, who had won four of six games on a three-city road trip, fattened their record to 5–2 by edging Kansas City, 1–0, in their home opener. Starters Hank Aguirre and John O'Donoghue battled each other under blue skies. Norm Cash scored the only run of the game, coming home on Don Demeter's double to left in the fourth inning. Larry Sherry recorded the final seven outs, including a diving stab of a bounding ground ball to retire the A's in the eighth with runners on second and third.

	R	H	E	Pitchers
Kansas City 000 000 000 —	0	5	0	O'Donoghue (6.1), Talbot (1.2)
Detroit 000 100 00x —	1	3	1	Aguirre (7.1), Sherry (1.2)

Winning Pitcher: Aguirre (2–0)   Losing Pitcher: O'Donoghue (1–1)
Save: Sherry
Attendance: 32,658   Time: 2:05   Weather: Sunny, 68 degrees

1966 (Friday, April 15) The Tigers stretched their season-opening win streak to four games with an 8–3 victory over Washington. With the Senators ahead 2–1 in the fourth, Dick McAuliffe cracked a grand slam to provide a lead the Tigers never relinquished. Norm Cash, Al Kaline, Don Wert, and Bill Freehan led an eleven-hit attack with two hits apiece, with Kaline opening the home season with a double and a home run. Orlando Pena pitched the final five innings in relief of starter Dave Wickersham to get credit for the win.

	R	H	E	Pitchers
Washington 002 001 000 —	3	5	1	Duckworth (3.2), McCormick (0.1), Narum (2), Cox (2)
Detroit 010 421 00x —	8	11	1	Wickersham (4), Pena (5)

Winning Pitcher: Pena (1–0)   Losing Pitcher: Duckworth (0–1)

Home Runs: (WAS) McMullen (1 on) (DET) McAuliffe (3 on), Kaline
Attendance: 36,674 Time: 2:32 Weather: 54 degrees

1967 (Tuesday, April 18)
Detroit improved to 4–3 for the year as Earl Wilson held the Angels to one run—that on a second-inning homer by Jimmie Hall—in a 4–1 triumph. Al Kaline broke the 1–1 tie with a solo shot in the sixth. The Tigers gained some breathing room in the eighth when Bill Freehan grounded into a forceout at second. The relay throw to first was in the dirt, allowing Don Wert and Gates Brown to both scamper home. The official scorer generously awarded Freehan two RBIs on the play.

		R	H	E	Pitchers
California	010 000 000 —	1	7	1	Lopez (6), Rojas (2)
Detroit	010 001 02x —	4	7	0	Wilson (9)

Winning Pitcher: Wilson (1–1) Losing Pitcher: Lopez (0–2)
Home Runs: (CAL) Hall (DET) Kaline
Attendance: 33,211 Time: 2:25 Weather: 46 degrees

1968 (Wednesday, April 10) Boston left fielder Carl Yastrzemski, last year's MVP, picked up where he left off, guiding the Bosox to a 7–3 victory over the Tigers with a pair of solo home runs. Teammate Rico Petrocelli knocked in three runs with a single and a double. Detroit starter and loser Earl Wilson smacked a home run in the third inning and Mickey Stanley, leading off and playing first base, contributed three hits. The setback was only temporary; the Tigers went on to win their next nine in a row and a world championship in October.

		R	H	E	Pitchers
Boston	021 002 101 —	7	10	1	Ellsworth (9)
Detroit	001 000 020 —	3	9	1	Wilson (5), Dobson (2), Patterson (2)

Winning Pitcher: Ellsworth (1–0) Losing Pitcher: Wilson (0–1)
Home Runs: (BOS) Yastrzemski 2 (DET) Wilson
Attendance: 41,429 Time: 2:44 Weather: 60 degrees

1969 (Tuesday, April 8) A full house of 53,572 rooters watched the Tigers begin defending their world championship crown with a 6–2 victory over Cleveland. Norm Cash doubled in two runs off Luis Tiant to tie the game in the third, and then Al Kaline drove a two-run homer to left in the sixth to give Denny McLain the win. Although the Tigers ultimately finished second in the new American League Eastern Division, McLain eventually captured his second straight Cy Young Award.

		R	**H**	**E**	**Pitchers**
Cleveland	110 000 000 —	2	3	0	Tiant (5),
					Hamilton (2),
					Pina (1)
Detroit	002 021 10x —	6	11	1	McLain (9)

Winning Pitcher: McLain (1–0)   Losing Pitcher: Tiant (0–1)
Home Runs: (CLE) Brown (DET) Kaline (1 on)
Attendance: 53,572 Time: 2:19 Weather: 70 degrees

1970 (Tuesday, April 14) Tiger bats pounded seven Cleveland pitchers for fifteen hits as Detroit boosted its record to 4–3 with a 12–4 thrashing of the Indians. Norm Cash and Jim Northrup had three hits apiece and Willie Horton, Don Wert, and Bill Freehan chipped in with two each. Mickey Lolich survived a twelve-hit Cleveland attack for his second win of the season.

		R	**H**	**E**	**Pitchers**
Cleveland	000 021 010 —	4	12	1	Hand (2),
					Hargan (2),
					Hennigan (0),
					Miller (0),
					Ellsworth (1),
					Paul (2),
					Higgins (1)
Detroit	004 051 20x —	12	15	1	Lolich (9)

Winning Pitcher: Lolich (2–1)   Losing Pitcher: Hand (0–2)
Home Runs: (DET) Cash (1 on) (CLE) Ford
Attendance: 46,819 Time: 2:55 Weather: 52 degrees

1971 (Tuesday, April 6) In Detroit's earliest home opener ever, Mickey Lolich enjoyed an easy afternoon against the Indians as the Tigers built up a 7–1 lead after four innings and then coasted to an

8–2 triumph. Lolich, destined for a twenty-five-win season, scattered six hits and struck out nine. The Tigers were paced by Willie Horton's single and double and Jim Northrup's triple and two RBIs. Lolich helped his own cause with a run-producing single in the second off Cleveland starter Steve Hargan. Despite the cold temperature, attendance was announced as 54,089, which remains the second-largest opening day crowd ever in Detroit.

			R	H	E	Pitchers
Cleveland	000 110 000	—	2	6	0	Hargan (2),
						Machemehl (1),
						Dunning (1),
						Pascual (3),
						Lamb (0.2),
						Austin (0.1)
Detroit	022 300 01x	—	8	9	1	Lolich (9)

Winning Pitcher: Lolich (1–0)   Losing Pitcher: Hargan (0–1)
Attendance: 54,089   Time: 2:44   Weather: 46 degrees

1972 (Saturday, April 15) A two-week players' strike forced the Tigers to open at home on a Saturday for the first time since 1912. Mickey Lolich's pitching line in a 3–2 win over Boston—two runs, six hits, nine strikeouts—was an exact replica of his home-opening performance the year before. Eddie Brinkman put Detroit on the board with a two-run homer in the second inning off Marty Pattin. Norm Cash scored the winning run in the seventh on a single by Bill Freehan. The victory proved more significant than it seemed at the time. Had the score been reversed, the Red Sox, not the Tigers, would have wound up winning the American League East pennant by a half-game.

			R	H	E	Pitchers
Boston	101 000 000	—	2	6	1	Pattin (6),
						Tatum (2)
Detroit	020 000 10x	—	3	6	0	Lolich (9)

Winning Pitcher: Lolich (1–0)   Losing Pitcher: Pattin (0–1)
Attendance: 31,510   Time: 2:18   Weather: Low 50s

1973 (Wednesday, April 11) Cold weather forced a one-day postponement of opening day festivities, but there wasn't much to cheer about at the corner as Baltimore won, 3–1. Detroit fell to 1–2 after

Jim Northrup misjudged a two-out line drive by Tommy Davis in the 12th inning, allowing two runs to score. Northrup broke in on the ball, then watched as it sailed over his head in center. A trio of Oriole hurlers held the Tigers to four hits, which included a second-inning home run by Norm Cash that accounted for all of the Tigers' scoring.

		R	**H**	**E**	**Pitchers**
Baltimore	000 000 100 002 —	3	8	0	Palmer (7), Jackson (2), Watt (3)
Detroit	010 000 000 000 —	1	4	0	Fryman (8), LaGrow (3.2), Timmerman (0), Hiller (0.1)

Winning Pitcher: Watt (1–0)   Losing Pitcher: LaGrow (0–1)
Home Run: (DET) Cash
Attendance: 46,389   Time: 3:06   Weather: Upper 30s

1974 (Tuesday, April 9) Detroit dropped to 2–3 when Mickey Lolich lost his second straight strong start of the season, 3–0 to the Yankees. Lolich, who had now allowed just three earned runs in two complete-game losses, received little support from his teammates. New second baseman Gary Sutherland started his career at Michigan and Trumbull with a bang, collecting four hits in as many at-bats. But Detroit stranded a dozen runners on the bases against three New York pitchers: Steve Kline, Fred Beene, and Sparky Lyle.

		R	**H**	**E**	**Pitchers**
New York	200 000 100 —	3	8	1	Kline (7.2), Beene (1), Lyle (0.1)
Detroit	000 000 000 —	0	8	2	Lolich (9)

Winning Pitcher: Kline (1–0)   Losing Pitcher: Lolich (0–2)
Save: Lyle
Attendance: 44,047   Time: 2:32   Weather: 38 degrees

1975 (Thursday, April 10) The Tigers began one of the worst seasons in their history—102 losses, including a near-record nineteen-game losing streak—in fitting fashion. Baltimore soundly trounced Detroit, 10–0. Oriole batters routed three Detroit pitchers. Lee May hit a three-run homer and Don Baylor went 4–4 with three RBIs.

Jim Palmer surrendered only three singles: one each to Nate Colbert, Aurelio Rodriquez, and Art James.

			R	H	E	Pitchers
Baltimore	300 102 022	—	10	13	0	Palmer (9)
Detroit	000 000 000	—	0	3	0	Coleman (6),
						Lemanczyk (2),
						Bare (1)

Winning Pitcher: Palmer (1–0)   Losing Pitcher: Coleman (0–1)
Home Run: (BAL) May (2 on)
Attendance: 40,139   Time: 2:04   Weather: 44 degrees

1976 (Thursday, April 13) The country's bicentennial fever produced few fireworks on opening day in Detroit, as the Milwaukee Brewers squeezed past the toothless Tigers, 1–0. It was the third straight year the Tigers were blanked in their home opener. This time Jim Slaton did the honors, allowing only a single to Ben Oglivie and a double to Aurelio Rodriquez. The Brewers were held scoreless until the ninth when they broke through on Charlie Moore's sacrifice fly off of John Hiller. Detroit fell to 1–1 with the loss.

			R	H	E	Pitchers
Milwaukee	000 000 001	—	1	8	0	Slaton (9)
Detroit	000 000 000	—	0	2	1	Bare (7.1),
						Hiller (1.2)

Winning Pitcher: Slaton (2–0)   Losing Pitcher: Hiller (0–1)
Attendance: 48,612   Time: 1:57   Weather: 61 degrees

1977 (Thursday, April 7) Kansas City defeated Detroit, 7–4, as Amos Otis led the Royals with a single, double, and a home run, accounting for three runs. Otis's two-run shot off Dave Roberts in the first gave Kansas City a quick 2–0 lead, but the big blow was a three-run homer by John Mayberry in the fifth, after the Tigers had crept to within a run of the Royals. Ron LeFlore and Tom Veryzer, with two hits each, accounted for half of the Tigers' total. LeFlore, Rusty Staub, Tito Fuentes, and Phil Mankowski each had one RBI.

			R	H	E	Pitchers
Kansas City	200 130 001	—	7	12	0	Splittorff (6),
						Bird (1), Gura (0.2),
						Littell (1.1)

Detroit   200 000 200 — 4   8   0   Roberts (5),
                                           Arroyo (3.1),
                                           Hiller (0.2)
Winning Pitcher: Splittorff (1–0)   Losing Pitcher: Roberts (0–1)
Save: Littell
Home Runs: (KC) Otis (1 on), Mayberry (2 on)
Attendance: 46,807   Time: 2:30   Weather: Low 40s

1978 (Friday, April 7) The opener was delayed one day by rain, but
the biggest crowd since 1971 still turned out to rock the stadium
with the chant: "We want the Bird!" Mark Fidrych bounced back,
at least temporarily, from arm problems, spinning a five-hitter
against Toronto. The Tigers won 6–2, thanks to home runs by Milt
May, Phil Mankowski, and Jason Thompson. Mankowski's three-
run blast broke up a 2–2 tie in the fourth, while Thompson's shot
landed on the roof in right field. The Tigers' keystone kids, Alan
Trammell and Lou Whitaker, made their first opening day starts,
each contributing a hit. Fidrych's glory was short-lived; injuries limited him to just two more starts in 1978 and led to his retirement
two seasons later.

			R	H	E	Pitchers
Toronto	020 000 000	—	2	5	0	Lemanczyk (3.2), Jefferson (4.1)
Detroit	011 300 10x	—	6	10	1	Fidrych (9)

Winning Pitcher: Fidrych (1–0)   Losing Pitcher: Lemanczyk (0–1)
Home Runs: (DET) May, Mankowski (2 on), Thompson
Attendance: 52,528   Time: 2:04   Weather: Clear, 67 degrees

1979 (Saturday, April 7) Two days of cold weather forced a rare
Saturday opener with Texas. Dave Rozema surrendered a single and
a home run to the first two Rangers he faced; it was downhill from
there as Texas rolled to an 8–2 victory. Fergie Jenkins went all the
way for the Rangers, scattering seven hits. Steve Kemp had a single
and a home run and Phil Mankowski added two singles and an RBI
for Detroit.

			R	H	E	Pitchers
Texas	200 021 300	—	8	8	4	Jenkins (9)
Detroit	010 100 000	—	2	7	2	Rozema (5.1), Burnside (1.1), Lopez (2.1)

Winning Pitcher: Jenkins (1–0)   Losing Pitcher: Rozema (0–1)
Home Runs: (TEX) Grubb (1 on) (DET) Kemp
Attendance: 43,708   Time: 2:40   Weather: Upper 30s

1980 (Friday, April 18) It was a long day at the office as Kansas City and Detroit engaged in a three-and-a-half-hour marathon that finally ended when the Royals scored three times in the top of the eleventh off Aurelio Lopez to win, 9–6. The Tigers chased starter Paul Splittorff with four runs in the first, but Dave Rozema couldn't hold the lead. Detroit regained the advantage with two runs in the eighth, but the bullpen failed. The Royals roughed up Pat Underwood and Jack Billingham for two runs in the ninth to tie the game, then exploded for a three-spot in the eleventh to win it. Alan Trammell led the Tigers' assault with three hits and two RBIs.

	R	H	E	Pitchers
Kansas City 000 040 002 03 —	9	15	0	Splittorff (0.2), Pattin (5), Christenson (2.1), Quisenberry (3)
Detroit 400 000 020 00 —	6	14	0	Rozema (4.2), Hiller (2.1), Underwood (1.1), Billingham (1.2), Lopez (1)

Winning Pitcher: Quisenberry (1–0)   Losing Pitcher: Lopez (0–2)
Attendance: 50,687   Time: 3:34   Weather: 65 degrees

1981 (Thursday, April 9) Richie Hebner broke open a 2–2 deadlock in the seventh inning with a three-run homer off Joey McLaughlin, in relief of starter Jim Clancy, to give Jack Morris his first opening day win, 6–2 over the visiting Blue Jays. Hometown stars this afternoon were Morris, who held Toronto to five hits, and Alan Trammell, who chipped in with a single and a triple.

	R	H	E	Pitchers
Toronto 001 010 000 —	2	5	1	Clancy (6), McLaughlin (0.2), Willis (0.1), Jackson (1)

Detroit   001 010   31x — 6   8   1   Morris (9)
Winning Pitcher: Morris (1–0)   Losing Pitcher: McLaughlin (0–1)
Home Run: (DET) Hebner (2 on)
Attendance: 51,452   Time: 2:40   Weather: 62 degrees

1982 (Thursday, April 15) After opening the season 2–4 on the road, Detroit came home and scored single runs in four different innings to beat Dave Steib and the Toronto Blue Jays, 4–2. Chet Lemon, Enos Cabell, and Richie Hebner each had a pair of hits for Detroit, and Cabell knocked in two runs. Kevin Saucier earned the victory with 3 2/3 innings of shutout relief. Elias Sosa, acquired from Montreal, picked up the save.

		R	**H**	**E**	**Pitchers**
Toronto	001 100 000 —	2	8	0	Steib (6.1),
					Garvin (1.2)
Detroit	100 011 10x —	4	9	0	Rozema (3.1),
					Saucier (3.2),
					Sosa (2)

Winning Pitcher: Saucier (1–1)   Losing Pitcher: Steib (0–1)
Save: Sosa
Attendance: 51,038   Time: 2:26   Weather: 63 degrees

1983 (Friday, April 8) The Tigers fell to 2–2 for the year as they all but gift-wrapped this opener to Chicago. Sloppy fielding, including a dropped ball and missed cut-offs, and a bases-loaded walk all contributed to a 6–3 defeat. Detroit forged a 3–0 lead in the third on RBIs by Kirk Gibson, Lance Parrish, and Larry Herndon, but Dennis Lamp and Jerry Koosman cooled the Tigers' bats after that. A series of base hits and misplays allowed the White Sox to chip away at starter Milt Wilcox with a run in the fifth, two in the sixth, and three in the seventh.

		R	**H**	**E**	**Pitchers**
Chicago	000 012 300 —	6	8	0	Lamp (6),
					Koosman (3)
Detroit	003 000 000 —	3	7	2	Wilcox (6.2),
					Lopez (1.1),
					Bailey (1)

Winning Pitcher: Lamp (1–0)   Losing Pitcher: Wilcox (0–1)
Save: Koosman
Attendance: 51,350   Time: 2:47   Weather: 49 degrees

1984 (Tuesday, April 10) Detroit ran its record to a perfect 6–0 as it jumped on Texas starter Dave Stewart for four runs in the first inning. Free-agent first baseman Darrell Evans slammed a three-run homer in his first Tiger Stadium at-bat to open the scoring. Dave Bergman and Howard Johnson knocked in the other runs. Dan Petry pitched a strong four-hitter for his second win of the season, one that saw the Tigers race to a record 35–5 start and claim their first world championship since 1968.

			R	H	E	Pitchers
Texas	100 000 000	—	1	4	0	Stewart(0.2),
						Schmidt (4.1),
						Henke (2), Bibby (1)
Detroit	401 000 00x	—	5	5	0	Petry (9)

Winning Pitcher: Petry (2–0)   Losing Pitcher: Stewart (0–2)
Home Run: (DET) Evans (2 on)
Attendance: 51,238   Time: 2:32   Weather: 53 degrees

1985 (Monday, April 8) The Tigers battled snow and falling temperatures to come from behind for an exciting opening day win. Trailing Cleveland 4–3 in the bottom of the eighth, Detroit scored two runs on Chris Pittaro's single and Lou Whitaker's sacrifice fly. Last year's MVP and Cy Young Award winner, Willie Hernandez, preserved the 5–4 win with a scoreless ninth inning. The game was notable for Sparky Anderson's short-lived experiment of playing rookie Pittaro at second base and moving Whitaker to third.

			R	H	E	Pitchers
Cleveland	100 003 000	—	4	6	1	Blyleven (4.2),
						Jeffcoat (0.1),
						Waddell (2.1),
						Camacho (0.2)
Detroit	000 120 02x	—	5	10	0	Morris (8),
						Hernandez (1)

Winning Pitcher: Morris (1–0)   Losing Pitcher: Camacho (0–1)
Save: Hernandez
Attendance: 51,180   Time: 2:49   Weather: Snow flurries, 30s

1986 (Monday, April 7) The Red Sox battered Jack Morris for four home runs, including Dwight Evans' shot to dead center on the game's first pitch. This was Kirk Gibson's day at Tiger Stadium—Gibby cracked two-run homers in the fifth and seventh innings, the latter giving the Tigers a 6–5 lead they never relinquished. Gibson finished the day with four hits in four at-bats, five ribbies, and a stolen base. Morris, with relief help from Bill Campbell and Willie Hernandez, picked up his second opening day win in a row.

		R	H	E	Pitchers
Boston	101 000 300 —	5	12	0	Hurst (4.2), Stewart (2.1), Crawford (0.2), Sambito (0.1)
Detroit	001 030 20x —	6	13	0	Morris (7), Campbell (1), Hernandez (1)

Winning Pitcher: Morris (1–0) Losing Pitcher: Stewart (0–1)
Save: Hernandez
Home Runs: (BOS) Dw. Evans, Rice, Baylor (1 on), Gedman (DET) Gibson 2 (1 on)
Attendance: 51,437 Time: 2:55 Weather: 69 degrees

1987 (Monday, April 6) Larry Herndon crushed a five-hundred-foot home run to straightaway center field in the sixth inning off Dennis Rasmussen, but that was the Tigers' only score in a ten-inning, 2–1 loss to the Yankees. New York scored an unearned run in the fourth off Jack Morris, and then won the game in the tenth on Rickey Henderson's run-scoring double.

		R	H	E	Pitchers
New York	000 100 000 1 —	2	9	0	Rasmussen (7), Righetti (3)
Detroit	000 001 000 0 —	1	5	1	Morris (9.2), Hernandez (0.1)

Winning Pitcher: Righetti (1–0) Losing Pitcher: Morris (0–1)
Home Run: (DET) Herndon
Attendance: 51,315 Time: 3:01 Weather: 50 degrees

1988 (Tuesday, April 12) The Tigers benefitted from the controversial new guidelines governing the balk rule in their curtain raiser against Texas. Rangers starter Bobby Witt was called for four balks in the first three innings, leading to three Detroit runs in the home team's 4–1 victory. Tom Brookens had two hits while Alan Trammell, Matt Nokes, and Jim Morrison each drove in a run. The

Tigers, after splitting six games in Boston and Kansas City to start the season, improved to 4–3 with the win.

		R	H	E	Pitchers
Texas	000 010 000 —	1	5	2	Witt (9)
Detroit	202 000 00x —	4	5	0	Tanana (7.1), Henneman (1.2)

Winning Pitcher: Tanana (2–0)   Losing Pitcher: Witt (0–2)
Save: Henneman
Attendance: 51,504   Time: 2:34   Weather: 64 degrees

1989 (Friday, April 7) After dropping their first two games in Texas, the Tigers flew home to put one in the win column with a 10–3 rout of Milwaukee. Held to just a two-run homer by Matt Nokes in the first six innings, Detroit then exploded for three runs in the seventh and five more in the eighth. Kenny Williams was the big gun, driving in three teammates with a single and a double. The Tigers' win produced false optimism for a season that ended with a last-place finish and 103 losses.

		R	H	E	Pitchers
Milwaukee	010 000 200 —	3	7	2	Weyman (6), Mirabella (1.1), Crim (0.2)
Detroit	000 200 35x —	10	9	0	Alexander (7.1), Hernandez (1.2)

Winning Pitcher: Alexander (1–0)   Losing Pitcher: Weyman (0–1)
Save: Hernandez
Home Runs: (DET) Nokes (1 on) (MIL) Braggs (1 on), Deer
Attendance: 51,473   Time: 2:45   Weather: 45 degrees

1990 (Thursday, April 12) Hot bats were on display on a cold afternoon, as the Tigers and Red Sox combined for eighteen runs and twenty-eight hits in an 11–7 Detroit win. Lou Whitaker started things off with a two-run dinger in the first inning off Mike Rochford. The Tigers went on to open a 10–1 lead after three innings. This was sweet revenge for the Tigers, who opened the campaign with three losses in Beantown. A new face in the lineup, third baseman Tony Phillips, went 4–4 with three RBIs, while old favorite Alan Trammell added two singles and two RBIs.

		R	**H**	**E**	**Pitchers**
Boston	100 130 101 —	7	15	2	Rochford (1.2),
					Gardner (0.1),
					Kiecker (4),
					Harris (2)
Detroit	244 010 00x —	11	13	0	Tanana (4.2),
					Lugo (3.1),
					Henneman (1)

Winning Pitcher: Lugo (1–0)   Losing Pitcher: Rochford (0–1)
Home Runs: (DET) Whitaker (1 on) (BOS) Pena
Attendance: 44,906 Time: 3:36 Weather: 36 degrees

1991 (Monday, April 8) Detroit put together three two-run innings to defeat the Yankees, 6–4. Alan Trammell, who always hit well on opening day, added to his reputation with a two-run homer in the first and a two-run double in the fifth, the latter tying the game at four runs apiece. In the seventh Cecil Fielder unknotted the tie, doubling in Milt Cuyler and Tony Phillips. Paul Gibson, the third of four Detroit pitchers, was awarded the win, while Mike Henneman earned the save.

		R	**H**	**E**	**Pitchers**
New York	102 100 000 —	4	10	1	Leary (6),
					Cadaret (0.1),
					Plunk (1.1),
					Farr (0.1)
Detroit	200 020 20x —	6	8	1	Tanana (5),
					Petry (1),
					Gibson (2),
					Henneman (1)

Winning Pitcher: Gibson (1–0)   Losing Pitcher: Cadaret (0–1)
Save: Henneman
Home Runs: (DET) Trammell (1 on) (NY) Maas (1 on), Blowers (1 on)
Attendance: 47,382 Time: 3:15 Weather: 72 degrees, showers

1992 (Monday, April 6) During the offseason Jack Morris, hero of the Minnesota Twins' dramatic 1991 World Series victory over Atlanta, showed his appreciation for his home state of Minnesota by signing a contract with Toronto. Tiger Stadium fans booed the bald-faced mercenary, who responded by scattering five hits and striking out seven in the Blue Jays' 4–2 victory. The ex-Tiger ace, handling his thirteenth consecutive opening-day assignment (a major-league record) lost his shutout in the ninth on a pair of upper-deck blasts by Cecil Fielder and Rob Deer.

		R	**H**	**E**	**Pitchers**
Toronto	100 101 010 —	4	10	0	Morris (9)
Detroit	000 000 002 —	2	5	0	Gullickson (6),
					Leiter (2),
					Lancaster (1)

Winning Pitcher: Morris (1–0)   Losing Pitcher: Gullickson (0–1)
Home Runs: (TOR) Borders, Olerud (DET) Fielder, Deer
Attendance: 51,068   Time: 2:46   Weather: Sunny, breezy, 56 degrees

1993 (Tuesday, April 13) The Tigers came home from a West Coast swing where they dropped four of six games. As was often the case during the summer, free agent acquisition Mike Moore was the beneficiary of the Tigers' potent offense—in this case, an overwhelming display of power that buried the Oakland As, 20–4. Travis Fryman, Rob Deer, and Mickey Tettleton blasted three-run homers to pace the biggest opening day rout in Detroit's history. The Tigers built up a 16–4 lead after four innings and then coasted. Cecil Fielder had four singles while Fryman accumulated five RBIs.

		R	**H**	**E**	**Pitchers**
Oakland	002 000 200 —	4	7	2	Davis (2.1),
					Mahler (1.1),
					Nunez (2.1),
					Boever (2)
Detroit	431 800 04x —	20	18	0	Moore (6.2),
					MacDonald (1.1),
					Henneman (1)

Winning Pitcher: Moore (1–1)   Losing Pitcher: Davis (0–2)
Home Runs: (DET) Fryman (2 on), Deer (2 on), Tettleton (2 on)
Attendance: 49,674   Time: 3:32   Weather: 56 degrees

1994 (Monday, April 11) The Baltimore Orioles played home wreckers, easily dispatching the Tigers by a 7–4 score. Newcomer Tim Belcher, signed as a free agent for $3.4 million, lost his second outing in a row as the Tigers fell to 2–5. Belcher surrendered six hits and walked seven, although it was a dropped fly ball by Junior Felix that opened the door for four unearned runs in the third. "The fans expect to see a lot better pitching from a major-league pitcher than that," Belcher admitted afterwards. Meanwhile, his counterpart, Ben McDonald, retired twenty-one of the first twenty-three men he faced.

			R	**H**	**E**	**Pitchers**
Baltimore	004 003 000	—	7	11	0	McDonald (7.2),
						Mills (0.2),
						Poole (0.2)
Detroit	000 000 022	—	4	4	1	Belcher (5.1),
						Krueger (0.2),
						Boever (3)

Winning Pitcher: McDonald (2–0)   Losing Pitcher: Belcher (0–2)
Home Run: (DET) Fryman
Attendance: 50,314   Time: 3:17   Weather: Overcast, windy, 50 degrees

1995 (Tuesday, May 2) The Tigers' one hundredth opener at Michigan and Trumbull was the most tumultuous in memory. The crowd, the smallest since the 1972 strike season, included many fans who repeatedly batted beachballs onto the field, threw objects at players, and ran out onto the diamond and delayed the game. Thirty-four people were arrested and ticketed. Lost in the commotion was an 11–1 lacing by the Indians, who were paced by four home runs and Dennis Martinez's seven strong innings. "Ugly day," summarized Cecil Fielder. The Tigers dropped to 2–4 for the season.

			R	**H**	**E**	**Pitchers**
Cleveland	401 001 320	—	11	16	0	Martinez (7),
						Plunk (1), Shuey (1)
Detroit	010 000 000	—	1	8	1	Bergman (3),
						Bohanon (4),
						Groom (1), Lira (1)

Winning Pitcher: Martinez (2–0)   Losing Pitcher: Bergman (0–2)
Home Runs: (CLE) Thome (2 on), Ramirez, Sorrento (2 on), Baerga (1 on)
Attendance: 39,398   Time: 3:23   Weather: Partly cloudy, 60 degrees

1996 (Tuesday, April 9) The Tigers had only four hits on a cold, snowy afternoon, but three sailed into the seats, producing a 10–9 victory over Seattle. The biggest blow came in the bottom of the fourth, after the Mariners touched starter Scott Aldred for four runs to build a 7–4 lead. With two outs and the bases loaded, Cecil Fielder lined a Bob Wells pitch 435 feet into the left-center-field stands. Detroit was the beneficiary of nine walks, including six in the six-run rally in the fourth. Seattle lost despite ten extra-base hits, including six doubles, two triples, and two home runs. The Tigers, coming off a western road trip, evened their record at 4–4. The freezing weather kept the announced crowd of 42,932 to an actual turnout of 35,600.

		R	H	E	Pitchers
Seattle	300 400 110 —	9	12	1	Wolcott (3.1),
					Menhart (0),
					Wells (3.2),
					Ayala (1)
Detroit	310 600 00x —	10	4	1	Aldred (3.1),
					Keagle (3.2),
					Myers (0.2),
					R. Lewis (0.1),
					B. Williams (1)

Winning Pitcher: Keagle (2–0)   Losing Pitcher: Menhart (0–1)
Save: B. Williams
Home Runs: (SEA) Jordan (1 on), Rodriquez (1 on)   (DET) Fryman (2 on), Trammell, Fielder (3 on)
Attendance: 42,932   Time: 3:05   Weather: Cloudy, 34 degrees, flurries

1997 (Monday, April 7)
After losing their last seventeen home games in 1996, the Tigers pounded Minnesota, 10–4, behind catcher Brian Johnson's four RBIs, which included a three-run homer in the fourth. Batterymate Justin Thompson started and got the victory, the first for a Detroit starter since the previous August 30—a span of thirty-three games. The Tigers, who were swept by the Twins in Minnesota before taking two of three in Chicago, boosted their record to 3–4 with the win. Biting winds, coupled with near-freezing temperatures, resulted in about ten thousand no-shows.

	R	**H**	**E**	**Pitchers**
Minnesota 100 001 200 —	4	9	3	Rodriguez (4), Aldred (2.1), Trombley (0.2), Guardado (0.1), Naulty (0.2)
Detroit 020 300 05x —	10	9	0	Thompson (6.2), Sager (1.1), Jones (1)

Winning Pitcher: Thompson (1–0) Losing Pitcher: Rodriguez (0–1)
Home Runs: (DET) Johnson (2 on)
Attendance: 42,749   Time: 2:55   Weather: Sunny, windy, 37 degrees

Bibliography

Ager, Susan. "The Fairy Tale Life of Tom Monaghan," *Detroit Free Press Magazine* (June 9, 1985).

Albom, Mitch. *The Live Albom*. Detroit: Detroit Free Press, 1988.

———. *Live Albom II*. Detroit: Detroit Free Press, 1990.

Alexander, Charles C. *Ty Cobb*. New York: Oxford University Press, 1984.

Allen, Lee. *The American League Story*. New York: Hill & Wang, 1962.

Angell, Roger. *Once More Around the Park: A Baseball Reader*. New York: Ballantine Books, 1991.

Angelo, Frank. *For the Children: A History of the Old Newsboys Goodfellows*. Detroit: Old Newsboys Goodfellow Fund, 1989.

Anderson, Sparky (with Dan Ewald). *Sparky!* New York: Prentice Hall Press, 1990.

Archer, Jim. "Fernando vs. The Bird: A Tale of Two Pitchers." *Baseball Research Journal* (1982).

Babson, Steve. *Working Detroit*. New York: Adama Books, 1984.

Bak, Richard. *Cobb Would Have Caught It: The Golden Age of Baseball in Detroit*. Detroit: Wayne State University Press, 1991.

———. *Turkey Stearnes and the Detroit Stars: The Negro Leagues in Detroit, 1919–1933*. Detroit: Wayne State University Press, 1994.

————. *Ty Cobb: His Tumultuous Life and Times.* Dallas: Taylor Publishing Co., 1994.

————. *Lou Gehrig: An American Classic.* Dallas: Taylor Publishing Co., 1995.

Barber, Red. *The Broadcasters.* New York: Dial Press, 1970.

Barrow, Ed. *My 50 Years in Baseball.* New York: Coward, McCann, 1951.

Batchelor, E. A. "D. A. C. Nines Were Country's Best." *D. A. C. News* (August 1925).

————. "Personal and Confidential: 'Ty' Tyson." *Detroit Saturday Night* February 7, 1931).

Beasley, Norman, and George W. Stark. *Made in Detroit.* New York: G. P. Putnam's Sons, 1957.

Beer, Matt. "Stormy Weather." *Detroit Monthly* (February 1987).

Bennett, Tom, et al. *The NFL's Official Encyclopedic History of Professional Football.* New York: Macmillan, 1977.

Benson, Michael. *Ballparks of North America: A Comprehensive Historical Reference to Baseball Grounds, Yards and Stadiums, 1845 to Present.* Jefferson, NC: McFarland & Co., 1989.

Betzold, Michael. "The House That Frank Built." *Detroit Free Press Magazine* (April 19, 1992).

Betzold, Michael, and Ethan Casey. *Queen of Diamonds: The Tiger Stadium Story.* West Bloomfield, Michigan: A & M Publishing Co., 1992.

Bingay, Malcolm. *Detroit Is My Own Home Town.* Indianapolis: Bobbs-Merrill, 1946.

————. *Of Me I Sing.* Indianapolis: Bobbs-Merrill, 1949.

Boyd, Brendan C., and Fred C. Harris. *The Great American Baseball Card Flipping, Trading and Bubble Gum Book.* Boston: Little, Brown & Co., 1973.

Broeg, Bob. *The Pilot Light and the Gas House Gang.* St. Louis: Bethany Press, 1980.

Bryan, Ford R. *Henry's Lieutenants.* Detroit: Wayne State University Press, 1993.

Bryson, Bill, and Leighton Housh. *Through the Years with the Western League, Since 1885.* Washington: Western League, 1951.

Cantor, George. *The Tigers of '68: Baseball's Last Real Champions.* Dallas: Taylor Publishing Co., 1997.

———. "The Green Green Grass of Home." *MICHIGAN: The Magazine of The Detroit News* (April 3, 1988).

Carney, Kim. *The Last, Best Detroit Tigers Fan.* Royal Oak, Michigan, 1991. Unpublished play.

Cauffiel, Lowell. "Squeeze Play." *Detroit Monthly* (May 1988).

Chafets, Ze'ev. *Devil's Night and Other True Tales of Detroit.* New York: Random House, 1990.

Chipp, Mel. "Inside-the-Park Home Runs." *Baseball Research Journal* (1980).

Cobb, Ty (with Al Stump). *My Life in Baseball: The True Record.* New York: Doubleday & Co., 1961.

Cochrane, Gordon S. *Baseball: The Fans' Game.* New York: Funk and Wagnalls, 1939.

Cohen, Richard M., David S. Neft, and Roland T. Johnson. *The World Series.* New York: Dial Press, 1976.

Conot, Robert. *American Odyssey.* New York: Wm. Morrow & Co., 1974.

Cope, Myron. *The Game That Was: An Illustrated Account of the Tumultuous Early Days of Pro Football.* New York: Thomas Y. Crowell, 1974.

Creamer, Robert W. *Babe: The Legend Comes to Life.* New York: Simon and Schuster, 1974.

Curran, Bob. *Pro Football's Rag Days.* New York: Bonanza Books, 1969.

Curran, William. *Big Sticks: The Phenomenal Decade of Ruth, Gehrig, Cobb, and Hornsby.* New York: Wm. Morrow and Co., 1990.

Cutting, A. J. " 'Old Slug' Went Down Swinging." *Heritage: A Journal of Grosse Pointe Life* (January 1989).

Daly, Bob, and Bob O'Donnell. *The Pro Football Chronicles.* New York: Collier Books, 1990.

Dewey, Donald, and Nicholas Acocella. *Encyclopedia of Major League Baseball Teams.* New York: Harper Collins, 1993.

Einstein, Charles (ed.). *The Baseball Reader.* New York: McGraw-Hill, 1983.

Falls, Joe. *Detroit Tigers.* New York: Collier Books, 1975.

———. "When the 'G-Men' Rallied a City." *MICHIGAN: The Magazine of The Detroit News* (June 5, 1983).

———. *The Detroit Tigers: An Illustrated History.* New York: Walker & Co., 1989.

Faulkner, Tom. "Balls, Strikes and Class Consciousness." *Detroit Free Press Magazine* (August 28, 1994).

Feller, Bob (with Bill Gilbert). *Now Pitching, Bob Feller.* New York: Birch Lane Press, 1990.

Fine, Sidney. *Frank Murphy: The Detroit Years.* Ann Arbor: University of Michigan Press, 1975.

———. "Chance and History: Some Aspects of the Detroit Riot of 1967." *Michigan Quarterly Review* (Spring 1986).

Fleming, G. H. *The Dizziest Season.* New York: Wm. Morrow & Co., 1984.

Freehan, Bill (with Steve Gelman and Dick Schaap). *Behind the Mask.* New York: Popular Library, 1970.

Fulk, David, and Dan Riley (eds.). *The Cubs Reader.* Boston: Houghton Mifflin Co., 1991.

Gerlach, Larry R. *The Men in Blue.* New York: Viking Press, 1980.

Goldstein, Richard. *Spartan Seasons: How Baseball Survived the Second World War.* New York: Macmillan, 1980.

Good, David L. "Detroit's Boys of Summer." *Detroit News Magazine* (April 5, 1981).

Green, Jerry. *Detroit Lions.* New York: Macmillan, 1973.

Greenberg, Hank (with Ira Berkow). *Hank Greenberg: The Story of My Life.* New York: Times Books, 1989.

Grimm, Joe. "The Next Best Thing to Playing Shortstop!" *Chronicle: The Quarterly Magazine of the Historical Society of Michigan* (Spring 1984).

Haig, Irv. "The Night It Rained Home Runs." *Baseball Digest* (March 1972).

Harrigan, Patrick. *The Detroit Tigers: Club and Community, 1945–1995.* Toronto: University of Toronto Press, 1997.

Harwell, Ernie. *Tuned to Baseball.* South Bend, Indiana: Diamond Communications, 1985.

Hawkins, John. *This Date in Detroit Tigers History.* Briarcliff Manor, N. Y.: Stein & Day, 1981.

Helyar, John. *Lords of the Realm.* New York: Villard Books, 1994.

Herskowitz, Mickey. *The Golden Age of Pro Football: A Remembrance of Pro Football in the 1950s.* New York: Macmillan, 1974.

Hill, Art. *I Don't Care If I Never Come Back*. New York: Simon and Schuster, 1980.

Honig, Donald. *Baseball When the Grass Was Real*. New York: Coward, McCann, Geoghagen, 1975.

———. *Baseball Between the Lines*. New York: Coward, McCann, Geoghagen, 1976.

———. *The Man in the Dugout*. Chicago: Follett, 1977.

Howard, Johnette. "No Relief." *Detroit Free Press Magazine* (February 21, 1988).

Hurlburt, John. "Detroit's Dazzling Debut." *Baseball Research Journal* (1980).

James, Bill. *The Bill James Historical Baseball Abstract*. New York: Villard Books, 1986.

Jordan, David M. *A Tiger in His Time*. South Bend, Indiana: Diamond Communications, 1991.

Kaline, Al (with George Vass). "The Game I'll Never Forget." *Baseball Digest* (May 1974).

Karras, Alex (with Herb Gluck). *Even Big Guys Cry*. New York: Holt, Rinehart & Winston, 1977.

Kermisch, Al. "From a Researcher's Notebook." *Baseball Research Journal* (1976).

Kerrane, Kevin. *The Hurlers*. Alexandria, Virginia: Redefinition Books, 1989.

Kirsch, George B. *The Creation of American Team Sports: Baseball & Cricket, 1838–72*. Urbana: University of Illinois Press, 1989.

Kool, Nancy. "Enlightenment and the Oldest Tiger." *Monthly Detroit* (April 1981).

Lansche, Jerry. *Glory Fades Away: The Nineteenth-Century World Series Rediscovered*. Dallas: Taylor Publishing Co., 1991.

Lapointe, Joe. "Detroit's Real Home Team." *Detroit Free Press Magazine* (September 23, 1984).

Levine, Peter. A. G. *Spalding and the Rise of Baseball*. New York: Oxford University Press, 1986.

Lieb, Fred. *Baseball As I Have Known It*. New York: Coward, McCann & Geoghegan, 1977.

———. *The Detroit Tigers*. New York: G. P. Putnam's Sons, 1946.

Linn, Ed. *Hitter: The Life and Turmoils of Ted Williams.* New York: Harcourt Brace & Co., 1993.

Lochbiler, Don. *Detroit's Coming of Age, 1873 to 1973.* Detroit: Wayne State University Press, 1973.

Lodge, John C. (with M. M. Quaife). *I Remember Detroit.* Detroit: Wayne State University Press, 1949.

Lowry, Philip J. *Green Cathedrals.* Cooperstown, N. Y.: Society for American Baseball Research, 1986.

Lutz, William W. *The News of Detroit.* Boston: Little, Brown & Co., 1973.

Mantle, Mickey (with Herb Gluck). *The Mick.* New York: Doubleday & Co., 1985.

McGraw, Bill. "The First Time." *Detroit Free Press Magazine* (April 5, 1987).

———. "One Hundred Years of Baseball in Detroit: Remembrance and Celebration." *Detroit Free Press Magazine* (April 5, 1981).

———. "Summer of '84." *Detroit Free Press Magazine* (April 3, 1994).

Mead, William B. *The Explosive Sixties.* Alexandria: Redefinition Books, 1989.

———. *Even the Browns.* Chicago: Contemporary Books, 1978.

Mosedale, John. *The Greatest of All: The 1927 New York Yankees.* New York: Dial Press, 1974.

Moss, Richard J. *Tiger Stadium.* Lansing: Michigan Department of State, 1976.

Murdock, Eugene. *Ban Johnson, Czar of Baseball.* Westport, Connecticut: Greenwood Press, 1986.

Murray, Mike (ed.). *Lions Pride: Sixty Years of Detroit Lions Football.* Dallas: Taylor Publishing Co., 1993.

Neft, David S., and Richard M. Cohen. *The Football Encyclopedia.* New York: St. Martin's Press, 1991.

Newcombe, Jack. "Black Mike of the Tigers." *Sport* (April 1960).

Nicholson, William G. "Bleacher Bums of Yesteryear." *Baseball Historical Review* (1981).

Obojski, Robert. *All-Star Baseball Since 1933.* New York: Stein & Day, 1980.

Okkonen, Marc. *Baseball Memories, 1900–1909.* New York: Sterling
    Publishing Co., 1992.

Pastier, John. "Diamonds Aren't Forever." *Historic Preservation*
    (July/August 1993).

Peterson, Joyce Shaw. *American Automobile Workers,* 1900–1933.
    Albany: State University of New York Press, 1987.

Reidenbaugh, Craig and Carter (eds.). *Take Me Out to the Ball Park.* St.
    Louis: The Sporting News, 1983.

Ribowsky, Mark. "Inside Track: Steve Kemp." *Inside Sports* (June 1982).

Rich, Marney. "The Fall and Fall of Denny McLain." *Detroit Monthly*
    (April 1986).

Smith, Curt. *Voices of the Game: The First Full Scale Overview of
    Baseball Broadcasting, 1921 to the Present.* South Bend, Indiana:
    Diamond Communications, 1987.

Smith, Fred. *The 995 Tigers.* Privately published, 1981.

———. *Tiger S.T.A.T.S.* Ann Arbor: Momentum Books, 1991.

Smith, Ron. *The Sporting News Chronicle of Baseball.* New York: BDD
    Illustrated Books, 1993.

Sobol, Ken. *Babe Ruth & the American Dream.* New York: Random
    House, 1974.

St. John, Bob. *Heart of a Lion: The Wild and Woolly Life of Bobby
    Layne.* Dallas: Taylor Publishing Co., 1991.

Strother, Shelby. *Saddlebags.* West Bloomfield, Michigan: A & M
    Publishing Co., 1991.

Stump, Al. *Cobb.* Chapel Hill, North Carolina: Algonquin Books, 1994.

Sugar, Bert R. *Hit the Sign and Win a Free Suit of Clothes from Harry
    Finkelstein.* Chicago: Contemporary Books, 1978.

Sullivan, George, and David Cataneo. *Detroit Tigers: The Complete
    Record of Detroit Tigers Baseball.* New York: Macmillan, 1985.

Thorn, John, and Pete Palmer (eds.). *Total Baseball.* New York: Warner
    Books, 1989.

Veeck, Bill (with Ed Linn). *Veeck—As in Wreck.* New York: Simon and
    Schuster, 1989.

Voelker, Don. "Michigan and Trumbull Before Baseball." *Michigan
    History Magazine* (July/August 1989).

Wagner, Bill. "The League That Never Was." *Baseball Research Journal* (1987).

Whittingham, Richard. *What a Game They Played.* New York: Harper & Row, 1984.

Whittingham, Richard (ed.). *The Fireside Book of Pro Football.* New York: Simon & Schuster, 1989.

"Why Our Hearts Belong to Baseball." *Detroit Free Press Magazine* (April 6, 1986).

Williams, Ted (with John Underwood). *My Turn at Bat.* New York: Simon & Schuster, 1988.

Wood, Bob. *Dodger Dogs to Fenway Franks.* New York: McGraw-Hill, 1988.

Woodford, Frank B. and Arthur M. Woodford. *All Our Yesterdays: A Brief History of Detroit.* Detroit: Wayne State University Press, 1969.

Wulf, Steve. "Detroit Jumped All Over 'Em." *Sports Illustrated* (October 22, 1984).

Young, Coleman (with Lonnie Wheeler). *Hard Stuff: The Autobiography of Mayor Coleman Young.* New York: Viking, 1994.

Zimbalist, Andrew. *Baseball and Billions.* New York: Basic Books, 1992.

Index

Bold indicates illustrated reference

Aaron, Hank, 316
Abbaticchio, Ed, 105
Abbott, Juliana Philinda, 55
Abstein, Bill, 105
Adams, Babe, 106–7
Adderly, Herb, 276
Advertising: at Bennett Park, 57,
    112; at Briggs Stadium, **206**; at
    Mack Park, 141; at Navin Field,
    141; radio-TV, 175, 222–3, 347,
    390; at Recreation Park, **12**, 25;
    at Tiger Stadium, 370, 397–8
Aetnas (Detroit), 22–3, 31
African National Congress, **352**
Agee, Claude, 238
Aguirre, Hank, 298, 305, 327
Akron Pros, 251
Alexander, Dale, 145–**146**, 147
Alexander, Doyle, 343, 346
All-England Eleven, 18

All-Star Games: (1941), 191–3, **200**,
    324; (1951) 217, 223, 316;
    (1971), 316
Alvord's gambling joint, 90
Amateur Athletic Union, 39
American Association, 43, 70,
    119–20
American Federation of Labor, 95
American Football League, 275, 281
American League, **69**–70, 72–9, 145,
    223, 230, 294, 315–6, 362, 374,
    380
American League Championship
    Series, 316; 1972 (Detroit-
    Oakland), 319–21; 1984
    (Detroit-Kansas City), 337;
    1987 (Detroit-Minnesota), 346,
    362
American Professional Football
    Association, 249–51. *See also*
    National Football League
American Revolution, 54–5

• 463 •

America's Agony, 293

Amole, Doc, 72

Anderson, Edwin J., 261

Anderson, Sparky, 85–6, 320–1, 334, 338, 340, 346–7, **354**, 362–3, 376, 381, 385, 395

Angus, Samuel, 75, 78, 80, 119

Antietam National Battlefield, 361

Arbitration, salary, 328–31, 343, 346–7

Archer, Mayor Dennis, 385–6, 393

Armour, Bill, **83**, 85

Associated Press, 341

Athletic Park, 66–8

Attendance, baseball: 380, 401–5; at Athletic Park, 67–8; at Bennett Park, 59–60, 68, 73, 75, 91–**96**, 97–8, 104–5, 113, 122; at Briggs Stadium, **180**, 186, 192, **198–9,** 201, 203, 209, 212–3, 215, 217, 219, 221, 236; at Burns Park, 76–8; at League Park, 42–3, 48; at Mack Park, 140, 144; at Navin Field, 122, 124, 127, **132**, 137–8, 145, 149–51, 154–5, 159–60, 162, 165, 167, 172, 179; at Recreation Park, 24, 29, 33; at River Rouge grounds, 68; at Tiger Stadium, 299–300, 309, 313, 316–20, 323, 337, 342–6, 370, 375, 381–2, 390, **396**–9; at Woodward Avenue grounds, 18, 20

Attendance, football: 248–9; at Briggs Stadium, 258–**263**, 266, 272–3; at Dinan Field, 254–6; at Navin Field, 252–4; at Silverdome, 288; at Tiger Stadium, 266, 284, 287

Auker, Eldon, 153, 162

Auto industry, 95–7, 123, 147–8, 325–6, 331

Baker, Del, 177, 189, 193

Baldwin, Lady, 32, **35**

Balsz, Lou, 42–3

Baltimore Colts, 271–2, **278**, 287

Baltimore Elite Giants, 203

Baltimore Orioles (American League), 305, 311, 316, 332–3, 344, 357, 369, 376, 381

Baltimore Orioles (National League), 45

Bando, Sal, 319

Barkley, Sam, 26

Barnard, E. S., 121–2

Barney, Lem, 281–**282**, 283

Barr, Terry, 276

Barrett, Jimmy, 62, 73

Barrow, Ed, 81–2

Barry, Dave, 19–20

Barry, Jack, **103**

Bartell, Dick, 195

Baseball America, 390

Baseball Chapel, 357

Baseball Writers Association, 94

Basic Agreement, 327–8, 371–2

Bassler, Johnny, 135, 137

Batchelor, Eddie, 39

Bat Day, **301**, 363–4

"Battle of the Overpass," 179

Baugh, Sammy, 258

Beaubien, Joseph, 52

Beckmann, Frank, 358

Belcher, Tim, 372, 381

Bell, Buddy, 386, 389–90, 398

Bell, George, 344

Bell, Jim, 241

Belle Isle, 176, 203, 251

Belle Isle Bridge, 96

Bench, Johnny, 316

Bennett, Charlie, 32, 34–**35**, 37, 45–6, 59, **114**

Bennett Park: **8**, **81–2**, **90–1**, **112**–5; advertisements, 57, 112; baseball attendance, 59–60, 68, 73, 75, 91–**96**, 97–8, 104–5, 113, 122; construction, 55–**56**, 57; expansion, 71, 94–5, 107; first doubleheader, 60; first game, 9–10, **50**, 58–9; first Sunday game, 91; football games, 249;

football gridiron laid out, 249; holiday doubleheaders, 60–1; origin of name, 57–8; outfield dimensions, 57, 95; rowdyism, 63–5, 111; seating capacity, 57, 94–5; ticket prices, 94–5, 107; torn down, 115, 117; wildcat stands, 107–**108**, 109–11; World Series games, **90–1**, 92–4, 97–**98**, 104–**106**, 107. *See also* Briggs Stadium, Navin Field, Tiger Stadium

Benton, Al, 199, 201

Benton, Jim, 261

Bergen, Mary, 166

Bergman, Dave, 335–6

Bersey, John S., 48

Bertoia, Reno, 347

Bess, Philip, 360

Bevacqua, Kurt, 337

Bingaman, Les, 268

Bingay, Malcolm, 75, 90, 120, 209–10. *See also* Iffy the Dopester

Black Bottom, 140–1

Black Sox scandal, 120

Blair, Paul III, 377

Blanda, George, 281

Blanding, Fred, 39

Bleachers, **162**–4, 185, 321–2, **349**, 360, 374

Blount, Tenny, 141

Blue, Lu, 138

Blue, Vida, 319, 321

Blue laws. *See* Sunday baseball

Bolling, Frank, 242

Book Cadillac Hotel, 210

Boone, Pat, 368

Borowy, Hank, 209

Boston Beaneaters, 45

Boston Red Sox, 125, 145, 228, 239, 305–6, 311, 316–9, 362

Boulevard Park. *See* League Park

Bowerman, Frank, 39

Bowman, A. C., 26

Box, Cloyce, 266

Brady, James J., 53–4, 259

Bressler, Rube, 88

Bridges, Tommy, 152–3, 166–9, 193, 199, 329, 358

Briggs, Mickey, 214, **218**, 371

Briggs, Spike, 215, **229**–30, **232**–3, 244–5

Briggs, Walter O., 77, 127, 151–2, 176–9, 181–**182**, 183–9, 201–3, 210–7, **224**, 226, 228–9, 233, 238, 242, 258–60, 351

Briggs Manufacturing Co., **182**–4, 229

Briggs Stadium: 189, 193, 196–7, **224–5**, 230, 233–**234**, 244, **262**–3, 270–1, 357; advertisements, **206**; All-Star Games, 191–3, **200**, 223; baseball attendance, **180**, 186, 193, 198–**199**, 201–3, 209,212–3, 215, 217, 219, 221, 236; first Lions game, 258; first Tigers game, 186; first night game, 215–**216**, 217; first television broadcast, 219–20; football attendance, 258–**263**, 266, 272–3; football gridiron laid out, 258; home runs hit out of, 192; largest crowds, 213; leased to Negro League teams, 203; maintenance, 184, **224**; name changed, 244–5; NFL playoff games, **246**, 267–**268**, 270–**274**; outfield dimensions, 185; parking, 237; prizefights, **194**, 202; seating capacity, 185; standing room only, 213; twilight starts, 202; World Series games, **197–8**, 199–201, 207–**208**, 209–10. *See also* Bennett Park, Navin Field, Tiger Stadium

Briggs Stadium Boycott Committee, 241

Briles, Nelson, 314

Brinkman, Eddie, 316, 319

Brock, Lou, **312**–4

Brodie, John, 272
Brogna, Rico, 399–400
Brookens, Tom, 332
Brooklyn Atlantics, 20
Brooklyn Dodgers, 218, 223, 225, 243, 356, 362. *See also* Los Angeles Dodgers
Brooklyn Excelsiors, 20, 22
Brooks Lumber Yard, 332
Brother Jonathan Wicket Club, 18
Brouthers, Dan, 27, 32–**35**, 45
Brown, Gates, 242, 299, 309, 327
Brown, Jimmy, 273
Brown, Kenyon, 292
Brown, Paul, 271, 273
Brown, Roger, 275, **277–8**
Brown, Three Finger, 92, 97
Brunet, George, 306
Brush, Alfred E., 26
Brush, Elijah, 24
Brush farm, 24, 26
Brusso, Noah. *See* Tommy Burns
Bruton, Billy, 296
Buelow, Fritz, 74
Bull Durham chewing tobacco, 112
Bullpen, 193–4, 238
Bunning, Jim, 234–5, 242, 298
Burke, Jimmy, 74
Burns, James, 42
Burns, James D., 71–**72**, 73–8, 89–91, 111
Burns, Tommy, 71
Burns Hotel, 71
Burns Park, 71, 75–8
Bush, Donie, 98–9, 125
Butler, Gold Brick, 59
Butsicaris, Jimmy, 297
Butzel Field, 184
Byrne, Bobbie, 105–6

Caddell, Ernie, 256
Cadillac, Antoine de la Mothe, 51
Cadillac Athletic Club, 71
Cadillaqua, 123
Cain, Bob, 226
Caldwell, Ray, **112**
California Angels, 305–7, 318

California League, 40
Callihan, Bill, **262**
Camden Yards, 369, 386
Cameron, William J., 99–102
Campaneris, Campy, 319
Campau, Bob, 44
Campau, Charles, 38
Campbell, Jim, 213, 293–4, 303, 316, 322, 327–30, 334, 349–50, 353, 355, 364, 367–8
Canton Bulldogs, 248, **253**
Capitol Records, 310
Carey, Paul, 357–8
Carlisle, Jack, 130
Carney, Kim, 361
Carr, Jay, 252
Carrigan, Bill, 92
Carroll, Cliff, 42
Cartwright, Alexander, 14
Casey, Doc, 72–4
Cash, Norm, **296**–99, 320, 329
Casinos, 392
Cass, Lewis, 16, 52
Cassady, Hopalong, 272
Cass Baseball Club, 22–3
Cass farm, 16
Cass Park, 16
Castillo, Marty, 336–7
Catholic Central High School, 259–**260**, 345
Cavanaugh, Mayor Jerry, 284
Cavaretta, Phil, 166, 169
Cedeno, Andujar, 390
Cepeda, Orlando, 313–4
Columbia Broadcasting System, 294
Chalmers, Hugh, 113
Chance, Frank, **98**
Chandler, Paul, 219–20
Chicago American Giants, 140, 203
Chicago Bears, 253–4, 256, 262, 276, 286–7
Chicago Cardinals, 258, 260–1
Chicago Cubs, 91–4, 97–8, 166–70, 207–**208**, 209–10, 212
Chicago White Sox, 22, 32, 113, 135, 137, 305, **308**, 381, 407
Children's Hospital, 297

Chipman, Judge J. Logan, 109
Christiansen, Jack, **265**–6, 289
Chrysler Corp., 229, 331
Church, Francis P., 102
Cieszkowski, Tom, 375
Cigarette girls, **174**
Cincinnati Reds, 62, 66, 197–201,
218, 320
Civil War, 18–9, 46
Clark, Danny, 137
Clark, Dutch, 255–**257**
Clark, Tony, **387**, 391
Clark Park, 78, 251
Clemens, Roger, 391
Clemente, Roberto, 316
Cleveland Browns, 246, 266–**268**,
270–1
Cleveland Bulldogs, 254
Cleveland Indians, 121–3, 139,
193–4, 203–4, 230, 243–4, **302**,
304, 316, 372, 380–1, 390
Cleveland Rams, 261. *See also* Los
Angeles Rams
Clifton, Flea, 167, 169
Clinton Elementary School, 366
Clutterbuck, Bryan, 377
Cobb, George, 42
Cobb, Ty, **6**, 39, **83**–9, 92, 97, **103**–4,
106, 112–3, **116**, 120, 122–3,
127–8, 130, 133–**134**, 135–40,
145, 225, 239, 329, 398
Cobo, Albert, 230
Cochrane, Mickey, 151–**153**, **155**,
157–8, 164, 166–9, 177, 186–7,
214
Cochrane Plan, 359
Codd, George, 39, 89
Cogdill, Gail, 275
Colavito, Rocky, 244, **296**, 298–9
Coleman, Joe, 316, 319–21
Collins, Eddie, 193
Collins, Ripper, 159, 163
Colorado Rockies, 383
Columbus (Western League), 58–9,
62
Columbus Panhandles, 249–50
Comiskey, Charles, 70, 73

Comiskey Park, 113
Common Ground Coalition, 364
Concessions, 107, 130–1, **171**, 203,
260, 340
Connolly, Tommy, 181
Conroy, Wid, **81**
Conway, Neil, 135–6, 215
Conway, Pete, **35**
Conzelman, Jimmy, **248**, 252–4
Cooke, Frederick A., **28**
Cooley High School, 367
Cooney, Johnny, 139
Cooper, Andy, 140
Coors Field, 383
Corktown, 53–4, 285
Corrigan Field, 251
Cosell, Howard, 221
"Couch Potatoes," 368
Coughlin, Father Charles, 189
Coveleski, Harry, 125
Craig, Roger, 347
Craig, William, 16
Cramer, Doc, 191, 201, 203
Crawford, Wahoo Sam, 79–80, **87**–9,
92, 97, 105, **112**–3, 329
Creekmur, Lou, 265–6
Cricket, 17–8, 238
Cronin, Joe, 62
Cronin, John, 72
Crosley Field, 113, 199–200, 215
Croul, Frank, 89–92
Crowder, Alvin, 159
Crowley, William S., 39
Cruz, Deivi, 398
Curtis, Chad, 381
Custer, Camp, 250
Cycle, hitting for the, 61–2

Dallas Cowboys, 284, 288
Daniels, Pepper, 140
Dauss, Hooks, 125, 132, **134**
David, Jimmy, 266, 274–5
Dayton Cadets, 249
Dayton Triangles, 250–1, 261
Dean, Dizzy, 159–**161**, 162, 221, 309
Dean, Paul, 159–**161**
Dearborn Independent, 102

Deer, Rob, 363
Delahanty, Jim, 99
DeLancey, Bill, 160
DeMan Brothers, 55
Denby High School, 260
Denny McLain at the Organ, 310
Deppert, John, Jr., 107, 109
Dequindre Park, 143
Derby, George, 30
Derringer, Paul, 199–200
Designated hitter, 145
Detroit: auto industry, 95–7, 123,
    147–8, 325–6; black popula-
    tion, 127, 140–41, 202,
    238–42, 325; city described, 28,
    30, 42, 51–5, 97, 325–7; crime,
    130–2, 327; defense work, 202;
    early amusements, 14–5, 54;
    economic conditions, 43–5,
    51–5, 147–51, 251, 325–6;
    expansion, 51–4; founding, 51;
    freeway systems, 237, 300;
    growth of suburbs, 236–7, 300;
    labor unrest, 179, 183–4; popu-
    lation, 52–5, 75; riots, 203–4,
    301–**304**, 305; urban renewal,
    223, 392–3
Detroit Amateur Baseball
    Federation, 251
Detroit Architectural Iron Works,
    118
Detroit Athletic Club, 23, 38–9, **41**,
    43, 70, 183
Detroit Baseball Club, 15–6, 19, 25
Detroit Board of Commerce, 121
Detroit City Railway, 26
Detroit Cougars, 309
Detroit Creams, 42–6. *See also*
    Detroit Tigers
Detroit Free Press, 15–6, 19, 22–3,
    46–7, 83, 142, 187, 209–10,
    216–7, 250–1, 381
Detroit Heralds, 249–51
Detroit Light Guard, 46–8
Detroit Light Guard Armory, 47
Detroit Light Guard band, 19, 48

Detroit Lions: 228–9, 245;
    announce new downtown stadi-
    um, 392–3; franchise moved
    from Portsmouth, 255; join
    Central Division, 281; largest
    crowds, 266; last scoreless tie,
    261; lineup integrated, 261–2;
    move to Briggs Stadium, 257–8;
    move to Pontiac, 284–6, 288–9;
    postseason games, **246**, 256,
    267–**268**, 270–**274**, 275–6, 284;
    radio broadcasts, 221, 255–6;
    smallest crowds, 261; sold, 259,
    261, 280; Thanksgiving Day
    games, 247–8, 256, 261, **265**–6,
    276–**277**, 279, 281, 287
Detroit Mystics, 251
Detroit News, 99–102, 212, 219–20,
    230, 237, 282, 307, 371
Detroit Opera House, 166
Detroit Panthers, 247, 252–4
Detroit Red Wings, 228–9, 256,
    375–6
Detroit Riding and Hunt Club, 176
Detroits (cricket team), 17
Detroits (baseball team), 19–22
Detroit Stars, 140–**141**, 142–6, 249,
    382
Detroit Tiger Tales, 210, 224
Detroit Tigers: announce new down-
    town stadium, 392–3; break
    ground on new stadium, 399;
    controversy over new stadium,
    358–61, 370–1, 382–9; finances,
    127, 149, 176, 211–2, 359, 370,
    372, 375–6; first airplane flight,
    223; first world's championship,
    166–70; free agency, 328–31,
    335, 342–3, 372; home uniform,
    243; interleague play, 398; join
    American League, **69**–70; length
    of games, 362–3; lineup inte-
    grated, 238–42; origin of nick-
    name, 46–8; payroll, 372, 376,
    381, 390, 394; postseason play,
    90–1, 92–3, 97–**98**, 104–**106**,

107, 159–**161**, 162–4, **165**–6, **168**–70, **197–8**, 199–200, 207–**208**, 209–10, **312**–4, 319–21, 337–**338**, 340–**342**; replacement players, 376–8; rivalry with Yankees, 133–**134**, 135, 138, 155–**156**, 157–8, 213–4, **219**, 294–**295**, 296–8; set strikeout record, 363, 391; sold, 67, 70–1, 75, 80, 94, 127, 176, 229–33, 292–3, 332–**333**, 364–6; standings, 401–4; value assessed, 393; Western League days, 40, 42–**50**, 55–**63**, 64. *See also* Detroit Creams

Detroit Tigers (football team), 247, 250–1

Detroit Tigers museum, 354

Detroit Times, 207, **232**, 256

Detroit Wolverines: **27–8**, 29–**35**, **36**–8, 66, 107, 109, 340; first game, 30; organized, 29; profits and losses, 30, 37–8; sold, 37–8; uniforms, 30–1; World Series, 33–**35**, **36**–7

Detroit Wolverines (football team), 254–5

Detroit Wolves, 145

Devil's Night, 327

DeWitt, Bill, 243

Dickey, Bill, 189

Dietz, Mike, 398

Dillon, Pop, 73–4

DiMaggio, Joe, 193, **200**, 214, **226**

Dinan Field, 254–7, 259, 263

Divine Child High School, 260

Doane, Dinger, 252

Dobson, Pat, 299

Doby, Larry, 226, 241

Dodge Main, 326

Doherty, John 389

Domino's Pizza, 332, 359

Donovan, Wild Bill, 79–80, 89, 105–6

"Don't Die on Third," 99–102

Doran, Jim, **268**, 270–1

Dorgan, Mike, 30

Doubleday, Abner, 13

Doubleheaders, 60–1, 151, 179, 212–3, 242–3

Dow, Bill, 368

Dowling, Pete, 73

"Down on the Corner," 368

Downtown Development Authority, 383–6, 392

Duluth Eskimos, 253

Dumon, E. E., 16

Dunedin, Florida, 377

Dungan, Sam, 44, 62–**63**

Dunlap, Fred, **35**

Durocher, Leo, 159

Dykes, Jimmy, **240**, 242–4

Eagle Art Gallery, 28

The Eagles, 368

Earl, Howard, 42

Early Risers, 16, 25

Easter, Luke, 241

Eastern Market, 49

Easterly, Ted, 122

Ebbets Field, 113, 218

Economic Club of Detroit, 359

Edison Electric Light Co., 26

Egan, Wish, 62, 184

Elberfeld, Kid, 62, 68–9, 73–4

Emmerich, Mike, 321

Engler, Gov. John, 377

ESPN, 294

Evans, Billy, 160

Evans, Darrell, 335–6, 340–1, 346

Everitt, Barney, 182

Everitt, Bill, 42

Evers, Hoot, 62, 184, 212–4, **219**, 223

Excelsiors (Chicago), 19–20

Excelsiors (Detroit), 22–3

Fairview Greens apartments, 145

Family Value Nights, 382

Fan Appreciation Day, 347, 368

Farkas, Andy, 258

Farmer, Silas, 53–4

Farr, Mel, 281
Faulkner, Tom, 373–4
Fears, Tom, 267
"Fearsome Foursome," 275, **278**
Federal League, 120, 124–5
Feller, Bob, 196–7
Fenway Park, 113, 117, 369
Ferry, Dexter, 16, 20–2
Ferry, Tony, 58
Fetzer, John, 230–**233**, 243, 291–4,
    306–7, 332–**333**, 347, 349–51,
    355, 358
Fidrych, Mark, 323, **324**–5, 330–1
Fielder, Cecil, 362, 366, 387, 390
Fife, Lyle, 261
Fifield, Jack, 67,
Fires, ball park, 142–**143**
Fireworks, **311**, 368
First World War, 127, **130**
Fisher, Ray, 112
Flagpole, **36**, 122, 146, 399
Flat Rock, 325
Flood, Curt, 314–5
Florida Marlins, 398
Fogarty, John, 368
Folsom, Frank, 16
Forbes Field, 104, 113
Ford Expressway, Edsel, 237
Ford, Henry, 95–7, 102, **155**
Ford, Henry II, 229
Ford, William Clay, 280, 284–6, 350,
    392
Ford, William Clay Jr., 392
Ford, Edsel, **155**
Ford Sunday Evening Hour, 102
Forest Citys (Cleveland), 21–2
Fort Dearborn, 54
Fort Pontchartrain, 51
Fortune, 353
Foster, Rube, 140, 141, 145
Fothergill, Bob, 62
"Four Horsemen," 252
Fox, Pete, 160, 166, 179
Fox Theater, 365, 399
Foxtown plan, 370–1
Foxx, Jimmie, **188**

Foytack, Paul, 242
Franklin Baseball Club, 15
Free agency, 328–31, 335, 342–3,
    372
Freehan, Bill, 299, **304**, **312**, 314–5,
    329
Fregosi, Jim, 306
French, Larry, 167–8
Frey, Glenn, 368
Friedman, Bennie, 254–5
Frisch, Frankie, 159, 164–**165**
Fryman, Travis, 62, 361, 376,
    379–81, 391
Fuentes, Tito, 328
Fyfe, Richard, **15**–7

Gaedel, Eddie, 230
Gainor, Del, 122
Galan, Augie, 169
Gallico, Paul, 163–4
Galvin, Pud, 31
Gambling, 30
Game of the Week, 221
Ganzel, Charlie, **35**
Garbey, Barbero, 336
Garland Stove Company, 25
Garvey's Stockyard Hotel, **76**–77
Gas House Gang, 159–61, **162**–4,
    165–6
Gatewood, Bill, 140
Gehrig, Lou, 154–**156**, 189–**190**, 191
Gehringer, Charlie, 62, 148, **153**–4,
    160, 166, 169, 177–**178**, 179,
    193–4, **195**–6, 229–30, 329
General Motors, 326, 392
Gentry, Rufus, 185
Gettysburg, Battle of, 18
Getzien, Pretzels, **28**, 31, **35**, 37
Gibbons, Jim, 275
Gibson, Bob, 313–5
Gibson, Kirk, 332, 337–**339**,
    340–**342**, 343–7, 381–2
Gibson, Sam, 139
Giddings, Judge James, 389
Gilmer, Harry, 279–**280**
Glanville, Jerry, 287–8

Gleason, Kid, 73–4
Glenalvin, Bob, 42, **44**
Glenn, Brandon, 399
Goebel Brewery, 222–3
Gold, Bernard, 232
Goodfellows football game, 233, 259–**260**
Goodfellows Fund, 53–4, 259–60
Gomez, Chris, 362
Gomez, Lefty, 157–8
Gone With the Wind, 356
"Goosebusters," 340
Gordon, Joe, 244
Gordon, Tom, 391
Goslin, Goose, 152–**153**, 157, 160, 166–7, 169
Gossage, Goose, 340
Grace Hospital, 26
Graham, Otto, 270–1
Grand Circus Park, 17, 223, 386
Grand Rapids (Western League), 60, 63–4, 70, 79
Grand Trunk Railroad, 67
Grange, Red, 253–4
Great Depression, 147–51
Green, George, 111
Green Bay Packers, 247, 253, **265**–6, 273, 276–**277**, 279, 283
Greenberg, Hank, **153**–4, 159–60, 166–7, 186–**188**, 189, 194–5, 201, 206–7, 209, 212–3, 341
Gregg, Vean, 122
Griffith, Clark, 158
Groomes, Mel, 261
Gross, Emil, 26, 29
Groth, Johnny, 184, 214
Ground rules: at Burns Park, 76; at League Park, 48; at Navin Field, 136; at Recreation Park, 29, 33–4
Grounds keepers, **174**, 184, **224**
Grove, Lefty, 187
Groza, Lou, 270
Grubb, Johnny, 336
Gutowsky, Ace, 256

Hack, Stan, 167–8
Hadley, Bump, 177
Hahn, Noodles, 62
Halas, George, 253
Hamilton, Earl, 72
Hammond Building, 42
Hamtramck, 54, 143–4, 263–4
Hamtramck High School, 259–60
Hamtramck Stadium, 143–5
Hand, Jack, 299
Hanlon, Ned, 32, 34–**35**, 45
Hansen, Harry, 233, 244
Harder, Mel, **178**
Harder, Pat, 267
Hard Rock Cafe, 392
Harper, George, 42
Harper, Walter, 26
Harper Hospital, 26, 32–3
Harris, Bucky, 151, 233
Harris, Fran, 220
Harris, W. W., 68
Hart, John, 380
Hart, Leon, 266–7
Hart Plaza, 51
Hartnett, Gabby, 167
Harvey, Doug, 314
Harwell, Ernie, 223, **298**, 302, 323–4, 355–8, 367
Hayes, Edgar, 152, **232**
Hegan, Mike, 62
Heilmann, Harry, **134**, 136–7, 173, 175, 217, 223, 329
Helms, Bubba, 341, 355
Hendrick, George, 321
Hendrie, George, 26
Henneman, Mike, 376, 381
Herman, Billy, 166–7, 169
Hernandez, Willie, 335–7
Herndon, Larry, 337, 344
Heydler, John, 145
Higgins, Pinky, 194, 199
Higginson, Bobby, 391, 394, 398
Higham, Dick, 30
Hill, Art, 191, 221–2
Hill, Ken, 389

Hill, Pete, 140
Hiller, John, 299
Hilltop Park, 123
Hinchman, Ford, 20
Hoerner, Joe, 314
Hoernschemeyer, Hunchy, 266–7
Hogsett, Chief, 147, 152
Holcomb, Doc, 282
Hollinger, W. M., 24
Hollinger's Nine, 24–7
Holmes, Ducky, 72–3
Holy Sepulchre Cemetery, 176
Homestead Grays, 203
Hoot Robinson's, 375
Horning, Steamer, 249
Hornung, Paul, 276
Horton, Tony, **304**
Horton, Willie, 241, 299–**300**, 303,
    313–5, 329
Houck, Sadie, 30
Houk, Ralph, 321
House, Frank, 184
Houtteman, Art, 184
Howard, Frank, 317
Howell, Roy Lee, 336
Hubert H. Humphrey Metrodome,
    346
Hudson Co., J. L., 15, 25, 237, **311**,
    326
Hughes, Chuck, 286–7
Hulbert, William, 30–1
Hunkin & Conkey, 118
Hunter, Brian, 394, 398–9
Hunter, Catfish, 319
Husting, Pete, 73–4
Hutchinson, Fred, 201, 214

I Don't Care If I Never Come Back,
    221–2
Iffy the Dopester, 209–10. *See also*
    Malcolm Bingay
Ilitch, Marian, 367
Ilitch, Mike, 364, **365**–72, 375–6,
    382–92, 399
Independence Hall, 361
Indianapolis (Western League),
    64–5, 73, 79

International League, 38
Irish Saloon, 375

Jackson, Joe S., 83, 94
Jackson, Reggie, 316, 319, 321
Jackson, Shoeless Joe, 122
Jamieson, Charlie, 139
Javier, Julian, 314
Jayne Playfield, 263–4
Jehovah's Witnesses, 352
Jennings, Hughie, 45, **85**–6, **98**, 127
Joe Louis Arena, 284, 349–50, 375–6
"John Deere Farm Report," 347
Johnson, Ban, 40, 48, 68–79
Johnson, Don, **208**
Johnson, Walter, 120
John, Tommy, **308**
Jones, Bumpus, 59
Jones, Ruppert, 336
Jones, Tom, 99, 105
Jones, Capt. W. V., 17
Joseph, Bernard, 131
Joseph, Walter, 131
Junker, Steve, 273
Jurges, Billy, 168

Kaline, Al, 234–5, 242, **295–6**, 298,
    310–4, 313, 318, 320, 327–9,
    358, 368–9
"Kaline's corner," **303**
Kansas City (Western League), 79,
    83
Kansas City Chiefs, 288
Kansas City Monarchs, 142–4, 203
Kansas City Royals, 337
Karras, Alex, 273, 275
KDKA (Pittsburgh radio station),
    172
Keeler, Wee Willie, 45, 86
Kell, George, **211**, 214–7, 222–3,
    298, 355–8
Kelsey, John, 39, **43**, 127
Keltner, Ken, 196–7
Kemp, Steve, 329, **330**–2
Key, Jimmie, 344
Kids' Row, 382
Killebrew, Harmon, 316

Killian, Ed, 89
King, Charles Brady, 95
King, Harvey, 16
Kinscherf, Carl, 261
Kiss, 369
Klein, Joe, 372, 385
Knickerbocker Baseball Club, 14
Knoop, Bobby, 306
Knorr, Fred A., 230–3, 292–3
Kolloway, Don, **226**
Kreig, Billy, 42
Kretlow, Lou, 184
Kreuter, Chad, 381
Kuenn, Harvey, **228**, **231**, 234–5,
    242–4
Kuhn, Bowie, 349
Kuntz, Rusty, 336–7, 340

Ladies Day, **150**, 243
LaFonde's Cigar Store, 186
Lajoie, Bill, 330, 334–5, 342
Lajoie, Nap, 113
Lambeau, Curly, 253
Lamonica, Daryle, 281
Landis, Judge Kenesaw Mountain,
    120, 138, 163–**165**
Landry, Greg, 281, 286
Lane, Frank, 244
Lane, Night Train, 275
Lane, Ray, 302–3, 358
Lary, Frank, **231**, 234–5, **240**, 243,
    276, 296
Lary, Yale, 264, 266, **269**–70
"The Last, Best Detroit Tigers Fan,"
    361
Lathers, Chick, 39
Lavelli, Dante, 270
Layne, Bobby, 262–**264**, 265–75
Leadley, Bob, 38
League Park, 42–6, **47**–9, 96
Lebeau, Dick, 275
Lee, Bill, 166
LeFlore, Ron, **322**–3
Leland Hotel, 203
Lemon, Bob, 72
Lemon, Chet, 331–2
Leno, Jay, 390

Leonard, Emil (Dutch), 205
Leonard, Hub (Dutch), 72, 138
Letterman, Dave, 390
Levin, Doron, 381
Lerchen, Bill, 39
Lezcano, Sixto, 322
Libby, Steve, 26
Lieb, Fred, 138
Life, 218
Lincoln, Abraham, 18
Lindbergh, Charles, 172
Lindell A. C., 297
Lipon, Johnny, 184, 201, 214
Little Caesar's Pizza, 365–6
Lodge, John C., 39, **41**, 89
Lofton, Kenny, 380
Lolich, Mickey, 299, 305, 313–6,
    318, 327
Lombardi, Ernie, 199
Lopez, Al, 233
Lopez, Aurelio, 336
Los Angeles Dodgers, 239
Los Angeles Rams, 266–7, 272, 283
Louis, Joe, **194**, 202
Lucci, Mike, 248
Lynn, Fred, 321

MacArthur, General Douglas, 227
Mack, Connie, 73, 151, 242, 381
Mack Park, 125, 140–**141**, 142–**143**,
    145, 250
Mady, Charles, 393
Magi, Vince, 367
Majestic Building, 71
Malnar, Jerry, 69
Mandel, Fred, 259, 261
Mandela, Nelson, **352**
Mann, Bob, 261–2
Manion, Clyde, 137
Mann, Bob, 261–2
Mansion House, 52
Mara, Tim, 255
Marine Corps, 356, 367
Maris, Roger, 294
Marsh, Joseph A., 31
Marshall, Bill, 250
Marshall, George, 258

Martin, Billy, 316, **320**–1
Martin, Charlie, 185–6
Martin, Pepper, 159, 163
Mascot, 382
"Massachusetts game," 14
Matchick, Tom, 299
Mathews, Eddie, 305, 307
Maxwell, Charlie, **239**, 242–3
May, James, 52
Maybury, William C., 66
Mayo, Eddie, 205, 207
Mazda, 325
McAllister, Lew, 72
McAuliffe, Dick, 302, 306–7, **308**–9,
    314, 320, 329
McCafferty, Don, 286–7
McCarthy, Charlie, 89
McCarthy, Eugene, 352
McCarver, Tim, 313–5
McCauley, Pat, 61–2
McCosky, Barney, 148–9, 184,
    191–2, 195, 201, **211**, 214
McDevitt, John, 353
McGraw, Bill, 315
McGraw, John, 45, 381
McGraw, Thurman, 266
McGrucken, Joe, 42
McHale, John, 232–3, **260**
McHale, John Jr., 382–3, 386, 394
McKinstry, Major David, 54
McLain, Denny, 299, 309–14,
    316–**317**
McLeod, Alex, 59
McMillan, Bo, 261, 263–4, 266
McMillan, James, 25–6
McMillan, Grace, 26
McSorley, J. B., 26
McWhirter, Nicki, 371
Medwick, Ducky, 159, **162**–4, **165**
Memorial Day, 60
Meusel, Bob, 62, 133
M'Fingal, 54
Michigan and Trumbull Avenues, 54.
    See also Bennett Park, Briggs
    Stadium, Navin Field, Tiger
    Stadium

Michigan Central Station, 210
Michigan Liquor Dealers Protective
    Association, 44
Michigan Radio Network, 173
"Milk Duds Tiger Trivia Quiz," 347
Miller, Marvin, 327, 330
Milliken, Governor William, 284
Mills, Merrill B., 38
Milwaukee (American League team),
    73–4, 79
Milwaukee Brewers, 316, 321–2,
    344, 373–4, 391
Minneapolis (Western League), 60,
    67–8, 79
Minnesota Twins, 305, 362, 389
Minnesota Vikings, 266, 286
Minor leagues, 221, 241, 367
Mitchell, Margaret, 356
Mize, John, 226
Monaghan, Tom, 332–**333**, 353–5,
    359, 364
Monday Night Football, 288
Moore, Mike, 376
Moriarty, George, 92, 99–**101**, 105,
    139, 145, 152
Morrall, Earl, 274
Morris, Jack, 332–3, 336–7, 343,
    346–**348**, 362
Morton, C. H., 26
Moss, Dick, 330–1, 343
Mossi, Don, 242
Motown Records, 326
Mount Clemens, 66–8
Mullin, George, 72, 89, 98–9, 105–6,
    112, 123, **126**
Mullin, Pat, 201
Murphy, Bob, 207
Murphy, Frank, 158
Museum of African American
    History, 392
Music Hall, 392
Mutuals (Jackson), 23
Myatt, Glenn, 139

Nagurski, Bronco, 256
Nance, Bill, 73

National Agreement, 70, 73, 78

National Association of Baseball Players, 15–6, 19–20

National Association of Professional Baseball Players, 23–4

National Bank of Detroit, 231–3

National Football League, 250–89, 338. *See also* American Professional Football Association

National Hockey League, 375–6

National Labor Relations Board, 377–8

National League, 24, 29–40, 43, 66, 70, 78–9, 145, 223, 398

National Police Gazette, 28

National Register of Historic Places, 359

National Trust for Historic Preservation, 361, 383

Naumoff, Paul, 281

Navarre, Francis, 52

Navarre, Robert, 51–2

Navin, Frank, 44, 80–2, 89–**93**, 94–5, 107–15, 117–**118**, 119–24, 127, 137–8, 142, 149–51, 160–1, 164–7, 170–**171**, 172, 175–6, 181–2, 237, 252

Navin, Grace, 176

Navin, Thomas J., 44, 70, 119–20

Navin Field: **148–149**, **156**–7, 187, 358; baseball attendance, 122, 124, **132**, 137–8, 149–51, 154–5, 159–60, 162, 165, 167, 172, 179; concessions, 130–1, **171**; construction, 117–9, **121**; expansion, 137–8, 176–**178**, 185; first game, 117, 122–3; flagpole, 122, 146; football attendance, 251, 253; football games, 249–54; ground rules, 136; Ladies Day, **150**; name changed, 186; opera concerts, 165–6; origin of name, 115; outfield dimensions, 122, 176–7;

parking, 237; radio broadcasts, **148**–9, 172–3, 175; rowdyism, 133, 158, **162**–165; seating capacity, 122, **131**, 137–8, 176; smallest crowd, 145; Ty Cobb Day, 139; ticket prices, 138; staging area during First World War, **130**; World Series games, 159–**161**, **162**–4, 165, 166–**168**, 169–70. *See also* Bennett Park, Briggs Stadium, Tiger Stadium

Negro leagues, 140–**141**, 142–5, 202–3

Neil Park, 78

Neun, Johnny, 138–9

Nevers, Ernie, 253

Newberry, John S., **15**–6, 25–6

Newhouser, Hal, 184, 205, 207–**208**, 209–10, 212, 214, 217, 329, 399

New Jersey Athletic Club, 39

Newsom, Bobo, **196**–9, 201

New York Athletic Club, 39

New York Cubans, 203

New York Daily News, 163–4

"New York game," 14

New York Giants, 223, 356

New York Giants (football team), 256, 261, 276

New York Mets, 390

New York Times, 270–1

New York Yankees, 133–**134**, 135, 138, **156**–8, 205, 212–4, 219, **240**, 242, 294–5, 311, 316, 323, 340, 358, 375, 390, 399

Nicknames, 30, 40, 46–8, 57–8, 73, 83, 94, 152, 154, 158–9, 187, 235, 243, **278**

Night games, 144, 215–**216**, 217, 236

Nokes, Matt, 343

Nonowski, Jim, 274

No-hitters, 31, 72, 126, 137, **227**, 297, 409

Northland, 237

Northrup, Jim, 299, 305, 309, 315, 320

Northwestern Association of
 Baseball Players, 19
Northwestern Baseball Tournament,
 19–20
Northwestern High School, 299
Northwestern League, 38

Oakland Athletics, 310, 319–21
Oakland Raiders, 248, 281
Odenwald, Jeff, 347
Olivares, Omar, 389
Olympia Stadium, 299
Olympic Games, 284
O'Neill, Steve, 204, **206**
Opening day: at Bennett Park, **50**,
 58–9, 62, 64–5, 72–3, 407–13;
 at Briggs Stadium, **180**, 186,
 244–5, 425–35; at League Park,
 42–3, 46, 48; at Navin Field,
 117, 122–3, **124–5, 178**, 414–25;
 at Recreation Park, 24–7, 30; at
 Tiger Stadium, 355, 377–**379**,
 380–1, 436–54
Opera Under the Stars, 165–6
Orchestra Hall, 341
Organ music, 310–1, 368
Orrell, Joe, 201
Osborn Engineering Co., 117–8, 176
Osborn, Gene, 358
O'Toole, Patsy, 158
Ott, Mel, 222
Overall, Orvie, 97
Overflow crowds, **8**, 29, 73–4, **90–1,
 96**, 122, **124–5**, 137–8, **156–8**,
 213
Owen, Marv, **153, 156**, 163, 167,
 169
Owens, Brick, 160
Owens, Steve, 281, **285**
Owens Park, 38
Oyler, Ray, 299, **302**, 309
Ozadowsky, Samuel. *See* Patsy
 O'Toole

Page, Joe, 214
Paige, Satchell, 140, 203

Paradise Valley, 203
Parker, Buddy, **246**, 256, **264**, 266–7,
 270–1
Parking, 237, 360, 367
Parrish, Lance, 332–4, 342–3, **348**
Pasek, Johnny, 151
PASS, 358, 370
Passeau, Claude, 192, 209
Pastor, Bob, **194**
Patrick, Van, 221–3, 278, 355
Pavlik, Roger, 389
Paws, 382
Pearl Harbor, 201, 215
Pecatonica (baseball team), 19
Peirce, David R., 16, 47
Peninsulars (cricket team), 17
Perfect game, 137
Petry, Dan, 332, 336
Petway, Bruce, 140
Philadelphia Athletics, 138–9, 215–7
Philadelphia Phillies, 334–5, 343,
 399–400
Phillips, Tony, 361, 376, 381
Pierce, Billy, 184
Pietrosante, Nick, 275–6
Pillette, Herman, 137
Pingree, Hazen S., 44, 46
Pittsburgh Pirates, 78–9, 104–7,
 212–3
Pittsburgh Steelers, 273
Playoffs, 316–7, 371. *See also*
 American League
 Championship Series
Plum, Milt, 274, 276, **280**
Poletown plant, 326
Political rallies, **352**
Pollard, Fritz, 251
Pontchartrain Hotel, 349
Pontiac, Chief, 55
Pontiac, Michigan, 284–6, **288**
PONY League, 367
Portsmouth Spartans, 255
Press facilities, 29, 94, 138, 185,
 213, 357, 393
Price, Jim, 310
Pride, Curtis, 391

Programs, game, **2**, **200**
Prohibition, 130–2
Promotions, ballpark, **301**, 347,
   363–4, 371, 382, 390, 397–8
Purple Gang, 131–2

Quigley, Capt., 55

Radcliffe, Ted, 140
Radio broadcasts, **148**–9, 153,
   170–3, 175, 255–6, 292, 302–3,
   355–8
Rapid Railway, 67
Rashid, Frank, 359
Rathbun, Bob, 358
Reach Baseball Guide, 104, 169–70
"A Real, Live Regular Town," 123
Recreation Park, **12**, 25–**32**, 33–4,
   36–8, 49, 107, 109
Recreation Park Co., 24–6
Reid, Philip, 46
Remick & Co., Jerome, 123
Renaissance Center, 392
Reuther, Walter, 179
Revolvers, 20
Reynolds, Debbie, 332
Rice, Fred, 189–91
Richards, George A., 255–**257**, 259
Richardson, Hardy, **27**, 32, **35**
Riots, 203–**204**, 301–**304**, 305
River Rouge grounds, 68
Riverside Park, 38
Rizzs, Rick, 358
Rizzuto, Phil, 214
Robertson, Charlie, 72, 137
Robeson, Paul, 251
Robinson, Bobbie, 144
Robinson, Frank, 316
Robinson, Jackie, 223, 225
Robinson, Theodore, 15
Rock Island Independents, 252–3
Rodriquez, Aurelio, 316
Roesink, John, 124–5, 141, 143–4,
   249–51
Rogell, Billy, **153**, **157**–8, 192, 195,
   230

Rolfe, Red, 226
Rolling Stone, 323
Roosevelt, Franklin D., 158
Rosetti Associates, 353
Rossman, Claude, 89
Rote, Tobin, 248, 271–**274**
Rounders, 14
Rowdyism, 22–3, 63–6, 76–7, 92,
   133, 158–9, **162**–3, 164–**165**,
   280, 307, 321–2, 341, **379**–81
Rowe, Jack, 32, **35**
Rowe, Schoolboy, **153**–4, 160–**161**,
   166–7, 199
Royal Oak Independents, 251
Rule changes, 31
Rulison, Professor, 29
Runnells, Tom, 376–8
Runner-up Bowl, 275
Russell House, 16
Ruth, Babe, **129**, 133–**134**, 135, 189,
   294, 362
Ryan, Nolan, 72, 297

Ste. Claire Hotel, 71
St. Louis (American Association),
   34, 37
St. Louis Browns, 79, 142, 179, 205,
   207, 212, 228, 232
St. Louis Cardinals, 159–**161**, **162**–4,
   165, **312**–5
St. Paul (Western League), 66–7, 70
St. Peter's Episcopal Church, 66
Salaries: 294; of Detroit Tigers, 128,
   184–5, 189, 194, 201, 327–31,
   342–3, 372, 376, 394; of
   Hollinger's Nine, 26, 29; of
   major league players, 128, 149,
   151, 328, 330–1, 375; of
   Western League players, 49
Salisbury, Harry, 26, 29
Salsinger, Harry, 80, 84–5, 120, 135,
   158, 203, 230, 357
Sanborn, Cy, 94
Sanders, Charlie, 248, 281, 286, **288**
San Diego Padres, 337–**338**,
   340–**342**

San Francisco 49ers, 266, 272–3, 275

Schaefer, Germany, 83–**84**, 85, 88, 99, **101**

Schalk, Ray, 62

Scheffing, Bob, 294, 299

Schembechler, Bo, 355, 358–60, 364

Schlesing, Steve, 368

Schmidt, Germany, 92, 105

Schmidt, Joe, 248, **269**, 275–6, 280–1, 287

Scoreboard, 55, 122, 185, 347, 351

Scorecards, **100**

Seating capacity: of Bennett Park, 57, 94–5; of Briggs Stadium, 185; of Navin Field, 122, **131**, 176; of new downtown stadiums, 392; of Tiger Stadium, 213, 353

Second World War, 201–2, **206**–7, 213, 260–2, 292, 356

Security guards, 347

Seibold, Nemo, 39

Seiver, Ed, 89

Shaffer, George, 38

Shapiro, Don, 306–7

Shattuck, Sgt. Lucius, 18

Shaughnessy, Tom, 26

Shaver, Bud, 256–7

Shea, Spec, 219

Sheridan, Pat, 346

Shibe Park, 191

Shreve, Lev, 38

Shubert, J. J., 165–6

Sierra, Ruben, 390

Silverdome, Pontiac, 286, **288**–9

Simpson, Allan, 390

Sisler, George, 62

Sisson, Harry, 176, 229–30

Skinner, Edna Mae, 153–4

Smith, Frank, 72

Smith, Fred, 172–3

Smith, Lyall, 217

Smith, Mayo, 306, 311–3, 316

Smith, Randy, 386, 394

Snyder, Charlie, 59

"Sock it to 'em, Tigers," 309

Sodowsky, Clint, 390

Sonnenberg, Gus, 252

Sopor, Mel, 181

Sorenson, Larry, 358

Spalding, Al, 31

Sparma, Joe, 305

Speaker, Tris, 127–8

Sporting Life, 46

The Sporting News, 138, 207, 251, 356

Sports Illustrated, 323

Sportsman's Park, 113, 207, 230

Square Deal Millers, 251

Stadium Bar, 268

Stallings, George, 46, 59–**60**, 64, 68, 74–7

Stanley, Mickey, 309, 329

Stark, George, 171–2

Starkey, Henry, 15

Starr, Bart, **277**, 279

State Fairgrounds, 284

Statler Hotel, 271

Staub, Rusty, 323

Stearnes, Nettie, 241

Stearnes, Turkey, 140–1, 144, 241

Stearns, Frederick K., 31–3, 37–9

Steinbrenner, George, 343

Steinfeldt, Harry, 62, 64

Stewart, Duff, 68

Stewart, Rod, 368, **369**

Stitzel, Howard, 175

Stone, John, 152

Stoner, Lil, 135

Strategic Fund, 384, 389

Strikes, player, 317, **326**, 331, 371–**373**, 374–**379**, 380–1

Stroh's Brewery, 223

Sumitomo Bank Ltd., 393

Summa, Homer, 139

Summers, Ed, 97

Sunday baseball, 65–8, 75–8, 89–92

Super Bowl, 281, 287

Swartwood, E., 26

Sweetan, Karl, 274

Swift, Bob, 209

"Take Me Out to the Ball Game,"
368
Tampa Smokers, 367
Tanana, Frank, 344–**345**
Taylor, Jimmy, 279
Team Marketing Report, 372
Tebbetts, Birdie, 201
Tecumsehs (London, Ontario), 22–3
Telegraphic re-creations of games,
170–3, 175, 251–2, 291–2
TeleNews Theater, 175
Television, 217–23, **225**, 277, 294,
323, 357–8, 366, 370–1
Templeton Co., John D., 118
Tenace, Gene, 319–20
Tettleton, Mickey, 361, 381
Texas Rangers, 364, 389
Thanksgiving Day football games,
256, 261, **265**–6, 276–**277**, 279,
281
Thomas, Gorman, 321–2
Thomas, Tommy, 62–**63**
Thompson, Jason, 323
Thompson, Justin, 394, 398
Thompson, Sam, **28**, 32–3, **35**, 59,
135
Thompson, William G., 29–31
Thomson, Bobby, 356
Thorpe, Jim, 248
Ticket prices: at Bennett Park, 94–5,
107; at Briggs Stadium, 234,
258;at League Park, 48; at
Navin Field, 138; at Recreation
Park, 32–3; at Tiger Stadium,
353, 372–3, 377, 390, 397–8; at
Woodward Avenue grounds,
18–20
Ticket scalpers, 347
Tiger Den, 372–4
Tiger Plaza, 367
Tiger Stadium: **282**–3, 323, **326**,
340–1, **349**, 390; advertising,
370, 397–8; All-Star Game, 316;
baseball attendance, 299–300,
309, 313, 316–20, 323, 337,
342–6, 370, 375, 381–2, 390,

396–9; Bat Day, **301**, 363–4;
bleachers closed, 321–2; concerts, 368, **369**; fireworks, **311**,
368; football attendance, 277,
287; football facilities, 284;
home runs hit out of, 297–8;
"Kaline's corner," **303**; largest
football crowds, 266; last football game, 287; maintenance,
351; named, 244–5; obstructed
view seats, 360; octopus thrown,
376; organ music, 310–1, 368;
political rallies, **352**; postseason
games, **312**–4, 319–21, 337–**338**,
340–**342**, 346, **349**; record
crowds, 213; renovation, 213,
349–53, 367; seating capacity,
213, 353; security guards, 347;
smoking banned, 347; sold to
city, 351; "stadium hug," **350**;
standing room only, 213. *See
also* Bennett Park, Briggs
Stadium, Navin Field
Tiger Stadium Fan Club, 353,
359–61, 368, 370, 388–9
Tighe, Jack, 233
Time, 271
Toledo, Ohio, 78
Toledo (Western League), 42–3
Toledo Mud Hens, 376
Topps baseball cards, 377
Torgeson, Lavern, 267
Toronto Blue Jays, 316, 336, 343–5,
362–3, 377, 391
Tournaments, baseball, 18–20
Tracewski, Dick, 385
Trammell, Alan, 323, 332–**335**,
337–**338**, 343–4, 381–2, **384**–5,
388, 391
Trendle, George W., 173
Trout, Dizzy, 204–5, 214, 221–2,
226, 329
Troy Haymakers, 24–7
Trucks, Virgil, 72, 201, 209, **227**
Trumbull, Elliott, 214, **218**
Trumbull, John, 54

Trumbull Avenue, 54, **82**
Trumbull Avenue police station, **82**
Tuttle, Bill, 347
Twenty-fourth Michigan Infantry
    Regiment, 18
Twitchell, Larry, **28**, **35**
Tyson, Ty, **148**, 173, 217, 220, **225**

Uhle, George, 151
Union Grounds, 24
Unions (Morrisiana, New York), 20
Uniroyal plant, 326
Unitas, Johnny, 272, **278**
United Auto Workers, 179, 325, 331
University of Detroit, 251, 254–7,
    259, 263
University of Illinois, 254
University of Michigan, 249, 251,
    254
University of Notre Dame, 252
University of Virginia, 249
"Unocal Where Are They Now?,"
    347

Van Brocklin, Norm, 267
Van Burkalow, P. N., 26
Van Depoele, Charles, 29
Vanderbeck, George Arthur, 11, 40,
    42–**45**, 46–9, 55–71
Van Poppel, Todd, 390
Veach, Bobby, 62, 125, **128**, 136–7
Veal, Coot, 239
Veeck, Bill, 230–2
Vernor, Benjamin, 20
Vernor, James, 20, 89
Virgil, Ozzie, 240–1
Vitt, Ossie, 193
Vosmik, Joe, 151
Voss, Tillie, 249, 251

Wabash Railroad, 291
Waddell, Rube, **61**–3
Wagner, Honus, 104, 107
Wakefield, Dick, 184–5, 201, 205
Walden Pond, 361
Waldmeir, Pete, 307

Walker, Bill, 160
Walker, Doak, 266–8, 271
Walker, Gee, 62, **153**, 160, 167, 179,
    186
Walker, Wayne, 275, 277, 279, 281
Walker & Co., 57
Wall Street Journal, 285, 330–1
Walter, John, 383
Warneke, Lon, 166
Washington, Gene, **282**
Washington Redskins, 258
Washington Senators, 205, 207, 227,
    241, 316
Waterfield, Bob, 261
Watkins, Bill, **35**
"The Wave," **290**, 337
Wayne State University, 258, 284
WDIV (Detroit station), 370
Webb, Skeeter, 209
Weger, Mike, **282**
Weidman, Stump, **27**, 30
Wells, David, 381
Wells, Eddie, 138
Wells, Jake, 38
Wert, Don, 311
Wertz, Vic, 214, 227
Wesley, Edgar, 140–1
West End Park. *See* Burns Park
Western League, 40, 42–**50**, 55–70
Western Market, 49, 55
Wheelock, Bobby, 38
Whitaker, Lou, 323, 332–**335**, 344,
    362, 376, 379–80
White, Deacon, 32, **35**
White, Frank, 62
White, Jo-Jo, **153**, 160
White, Whizzer, 260
Wiggins, Alan, 340
Wilcox, Milt, 332, 337
Wildcat stands, 107–**108**, 109–11
Williams, Paul, 220
Williams, Sam, 275, **278**–9
Williams, Ted, 191–3, **200**, 214
Wills, Maury, 239
Wilson, Chief, 105
Wilson, Earl, 299

Wilson, George, 271, 273, 279
Wilson, Glen, 334–5
Wilson, Jimmie, 199
Wilson, Ralph, 309
WJBK (Detroit station), 306
WJR (Detroit station), 255–6, 303, 355, 358
WKMH (Detroit station), 230
WKZO (Kalamazoo station), 292
Wockenfuss, John, 334–5
Wood, George, 30
Wood, Jake, 296
Woodbridge, Dudley, 49, 55
Woodbridge, William, 49, 52, 55
Woodbridge Grove, 49, 55
Woodward Avenue grounds, 18–20
Women's baseball teams, 29
World Series: 78–9, 158, 218–9, 251–2, 315–6, 375; 1887 (Detroit-St. Louis), 33–**35**, **36**–7; 1907 (Detroit- Chicago), **90–1**, 92–4, 181; 1908 (Detroit-Chicago), 97–**98**; 1909 (Detroit-Pittsburgh), 104–**106**, 107; 1934 (Detroit-St. Louis), 159–**161**, **162**–4, **165**; 1935 (Detroit-Chicago), 166–**168**, 169–70; 1940 (Detroit-Cincinnati), **197–8**, 199–201; 1945(Detroit-Chicago), 207–**208**, 209–10; 1968 (Detroit-St. Louis), **312**–5; 1984 (Detroit- San Diego), 337–**338**, 340–**342**
World's Fair, 217–8
Wright, Frank Lloyd, 332, 354
Wright, Rasty, 38
Wrigley Field, 113, 167, 176, 209, 369, 399
WWJ (Detroit station), **148**, 172–3, 219–20
WXYZ (Detroit station), 173, 175, 230
Wyandotte Arrows, 251
Wyse, Hank, 209

Yankee Stadium, 138, 177, 200, 245
Yawkey, William H., 80–2, **93**–4, 107, 119, 121
Yeager, Joe, **69**, 72
"Yes, Virginia, There Is a Santa," 102
York, Rudy, 177, 179, 192, 194–5, 199, 209
Yost, Fielding, 172
Young, Coleman, 325–7, 353–**354**, 388
Young, Cy, 78

Zeller, Jack, 189, 194

Photo Credits

Burton Historical Collection: 27 left, 35, 53, 56, 60, 69, 82, 83, 85, 108 both, 126, 129, 132, 146, 150 both, 153, 162, 163, 200 left, 206 both, 208, 211, 216 bottom, 219, 227, 229, 263, 264, 277, 280, 283, 285, 288, 296, 298, 302, 303, 304 both, 312, 333, 339, 342, 348 bottom, 352 both

Joe Carachiola: 290, 330, 335, 348 top, 349

Detroit Free Press: 379, 384

Detroit Lions: 262, 278

Detroit News: 98, 143, 148, 204, 282, 365

Detroit Tigers: 178 bottom, 188, 228, 345, 387

Dick Clark: 27 right, 196, 200 right

Designated Hatter: 1

Library of Congress: 90-91, 253

Manning Brothers: 76, 131, 149, 216 top

Michigan State Archives: 12, 15 both, 32, 194, 198, 224 both, 257 right

National Baseball Library: 44, 63, 101, 103 top, 190, 197

Osborn Engineering Co.: 121, 124-125

Selek/Bak Collection: 8, 10, 21, 28 both, 36, 41, 43, 45, 47, 50, 61, 72, 81, 84, 87, 93, 96, 100, 103 bottom, 106, 112, 114, 116, 118, 128, 130, 134, 141, 155, 156 both, 157, 161, 168, 171, 174 both, 178 top, 180, 182 both, 195, 202, 225, 226, 231, 232, 233, 234, 239, 240, 246, 248, 257 left, 260, 265, 268, 269, 274, 295, 300, 301, 308 both, 311, 317, 318, 320, 322, 324, 326, 338, 350, 354, 356, 366, 369, 373, 382

Elliott Trumbull: 218

Joe Vaughn: 396

Titles in the Great Lakes Books Series

Freshwater Fury: Yarns and Reminiscences of the Greatest Storm in Inland Navigation, by Frank Barcus, 1986 (reprint)

Call It North Country: The Story of Upper Michigan, by John Bartlow Martin, 1986 (reprint)

The Land of the Crooked Tree, by U. P. Hedrick, 1986 (reprint)
Michigan Place Names, by Walter Romig, 1986 (reprint)

Luke Karamazov, by Conrad Hilberry, 1987

The Late, Great Lakes: An Environmental History, by William Ashworth, 1987 (reprint)

Great Pages of Michigan History from the Detroit Free Press, 1987

Waiting for the Morning Train: An American Boyhood, by Bruce Catton, 1987 (reprint)

Michigan Voices: Our State's History in the Words of the People Who Lived It, compiled and edited by Joe Grimm, 1987

Danny and the Boys, Being Some Legends of Hungry Hollow, by Robert Traver, 1987 (reprint)

Hanging On, or How to Get through a Depression and Enjoy Life, by Edmund G. Love, 1987 (reprint)

The Situation in Flushing, by Edmund G. Love, 1987 (reprint)

A Small Bequest, by Edmund G. Love, 1987 (reprint)

The Saginaw Paul Bunyan, by James Stevens, 1987 (reprint)

The Ambassador Bridge: A Monument to Progress, by Philip P. Mason, 1988

Let the Drum Beat: A History of the Detroit Light Guard, by Stanley D. Solvick, 1988

An Afternoon in Waterloo Park, by Gerald Dumas, 1988 (reprint)

Contemporary Michigan Poetry: Poems from the Third Coast, edited by Michael Delp, Conrad Hilberry and Herbert Scott, 1988

Over the Graves of Horses, by Michael Delp, 1988

Wolf in Sheep's Clothing: The Search for a Child Killer, by Tommy McIntyre, 1988

Copper-Toed Boots, by Marguerite de Angeli, 1989 (reprint)

Detroit Images: Photographs of the Renaissance City, edited by John J. Bukowczyk and Douglas Aikenhead, with Peter Slavcheff, 1989

Hangdog Reef: Poems Sailing the Great Lakes, by Stephen Tudor, 1989

Detroit: City of Race and Class Violence, revised edition, by B. J. Widick, 1989

Deep Woods Frontier: A History of Logging in Northern Michigan, by Theodore J. Karamanski, 1989

Orvie, The Dictator of Dearborn, by David L. Good, 1989

Seasons of Grace: A History of the Catholic Archdiocese of Detroit, by Leslie Woodcock Tentler, 1990

The Pottery of John Foster: Form and Meaning,
by Gordon and Elizabeth Orear, 1990

The Diary of Bishop Frederic Baraga:
First Bishop of Marquette, Michigan,
edited by Regis M. Walling and Rev. N. Daniel Rupp, 1990

Walnut Pickles and Watermelon Cake: A Century of Michigan Cooking,
by Larry B. Massie and Priscilla Massie, 1990

The Making of Michigan, 1820–1860: A Pioneer Anthology,
edited by Justin L. Kestenbaum, 1990

America's Favorite Homes: A Guide to
Popular Early Twentieth-Century Homes,
by Robert Schweitzer and Michael W. R. Davis, 1990

Beyond the Model T: The Other Ventures of Henry Ford,
by Ford R. Bryan, 1990

Life after the Line, by Josie Kearns, 1990

Michigan Lumbertowns: Lumbermen and Laborers in Saginaw, Bay
City, and Muskegon, 1870–1905, by Jeremy W. Kilar, 1990

Detroit Kids Catalog: The Hometown Tourist by Ellyce Field, 1990

Waiting for the News, by Leo Litwak, 1990 (reprint)

Detroit Perspectives, edited by Wilma Wood Henrickson, 1991

Life on the Great Lakes: A Wheelsman's Story,
by Fred W. Dutton, edited by William Donohue Ellis, 1991

Copper Country Journal: The Diary of Schoolmaster Henry Hobart,
1863–1864, by Henry Hobart, edited by Philip P. Mason, 1991

John Jacob Astor: Business and Finance in the Early Republic,
by John Denis Haeger, 1991

Survival and Regeneration: Detroit's American Indian Community,
by Edmund J. Danziger, Jr., 1991

Steamboats and Sailors of the Great Lakes,
by Mark L. Thompson, 1991

Cobb Would Have Caught It: The Golden Age of Baseball in Detroit, by Richard Bak, 1991

Michigan in Literature, by Clarence Andrews, 1992

Under the Influence of Water: Poems, Essays, and Stories, by Michael Delp, 1992

The Country Kitchen, by Della T. Lutes, 1992 (reprint)

The Making of a Mining District: Keweenaw Native Copper 1500–1870, by David J. Krause, 1992

Kids Catalog of Michigan Adventures, by Ellyce Field, 1993

Henry's Lieutenants, by Ford R. Bryan, 1993

Historic Highway Bridges of Michigan, by Charles K. Hyde, 1993

Lake Erie and Lake St. Clair Handbook, by Stanley J. Bolsenga and Charles E. Herndendorf, 1993

Queen of the Lakes, by Mark Thompson, 1994

Iron Fleet: The Great Lakes in World War II, by George J. Joachim, 1994

Turkey Stearnes and the Detroit Stars: The Negro Leagues in Detroit, 1919–1933, by Richard Bak, 1994

Pontiac and the Indian Uprising, by Howard H. Peckham, 1994 (reprint)

Charting the Inland Seas: A History of the U.S. Lake Survey, by Arthur M. Woodford, 1994 (reprint)

Ojibwa Narratives of Charles and Charlotte Kawbawgam and Jacques LePique, 1893–1895. Recorded with Notes by Homer H. Kidder, edited by Arthur P. Bourgeois, 1994, co-published with the Marquette County Historical Society

Strangers and Sojourners: A History of Michigan's Keweenaw Peninsula, by Arthur W. Thurner, 1994

Win Some, Lose Some: G. Mennen Williams and the New Democrats, by Helen Washburn Berthelot, 1995

Sarkis, by Gordon and Elizabeth Orear, 1995

The Northern Lights: Lighthouses of the Upper Great Lakes,
by Charles K. Hyde, 1995 (reprint)

Kids Catalog of Michigan Adventures, second edition,
by Ellyce Field, 1995

Rumrunning and the Roaring Twenties:
Prohibition on the Michigan-Ontario Waterway,
by Philip P. Mason, 1995

In the Wilderness with the Red Indians,
by E. R. Baierlein, translated by Anita Z. Boldt,
edited by Harold W. Moll, 1996

Elmwood Endures: History of a Detroit Cemetery,
by Michael Franck, 1996

Master of Precision: Henry M. Leland, by Mrs. Wilfred C. Leland
with Minnie Dubbs Millbrook, 1996 (reprint)

Haul-Out: New and Selected Poems, by Stephen Tudor, 1996

Kids Catalog of Michigan Adventures, third edition,
by Ellyce Field, 1997

Beyond the Model T: The Other Ventures of Henry Ford,
revised edition, by Ford R. Bryan, 1997

Young Henry Ford: A Picture History of the First Forty Years,
by Sidney Olson, 1997 (reprint)

The Coast of Nowhere: Meditations on Rivers, Lakes and Streams,
by Michael Delp, 1997

From Saginaw Valley to Tin Pan Alley: Saginaw's Contribution to
American Popular Music, 1890–1955, by R. Grant Smith, 1998

These Men Have Seen Hard Service: The First Michigan
Sharpshooters in the Civil War, by Raymond J. Herek, 1998

Toast of the Town: The Life and Times of Sunnie Wilson,
by Sunnie Wilson with John Cohassey, 1998

Bridging the River of Hatred: The Pioneering Efforts of Detroit Police Commissioner George Edwards, 1962–1963, by Mary M. Stolberg, 1998

A Place for Summer: A Narrative History of Tiger Stadium, by Richard Bak, 1998